English Transcription

M. Luisa Garcia Lecumberri
University of the Basque Country

and

John A. Maidment
University College London

HODDER
EDUCATION
PART OF HACHETTE UK

First published in Great Britain in 2000 by
Hodder Education, part of Hachette UK
338 Euston Road, London NW1 3BH

www.hoddereducation.com
© 2000 M. Luisa Garcia Lecumberri and John A. Maidment

The advice and information in this book are believed to be true and
accurate at the date of going to press, but neither the authors nor the publisher
can accept any legal responsibility or liability for any errors or omissions.

British Library Cataloguing in Publication Data
A catalogue record for this book in available from the British Library

Library of Congress Cataloging-in-Publication Data
A catalog record for this book is available from the Library of Congress

ISBN 978 0 340 75978 3
Typeset in 10/12pt Times by Academic & Technical Typesetting, Bristol
Printed and bound by CPI Group (UK) Ltd., Croydon, CR0 4YY.

What do you think about this book? Or any other Hodder Education title?
Please send your comments to www.hoddereducation.com

What do you think about this book? Or any other Hodder Education title?
Please send your comments to www.hoddereducation.com

CONTENTS

Introduction

This book is designed to help you develop and improve your skills in transcribing English phonetically. Anyone who is interested in the way modern English sounds can benefit from working through the lessons in this book, each of which deals in detail with a particular aspect of the pronunciation of English, provides an overview of the theoretical background and backs this up with a number of exercises of different kinds. Model answers to all the exercises in the book may be found in the Appendix. There is also a glossary where you can find definitions of all the technical terms and abbreviations used in the lessons.

Phonetic transcription is a useful learning technique for two different kinds of people. For native speakers of English who wish to know more about English pronunciation, transcription is one way of reinforcing the idea that the spoken and written representations of language are completely different things. Transcription helps you to realise what you *actually* say, rather than what you *think* you say. Anyone who does phonetic transcription regularly is likely to be surprised fairly often at the discovery of some new phenomenon that they had not been aware of before. We certainly found this when preparing the transcribed texts for the book. For learners of English as a foreign or second language, transcribing texts helps to make one aware of the target one should be aiming for and of the pronunciation (or range of pronunciations) one can expect to hear from native speakers. The spelling system of English (its **orthography**) is notoriously unhelpful when it comes to learning the pronunciation of the language.

For both types of user, phonetic transcription can make you realise that the pronunciation of a word can differ, sometimes quite radically, depending on the sort of environment in which the word is said. A couple of simple examples should help to make this clear.

If anyone were to ask a native speaker of English how the word *from* is pronounced, the most probable answer would be /frɒm/. This is the form of the word which is used when the word is said in isolation and not part of a longer utterance. This form is called the word's **citation form**. The same form can also be heard as part of a longer utterance (a piece of **connected speech**), for example in the question, *Where do you come from?*

However, in the answer to this question it is very likely that the word will not be pronounced /frɒm/, but /frəm/, for example in *I come from Manchester*. Another, slightly more complicated, example concerns words such as *couldn't* and *shouldn't*. Some of the possible variations of the pronunciation of the first of these are set out below:

Orthographic form:	*couldn't*
Citation forms:	/kʊdənt/ or /kʊdn̩t/
Connected speech forms:	/kʊdənt/ or /kʊdn̩t/ or /kʊdn̩/ or /kʊdən/

Example: *I couldn't answer that question.*

/kʊbm̩p/ or /kʊdəmp/ or /kʊbm̩/ or /kʊdəm/
Example: *I couldn't make up my mind*

/kʊgŋk/ or /kʊdəŋk/ or /kʊgŋ̩/ or /kʊdəŋ/
Example: *I couldn't go.*

Fortunately, these types of variation in phonetic form are not random or arbitrary. They are, for most part, common to all languages and are the result of a universal tendency for speakers to economise on the amount of effort they put into the movements necessary to produce speech. Although there are differences in detail between one language and another, the speech of speakers of all languages displays this type of feature which can be explained by reference to a small number of **connected speech processes**. Many of the lessons in this book are designed to make you familiar with the common connected speech processes of English and to give you practice in including them in your transcriptions. A transcription of a piece of English text of more than a few words which did not include an example of the operation of at least one connected speech process would probably be an inaccurate and unrealistic representation of how that text would be spoken by an English native speaker. To put this another way: if you wish to produce a transcription of a piece of English which is accurate and realistic, it is no use simply looking each word up in a pronouncing dictionary, where typically what is recorded is the citation form, and then stringing these pronunciations together. English people simply do not speak that way. Neither do speakers of any other language.

A transcription of a piece of text in English may differ greatly depending on the **accent** being transcribed and the **style** of speech which is represented.

The way English is pronounced is, of course, different in different areas. Someone who comes from Scotland will very probably not sound the same as someone from Australia, so transcriptions representing the speech of the two speakers should not look the same. In this book we concentrate exclusively on an accent of British English known as **Received Pronunciation (RP)** or **Southern British Standard (SBS)**. This accent has a number of advantages. First, it is very well described in the literature on the pronunciation of English. Second, it is very widely used for the purposes of teaching English as a foreign or second language. Third, there are a number of pronouncing dictionaries available which use RP as their model and most general-purpose dictionaries, in Great Britain at least, use RP as the basis for the pronunciations they give.

People sound different on different occasions. In a formal situation, such as an interview, most people tend to speak more precisely and to avoid some of the connected speech processes which change or delete sounds. The same may be true when people are speaking to someone whom they do not know well. When people are in a relaxed, casual situation and are speaking to people they know well and feel at ease with, they tend to produce speech where the citation forms of words are changed or reduced. These differences are differences of speech style. The style aimed at throughout this book is a relaxed, informal one. In some of the earlier lessons, where some of the connected speech processes have not yet been introduced, a reading of the transcriptions given might sound rather more formal.

The structure of each lesson in this book is as follows. The topic of the lesson is introduced and explained with plenty of examples. The topic is then illustrated in a transcribed passage which contains a number of occurrences of the relevant phenomenon. These occurrences are highlighted in the transcription. Then there are a number of exercises of various types to help you make sure you have understood the topic and can produce transcriptions containing the feature concerned. For instance, you may be asked to look at a passage in orthography and to identify places in the passage where the phenomenon might occur. Or you might be given a transcribed passage where the phenomenon is not included and your task is to edit the transcription to show it at appropriate points. The final exercises in each lesson are always a number of passages for you to transcribe. Again, you can be sure that the relevant phenomenon occurs quite a few times in these passages.

The book consists of eight lessons. Each lesson introduces a new topic (or in some cases a number of related topics) and explains the theoretical background with a lot of examples. There are exercises for you to do in each lesson and the answers to all the exercises can be found in the Appendix. Although you can, of course, do the lessons in any order you wish, it would perhaps be wiser to follow the order given, since the exercises are cumulative, in the sense that features introduced in earlier lessons are included in later exercises without any further explanation. The last section of the book consists of a number of passages for you to transcribe as further practice.

Since this book is primarily about transcribing, the theory has been kept as short and simple as possible. You can find out more about the theoretical issues mentioned in textbooks such as *Gimson's Introduction to the Pronunciation of English* (Cruttenden, 1994), *English Phonetics and Phonology* (Roach, 1991), *Speech Sounds* (Ashby, 1995) or one of the other texts on English phonetics and phonology which you can find in the Bibliography. If you are interested in transcribing or learning about the sounds of American English, we can recommend two very accessible books: *Applied Phonetics: The Sounds of American English* (Edwards, 1992) and *Applied Phonetics Workbook* (Edwards and Gregg, 1997)

It is impossible to learn to transcribe without getting involved with some technical terminology. We have tried to keep this to a minimum and have given explanations of the terms used. There is a glossary with brief definitions of technical terms at the end of the book. Terms included in the glossary are printed in **bold type** on their first appearance in the text.

If your native language is not English, phonetic transcription is one way of improving your pronunciation of English. However, this course cannot solve *all* your problems. The spelling system of English is so complex and full of exceptions and special cases that the only foolproof way of finding out how an unknown word is pronounced is to look the word up in a good pronouncing dictionary. A good example is provided by the word *acorn*. The vast majority of words which begin with the letters *ac* are pronounced either /ək/ if the first syllable is **unstressed** (such as *across*, *accept*) or /æk/ if the first syllable is **stressed** (such as *accident, acrid*). But *acorn* begins with /eɪ/. There is no way of predicting this and, apart from the verb *ache* and related forms, such as *aching, achy,* this is the only common word beginning with *ac* which is pronounced like this. One suggestion for a pronouncing dictionary is the *Longman Pronunciation Dictionary* (Wells, 1990).

Transcribing phonetically is a skill which needs regular practice. It is much better to do a little transcription fairly often rather than a lot all at once. Some of the passages in this book are fairly long, but that does not mean that you need to transcribe the whole passage in one sitting. We advise transcribing sections of 100 words or so and then checking on your progress with the help of the answers in the Appendix.

If you are working without a teacher, but you know someone else who is also learning to transcribe, it is a good idea to swap transcriptions and try to spot each other's errors (and good points!), before looking at the answer provided. Another useful activity is to work on a transcription in a group, where you can learn from one other.

Finally, a word about the transcriptions we have provided as answers. These must be viewed as specimen answers only. We have provided notes to point out some alternatives to the pronunciation chosen. However, it would make this book enormously long and difficult to read if we attempted to mention every possible alternative. If your transcription does not agree with ours on a particular point then that does not *necessarily* mean that your version is wrong. What you *can* be sure of, though, is that our version is acceptable.

Acknowledgements

The authors acknowledge the encouragement and technical support provided by their two universities, the Department of Phonetics at University College London, and the University of the Basque Country. Warmest thanks go to all the authors of the passages used in this book: Molly Bennet, Federico Eguiluz, M. Mar and M. L. Garcia Lecumberri, Tirion Havard, M. Luisa Lecumberri, John Maidment, Rakesh Odedra, Gary Padbury, Wendy Plimmer, Jennifer Shepherd, Heather Visser, Dorothy Wilson and Kathleen Wilson. They all generously allowed us to alter their original versions in the process of adapting them for the various tasks. We take full responsibility for the final versions.

References

Ashby, P. 1995: *Speech Sounds*. London: Routledge.

Cruttenden, A. (Ed.). 1994: *Gimson's Introduction to the Pronunciation of English*. London: Edward Arnold.

Edwards, H. T. 1992: Applied Phonetics: The Sounds of American English. San Diego, CA: Singular Publishing.

Edwards, H. T. And Gregg, A. L. 1997: *Applied Phonetics Workbook: A Systematic Approach to Phonetic Transcription*. San Diego, CA: Singular Publishing.

Roach, P. 1991: *English Phonetics and Phonology*. Cambridge: Cambridge University Press.

Wells, J. C. 1990: Longman Pronunciation Dictionary. London: Longman.

Lesson 1

Symbols and terminology

In this lesson we shall introduce the symbols that will be used throughout the book. There are various sets of symbols used for the transcription of English. In this book we shall use the symbols in the *Longman Pronunciation Dictionary* (Wells, 1990). The basic terminology used to describe speech sounds will also be introduced in this lesson.

Consonant symbols

There are 24 consonant sounds in RP English. They may be classified according to their place and manner of articulation and voicing, as set out in Table 1.1 below. In the table, the first of a pair of symbols represents a **voiceless** sound and the second a **voiced** sound. Each of the above consonants is illustrated by a *keyword* in Table 1.2 which follows. The consonant is usually found at the beginning of the keyword, but for some sounds which cannot occur initially in a word the consonant is in **bold type**.

    Voicing: A voiced consonant is one which is accompanied by vibration of the vocal folds. If you pronounce a long /z/ sound, as if imitating the buzzing of a bee, and at the

Table 1.1 Consonant symbols

	bilabial		labiodental	dental	alveolar		post-alveolar		velar		glottal	palatal
plosives	p	b			t	d			k	g		
nasals	m				n				ŋ			
fricatives			f v	θ ð	s	z	ʃ	ʒ			h	
affricates							tʃ	dʒ				
approximants	w				l		r					j

Table 1.2 Consonant keywords and their transcriptions

consonant	keyword	transcription	consonant	keyword	transcription
p	pie	/paɪ/	ʃ	shy	/ʃaɪ/
b	buy	/baɪ/	ʒ	measure	/meʒə/
t	tie	/taɪ/	tʃ	chore	/tʃɔː/
d	die	/daɪ/	dʒ	jaw	/dʒɔː/
k	cow	/kaʊ/	h	high	/haɪ/
g	guy	/gaɪ/	m	my	/maɪ/
f	fee	/fiː/	n	nigh	/naɪ/
v	vie	/vaɪ/	ŋ	sing	/sɪŋ/
θ	thigh	/θaɪ/	w	why	/waɪ/
ð	thy	/ðaɪ/	l	lie	/laɪ/
s	sigh	/saɪ/	r	rye	/raɪ/
z	zoo	/zuː/	j	you	/juː/

same time place your thumb and finger on your throat, you should be able to feel the vibrations. For some voiced sounds, specifically voiced plosives, the vibration of the vocal folds does not always continue throughout the sound, but starts immediately after the end of the sound. Voiceless sounds have no vocal fold vibration. Try a long /s/ sound, imitating the hissing of a snake. You should not feel any vibrations in your throat.

The voiceless consonants of RP English are:

p t k f θ s ʃ tʃ h

The voiced consonants of RP English are:

b d g v ð z ʒ dʒ m n ŋ w l r j

Exercise 1.1 Look at the following short passage and try to identify all the voiceless consonants in it.

> *I haven't got a car at the moment. My car was stolen last Friday. I left it at the station all day and when I got back in the evening it had vanished. I hope the insurance company will send me a cheque soon, so that I can go and buy another one.*

Exercise 1.2 Which of the following words contain only voiced consonant sounds?

> much, moody, number, yellow, roses, knees, youth, loses, doses, dozes, wishing, leisure, those, under, jeans, this, his, wins, garage, universal.

Place of articulation: All speech sounds are made with a stream of air moving through the vocal tract. For all the sounds of English, most of the time, the airstream is set in motion by the lungs and travels up the windpipe (also called the trachea), through the voice-box (the **larynx**) where the vocal folds are situated, through the pharynx and then through the oral cavity or the nasal cavity (or both). Speech sounds are made by interfering with this stream of air, usually at some point within the oral cavity. The exact point of such interference is known as the **place of articulation (poa)** of the sound. RP English makes use of the following places (Table 1.3).

Table 1.3 Places of articulation

bilabial	the two lips approach one another to interfere with the airstream; RP English bilabial sounds are /p b m/
labiodental	the lower lip approaches the upper front teeth; RP labiodental sounds are /f v/
dental	the tip of the tongue approaches the back of the upper front teeth; RP dental sounds are /θ ð/
alveolar	the tip of the tongue approaches the area just behind the upper front teeth; this area is known as the **alveolar ridge**; RP alveolar sounds are /t d n s z l/
post-alveolar	the tip or the blade of the tongue approaches the rear part of the alveolar ridge; RP post-alveolar sounds are /ʃ ʒ tʃ dʒ r/
palatal	the middle part of the tongue approaches the roof of the oral cavity; the only palatal sound in RP English is /j/
velar	the back part of the tongue approaches the soft part at the back the roof of the oral cavity; this is known as the soft palate or **velum**; RP English velar sounds are /k g ŋ/
glottal	the two vocal folds in the larynx approach each other to interfere with the airstream; the only glottal consonant in RP English is /h/; however, there is another glottal sound with you will become familiar in a later lesson; this is known as a glottal stop [ʔ]
labial-velar	this is a complex place of articulation; the back of the tongue approaches the velum as for velar sounds, but at the same time the lips are rounded and protruded; the only labial–velar sound in RP English is /w/.

Exercise 1.3 Look at the following passage and try to identify the place of articulation of the first consonant of each word (if it begins with a consonant).

Last Tuesday my brother came to see me. He wanted to borrow my videorecorder because his is not very reliable. My nephew's birthday is next Thursday. They are going to have a party for some friends and they want to show some films.

Manner of articulation: At each place of articulation it is possible to interfere with the airstream in a number of different ways. This aspect of sound production is known as **manner of articulation (moa)**. See Table 1.4 for the manners for consonant sounds which RP English uses.

Exercise 1.4 Sort the following words into five classes on the basis of the manner of articulation of their initial consonant sound.

sixty, five, generous, lesson, doubt, give, quite, xylophone, usual, thrown, then, monster, hope, chemist, knot, cherry, physics, yacht, wrong, rubber

Sonorant, obstruent and **stop**: Two other very useful terms when dealing with consonants are **sonorant** and **obstruent**. These refer to large classes of manners of articulation. Sonorant consonants are the following: nasals and approximants (both median and lateral). Vowels are also sonorant. Obstruent consonants are the following: plosives, affricates and fricatives. The term **stop** also refers to manner of articulation. Stops are those sounds which have a complete closure in the oral cavity: plosives, affricates and nasals.

Table 1.4 Manners of articulation

plosive	the airstream is completely blocked for a short time and the blockage is released rapidly, causing the compressed air to burst out of the vocal tract; RP English plosive consonants are /p b t d k g/
fricative	the vocal tract is narrowed so that the airstream becomes turbulent and produces friction noise; RP fricatives are /f v θ ð s z ʃ ʒ h/
affricate	as for plosives, the airstream is blocked, but the blockage is released much more slowly and a short period of friction is heard; RP affricates are /tʃ dʒ/
approximant	the vocal tract is narrowed, but not enough to cause air turbulence; there is therefore no friction noise; RP approximants are of two kinds: **median approximants** where the air escapes over the centre of the tongue and **lateral approximants** where there is a blockage in the centre but the sides of the tongue are lowered so that air can escape laterally; the median approximants of RP are /w r j/ and the only lateral approximant in RP is /l/
nasal	as for plosives and affricates, nasals are produced with a complete blockage in the oral cavity; however, air is allowed to escape continuously through the nasal cavity; RP nasals are /m n ŋ/

Exercise 1.5 Sort the following words into three sets depending on whether they begin with an obstruent, a sonorant or a stop. Notice that some words will appear in more than one set.

choose, soap, metal, ripe, coast, white, told, youth, lorry, friend, thought, boast, purple, gate, violet, nasty, quiet

Vowels

RP English vowels are of two different sorts called **monophthongs** and **diphthongs**. A monophthong or simple vowel is a vowel sound which has a constant quality. A diphthong, on the other hand, changes its quality. It has a starting quality which is different from its ending quality. The monophthongs of RP are laid out in Table 1.5 and the diphthongs in Table 1.6.

Table 1.5 RP Monophthongs

vowel symbol	keyword	transcription
iː	leek	/liːk/
ɪ	lick	/lɪk/
e	leg	/leg/
æ	lack	/læk/
ʌ	luck	/lʌk/
ɑː	lark	/lɑːk/
ɒ	lock	/lɒk/
ɔː	lord	/lɔːd/
ʊ	look	/lʊk/
uː	Luke	/luːk/
ɜː	lurk	/lɜːk/
ə	butter	/bʌtə/

Table 1.6 RP Diphthongs

vowel symbol	keyword	transcription
aɪ	tie	/taɪ/
eɪ	day	/deɪ/
ɔɪ	toy	/tɔɪ/
aʊ	now	/naʊ/
əʊ	no	/nəʊ/
ɪə	dear	/dɪə/
eə	dare	/deə/
ʊə	tour	/tʊə/

Vowel length: RP English vowels are either long or short. The long vowels are all the diphthongs plus the five monophthongs /iː ɑː ɔː uː ɜː/. All the other vowels are short.

Vowel features: The monophthongs of RP English may be classified in three different ways according to (1) their **lip posture**, (2) their **location** and (3) their **height**.

Lip posture has two values in RP English:

- **rounded**: for the vowels /ɔː ɒ ʊ uː/
- **unrounded**: for the vowels /iː ɪ e æ ɑː ʌ ɜː ə/

Location has three values in RP English:

- **front**: when the highest point of the tongue lies below the hard palate – this is true for the vowels /iː ɪ e æ/
- **back**: when the highest point of the tongue lies below the soft palate, as for the vowels /ɑː ɔː ɒ ʊ uː/
- **central**: when the highest point of the tongue lies in an intermediate position at the junction of the hard and soft palates – this is so for the vowels /ʌ ɜː ə/

Height has three values in RP English:

- **close** or **high**: when the highest point of the tongue is close to the roof of the mouth, as for the vowels /iː uː/
- **open** or **low**: when there is a considerable distance between the highest point of the tongue and the roof of the mouth, as for the vowels /ɑː ɒ/
- **mid**: when the highest point of the tongue is midway between close and open, as for the vowels /ɪ e æ ʌ ɜː ɒ ɔː/; the mid-vowels of RP English can be further subdivided into **close-mid** or **mid-high**: /ɪ ʊ/, **open-mid** or **mid-low**: /æ ʌ ɔː/ and just mid /e ɜː ə/

For the purposes of this book the most important distinction which rests on vowel features is between high/mid-high and the rest.

Exercise 1.6 In the following passage identify all the high and mid-high monophthongs.

There are three reasons I should give if anyone asked why it is a good idea to learn English transcription. First, it helps you to realise what you say as opposed to what you think you say. Second, it teaches you that written language is not the same as spoken language. Third, it can be quite a lot of fun.

Exercise 1.7 Transcribe the following simple words.

band	hall	jump	weep	love	quit
ask	top	miss	juice	out	time
bless	cliff	drop	hoop	bead	turn
trap	dive	fear	grow	load	fair
boil	work	want	lose	close	boot
cook	pull	dome	why	cross	chair

Lesson 2

Transcription hints

In Lesson 1 we introduced the basic symbols to be used in the phonetic transcription of English and some of the basic terminology needed to describe speech sounds. Here, we will look at some refinements to the symbol set and give some hints on how to avoid common errors when transcribing.

Neutralisation symbols

In modern RP English a number of changes have taken place which affect vowel qualities. Fifty years or more ago a word like *city* was pronounced /sɪtɪ/. Nowadays it often gets pronounced /sɪtiː/, although the earlier pronunciation is still heard. What is more troublesome is that many speakers use a vowel which is intermediate between /iː/ and /ɪ/. This means that in some circumstances the difference between the two vowels is becoming blurred or **neutralised**. In order to cope with this situation an extra symbol needs to be employed. Our transcription of words like *city* uses the symbol /i/ (without the length mark) for the second vowel: /sɪti/. This can be interpreted as meaning: for the second vowel of the word some speakers use /iː/, some speakers use /ɪ/ and some speakers use a vowel which is neither /iː/ nor /ɪ/, but somewhere in between. The same situation is true for the two vowels /uː/ and /ʊ/. In a phrase such as *to a party*, the first word may be /tuː/ or /tʊ/ or the vowel may be somewhere between /uː/ and /ʊ/. In cases like this we shall use the neutralisation symbol /u/ and write /tu ə pɑːti/. (Notice that the second vowel in *party* is also written with a neutralisation symbol.) You must be careful to realise that these neutralisation symbols are not appropriate in all situations. There is no doubt that native speakers of RP English use /iː/ and never /ɪ/ in a word like *bean*, so it would be wrong to write /bɪn/ when transcribing this word. Similarly, the word *bin* is always /bɪn/, never /biːn/ or /bin/. Neutralisation of /iː/–/ɪ/ and /uː/–/ʊ/ is always found in unstressed[1] syllables. It is most common at the ends of words or morphemes. If there is a following consonant,

---

[1] If you are not sure about stress, please be patient. This is one of the topics dealt with in Lesson 3.

it must belong to a different morpheme (that is to say, the neutralised high vowel may be found word-finally even though sometimes it appears followed by other sounds if a morpheme is added).

One further point concerns words such as *before* and *remember*. If you look these up in a pronouncing dictionary you will probably find that the recommended pronunciation has /ɪ/ in the first syllable. However, many younger speakers these days use /iː/ in words like this. In the transcriptions in this book we have used the neutralisation symbol wherever we think there is a likelihood of hearing some native speakers of RP English using /ɪ/ and others using /iː/ or of speakers using a vowel which is difficult to identify as either /ɪ/ or /iː/. So we transcribe the above words /bifɔː/ and /rimembə/.

Vowel monophthonging

Traditionally, words such as *poor*, *sure*, *tour* were pronounced with the diphthong /ʊə/. This diphthong is slowly disappearing in modern RP and is being replaced by the long, back, rounded monophthong /ɔː/. This means that some pairs of words which used to be distinct now sound identical. For example, *more* and *moor* used to be /mɔː/ and /mʊə/. Now many people pronounce them both /mɔː/. In this book we shall use the monophthongal pronunciation wherever possible. The only words which consistently use the /ʊə/ diphthong are those spelt with the letter combination *ewer*: words such as *brewer*, *sewer*, *ewer*, *fewer*. These can never be pronounced with /ɔː/. The other situation where /ʊə/ is retained is when a word ending in /uː/ and is spelled with *ue* has the ending *r* attached to it, as in *truer* and *bluer*. These words retain the diphthongal pronunciation. Actually, for many speakers, the vowel quality at the beginning of the diphthong may be /uː/ rather than /ʊ/, so it is better to use the neutralisation symbol /u/. So, the above words would be transcribed /bruə suə juə fjuə truə bluə/.

Plurals, possessives and past tenses

One very frequent type of error that occurs when people are beginning to transcribe English arises from a failure to realise that identical spellings can have different pronunciations. This is true of the plural form of nouns in English. Most nouns add an orthographic *s* to make their plural form: *book–books*, *dog–dogs* and so on. However, the pronunciation of the **plural morpheme** varies according the noun to which it is added. The general rule is that the plural morpheme must agree in voicing with the last *sound* of the noun. So, nouns which end in a voiced consonant or a vowel add /z/ and those that end with a voiceless consonant add /s/.

Examples:

robes	/rəʊbz/
ropes	/rəʊps/
doors	/dɔːz/
wells	/welz/
homes	/həʊmz/
troughs	/trɒfs/

Exercise 2.1 Transcribe the plurals of the following nouns:

   weight, dove, town, rod, lamb, idea, song, track, view, myth

Of course, some nouns have irregular plural forms. There are well-known examples such as *child–children, ox–oxen, goose–geese, mouse–mice*. Some nouns do not have a distinct plural form: *deer, fish, sheep*, for example. However, there are other nouns which are what one might call, 'semi-regular'. They do add an *s* in the spelling, but other changes take place as well. Most (not all) of these nouns end in *fe* in the spelling: *knife–knives* /naɪvz/, *life–lives* /laɪvz/, *wife–wives* /waɪvz/. It is easy to see from the spelling that these are not completely regular. Some nouns look regular, but are in fact pronounced in an irregular way. The most common of these are: *house–houses* /haʊzəz/ and *youth–youths* /juːðz/.

The noun *house* is also an example of another phenomenon connected with plural formation. Nouns which end in one of the following consonants /s z ʃ ʒ tʃ dʒ/ (these consonants are known as **sibilants**) add a vowel before the plural ending. The vowel is /ɪ/ for some speakers and /ə/ for others. In this case the plural ending itself is always pronounced /z/.
   Examples:

buses	/bʌsəz/	*roses*	/rəʊzəz/
sashes	/sæʃəz/	*garages*	/gærɑːʒəz/
batches	/bætʃəz/	*ridges*	/rɪdʒəz/

Most of the above features of the pronunciation of the plural morpheme are also true for the pronunciation of the possessive morpheme which is written *'s* in the singular and *s'* in the plural. Again, the ending must agree in voicing with the last sound of the noun and if the last sound is a sibilant a vowel is inserted.
   Examples:

John's	/dʒɒnz/	*Luisa's*	/luːiːzəz/
Pete's	/piːts/	*boss's*	/bɒsəz/
Greeks'	/griːks/		

Notice, however, that nouns which have irregular plurals have perfectly regular possessive forms. For example, *wife's* /waɪfs/, *house's* /haʊsəz/.
   Exactly the same rules apply when *s* is added to a verb to form the third-person singular simple present tense form.
   Examples:

loves	/lʌvz/	*hears*	/hɪəz/
drops	/drɒps/	*washes*	/wɒʃəz/

And again when *'s* is added to the end of a word as a contraction of *is* or *has*.
   Examples:

John's here	/dʒɒnz hɪə/
John's come	/dʒɒnz kʌm/
Dick's here	/dɪks hɪə/
Dick's come	/dɪks kʌm/
Rose's here	/rəʊzəz hɪə/
Rose's come	/rəʊzəz kʌm/

A very similar phenomenon is found when verbs take an *ed* ending to form the simple past tense or past participle. The ending is pronounced as an alveolar plosive (/t/ or /d/) which agrees in voicing with the last sound of the verb. If the verb itself ends in an alveolar plosive then a vowel (/ɪ/ or /ə/) is inserted and the ending is always /d/.

Examples:

loved	/lʌvd/	*agreed*	/əgriːd/
laughed	/lɑːft/	*wished*	/wɪʃt/
wanted	/wɒntəd/	*ended*	/endəd/

Exercise 2.2 Transcribe the following simple phrases.

- He missed it
- Bill's brother's passed
- He makes badges
- She repairs watches
- Jack's started school
- He misses his friends' company

Be sure to remember that all of the above rules only apply when an extra morpheme is added. It is not true, for example, that /s/ can never follow a voiced sound. Here are some words where it can: *bounce* /baʊns/, *toss* /tɒs/, *else* /els/. In all these cases, the /s/ is already part of the word, it has not been added as a suffix.

Smoothing

When the diphthongs /eɪ aɪ aʊ əʊ/ are immediately followed by /ə/ in words such as *player*, *higher*, *power*, *lower* a phenomenon known as **smoothing** may occur. The end target of the diphthong is left out and the resulting vowel sequences are /eə aə aə ɜː/. These symbols suggest that the smoothed version of /aɪə/ and /aʊə/ are identical. However, this is not true for all speakers. The use of the symbol /a/ in both /aɪ/ and /aʊ/ reflects the fact that in modern RP English there is not much phonetic difference between the starting points for these two diphthongs. However, /aʊ/ usually has a slightly backer start point. To reflect this in the smoothed versions, we shall use the symbol /aə/ for a smoothed /aɪə/ and /ɑə/ for a smoothed /aʊə/, for example: *tyre* /taə/, *tower* /tɑə/. Notice that the smoothing of /əʊə/ results in a monophthong.

Exercise 2.3 Transcribe the following, showing smoothing where possible.

- hours
- wiring
- showered
- grower

Connected speech

So far in this book we have concentrated mainly on the transcription of isolated words. Finally in this lesson we will look at a small piece of connected speech and give some hints on how to go about transcribing it. The remainder of the book focuses on some of the most common features of connected speech and practises their use in transcription.

Here is a brief passage in ordinary spelling. It is followed by a phonetic transcription.

I saw Fred the other day. I must say he's gained a lot of weight, hasn't he? He looks so .
different from the last time I saw him a year ago that I hardly recognised him. Have you
seen him recently? Well, apart from looking fat, he seems quite well.

| aɪ sɔː *ˈfred ði ˈʌðə ˈdeɪ | aɪ ˈmʌs seɪ ɪz ˈgeɪnd ə ˈlɒt əv ˈweɪt | ˈhæzənt i | hi
ˈlʊks ˈsəu ˈdɪfrənt frəm ðə ˈlɑːs taɪm aɪ ˈsɔːr ɪm ə ˈjɪər əˈgəu | ðət aɪ ˈhɑːdli
ˈrekəgnaɪzd ɪm | həv ˈjuː siːn ɪm ˈriːsəntli | wel əˈpɑːt frəm ˈlʊkɪŋ ˈfæt | hi
ˈsiːmz kwaɪt ˈwel |

Look through the transcription carefully. Here are some things to notice.

- There are no capital letters. These are not used in phonetic transcription.
- There are no normal punctuation marks – no commas, full stops, question marks.
- The mark ' is used to indicate stressed syllables. For more details see Lesson 3.
- The symbol | is used to mark a point where a speaker of the text might introduce a brief pause. Quite often this coincides with a place where there is a punctuation mark in the text, but *not always*. The symbol | is called a **word group boundary** or **potential pause**.
- * is used to indicate that the following word is a name.
- Many words in connected speech are pronounced (and therefore should be transcribed) differently in different environments. For example, the word *he* is transcribed /i/ in the phrase *hasn't he*. It is quite normal for the /h/ not to be pronounced here, but in the very next phrase *he looks so different . . .* we have transcribed the word /hi/. This is because immediately following a pause it is not usual to omit /h/ in RP English. There is more detail on this topic in Lesson 3. Another example is the word *saw* which appears twice in two different forms.
- There are a number of letters of the alphabet which are not used as symbols for transcribing English. These are *c o q x y*. In transcriptions the only symbols you are supposed to use are the phonetic symbols introduced in Lesson 1 and in this lesson.
- Be careful to think about how speech sounds and to avoid being misled by the spelling. Look at the words *recently* and *recognised*. They both contain the letter *c*. Does this sound the same in the two words? No, of course it doesn't. In the first it has the sound /s/ (a voiceless alveolar fricative) and in the second the sound /k/ (a voiceless velar plosive).
- The ordinary spelling version uses letters which do not correspond to any sound at all. Some examples of these 'silent' letters are:

e in *gained, recognised, quite*
r in *other, hardly, apart*

Exercise 2.4 As a final exercise for this lesson, try reading aloud the following short transcription and then check with the answers section.

| ˈwaɪ dʒu ˈwɒnt tə ˈliːv səu ˈɜːli | ˈaɪd əv ˈθɔːt | ðət wi kʊd ˈget ðeər ɒn ˈtaɪm
| ɪf wi ˈleft ət əbaut ˈhɑːf pɑːs ˈten | ɪf wi ˈliːv ət ˈnaɪn | wil əˈraɪv ˈfɑː tu ˈɜːli | ən
wil ˈhæv tə ˈstænd əraund ɪn ðə ˈkəuld | ˈweɪtɪŋ fə ði ˈʌdəz tə ʃəu ˈʌp |

From now on and throughout the rest of this book, we shall transcribe passages rather than single words or phrases in order to demonstrate and study processes which occur in connected speech. If you feel you need to do additional practice on single word transcription before attempting the passages, we can suggest *Practical Phonology* (Bogle, 1996), *Making Sense of Spelling and Pronunciation* (Digby and Myers, 1993) or *English Spelling* (Carney, 1997). You will also find it is useful to look at the transcription examples and do the exercises in the textbooks on English phonetics, phonology and pronunciation which you can find in the Bibliography at the end of the book.

References

Bogle, D. 1996: *Practical Phonology*. Edinburgh: Moray House.
Carney, E. 1997: *English Spelling*. London: Routledge.
Digby, C. and Myers, J. 1993: *Making Sense of Spelling and Pronunciation*. Hemel Hempstead: Prentice Hall International.

Lesson 3

Stress, rhythm and weak forms

Stress

In many languages, including English, when a word has more than one syllable and when it is pronounced in isolation, that is to say, when it is in its citation form, one of its syllables will be more prominent and audible than the others. This most audible syllable bears the main **lexical stress** or **accent** of the word. Lexical stress is predictable in some languages. For example, in Czech the first syllable of the word bears the main lexical stress, whereas in Polish it is the penultimate syllable. Lexical stress in English is not predictable in this way. Look at the examples below, where the syllable bearing the main lexical stress is preceded by '.

Examples:

butter /'bʌtə/	*except* /ɪk'sept/	*seventy* /'sevənti/
attention /ə'tenʃən/	*referee* /refə'riː/	

You can see that for two-syllable words, the first or the second syllable can bear main lexical stress and for three-syllable words the first, second or third can be stressed.

When words are put together into phrases or sentences in connected speech, some words retain their lexical stress and others lose it and in connected speech one-syllable words can bear stress. Look at the example below:

The 'fight between the 'cat and the 'dog

In this utterance of this phrase there are three stressed syllables *fight, cat* and *dog*. These all happen to be one-syllable words. The word *between* does not bear a stress at all, although if we were to say this word in isolation, the second syllable would bear the main lexical stress: /bi'twiːn/. Moreover, a word may bear stress when it appears in connected speech on a different syllable from that which carries the main lexical stress when the word is said in isolation.

Example:

citation form	*afternoon*	/aːftə'nuːn/
connected speech form	*afternoon tea*	/'aːftənuːn 'tiː/

The stresses we marked in the phrase above about *the cat and dog* and in *afternoon tea* are not lexical stresses but **sentence stresses** or **rhythmic stresses**. As we have seen, the two types of stress do not always coincide. In this book, when we use the term **stress**, we mean rhythmic stress, unless we explicitly say otherwise. We will not use the word *accent* to refer to syllable prominence at all.

Rhythm

Rhythm could be defined as the periodic repetition of an event. Languages can have one of two different types of rhythm depending on the type of event that is repeated periodically. *Syllable-timed* languages are those in which syllables are repeated periodically, that is, all syllables take *approximately* the same amount of time. To put this another way, for each syllable there is a rhythmic beat which occurs at more or less equal time intervals. French and Spanish are examples of syllable-timed languages. In *stress-timed* languages it is stresses which occur at approximately equal intervals, that is, there is more or less the same amount of time between stresses. English is a stressed-timed language.

Stress-timing can be seen at work in the following example:

```
w         x    y                z
'David had 'seen 'helicopters at the 'airport.
```

Since it is stresses that occur at approximately equal intervals, stress-timed rhythm requires that more or less the same amount of time be spent in the pronunciation of the three syllables between w and x, for the one syllable between x and y, for the six syllables between y and z and for the two syllables between z and the end of the utterance. It is therefore necessary to compress the duration of syllables more in the stretch between y and z : *'helicopters at the*, than in the one between w and x: *'David had*, whereas the syllable between x and y, *'seen* and the ones after z *'airport* will be relatively long. When there is a need to hurry over some words, it is mainly unstressed syllables that get shortened. Therefore, stress-timing requirements are responsible for many of the phonetic weakenings found in English, such as the reductions found in weak forms.

Weak forms

As we have already said, when words are isolated, that is, out of context, we use their *citation forms*. In that case, all words have at least one stressed syllable. However, some words may not be stressed in connected speech and there are words which are rarely stressed. These words which are not usually stressed are words that have little lexical meaning (**grammatical** or **form** words). Prepositions, pronouns, auxiliary and modal verbs, conjunction and articles are grammatical words. On the other hand, words which often keep the stress in connected speech because they carry considerable semantic weight (**lexical** or **content** words) are nouns, main verbs, adjectives and adverbs.

Phonetic weakenings and reductions mostly affect unstressed syllables. Sounds in unstressed syllables are frequently weakened, for instance by shortenings, elisions etc. In English these processes have produced historically important changes in the pronunciation of unstressed syllables, particularly in vowels, and are now the usual pronunciations of words. For instance, historical /'ɔːfʊl/ for *awful* is no longer the usual pronunciation; its reduced form is much more likely: /'ɔːfəl/. In some grammatical words, on the other hand, both the full and reduced pronunciation co-exist. The choice between these pronunciations depends largely on whether the word is stressed or unstressed in connected speech.

Because grammatical words are usually unstressed, their reduced or weak pronunciations are very frequent, even more so than their full forms. There is, accordingly, a weak, normal pronunciation and a full, strong one which is used when the word is stressed for some reason and in some other circumstances we shall see below. These pronunciations are known as the **weak form** and **strong form** respectively.

Not all grammatical words have an alternation between weak and strong pronunciations. For instance, only monosyllabic grammatical words may have a weak form. Conversely, some words present several different weak forms.

Changes affecting grammatical words are systematic since they follow general language rules and properties of sounds. For instance, the more centralised a vowel, the weaker it is. The greatest weakening for any sound is **elision**.

Vowel changes

Weakening makes all vowels move to the centre of the vowel space. They will first move to the central vowel quality nearest to their original one as in Table 3.1

Table 3.1 Vowel changes

strong vowel		weak vowel	example
/iː/	→	/ɪ/, /i/	*be*
/uː/	→	/ʊ/, /u/	*do*
/e/	→	/ə/	*them*
/æ/	→	/ə/	*and*
/ʌ/	→	/ə/	*but*
/ɑː/	→	/ə/	*are*
/ɒ/	→	/ə/	*of*
/ɔː/	→	/ə/	*for*
/ɜː/	→	/ə/	*her*

In the case of grammatical words which have the vowel /ʊ/ in their citation form, such as *could*, they can stay unchanged when unstressed since this vowel is already weak, or they may be further weakened to schwa /ə/:

/kʊd/   /kəd/   *could*

By the same token grammatical words which have the vowel /uː/ in their strong form may go a further step in weakening, which would make the vowel /ʊ/ go to /ə/, for example:

/duː/ → /dʊ/ → /də/   *do*
/juː/ → /jʊ/ → /jə/   *you*

The last pronunciation of these words (which is only possible when the following sound is a consonant as we shall see below) is considered to be very informal in RP, but is usual in other varieties of English.

Consonant changes

Consonant changes are not an intrinsic part of weak forms but an optional step in a scale of weakening which depends on the speech register that is used. Many of the consonant changes that we will mention are not exclusive to weak forms. They can be seen to occur in lexical words, too, depending on the phonetic context and register. Nevertheless, grammatical words are favourable environments for these changes. The following changes are very often found in weak forms

- /h/ may be elided if it is not at the very beginning of the utterance (following a potential pause):

  /ˈtel hɪm/ → /ˈtel ɪm/   *tell him*

but not in

  /hi ˈkeɪm/ *he came*

- · /d/ and /t/ may be elided when at the end of a word and preceded by another consonant:

  /ˈænd/ → /ənd/ → /ən/   *and*

This matter of elision will be dealt with more fully in Lesson 6.

Table 3.2 lists the most common words which have strong and weak forms in RP English. Notice that all these words consist of a single syllable and that they nearly all belong to one of the four classes: auxiliary verb, conjunction, preposition, pronoun. The symbols /l̩/ and /n̩/ in this table represent syllabic consonants. (*See Lesson 5 for an explanation.*)

Use of weak forms in RP

Grammatical words in connected speech are used in their weak form most of the time but take into account the following restrictions.

(I) When the word is stressed because of emphasis or contrast, the strong form is compulsory:

  /ənd/ → /ˈænd/ in *I didn't say apples or pears, I said apples and pears*

(II) When prepositions and auxiliary verbs appear in grammatical structures such as the following, they are used in strong form:

Table 3.2 Common words with strong and weak forms in RP English

word	strong form	weak form	word	strong form	weak form
a	/eɪ/	/ə/	his	/hɪz/	/ɪz/
am	/æm/	/əm/	just	/dʒʌst/	/dʒəst/
an	/æn/	/ən/	me	/miː/	/mɪ/, /mi/
and	/ænd/	/ənd/, /ən/, /n̩d/, /n̩/	must	/mʌst/	/məst/
are	/ɑː/	/ə/	of	/ɒv/	/əv/
as	/æz/	/əz/	shall	/ʃæl/	/ʃəl/, /ʃl̩/
at	/æt/	/ət/	she	/ʃiː/	/ʃɪ/, /ʃi/
be	/biː/	/bɪ/, /bi/	should	/ʃud/	/ʃud/, /ʃəd/
been	/biːn/	/bɪn/	some	/sʌm/	/səm/, /sm̩/
but	/bʌt/	/bət/	than	/ðæn/	/ðən/, /ðn̩/
can	/kæn/	/kən/, /kn̩/	that	/ðæt/	/ðət/
could	/kud/	/kud/, /kəd/	the	/ðiː/	/ðɪ/, /ði/, /ðə/
do	/duː/	/du/, /du/, /də/	them	/ðem/	/ðəm/, /əm/
does	/dʌz/	/dəz/	there	/ðeə/	/ðə/
for	/fɔː/	/fə/	to	/tuː/	/tu/, /tu/ /tə/
from	/frɒm/	/frəm/	us	/ʌs/	/əs/
had	/hæd/	/həd/, /əd/	was	/wɒz/	/wəz/
has	/hæz/	/həz/, /əz/	we	/wiː/	/wɪ/ /wi/
have	/hæv/	/həv/, /əv/	were	/wɜː/	/wə/
he	/hiː/	/hɪ/, /ɪ/ /hi/, /i/	who	/huː/	/hu/ /hu/
her	/hɜː/	/hə/, /ə/	would	/wud/	/wud/, /wəd/
him	/hɪm/	/ɪm/	you	/juː/	/ju/, /ju/, /jə/

That's the picture I was looking <u>at</u>	/æt/ not /ət/
You were later than I <u>was</u> this morning	/wɒz/ not /wəz/
He can sing well, but I <u>can</u> too	/kæn/ not /kən/ or /kn̩/
He's younger than I <u>am</u>	/æm/ not /əm/
They were being looked <u>for</u> by the police	/fɔː/ not /fə/

The underlined words above are not likely to bear stress, but nevertheless appear in the strong form. The reason is that a word which normally follows the underlined preposition or auxiliary verb has either been deleted or moved to some other position in the sentence, leaving the auxiliary or preposition behind. The auxiliary or preposition is said to be *stranded*. Take the first sentence, for example. The word *at*, being a preposition, is normally followed by a noun or noun phrase which it is said to govern. The noun phrase which *at* governs in this sentence is *the picture*. Because of the grammatical structure used, this phrase does not immediately follow the preposition, therefore the preposition is stranded. In the second and third sentences the verbs *was* and *can* are not followed by an adjective or a verb, respectively. They have been deleted in order to avoid repetition. Again, the auxiliaries are stranded. **Stranding** often takes place at the end of the sentence, but not always, as you can see from some of the sentences above.

One final detail about stranding is that the auxiliary verb *have* in structures where it is immediately preceded by another auxiliary, such as *can't, could, couldn't, must, mustn't, should, shouldn't, will, won't, would, wouldn't*, is normally used in its weak form even if it is stranded. In the following sentences *have* is pronounced /əv/ or /həv/ not /hæv/.

He left before he should have
I told them to do it, but they won't have unfortunately

It must be borne in mind that stranding does not apply to other words which have weak forms, such as conjunctions or pronouns.

(III)   A preposition preceding a pronoun can be used in strong or weak form:

I was looking for you   /fə ju/ or /fɔ: ju/.

(IV)   Some words can function either as an auxiliary verb or as a main verb. When such words are used as auxiliary verbs, they may be pronounced in the weak form, but if they constitute a main verb, even if they are unstressed, they must be used in strong form:

We have our holiday in August   /hæv/ not /həv/ or /əv/
We have to go   /hæv/ not /həv/ or /əv/
You have seen them   /həv/ or /əv/ if unstressed

Other words to which this applies are *has, had, do* and *does*. The various forms of the verb *to be* are an exception to this rule, since they can appear in weak form even if they are functioning as the main verb:

They are happy   /ə/ if unstressed
We were friends   /wə/ if unstressed

(V)   There are a number of words which need special mention. For these words the use of weak or strong forms is determined by their function in the utterance or by their meaning.

her   /hə/, /ə/

As a possessive adjective, /h/ is not usually dropped, for instance in *This is her car* is pronounced with /hə/. As a personal pronoun /ə/ may be used, as in *It belongs to her*.

just   /dʒʌst, dʒəs/

This word can mean 'only' or 'simply' as in *I'll just telephone him*. In this meaning the word is usually found in its weak form. Another meaning is 'precisely' or 'exactly' as in *I arrived just in time*. With this meaning the word is usually stressed and therefore used in its strong form. A third meaning is 'a short time ago' or 'a short time before'. This is usually found accompanying a verb in the present perfect or past perfect tense as in *I've just seen him* or *She'd just written him a letter*. In this usage the word can be weak if unstressed, but must be strong if it is stressed.

some   /sʌm/, /səm/, /sm̩/

This is a rather troublesome word because it has so many different meanings. It is used in its strong form when it precedes countable singular nouns and it means 'a certain': /sʌm/ in *Some animal was shot*, or when it precedes certain non-countable nouns and means 'a considerable amount of', so /sʌm/ in *I haven't seen you for some time*. It is also strong when used as a pronoun as in

Some of the boys ran or *I bought some.* In other cases the weak form is normally used: /səm/ *I need some money.* However, notice the following important point: *some* can mean 'part of the whole', in which case it is usually stressed and strong, or it can simply be the plural equivalent of 'a' or 'an' as in singular: *a person,* plural *some people.* So a sentence like *I met some people at the party* could mean 'I met some [but not all] of the people at the party' in which case *some* will be strong, or it could mean 'I met a few people at the party' in which case *some* will be weak.

that   /ðæt/, /ðət/

Strong form as an adjective or pronoun /ðæt/: *That boy is sad.* Weak form as a relative pronoun or conjunction /ðət/: *He's the man that I was talking about* (pronoun), *I know that you have a bike* (conjunction).

there   /ðeə/, /ðə/

Strong form as an adverb: /ðeə/ in *I bought it there.* Weak form in existential construction: /ðə/ in *There is a dog in the garden.*

(VI)   Some words with more than one weak form have their choice determined by the phonetic context.

do

/duː/, /du/ before a vowel as in *Do I know you?*
/də/ before a consonant as in *Do they want to?* (casual pronunciation).

the

/ðɪ/, /ði/ before a vowel as in *The apples were good.*
/ðə/ before a consonant as in *The children left.*

to

/tuː/, /tu/ before a vowel as in *He spoke to everybody.*
/tə/ before a consonant as in *I gave it to my neighbour.*

you

/juː/, /ju/ before a vowel as in *You always say that.*
/jə/ before a consonant as in *You can't be serious* (casual pronunciation).

Notice, however, that the various weak forms of the word *and* are not restricted to specific environments. The use of /ənd/, /ən/, /n̩d/ or /n̩/ is essentially random.

(VII)   Contracted negative forms of auxiliary verbs, including the verb *to be*, do not have weak forms. So, for example, *aren't* is always /ɑːnt/. Be careful with some of these negative contractions because they may differ considerably from the affirmative strong form as in *can't* /kɑːnt/, *don't* /dəunt/ and *won't* /wəunt/.

(VIII)   Possessive pronouns, such as *yours*, *his* and *hers*, are never used in weak forms. So, *That hat is his* must show the full form /hɪz/, whereas *That is his cake* can be found with /ɪz/.

(IX)   Finally, there are a number of other words which are deceptive in that they look as though they ought to have weak forms, because they are grammatical words with only one syllable. The most common of these are the words *on, off* and *up*. These do not have weak forms in RP English. *On* is always /ɒn/, *off* is always /ɒf/ and *up* is always /ʌp/ and *or* is /ɔː/ /ɔːr/ most of the time, except for very casual speech and close-knit structures such as *one or two* in which it may be found weakened to /ə/. Also, single-syllable grammatical words where the vowel is a diphthong, such as *out, round* and *while*, do not have weak forms.

Here is a transcribed passage in which you can find many grammatical words in the weak or in the strong form. Try to read it bearing in mind that '|' means there is a potential pause. You will see that the transcription has been annotated. Each superscript number refers to a relevant explanation or comment on the following page. A group of asterisks (***) after the comment means that we will not repeat it in future lessons. Remember that there may be other possible pronunciations for some of the words in the passage, certainly in other varieties of English but also within RP. You can find an orthographic version for this passage in the answers section at the end of the book.

Sample transcription

| wen aɪ ˈθɪŋk əv maɪ ˈjɪəz[1] ət juːniˈvɜːsɪti | ˈwʌn əv ðə ˈθɪŋz[1] aɪ rɪˈgret | ɪz ðə ˈfækt ðət aɪ dɪd ˈnɒt teɪk ˈsʌm[2] sʌbdʒəkts[3] ˈsɪərɪəsli | ənd[4] aɪ ˈəunli dɪd iˈnʌf ˈwɜːk tə ˈskreɪp ˈbaɪ | ˈsʌmhau | ðeɪ əv[5] ˈɔːl kənˈtraɪvd[6] tə ˈkʌm bæk ˈhɔːntɪŋli | sɪns aɪ əv[5] ˈendəd[7] ʌp ˈniːdɪŋ tə ˈnəu əbaut ðəm fə maɪ ˈwɜːk | ˈwɒt ə ˈlɒt əv ˈweɪstəd[7] ɒpəˈtjuːnɪtiz[1] | ət ðə ˈtaɪm | fə wɒtˈevə ˈriːzən | aɪ ˈkʊdənt ˈsiː eni ˈɪntərəst ɪn ðəm | ə ˈlɒt əv ɪt wəz maɪ ˈəun ˈfɔːlt | fə ˈspendɪŋ maɪ ˈtaɪm ɪn ˈʌðə pəˈsjuːts[3] | sʌtʃ əz ˈpleɪɪŋ ˈkɑːdz[1] wɪð maɪ ˈklɑːsmeɪts[3] | ɔː ˈgəuɪŋ tə ðə kæfəˈtɪərɪə | fə ˈlɒŋ ˈtʃæts[3] ənd[4] ˈnjuːmərəs ˈkɒfiz[1] | bət aɪ məst ˈɔːlsəu pɔɪnt ˈaut ðət ɪt ˈɒftən[8] wəz ðə ˈlektʃərəz[1] ˈfɔːlt | ˈnau aɪ əm ˈθrəuɪŋ ˈstəunz[1] ɪn maɪ ˈəun ˈglɑːshaus | bət ɪt ˈhæz[9] tə bi ˈsed | ðə wəz ðɪs ˈkɔːs | wɪtʃ went ˈtəutəli ˈəuvə maɪ ˈhed | ənd[4] tə ðɪs ˈdeɪ | aɪ ˈdaunt[10] nəu ˈhau aɪ ˈpɑːst[11] ɪt | ðə ˈlektʃərə wəz ə ˈveri naɪs ˈmæn | ə bɪt ˈʃaɪ | ənd[4] wɪð ə məˈnɒtənəs ˈvɔɪs ˈkwɒlɪti | wɪtʃ ˈment ðət ju wər[12] ˈiːzɪli ˈsent tə ˈsliːp | bət ðə ˈwɜːst wɒz[13] ðət i[5] ˈnjuː tuː ˈmʌtʃ | ɔː ˈrɑːðə | hi[14] ˈdɪdənt nəu ˈhau tə ˈpɪtʃ θɪŋz[1] ˈləu ɪnʌf fə ˈstjuːdənts[3] tə ˈfɒləu | hi[14] ˈfaɪnəli ˈgeɪv ʌp ˈtiːtʃɪŋ | ənd[4] bɪˈkeɪm ə ˈfʊltaɪm rɪˈsɜːtʃə | wɪtʃ aɪ ˈθɪŋk ɪz ˈwɒt i[5] wəz kʌt ˈaut fɔː[13] | aɪm ˈnɒt traɪɪŋ tə ˈʃɪft ˈɔːl ðə ˈbleɪm fə ðə ˈkɔːsəz[15] aɪ ˈweɪstəd[7] | laɪk aɪ ˈsed | ɪt wəz ˈɔːlsəu ˈdjuː tə maɪ ˈɪntərəsts[3] ˈliːnɪŋ təwɔːdz ˈʌðə ˈθɪŋz[1] | ˈstɪl | ˈsəuʃəlaɪzɪŋ ɪz əˈnʌðə ˈskɪl ðət ˈhæz[9] tə bi ˈlɜːnt | ənd[4] ɪz ɪmˈpɔːtənt fə jɔː ˈfjuːtʃə | ˈdaunt[10] ju ˈθɪŋk |

Comments to the sample transcription

1.   When it is a morpheme or contraction, 's' agrees in voicing with the previous sound. In this case the previous sound is voiced so the morpheme is pronounced /z/. ***

2. Here *some* means 'part of the whole', and therefore it is stressed and used in the strong form.
3. When it is a morpheme or contraction, 's' agrees in voicing with the previous sound. In this case the previous sound is voiceless so the morpheme is pronounced /s/. ***
4. /ənd/ and /ən/ are alternative weak forms for *and*. ***
5. /h/ can be deleted here because it is not following a potential pause. ***
6. The regular past tense morpheme agrees in voicing with the previous sound. In this case the previous sound is voiced so the morpheme is pronounced /d/. ***
7. The regular past tense morpheme is pronounced /əd/ or /ɪd/ when the previous sound is /t/ or /d/.
8. /ɒfən/ is an alternative pronunciation.
9. The strong form is used because the verb is not being used as an auxiliary.
10. The strong form must be used because it is a negative contraction.
11. The regular past tense morpheme agrees in voicing with the previous sound. In this case the previous sound is voiceless so the morpheme is pronounced /t/. ***
12. /r/ is pronounced here because the next word begins with a vowel sound and there is no pause in between (*see Lesson 4*). ***
13. The strong form is used because the grammatical word is stranded.
14. /h/ cannot be deleted here because it is following a potential pause. ***
15. The morpheme 's' is pronounced /əz/ or /ɪz/ when it follows a sibilant consonant /s z ʃ ʒ tʃ dʒ/. ***

Exercise 3.1 Look at the following passage which is given in orthography. Try to identify all the weak forms of the grammatical words in it. Check your version at the end of the book, where you can also find this text transcribed and commented.

A group of people were sitting having a drink in a bar and one man was boasting about how tough he was. After a while, everyone else got fed up with listening to this, so someone said, 'All right. You say you're so tough, but I bet you can't spend the night alone on the top of the mountain without a coat or anything to keep you warm.' The man took on the bet and the next night he climbed the mountain alone. He found a sheltered spot and sat down. He had brought a book with him and he lit a candle so that he was able to read. He spent the coldest, most miserable night of his life. In the morning, he staggered down the mountain half-dead and went to find his friends and to claim his winnings. 'Are you sure you didn't have a coat?' they asked him. 'I was dressed just as I am now,' he said. 'And you didn't light a fire? Not even a candle?' 'Oh, yes. I had a candle, but only in order to read my book.' 'The bet's off,' they said and went away laughing. The man was very annoyed, but he didn't say anything. A few weeks later, he invited them all to dinner at his house. They all arrived on time and sat waiting for the meal to be served. An hour went by, two hours, but still no food appeared. Finally, they began to lose patience and asked the man what he was playing at. 'All right,' he said. 'Let's go into the kitchen and see if the food's ready.' They all followed him into the other room where they saw a huge pot of water on a stand and underneath was a single lighted candle. The man put his finger into the water. 'No. It's not ready yet. I can't understand it. The candle's been there since yesterday.' His friends laughed and took him out for an expensive meal at the nearest restaurant.

Here there are four passages for you to transcribe. Pay special attention to the use of weak forms and remember the hints which we gave you in the previous lessons. After doing each one of them, compare it to our version at the end of the book and study the comments carefully. We suggest you do not start a new transcription until you have fully understood the last one you have done. It may be a good idea to revise the explanations given in this lesson and the previous ones if you find you do not understand the transcription comments or that you are making quite a lot of mistakes.

Exercise 3.2 Transcribe the following passage including all we have covered so far with special attention to weak forms.

- How did you get here this morning? I didn't see you at the station.
- I came by car, but I wouldn't do it again.
- Why not? The traffic isn't too bad, is it?
- It was this morning. There are a lot of roadworks just the other side of the river.
- Oh, yes. I'd completely forgotten about those. So why didn't you catch the train?
- The alarm clock didn't go off. There must have been a power cut last night, because the numbers were blinking. And then the traffic made me 20 minutes late.
- Oh, dear. Mr Jenkins wouldn't like that.
- He certainly didn't like it. He got rather unpleasant about it.
- I'm not surprised. He's been getting more and more bad-tempered lately. Everybody's noticed it. Ever since he had that meeting at the head office, he has been quite unbearable.
- Yes. I know he's got a lot on his plate at the moment, but there's really no need to be rude to someone in front of everybody else. He made me feel as if I had just killed somebody. I tell you. I think he means to make me pay for this.
- Oh, I shouldn't worry too much about it. He'll have forgotten all about it by tomorrow. He always does. It's one of his few good qualities.
- He will if I'm not late again, but this is the fourth time I've been late this month. When it's not roadworks, it's a broken down bus. I really must manage to get here on time from now on.
- I'd do my very best if I were you. You mustn't underestimate him, not with all these goal-achieving policies he's always ranting about. Besides, there are quite a few people around that would love to have a go at your job. Nothing personal, you understand. It's just pure climbing.
- Oh, I do know. And I will try. Like you said, this place is teeming with competitors and getting on the wrong side of Jenkins is not the best way to keep them at bay. I've already changed jobs twice in the last three years. I don't want to go through all that again.

Exercise 3.3 Transcribe the following passage including all we have covered so far with special attention to weak forms.

I have lived in London for ten years now. It seems such a long time, when I actually stop and think about it. Ten years! More than a third of my life. When I think of home however, Sheldon always comes to mind – a tiny village in the heart of the Blackdown Hills, hidden in the depths of Devon. I love going home at this time of year. Spring is maturing like an adolescent girl; the leaves unfurling, modestly extending their fresh, green growth. The fields reverberate with the hesitant bleating of newborn lambs and the hedges and trees are filled with the expectant rustle of new life in creation. London, however, remains oblivious to the fertility of spring. We are buried in ourselves. There are delays on the Northern Line again. A signal failure at some station makes all trains late. The *Big Issue* vendor at the underground ticket office shouts in your face. The crowds push and shove in the direction of the super-market, mouths watering in anticipation of their evening meal. I take a walk down the road to post a letter. London kills me. Red buses shuddering past me, belching thick smoke which clings to the back of my throat. In this city, you learn to walk fast, avoid all eye-contact and maintain the air of someone on an errand. It's called self-preservation. If you slow down, or catch a stranger's eye, then who knows what might happen? It is safer to remain within the bubble of anonymity. I want to go home – my home – where I can sit under the eucalyptus tree in the dusk and watch the horizon darken as the sun sets and the bats start their nightly hunt for juicy insects.

Exercise 3.4 Transcribe the following passage, including all we have seen so far, with special attention to weak forms.

I haven't got a car of my own, but sometimes I borrow one from a friend and drive to see my brother and sister-in-law, who live about 60 miles from London. I have done the journey in all kinds of weather, but the worst time I ever had was on a very foggy day in the middle of November. When I started the drive, the weather was a bit misty, but I didn't think it was bad enough to postpone my trip, or to go by train, which, although it was possible at that time, wasn't very easy or conve-nient. Anyway, I got about 20 miles outside London and the mist started getting thicker and thicker. I was getting more and more nervous, because I am not a very confident driver at the best of times. I suppose I don't get enough practice. I really hate fog, even when I'm not driving, but when you're behind the wheel of a car, it seems ten times worse, doesn't it? I had to drive extremely slowly and the journey took me almost an hour longer than it normally does. Finally, I got to the place where I had to turn off the main road into the small country lane which leads to the village where my brother lives. At least I thought I had got to the right lane. After about a mile, I passed a house which I could just make out in the fog, but which I didn't recognise at all. I didn't fancy turning round and going back to the main road, because I thought it would be dangerous getting back into the flow of traffic in such poor visibility. I decided to press on and see if I came to any signposts which would put me back on the right track. That was my silliest mistake. The next hour was like a nightmare. I got deeper into the coun-tryside and the fog got even thicker. At one point, I lost the road altogether and found myself driving across a field through a herd of rather surprised cows. Once I missed by inches going into a rather deep ditch. Finally, I came to a signpost with the name of my brother's village on it. It was ten miles back in the direction I had just come. The next time I visit my brother in November, I shall listen very carefully to the weather forecast before I set out. Better still, I shall get him to visit me.

Exercise 3.5 Transcribe the following passage, including all we have covered so far, with special attention to weak forms.

The game's something like baseball, something like football, but let me tell you, it's much better than either. It's played on a flat park which has a square marked in the middle and a limit round the outside. The square is where the batman stands. He has a bat made of wood and shaped something like a garden spade. The batman cannot leave the area which is marked off at any time during his round on the pitch. If he does, he loses one of his three lives. The ballman stands anywhere he wants outside the square and throws the ball to the batman. The ball must land within the square. If it doesn't, the batman gets a point. Otherwise he has to hit the ball before it bounces a second time, but he can't hit it before it bounces at all. If the ball bounces a second time inside the square, the batman loses two of his lives. Let's assume the batman hits the ball. He can get two points if the ball goes over the limit without touching the ground, and one point if it does touch down. Both the batman's team and the ballman's team have fieldmen on the park. Exactly how many is decided by the ballman for each new round. Sometimes there are 20 or more. The batman's team must always have as many as the ballman's team. If a fieldman of the ballman's team gets the ball, he must try to get it back to the square and drop it in. He can do this by running with the ball, or throwing it to another fieldman on his team. If he succeeds, the batman doesn't score anything. The batman's team's fieldmen have to try to stop this happening and to get the ball across the limit, again by throwing it or by running with it. This phase of the game is more like war than anything. About the only thing that fieldmen aren't allowed to do is to hit an opponent with their fists. Almost anything else goes. Fieldmen need to be really tough, I can tell you. Most of them are about eight feet tall, and you wouldn't want to meet any of them in an alley on a dark night. A few years ago the game was played without any protective gear, but there were many accidents and often players got seriously injured. Nowadays if you saw the players for the first time, you would think they belonged to a commando unit or to a science fiction film. They are padded from head to toe. They wear crash helmets and protections on all their joints and soft parts, specially the fieldmen, but they don't wear gloves. That is because you can get a better grip with your bare hands. Batmen do use gloves so that the bat does not slip. Old-timers think these new outfits make it a softer game, so they are not in favour of players using them. But I'm sure the players are.

You have now done quite a few exercises on the basics of English transcription. If you think you have mastered the symbols, smoothing, weak forms and the rest, you can go on to Lesson 4. However, if you are not very sure you are doing well, we suggest you carry on practising with the five texts that follow. It is important that you feel confident in doing what we have covered so far before you go on to the next lesson.

Exercise 3.6 Transcribe the following passage, including all we have dealt with up to now, with special attention to weak forms.

I recently went to London to meet a friend I had not seen for some time. I arranged to meet her at Victoria station and travelled by train, instead of driving as usual. The train was a few minutes late due to maintenance work on the line. It was not crowded as it was too late for commuters to be using it and we had a comfortable journey. My friend was waiting for me by the arrivals and departures board and as we had both breakfasted earlier than usual, we went into the station café and had a cup of coffee. When we had finished our drink, we went by tube to South Kensington to the Victoria and Albert Museum. It was difficult to decide where to go first, as there was so much of interest to see, but we finally chose an exhibition on dress, where we saw costumes from the eighteenth century onwards, some of them for day wear, but mostly for evening wear, and all for well-off people. Some of the ball gowns were magnificent. We then looked at Islamic art, mostly pottery, ceramics and carpets. The latter were very beautiful, with intricate patterns and rich colours. There were also lovely plates and ewers, and carved wood inlaid with ivory. We also enjoyed looking at European medieval carvings and silver cups. We had lunch in the cafeteria in the museum, and having admired some stained glass and church embroideries, we left the museum and went to look at more recent work in Harrods department store. We spent most of our time there in the food halls, where our mouths watered as we passed piles of fruit and vegetables from all parts of the world, luscious chocolates, spiced, smoked and fresh meats. There were also pies, pates, cheeses, pickles and preserves. My friend said it must be possible to buy anything you wished for, as long as you had enough money. All too soon it was time to catch my train home. This time it was filled with commuters and some people couldn't find a seat and had to stand for a long time, until others reached their destination and got out. The early part of the journey was through the London suburbs. When we were waiting for the signals to change in our favour near Clapham Junction, I saw a fox walking along beside the track where there was a grassy space between the rails. He seemed quite unconcerned about the train. He came to a place where there was a scatter of feathers and I wondered if he had caught a pigeon the previous evening and had come back to see if he could catch another for his dinner. There was no more excitement after that, though the embankments were looking beautiful with cherry blossom and lilac in the gardens, fresh green foliage and wild flowers. I had a very enjoyable day though I felt pleasantly tired at the end of it.

Exercise 3.7 Transcribe the following passage, including all we have dealt with so far, with special attention to weak forms.

My friend and I both have very energetic dogs, so first thing in the morning we like to take them for a walk to burn up a little bit of their energy and keep fit ourselves at the same time. We are lucky to have a park nearby, usually known as *The Hill*. It is really two hills, one open and rocky with wild places covered in bracken and gorse. There is a system of paths that have been surfaced with tarmac so that we can keep our shoes dry, even on very rainy days. We don't usually see much wildlife: birds, squirrels and a rabbit or two, but I'm told that at the less disturbed times of early morning, late evening and night time, badgers, foxes, hedgehogs, lizards, all enjoy the hill, adding to the fun for the dogs, because there are interesting scents to pick up, and trails to follow. The second hill has a conifer wood, with a soft floor of pine needles and a deciduous wood, where children delight to search for horse chestnuts, which are known as conkers, in the autumn. For the rest of us, there are beautiful views to enjoy. To the south and west you can see the Dublin mountains. Each season has its delights: the green of spring with the white blackthorn blossom, is followed by the hawthorn and alder blossom, heavy with scent which attracts the bees. The gorse blooms in spasms from spring on, but puts on its real show of gold in late summer, to complement the purple of the heather and gradually the bracken turns its lovely red brown colour. Even in winter, the mountains look lovely, sometimes misty, other times powdered with snowfalls that we miss, as we are near the sea. The snow is not often deep, but it outlines the farms, hedges and fields and also the rocky outcrops and seams. If we turn to face east, we can see the sea, always with a lace of white foam on the distant beach. In fine weather, there are little fishing boats and men hauling up lobster and crab pots. Tankers and cargo ships sail up to dock upriver in Dublin port, and the ferry from Wales can be seen making for one of the two harbours nearby. Below us, there are beautiful houses skirting the coastline. Most of them are quite old, but they look splendid, since they belong to people who are very well-off, a few famous artists amongst them, and who can afford to keep them in excellent condition. To the north you can see the city with early sunshine glinting on cars as people make their way to work. Across the bay is the north side equivalent to our hill. It's a favourite place to go on outings. If it's not raining, we like to take a picnic basket with us and spend the afternoon there, sipping tea or coffee and eating a few sandwiches and cakes whilst we watch the gulls dipping into the sea. The train speeds by below us towards the city and the other side of the bay. At last I turn downhill, invigorated but reluctant to leave, although I'm looking forward to tea and toast before starting on housework and shopping.

Exercise 3.8 Transcribe the following passage, including all we have seen so far, with special attention to weak forms.

My father was a sailor, and I was born far away from home, in the south. Since my father had to travel often to that part of the country, my family went to live there, and that was where I was born. When I was just six months old, we all came back north to the town where my parents had their house. There I grew up and had a very happy childhood. Life was simple and safe. I used to meet other children in the street to play after school. I remember one day when my brother got very angry because I had lost in a game of marbles and he had to go and win them all back. Things carried on peacefully until the war. I was only seven when our town was bombed and we were left with the clothes we were standing in, nothing else. I was very upset about losing a very pretty doll I had and a tartan dress with matching velvet jacket. My mother had had them made for me to wear after my first communion. That was the nineteenth of April, at the convent nearby. It was a beautiful day and very special because it made me feel very important. After the war we went to live in a university town in the west, whilst my brother studied law. They were really hard times. We all had to make do with whatever was available. I remember how cold it was in the winter. My mother made me a coat out of a blanket. She dyed it blue, but the stripes going across still showed. When father came to visit, he brought us wonderful things that were not to be found anywhere at home: salted butter, tinned meat from Argentina, chocolate and coffee. It made us feel privileged. I'll never forget how upset I was when I found out about Father Christmas. It happened one afternoon. My mother and brother went out shopping and took a long time to come back. When they arrived, I heard the creaking from the lid of a big wicker trunk we had in a cupboard. I waited until they weren't looking and then went very carefully to the cupboard and lifted the lid a little bit and there they were, the toys. I thought 'If I get these toys as presents tomorrow, I'll know who Father Christmas is'. And so it was. The following morning I opened the presents I had seen the day before. When my brother finished his studies, we moved to a city not far from our old home. My parents wanted to go back to their part of the country, but since they had to start from scratch, they chose a city so that we had more opportunities to study and find jobs. I went to secondary school and then trained to be a teacher. I worked at a primary school for nine years, teaching small children how to read and write. It amuses me nowadays when I find that some of those young pupils of mine have become important people or highly qualified professionals. It also fills me with pride, even if my contribution to their careers was only a minor one. Like everyone, I have had good and bad times in my life. My marriage has been a very happy one and we had three great children. Many years have gone by, but I feel fortunate because I have a family who loves me and takes care of me, and two granddaughters. I love spending time with them and watching them grow up. Last Christmas I saw the wonder in their eyes when they came into the room and saw their presents. Their flushed faces and innocence brought a lot of memories back. I hope they don't hear the sound of a creaking lid for a long time yet.

Exercise 3.9 Transcribe the following passage, including all we have seen so far, with special attention to weak forms.

The young woman walked down the eighteenth-century London high street with her long skirt billowing in the wind and the hem tapping at her ankles. She was lost in thought and was taken aback when her day-dreaming was disturbed by a young gentleman. 'Good morning Lady Helen,' said the man. The woman was confused. Having only recently arrived, she knew no one in the capital and did not answer to the name of Helen, but Jane. Recognizing the mistake, the man apologized for his error. She was about to turn away from the young man, who was extremely well-dressed and seemed to be very well-off, when he commented on the colour of her eyes and the beauty of her expression. The conversation continued until eventually the man, who introduced himself as Lord Charles, insisted that she join him for tea at his apartment nearby. The apartment, although modest, was far more glamorous than anything she had ever seen before. The maid served them tea and cucumber sandwiches and the lord discussed his contacts and his imminent trip to the continent. Since she had told him that she was fluent in French, German and Spanish, he suggested that she accompany him on his journey the very next week. Jane was at first speechless but with only a little more persuasion, she agreed. The lord felt that it was necessary for the woman to obtain a new wardrobe so that she would have more suitable clothes for the weather and company that they would meet. For this the lord gave her a list of shops on Bond Street where he had an account. The next question was that of jewellery. Lord Charles was meeting a jeweller friend of his later that day and could buy watches, ear-rings and rings that would be suitable for the trip. The problem was that the lord might not get the correct size. Then he appeared to stumble across a solution. Jane was wearing a selection of jewels. Perhaps if he could borrow them for the day, he could show them to the jeweller who would then be able to obtain a perfect match. Reluctantly, Jane agreed, having established that she was to return the following day and have the items returned to her. The next day Jane went back to the flat and was alarmed to discover the place completely empty. With time she realized that the man she had trusted was a fraud and vowed that she would have justice served upon him. For weeks she walked the streets of London looking for Lord Charles. Then, one day she saw him. She approached him directly and demanded that he return what was hers. Taken aback, the man blundered, claiming that he didn't know who the woman was, he continued to make his way down the street. Jane followed him until she saw a policeman. Then she insisted that the man be arrested for the theft of her jewellery.

Exercise 3.10 Transcribe the following passage, including all we have seen so far, with special attention to weak forms.

The man who was arrested was known as Harold Fox and it was assumed that the name Lord Charles had been an alias to hide his true identity. An announcement was made in the newspapers and 15 women came forward to admit that they too had been victims of such a crime. It appeared that Mr Fox had used a selection of names and that all of his characters had similar histories. Despite Mr Fox's adamant denial of the offence, an identity parade was arranged and eight of the victims positively identified him as the person who had tricked them out of their possessions. Throughout the whole trial, Mr Fox maintained his innocence, claiming that he was able to prove that he was not the person who had committed those crimes, regardless of which, he was found guilty on several counts of dishonesty. Distraught and in disbelief, Mr Fox was taken to the cells where he continued to claim that there was a miscarriage of justice and that his innocence could be proven. He wrote to the Home Office, the prison governor and the chief of police for the entire 14 years of his sentence but to no avail. Eventually, he was released from gaol and re-entered the world, an older and much weaker man. Nevertheless, he persevered in his mission to clear his name and made every effort to contact the authorities. Again no one listened. Several months after his release from prison, he was approached by a young woman he had never seen before. She began accusing him of having taken her jewellery. He was arrested immediately and this time he was sentenced to 20 years. As the days turned into weeks and the weeks into months, Mr Fox gradually gave up his fight and began to accept that it was God's will that he should suffer for what he hadn't done. Then, out of the blue, it was reported in a newspaper that a man had been arrested for stealing jewellery from young women. This man had admitted to assuming the name of Lord Charles and others, thus proving that Mr Fox had been innocent all the time. Research into the case shortly after showed that Mr Fox had been in Peru at the time of the original offences and could not, by any stretch of the imagination, have been responsible for the crimes he had been punished for. Mr Fox received some compensation for the miscarriage of justice, but perhaps more importantly, a court of appeal was established in Great Britain for the first time.

Lesson 4

Sandhi r

English accents may be classified into two different groups depending on where the sound /r/ is allowed to occur. These two accent groups are known as 'rhotic' and 'non-rhotic' accents. RP English is a non-rhotic accent. In rhotic accents, for instance General American and Irish English and Scottish English, /r/ is pronounced whenever it appears in the spelling. On the other hand, in many British accents including RP and in Australian English, the sound /r/ is only pronounced when it is followed by a vowel sound. Accordingly, /r/ is not pronounced in *bar*, *bars* or in *bare, bared* because /r/ is followed by a consonant or by a pause but it is pronounced in *barring, baring* because /r/ is followed by vowel sound.

When the spelling of a word ends in *r* or *re*, the /r/ is usually pronounced if the next word begins with a vowel sound, although it is not wrong to leave it out:

bar and pub /bɑːr ənd pʌb/ or /bɑː ənd pʌb/
bare it /beər ɪt / or /beə ɪt/

If the orthographic *r* is in the middle of a word and is followed by a vowel, /r/ must be pronounced:

baring /beərɪŋ/   *NEVER*   /beəɪŋ/

The pronunciation of word-final orthographic *r* or *re* when followed by a vowel in the next morpheme or word is known as **linking r**.

Note that in non-rhotic accents, not all vowels can be followed by /r/. In RP English the high vowels or the diphthongs ending in one of these vowels /iː/, /ɪ/, /i/, /uː/, /ʊ/, /u/, are never followed by /r/.

By analogy with linking r, some speakers pronounce /r/ after certain vowels when the next word begins with a vowel, even though there is no 'r' in the spelling. For example:

draw it /drɔːr ɪt/

This non-orthographic pronunciation of /r/ is known as **intrusive r**. It must be borne in mind that intrusive r is an analogical process and therefore only found after those vowels which can be followed by an orthographically motivated /r/, that is, linking r.

So intrusive r is not possible after high vowels, since, as we saw above, linking r is not found in that position either.

Intrusive r is acceptable between words, but is sometimes frowned upon when it occurs within words, as in

drawing /drɔːrɪŋ/

It must be noted, however, that many speakers of present day RP pronounce /r/ in this sort of word.

Linking r and intrusive r are known jointly as **sandhi r** (sandhi is a Sanskrit word meaning *putting together*). Finally, it must be noted that what has been said about sandhi r only applies to non-rhotic English accents. Rhotic accents, on the other hand, pronounce /r/ following the spelling so that there is no occasion to consider it a linking phenomenon.

Here is a transcribed passage in which you can find many instances of sandhi r which have been highlighted. Remember that each superscript number refers to a comment on the following page. The orthographic version for this passage is in the answers section at the end of the book.

Sample transcription

| aɪ ˈnevə[r] ɪˈmædʒɪnd ðət aɪ wʊd ˈmuːv əˈweɪ frəm ðə ˈtaɪni lɪtəl ˈvɪlɪdʒ weə[r] aɪ gruː[1] ˈʌp | tə ˈsetəl ˈdaʊn ɪn sʌtʃ ə ˈbɪg ˈsɪti | əz *ˈlʌndən | ɪts ˈəʊnli ˈnaʊ ðət aɪ[1] ʌndəˈstænd waɪ maɪ ˈfæməli wə nɒt səʊ ˈkiːn ɒn ði[1] aɪˈdɪə[r][2] əv əs ˈliːvɪŋ | ˈnaʊ[1] aɪ hæv[3] ˈtuː jʌŋ ˈkɪdz | *ˈlɪndə[r][2] ənd *ˈpɔːl | ənd ə ˈhʌzbənd tə ˈkeə[r] əbaʊt | aɪ ˈrɪəlaɪz ðə dɪsədˈvɑːntədʒɪz ə ˈtʃaɪld ˈhæz[3] ɪn ə ˈsɪti | ˈlʊkɪŋ ˈbæk tə ðə ˈdeɪz wen aɪ wəz ə ˈsmɔːl ˈɡɜːl | aɪ rɪˈmembə[r] əbʌv ˈɔːl | haʊ[1] ɪndɪˈpendənt wi[1] ˈɔːl ˈwɜː[4-5] | ən ˈhaʊ mʌtʃ ˈfriːdəm wi ˈhæd[3] | wi ˈjuːst[6] tə ɡəʊ tə ˈskuːl ɒn ɑə[7]r ˈəʊn | raɪd ˈbaɪsɪkəlz | pleɪ ˈhaɪd ənd ˈsiːk ɪn ðə ˈpɑːk | ˈhɒpskɒtʃ ɪn ðə ˈstriːt | ˈswɪm ɪn ðə ˈstriːm | ən ˈraɪd ɒn ðə ˈswɪŋ | wɪtʃ wi ˈjuːst[6] tə ˈmeɪk frəm ə ˈtriː[1] ɪn ðə ˈwʊdz | wi wʊd ˈlɪtərəli ˈpleɪ fə[r] ˈɑəz[7] | ˈhævɪŋ ˈɡreɪt ˈfʌn | ɪt wʊd biː[1] ˈɔːlməʊst ˈdɑːk bɪfɔː[r] aɪ ɡɒt ˈhəʊm | jet aɪ ˈnevə sɔː[r][2] ˈaɪðə maɪ ˈmʌðə ɔː maɪ ˈfɑːðə kənˈsɜːnd əbaʊt ɪt | sɪns ðeɪ ˈnjuː wi wə[r] ˈɔːl ˈseɪf | ənd wi wʊd ˈkʌm həʊm ˈwen wi felt ˈhʌŋgri[1-5] | aɪ wʊd ˈlaɪk maɪ ˈtʃɪldrən tə hæv[3] ˈplenti[1] əv ˈfʌn ˈtuː[1-5] | ənd ˈduː[1-3] ˈaʊtdɔː[r] ækˈtɪvɪtiz | bət ɪts ɪmˈpɒsɪbəl fə[r] ə ˈtʃaɪld ˈhɪə[r] ɪn ðə ˈsɪti | tə ˈhæv[3] ðə ˈkaɪnd əv ˈfriːdəm ˈaɪ[1] əndʒɔɪd | ðeɪ ˈsɜːtənli ˈkænɒt ɡəʊ[1] ˈaʊt ɒn ðeə[r] ˈəʊn | ˈkɑːz ə[r] ə ˈdeɪndʒə[r] aɪm ˈveri[1] əˈweə[r] ɒv[4] | ˈnɒt tə ˈmenʃən ˈməʊtəbaɪks | ðə ˈrʌʃ ɑə[7]r ɪz pəˈtɪkjʊləli ˈbæd | wɪð ˈevri wʌn ˈspiːdɪŋ ənd ˈdraɪvɪŋ laɪk ˈmeɪniæks | ˈðen ðə[r] ɪz ðə ˈvaələns[7] | ɪts ˈnɒt iːvən ˈseɪf fə[r] ən ˈædʌlt tə ˈwɔːk əraʊnd | wɪðaʊt ðə ˈfɪə[r] əv getɪŋ ˈmʌɡd ɔː[r] əˈsɔːltɪd | ˈeniweɪ[1-5] | aɪ ˈtraɪ tə teɪk maɪ ˈsʌn ənd ˈdɔːtə[r] aʊt tə ˈpleɪ əz ˈmʌtʃ əz aɪ ˈkæn[4] | ɒn ˈsʌmə[r] ˈiːvnɪŋz wi ˈɡəʊ tə ðə ˈpɑːk | ən teɪk ˈpɪknɪks wɪð əs | ðə[r] ɪz ən ədˈventʃə[r] ˈeərɪə[r][2] ɪn ðə ˈpɑːk | weə[r] ə ˈlɒt əv ˈtʃɪldrən get təˈɡeðə[r] ən ˈpleɪ | bət ðeɪ ˈdəʊnt[8] hæv[3] ði[1] ɒpəˈtjuːnɪti[1] əv ˈduːɪŋ ˈveri meni ˈθɪŋz ɒn ðeə[r] ˈəʊn | nɔː[r] əv ˈrʌnɪŋ əˈraʊnd | ɔː ˈsaɪklɪŋ ɔːl ˈəʊvə ðə ˈpleɪs əz ˈwiː[9] dɪd | ˈsʌmtaɪmz aɪ ˈwʌndə weðə[r] ˈɑːftə ˈɔːl | aɪ ˈʃʊd əv muːvd əˈweɪ[1-5] | aɪ dʒɜst ˈhəʊp ðə ˈkɪdz dəʊnt[8] ˈfiːl ðeɪ[1] ə[r] ˈæktʃuəli mɪsɪŋ ˈaʊt | ˈmeɪbi[1-5] | əz ðeɪ ˈseɪ | ju ˈdəʊnt[8] ˈmɪs | wɒt ju[1] əv ˈnevə[r] ɪkˈspɪərɪənst |

Comments on sample transcription

1. Sandhi r is not possible because it cannot follow a high vowel.
2. Notice the intrusive r.
3. The strong form is used because here the verb is not an auxiliary.
4. The strong form is used because the grammatical word is stranded.
5. Sandhi r is not used when the two vowels are separated by a potential pause.
6. *used* is pronounced /juːzd/ when it means *employed* or *utilised* but /juːst/ when it means *accustomed*.
7. Smoothing (see Lesson 2).
8. Strong form because it is a negative contraction.
9. The strong form is used because the grammatical word is emphasised and therefore stressed.

Exercise 4.1 Look at the following passage which is given in orthography. Try to identify all the occasions where sandhi r could be used. Check your version at the end of the book, where you can also find this text transcribed with comments.

> My exams are over and I have some breathing space now for a few months, before I have to start thinking about revising again. I was very insecure about my ability to study again when the course began. I felt as though my brain had been atrophied for all those years since I left college. And to make the matter even worse, most of the students in my class were much younger than me. However, I'm happy to report that I did very well, so now I'm more at ease and can relax and really enjoy the lessons. My class is made up of a very diverse group of people, coming from a variety of countries, cultures, religions and economic backgrounds. It is interesting to discover all the various reasons that brought all these students to this particular area of the world and I have learnt a lot more in this place than a new language by listening to their sometimes harrowing stories. Many of them are refugees and were faced with the dilemma of leaving it all behind or risking prison or worse. It is once more evident to me how easily things come to a western European and how very much we take for granted things like fair law and justice. Over a few months all of us in the class have become a close-knit group, since we share a common problem that crosses all barriers. We are all struggling to understand the same new culture and settle into the same new country. And everyone has funny things to relate about the lack of progress we sometimes find. There is no one who understands better about the difficulties we face than a fellow foreigner in the same boat. It doesn't matter if they come from the other end of the world. We are all far away from home and missing those we left behind, so we console, cajole and encourage each other along frequently.

Exercise 4.2 Now we ask you to look at the following transcription and insert all the possible instances of sandhi r that you can find. You will find an edited version with explanations and comments as well as the orthographic version at the end of the book.

| *ˈemə ənd hə ˈjʌŋgə ˈsɪstə *ˈænθɪə ə ˈkʌmɪŋ tə ˈsteɪ | maɪ ˈbrʌðə ənd ɪz ˈwaɪf ə ˈgəʊɪŋ əˈweɪ fə ə ˈlɒŋ wiːkˈend ɒn ðeə ˈəʊn | səʊ ðeə ˈdɔːtəz wɪl bi ˈleft wɪð ˈʌs | əv ˈkɔːs | aɪ əv ˈnəʊn ðɪs fə ə ˈwaɪl | ənd əv ˈgɒn əˈbaʊt maɪ ˈdeɪli ˈbɪznɪs wɪð maɪ ˈjuːʒʊəl ˈtʃɪəri ˈætɪtjuːd | ɪt ɪz ˈəʊnli ɪn ðə ˈlɑːst fjuː ˈdeɪz | ˈnaʊ ðət ðeə əˈraɪvəl ɪz

ˈɔːlməʊst əˈpɒn əs | ðət aɪ əv ˈnəʊtɪst ˈkliə ɪndɪˈkeɪʃənz əv ˈstres ɪn mi | maɪ ˈhændz ʃeɪk ˈslaɪtli frəm ˈtaɪm tə ˈtaɪm | ənd maɪ ˈθrəʊəweɪ rɪˈmɑːks əbaʊt haʊ ˈɡɑːstli ɪt wɪl ɔːl ˈbiː | həv bɪˈɡʌn tə siːm ˈkʌləd wɪð ðə ˈtaɪniəst ˈtʌtʃ əv ˈhɪstɪərɪə ən ˈsaʊnd ə lɪtəl ˈstreɪnd | aɪ ˈdəʊnt wɒnt ju tə ˈɡet mi ˈrɒŋ | aɪ ˈlʌv ðəm bəʊθ ˈdɪəli | ˈteɪkən ɪndɪˈvɪdʒəli maɪ ˈniːsɪz ə əˈfekʃənət | ˈɪntərəstɪŋ ən dɪˈlaɪtfəl | ðə ˈtrʌbəl ˈɪz | ðeɪ ə ˈnɒt ˈkʌmɪŋ ɪndɪˈvɪdʒəli | ðeɪ ə tə bi ˈwɪð əs təˈɡeðə ənd fə ət ˈliːst ˈfɔː həʊl ˈdeɪz | *ˈænθɪə ɪz nɒt ˈəʊnli *ˈeməz jʌŋɡə ˈsɪstə | ʃi ɪz ˈɔːlsəʊ hə ˈenəmi | ənd ðə ˈfiːlɪŋ ɪz ˈmjuːtʃuəl | ˈhaʊ ˈtuː sʌtʃ ˈwel brɔːt ʌp ˈtʃɪldrən kən ˈmænɪdʒ tə ɡəʊ ɒn ˈfaɪtɪŋ iːtʃ ˈʌðə ɪn sʌtʃ ə kənˈsɪstənt ˈmænə | ɪz ˈhɑːd tu ɪkˈspleɪn | ðeə ænɪˈmɒsəti dɪd ˈnɒt ˈɡrəʊ əʊvə ˈeniθɪŋ ɪn pəˈtɪkjʊlə aɪ maɪt ˈæd | ɪt wəz ˈðeə frəm ðə bɪˈɡɪnɪŋ | ðə ˈdeɪ *ˈeмə wəz ɪntrəˈdjuːst tə hə ˈnjuːbɔːn ˈsɪblɪŋ | wəz wʌn əv ˈɒmɪnəs fəˈbəʊdɪŋ | *ˈeмə ət ðə ˈtaɪm wəz ˈəʊnli ˈtuː | ʃi wəz ˈbrɔːt ɪn tə ˈsiː ðə ˈbeɪbi | ənd ɑːftə ə ˈkwɪk ˈlʊk ət ðə ˈtaɪni ˈbʌndəl | ʃi ˈsnɔːtɪd ˈlaʊdli | ˈtɜːnd ɒn hə ˈhiːl ənd ˈleft | ʃi rɪˈfjuːzd tə ˈtɔːk tu ˈenibɒdi fə ə ˈnʌmbə əv ˈdeɪz | ənd ɪt wəz ˈnɪə ə ˈmʌnθ | bɪfɔː ˈeniwʌn kʊd pəˈsweɪd ə tə ˈspiːk tə hə ˈmʌðə əˈɡen | ði aɪˈdɪə əv ˈtraɪɪŋ tu entəˈteɪn ðiːz ˈtuː lɪtəl ˈɡɜːlz | fə ˈeniθɪŋ ˈəʊvə ən ˈaə ɪz ˈfɪlɪŋ mi wɪð ˈpænɪk | aɪ əv ˈtraɪd tə prɪˈpeə əz ˈmʌtʃ əz aɪ ˈkæn | aɪ əv ˈbɔːt ðə ˈdʒeli | əbaʊt ˈten ˈpækɪts əv ɪt | ɪn ˈevri ˈfleɪvə aɪ kʊd ˈfaɪnd | aɪ ˈnəʊ ðət wɒtˈevə ɪz *ˈeməz ˈfleɪvə əv ðə ˈmʌnθ | *ˈænθɪə ɪz ˈbaʊnd tə ˈheɪt ɪt | ðə ˈlɑːst taɪm ðeɪ ˈkeɪm tə ˈvɪzɪt | aɪ meɪd ˈɒrɪndʒ ˈdʒeli | *ˈeмə əˈdɔːd ɪt | *ˈænθɪə tʊk ˈwʌn smɔːl ˈspuːnfʊl | ˈskruːd ʌp hə ˈfeɪs ənd ˈsed ðət ɪt ˈteɪstɪd ˈnɑːsti | aɪ wɪl ˈtraɪ ˈteɪkɪŋ ðəm fə ə ˈwɔːk tə ˈfiːd ðə ˈdʌks ɒn ðə ˈvɪlɪdʒ ˈpɒnd | bət aɪm ˈʃɔː ɪt wɪl bi ðə ˈbest aɪˈdɪə ɪn ðə ˈwɜːld fə ˈwʌn əv ðəm | ənd ði ˈʌðə wʌn wɪl ˈstɪk aʊt hə ˈləʊə ˈlɪp | ˈstæmp hə ˈfʊt ənd ˈseɪ ðət ʃi ˈheɪts sɪli ˈdʌks | aɪ ˈwʌndə ɪf ɪt wɪl bi ði ˈeldəst hu wɪl ˈflætli rɪˈfjuːz tə hæv ˈbɔɪld ˈeɡ fə ˈbrekfəst | ɔː ˈɡəʊ fə ə ˈsaɪkəl ˈraɪd | ɔː ˈiːvən wɒtʃ ə ˈvɪdiəʊ ət ˈhəʊm | ˈhaʊ kən ˈtuː ˈtʃɪldrən əv ˈfɔː ənd ˈsɪks | ˈmænɪdʒ tə ˈsʌmən ði ˈenədʒi tə dɪsəˈɡriː ɒn ˈæbsəluːtli ˈevriθɪŋ | aɪ ˈsʌmtaɪmz səˈspekt ðət ðeɪ ˈkʌm tə ˈsiːkrət əˈɡriːmənts wen ˈnəʊwʌn ɪz ˈprezənt | əz tə ˈwɪtʃ ˈsaɪd əv ðeə ɪnˈevɪtəbəl dɪsəˈɡriːmənt ɒn ˈevri ˈsʌbdʒɪkt | ˈiːtʃ wɪl ˈteɪk | ˈmeɪbi ɪts ˈɔːl ə ˈplɔɪ tə draɪv ˈædʌlts ʌp ðə ˈwɔːl |

The following three passages are for you to transcribe. Pay special attention to the use of sandhi r and remember the hints which we gave you in the previous lessons. After completing each one compare it to our version at the end of the book and study the comments carefully.

When you finish these transcriptions, take some time to look at your progress so far. If you are making quite a lot of mistakes or there are things you do not understand, you should revise these first four lessons *very carefully* before starting on Lesson 5.

Exercise 4.3 Transcribe the following passage, including all we have seen so far, with special attention to sandhi r.

When he heard of the offer of a house on a small island, he went for it. He had lately been feeling unhappy in the big city. His work wasn't going anywhere at all. He sat in front of the computer every morning, steaming cup of coffee in his hand. He would stare at the blank screen, daring it to defeat him. After about an hour of wrestling, he would surrender and start to wander endlessly around the flat. Then last Wednesday he got a break. The day before he had bumped into Anna in the pub. She had recently inherited a house off the west coast – well, rather an old cottage, she said. She'd thought about selling it. However, her agent said it wouldn't fetch a good price because of its remote location. Besides, it would be a nice place for Anna to spend the summer at. In the winter it could be rented out, but she had to find some time to travel out there and sort it out. There were a couple of things that had to be done to it before any decisions were taken – a coat of paint, maybe a window shutter in need of adjusting, and a few tiles here and there ought to be replaced. Apart from that, there was nothing the matter, Anna said. He was really taken with the idea of it and even hinted that he enjoyed working with his hands. Anna rang the following morning. She had been thinking about the house and his enthusiasm over it. Would he be interested in moving in rent-free? In exchange he would just have to fix up whatever he thought necessary. He could stay until the summer if he wanted to. Anna of course would pay for all the materials that were used. She had hardly finished speaking when he accepted. What a wonderful idea it was! And it was perfect timing too. He really wanted to get out there and enjoy the lack of distractions other than nature and healthy work. He was now standing in the kitchen of the house – fair enough, she had said cottage – and feeling the weight of the world on his shoulders. When he first saw it, it hadn't looked too bad – a few slates missing from the roof, and only one shutter in its right place, nothing major it seemed – but when he walked in, he started realising what he had let himself in for. This was surely not a matter of fixing, but of gutting out and building from scratch. None of the lights worked. How could they when the electricity didn't either? The fuse box was burnt to a cinder and nothing short of new wiring would solve that. Turning on a tap made the pipes rattle as if they were about to take off, but no water actually came out. The ceiling beams had been eaten by an army of termites. All floorboards creaked when stepped on and several showed their true nature and broke under his probing foot. He had a funny feeling that the house meant to collapse and bury him forever under its weight.

Exercise 4.4 Transcribe the following passage, including all we have seen so far, with special attention to sandhi r.

Freddy grew up in the city with his brother Alex and their parents, but his fondest memories, the ones he tells of time and time again, are of their holidays in the country. They owned a beautiful house. It's still there and now it belongs to Freddy since he bought his brother out. Alex has lived abroad for over 30 years and is not likely to come back now. The house is white with dark green windows, a veranda and balconies. There is a porch downstairs, roofed by a vine trellis. The walls in the porch are covered to waist height with Moorish-looking tiles in all colours. There is quite a lot of land surrounding the main building, mostly taken up by a wild-looking garden with fruit trees, bushes and flowers. Freddy stays there all through the summer and early autumn and goes for an afternoon during the rest of the year at least once a week. It's too cold to stay overnight in the winter, as the only available heating is that provided by the fireplace in the sitting room and the Aga in the kitchen. The garden slopes down towards the village, since the house is conveniently situated, slightly removed from and above all the others.

Freddy's father Albert bought the house in the 1920s. He had gone to Cuba at the beginning of the century with his two brothers. They worked very hard like most emigrants, and, like some of them, Albert made quite a lot of money and came back home to be a gentleman of leisure and found a family. Before embarking on the latter aim, he bought the house and surrounding land and invested the rest of his fortune wisely. After a while a young girl in the village caught his eye. He lost no time in setting things in motion. He spoke to the village priest and was assured of the girl's character and family background. After obtaining similar unimpeachable credentials for Albert, the priest put in a good word with the girl's parents and within a few months they were married. Freddy and Alex had a very strict and religious upbringing. Albert had all the time in the world to keep an eye on the running of the household and his children. Nevertheless, the two boys were always known for their imaginative pranks. They were aware of the consequent punishments, but they accepted the penances as the natural price that had to be paid for achieving their ends. Their mother would try to cover up as much as she could for them, but she never understood what it was that made them so unruly, when, and this was evident to all, they were such good and kind-hearted boys. One winter in the city Alex spent a few pleasurable hours throwing eggs down from his window at all the passers-by who caught his fancy. He also carried a little notebook where he kept a record of all the street lights he had broken, or rather stoned. Freddy was a keen guitar player and consequently his presence was much required at all parties and gatherings, since no one owned a record-player at the time. Being so popular a fellow, it was easy for him to forget parental curfews. On one occasion he got back after eight a.m. to find his father on the porch waiting for him. 'Don't even think of going to bed,' Albert said, 'before all those sacks are absolutely full of potatoes.' Then he resumed his newspaper reading on the porch seat. The workmen took pity on Freddy and helped him by sneaking a few potatoes into his sacks when Albert wasn't looking. Still, he was digging in the garden until lunchtime. All through the summers both brothers would often get the local cabby to give them rides to the various parties in surrounding villages. Since they didn't have any money, their account with the driver ended up at such a high figure they were forced to go to Aunt Sally for funds. She was their father's sister and one of the most innocent, kindest persons you would ever encounter in this world. She was unmarried and lived on her own at the other end of the village. Freddy and Alex would always turn to her in a scrape. Quite a number of times they returned looking horribly scruffy after a particularly fun outing. Going home in such a state would have been looking for unnecessary trouble, so they would pop into Sally's house first, spin her an incredible yarn, and get a full meal whilst their clothes were being cleaned and ironed. Then they would go home looking as neat as two pins. It is unimaginable what the two of them would have got into had Albert been a father of a less strict kind. And yet, without so many rules to be broken and a less formidable opponent, they might have thought it wasn't worth their while. Probably for them half the fun was besting Albert.

Exercise 4.5 Transcribe the following passage, including all we have seen so far, with special attention to sandhi r.

They walked into the restaurant, but Cordelia's heart just wasn't in it. Should she leave it for tonight? After all it was their anniversary. Or should she come out with it right there and then in front of a room full of people. 'Would you like a table next to the window, Madam, or out in the conservatory?' Her uneasy thoughts were interrupted and quite honestly she did not care in the least where they sat. She had more important things on her mind. 'Let's sit next to the window,' she replied, thinking that if this did get a bit too hot to bear, she could always make a quick get-away through the nearest door or even across the patio. They took their allocated seats. George as usual pulled the chair out and made sure of her comfort, before he sat down himself. He got the wine menu. 'We'll have champagne,' he decided. It was only proper on their anniversary. Cordelia acknowledged the gesture, although she wasn't about to fall for it. Her mind was elsewhere at the time. She was trying to remember exactly when she had become suspicious. There was nothing clear at first, just that he wasn't around as much as he used to be, but he was a busy man, and at different times of the year his job did make demands on him. Cordelia had used these excuses over and over again, but she knew in her heart that her instincts were always right. It had been proved many a time, even when the dreadful Mrs Shaw announced that she had seen George, her own George, at the museum cafeteria in the company of another woman. She had denied that there was anything untoward happening. It had been a previously arranged business dinner. And yes, Cordelia had known all about it. Unfortunately, she too had been engaged that evening and therefore unable to attend. When she got home that night, she didn't bring up the subject with her husband, and with time she had managed to convince herself that maybe what she had told Mrs Shaw was true. His absences became more and more frequent. He started going away for a long weekend every now and then, and after a while every third week, claiming that he had a weekend conference. It was such a bore, he claimed. How he would have just loved to stay at home and spend the time with her instead, but the mortgage needed to be paid and money had to be earned. When he came back, he was distracted. A difficult meeting, he said. It had brought up much to think about. Cordelia always showed sympathy, but she knew when he was lying and was insulted that he thought he could pull the wool over her eyes. Had he learnt nothing about her in all their years together under the same roof? In her isolation and loneliness she had begun to look into herself for a solution, for a reason why George no longer loved her. She found no answer inside. Her intuition told her it was an outside cause. In the course of this inner appraisal Cordelia admitted the fact that whatever unconscious mistakes she might have made, she deserved better as a human being and would have to go after it. She would tell him tonight. He had to choose. It was her or the other one. His deceit would not be tolerated from now on. It had to end. Quite honestly, she didn't mind what his decision was, not any longer actually. What a surprising and comforting thought! I don't care any more.

Lesson 5

Consonant syllabicity

All syllables must have a nucleus. The nucleus may optionally be preceded by an **onset**, consisting of one or more consonants and it may optionally be followed by a **coda**, again consisting of one or more consonants. Sounds which may perform the function of syllable nucleus are said to be **syllabic**. Vowels are syllabic, whereas, in most languages, consonants are not syllabic, that is, they cannot be syllable nuclei. In English, too, consonants are generally non-syllabic, but there is a process known as **syllabic consonant formation (SCF)** which makes consonants such as /n/ and /l/ syllabic, that is to say, syllable nuclei. In SCF, a sequence of /ə/ followed by one of the above consonants may merge so that the vowel disappears, but gives its syllabic characteristic to the consonant. Syllabic consonants are represented with the diacritic /ˌ/ underneath. The most likely consonants to become syllabic in English are /n/ and /l/, under certain conditions. For both consonants the sequence /ə/ plus /n/ or /l/ must be in the same syllable, but there are other requirements for SCF to be possible. These conditions are more restrictive for the nasal than for the lateral.

The alveolar nasal /n/ may become syllabic in the following environments:

- When the sequence is preceded by a consonant, which must be an obstruent (plosive, fricative or affricate). Nasal syllabicity is more likely if the preceding consonant is an alveolar.

    listen /lɪsən/ → /lɪsn̩/
    pardons /pɑːdənz/ → /pɑːdn̩z/

- If the sequence is preceded by more than one consonant, SCF is sometimes possible but not if one of the preceding consonants is a nasal:

    golden /gəʊldən/ → /gəʊldn̩/

    BUT NOT

    London /lʌndən/ → /lʌndn̩/

The details of which consonant sequences may be followed by SCF involving /ən/ are rather complicated. Our advice is to confine SCF to those situations where the sequence is preceded by a single consonant, although you will hear RP speakers using /n̩/ in other circumstances. On the other hand, if the sequence /ən/ precedes the stressed syllable, syllabicity is not very frequent, so you may simply ignore it:

/kənˈdens/ or /kn̩ˈdens/

SCF involving the alveolar lateral only requires that the sequence be preceded by at least one consonant, other than /w j r/ (approximants).

parcel /pɑːsəl/ → /pɑːsl̩/
pistol /pɪstəl/ → /pɪstl̩/
handle /hændəl/ → /hændl̩/
panel /pænəl/ → /pænl̩/ /pænl̩ɪŋ/

Notice that if a morpheme starting with a weak vowel is added after the syllabic nasal or lateral, syllabicity for the consonant may be lost (**de-syllabicity**), since the consonant may become the onset of the following syllable:

listen /lɪsən/ → /lɪsn̩/→ /lɪsn̩ɪŋ/ OR /lɪsnɪŋ/
rattle /rætəl/ → /rætl̩/→ /rætl̩ɪŋ/ OR /rætlɪŋ/

As you can see in the above examples, the last pronunciation given for the words *listen* and *rattle* may be considered as being the result of a straightforward deletion of the vowel /ə/. We shall deal with this and other types of deletion in Lesson 6.

Here is a transcribed passage with a lot of syllabic consonants in it. We have commented on particular points but remember we tend not to repeat comments which were signalled with *** in previous lessons nor explanations which were provided for the specific topic of each lesson. You can find the orthographic version for this transcription in the Appendix at the end of the book.

Sample transcription

| ˈmeni ˈkʌntriz əv ɪntrəˈdjuːst ˈdʒʊəriz | ðɪs ɪz ˈdʌn ɪn ən əˈtempt tə ˈbrɪŋ ˈdʒʌstɪs ˈkləʊsə tu ˈɔːdɪnəri ˈpiːpl̩ | səʊ ðət wi ˈɔːl teɪk ˈpɑːt ɪn ði ˈæplɪkeɪʃn̩ əv ðə ˈlɔː | ɪn ˈsʌtʃ ˈkʌntriz | ˈdʒʊərəz ə ˈrændəmli səˈlektɪd frəm ði iˈlektərəl[1] ˈsensəs | ənd huˈevər ɪz ˈtʃəʊzn̩ hæz[2] ði ɒblɪˈɡeɪʃn̩ tu ˈækt əz ə ˈdʒʊərər | ɪn eni ˈkeɪs ðət ɡəʊz ˈʌp fə ˈtraəl[3] ɪn ðə ˈləʊkl̩ ˈkɔːts | ðɪs ɪz ˈnəʊn əz ˈdʒʊəri ˈsɜːvɪs | ˈfɪftiːn ˈpɜːsn̩z ər əˈpɔɪntɪd | frəm huːm ˈtwelv wɪl hæv[2] tə teɪk ˈpɑːt ɪn ə ˈtraəl[3] | ðə diˈfens kn̩ riˈdʒekt ʌp tə ˈθriː ˈkændɪdeɪts ɒn ˈdɪfərənt[4] ˈɡraʊndz | sʌtʃ əz biːɪŋ ˈpredʒʊdɪst əɡenst ðə diˈfendənt[5] | wʌns juv biːn ˈtʃəʊzn̩ | ðəz ˈlɪtl̩ ˈtʃɑːns əv biːɪŋ ˈeɪbl̩ tə ɡet ˈaʊt əv ɪt | ˈdʒʊəri sɜːvɪs ɪz kn̩ˈsɪdəd[6] ə ˈraɪt | bət ˈɔːlsəʊ ə ˈdjuːti | ən ɒblɪˈɡeɪʃn̩ | waɪ ʃʊd ˈenibɒdi ˈwɒnt tu əˈvɔɪd ɪt | ˈwel | ˈmeni ˈpiːpl̩ wʊd bi ˈɒnəd tə bi ˈɑːskt tə fɔːm ˈpɑːt əv ə ˈdʒʊəri | bət ˈʌðəz hæv[2] ˈstrɒŋ rezəˈveɪʃn̩z | nɒt ˈevribɒdi fiːlz ˈkeɪpəbl̩ əv ˈbeərɪŋ ðə rɪspɒnsəˈbɪləti ðət ɪt ɪnˈvɒlvz | aɪ ˈriːsn̩tli wɒtʃt ə teliˈvɪʒn̩ ˈprəʊɡræm | ɪn wɪtʃ ˈveəriəs ˈpiːpl̩ hu əd biːn ˈdʒʊərəz | ˈtəʊld əv ðeər ɪkˈspɪəriənsɪz | ˈɔːl əv ðəm əd ˈtraɪd ˈmɜːdə ˈkeɪsɪz | ðə wəz ə ˈleɪdi hu əd biːn ˈθretn̩d | ˈʃiː ənd hə[7] ˈfæmɪli | baɪ ˈfrendz əv ði əˈkjuːzd | ðə pəˈliːs kʊd ˈəʊnli səˈdʒest ðət ʃi kɔːl ˈnaɪn naɪn ˈnaɪn | ɪf ˈeniθɪŋ ʃʊd ˈhæpn̩ | əˈnʌðə mæn wəz səʊ ˈdevəsteɪtɪd baɪ ðə ˈhəʊl ˈθɪŋ | ðət i ˈstɪl hæd[2] ˈtɪəz ɪn ɪz ˈaɪz wen i ˈtɔːkt

əbaut ɪt | fə 'hɪm[8] | ɪt 'wɒznt[9] 'əʊnli ðə 'bɜːdn̩ əv 'hævɪŋ tə di'saɪd weðə 'sʌmwʌn wəz 'ɡɪlti ɔː 'nɒt | ɪt wəz ðə 'həʊl 'traəl[3] | 'lɪsnɪŋ[10] tu 'ɔːf| 'diːteɪlz əbaut ðə 'vɪktɪmz 'deθ | 'lʊkɪŋ ət ðə 'fəʊtəʊɡrɑːfs | ðə 'wepn̩z | ðə 'θɪŋ ðət keɪm ə'krɒs əz 'hɑːdɪst ɒn ðə 'dʒʊərəz | wəz ðə 'fækt ðət ðeɪ wə 'nɒt ə'laʊd tə 'tɔːk tu 'enibɒdi | əbaut 'wɒt wəz 'hæpnɪŋ[10] 'evri 'deɪ ɪn 'kɔːt | ðeə 'fæmɪli 'laɪvz əd biːn dɪs'rʌptɪd | bikɒz ðeɪ wər 'ʌneɪbl̩ tə seɪ 'waɪ ðeɪ wə 'fiːlɪŋ 'ləʊ ɔːr ʌp'set | ənd 'ðeəfɔː 'nəʊwʌn kʊd 'help ðəm 'kəʊp wɪð ɪt | aɪ sə'pəʊz 'ðiːz wə tu ə 'sɜːtn̩ ɪk'stent ɪk'sepʃən|[11] 'keɪsɪz | 'məʊst piːpl̩ 'əʊnli ə'tend 'maɪnə 'traəlz[3] | 'θɪŋz laɪk 'θeft | 'fɔːdʒəri ɔː 'bɜːɡləri | 'stɪl | ðeər ɪz 'ɔːlweɪz ðə 'tʃɑːns ðət 'wʌn əv əs wɪl get 'kɔːld fər ə 'kæpɪt| 'keɪs |

Comments on sample transcription

1. Syllabic /l/ is impossible here because /ə/ is preceded by an approximant.
2. The strong form is used because the verb is not being used as an auxiliary.
3. Smoothing (see Lesson 2).
4. Syllabicity is not possible because /ən/ is preceded by a sonorant. In nasal syllabicity, the preceding consonant must be a plosive, fricative or affricate.
5. Syllabicity is not possible because /ən/ is preceded by two consonants, the first of which is a nasal.
6. Syllabicity in the syllable preceding the stress is not very common.
7. /h/ is not deleted because *her* is acting as an adjective. ***
8. The strong form (in which case no /h/ deletion) is used because the word is being emphasised, therefore stressed.
9. The strong form is used because it is a negative contraction. ***
10. De-syllabicity because /n/ becomes the onset of the following syllable since it begins with a vowel. It could also be seen as a case of /ə/ elision (see Lesson 6). The pronunciation ending in /nɪŋ/ with syllabic nasal is also possible.
11. /ɪk'sepʃn̩/ is a possible alternative pronunciation and so is /ɪk'sepʃnəl/.

Exercise 5.1 Look at the following passage which is given in orthography. Try to identify all the possible syllabic consonants in it. You can find the answer and its transcribed version at the end of the book.

It is a widely held belief that whenever two English people meet, they will start talking about the weather. I am not sure that is entirely true, but I can see the reason why the English should be so interested in this subject. For one thing, English society is one which, unlike some others, doesn't easily tolerate total silence, even between strangers. The exception to this is, of course, when the English are on trains. It is another supposed typical trait of the national character that the English never speak to one another on a train. Apart from this, the weather makes a nice neutral topic of conversation for a few minutes. One cannot blame anybody for the weather, so talking about it is unlikely to cause any ill-feeling. You can, of course, blame the weather forecasters for getting their predictions wrong and the English frequently do this. The other thing about the weather in England is that it is certainly worth talking about. Things change so rapidly here. You can experience three or more different types of weather in a single day. Quite recently I left home early in the morning and drove to the station in terrible fog and frost. By the middle of the morning it was sunny and warm, but I came home in the evening and had to drive through an awful storm with wind, rain, thunder and lightning. Given this uncertainty, it is hardly surprising that we comment on the weather so often. I find it difficult to envisage what it is like living in a completely predictable climate. It must be so boring to wake up every day and know for certain what the temperature is going to be within a few degrees and whether there will be any rain or not. It is hard to imagine two people who live in an oasis on the edge of a desert saying things like 'it's turned out nice again, hasn't it?', but for the English such a remark has some meaning.

Exercise 5.2 The following transcribed passage could contain syllabic consonants, but these have not been included. Retranscribe it showing the occurrence of syllabic consonants.

| *'neɪθən lʌvd 'miːt | ʌn'fɔːtʃənətli 'hiː ənd hɪz 'waɪf wə 'veri 'pɔːr ənd ðeɪ 'kʊdənt 'juːʒuəli ə'fɔːd ɪt | ðeɪ 'hædənt iːtən 'miːt fə 'sevərəl 'wiːks | ənd *'neɪθən wəz 'getɪŋ ə 'terɪbəl 'kreɪvɪŋ fər ɪt | i'ventʃuəli i 'kʊdənt 'stænd ɪt eni 'lɒŋgə | səʊ i 'geɪv ɪz 'waɪf sʌm əv ðə 'mʌni i əd biːn 'seɪvɪŋ tə 'baɪ səm 'njuː 'ʃuːz | 'lɪsən | ju məst 'gəʊ ənd baɪ səm 'miːt tə'deɪ | ðəz i'nʌf 'ðeə fər əbaʊt 'sevən 'paʊndz əv 'stjuːɪŋ 'biːf | 'meɪk ə 'hjuːdʒ 'stjuː | aɪ dəʊnt 'keə wɒt 'vedʒətəbəlz ju pʊt 'ɪn ɪt | bət ɪt 'mʌst hæv 'miːt | ðen *'neɪθən went 'ɒf tə 'wɜːk | ənd 'ɔːl 'deɪ i felt 'hæpi ət ðə 'θɔːt əv ðə 'maːvələs 'stjuː i wəz 'gəʊɪŋ tə 'get ɪn ði 'iːvnɪŋ | 'miːnwaɪl | *'neɪθənz 'waɪf set 'ɒf fə ðə 'bʊtʃə tə 'baɪ ðə 'miːt | ʃi 'wɒzənt əz 'fɒnd əv 'miːt əz *'neɪθən wɒz | 'hɜː greɪt 'pæʃən wəz 'tʃɒkələt | ənd ʃi 'hædənt iːtən eni əv 'ðæt fə 'mʌnθs | 'raɪt nekst tə ðə 'bʊtʃəz 'ʃɒp | ðə wəz ə kən'fekʃənə | wɪð ə 'wɪndəʊ dɪ'spleɪ | 'fʊl əv ðə 'məʊst dɪ'lɪʃəs lʊkɪŋ 'θɪŋz ʃi əd 'siːn fə 'jɪəz | ʃi 'kʊdənt ri'zɪst ɪt | ʃi went 'ɪn ənd 'spent ɔːl əv ðə 'mʌni *'neɪθən əd 'gɪvən ə | ðæt 'iːvnɪŋ *'neɪθən keɪm həʊm 'biːmɪŋ ɔːl 'əʊvə | hɪz 'waɪf pʊt ə 'pɒt əv 'stjuː ɒn ðə 'teɪbəl | ənd 'sɜːvd ɪm ə 'bɪg 'pleɪtfʊl | ɪt wəz ə 'wʌndəfəl 'stjuː kənteɪnɪŋ 'biːnz | ənd pə'teɪtəʊz ənd 'lentəlz | ənd 'ɔːl sɔːts əv 'ʌðə 'vedʒətəbəlz | bət *'neɪθən 'kʊdənt 'faɪnd iːvən ə 'lɪtəl piːs əv 'miːt | hi 'sɜːvd ɪmself ə 'kʌpəl əv 'taɪmz | 'fɪʃɪŋ ə'raʊnd ɪn ðə 'pɒt | bət 'stɪl i 'faʊnd nəʊ 'miːt | 'dɪdənt ju 'baɪ ðə 'miːt aːskt *'neɪθən | əʊ aɪ 'sɜːtənli 'dɪd sed ɪz 'waɪf | bət ðə məʊst 'hɒrɪbəl 'θɪŋ hæpənd | wen aɪ keɪm 'həʊm frəm ðə 'bʊtʃər aɪ 'rɪəlaɪzd aɪ əd fə'gɒtən tə get 'sɔːlt | səʊ aɪ 'went tə ðə 'neɪbə tə 'bɒrəʊ sʌm | 'wen aɪ gɒt 'bæk | aɪ 'əʊpənd ðə 'dɔːr ənd sɔː ðə 'kæt 'næpɪŋ ʌndə ðə 'teɪbəl | ɪt wəz 'klɪər ɪt əd 'iːtən ɔːl ðə 'miːt | *'neɪθən gɒt 'ʌp ənd went ɪn 'sɜːtʃ əv ðə 'kæt wɪð ə 'terɪbəl 'lʊk ɒn ɪz 'feɪs | hi keɪm 'bæk ənd 'pʊt ɪt ɪn ə 'kɒtən 'bæg | ənd pʊt ðə 'bæg ɒn ðə 'kɪtʃən 'skeɪlz | ðə 'kæt weɪd 'dʒʌst əʊvə 'sevən 'paʊndz | ɪf 'ðɪs ɪz ðə 'kæt | 'weər ɪz ðə 'miːt | ənd ɪf 'ðɪs ɪz ðə 'miːt | 'weər ɪz ðə 'kæt graʊld *'neɪθən|

Here there are three passages for you to transcribe. Include as many syllabic conso-nants as you can and the processes that we have seen so far (weak forms, sandhi r etc.). After completing each one, compare it to our version at the end of the book. If you find you are making many mistakes or that you do not understand the comments, we advise you to go back and revise previous lessons and transcriptions before you go on.

Exercise 5.3 Transcribe the following passage, including all the processes seen so far, with special attention to syllabicity.

Since we moved here a year ago I have been very frustrated by my inability to communicate fluently. I have much, some would say too much, to say on any given subject. I have always been known as someone who is willing, even eager, to share her opinions on almost any topic, and suddenly have found myself with this curious new disability that prevents me from doing so. By the time I have formulated my vital contribution to a discussion in progress, the conversation has moved on and I have to begin processing all over again. I find myself regularly and literally at a loss for words, an unfamiliar dilemma for me. The most important benefit of these classes, therefore, is that they have started reopening those verbal floodgates. I can converse again and so now I'm back on home ground on my old soapbox, pontificating again to anyone who'll listen. The only difference is that now I hold forth in another language and that other people get more chances to speak, since I still have to stop to think more frequently than in my native language. I still have much to learn and make the silliest mistakes regularly. My kinder friends say it's part of my charm and they must have sore tongues from biting them so often to resist the temptation to correct me constantly. I find humour the most difficult aspect to master and fear I may never get it. I am still translating sayings literally and being left in confusion as a result. I tend to switch off in a conversation if no one is speaking directly to me, as I have to concentrate so hard. So sometimes I suddenly realize that everyone is looking at me expectantly, awaiting a response. Then I have to admit that I haven't got a clue as to what they've been talking about and could I get a quick recap please. I am making progress, however. Every time I'm able to answer someone without consciously needing to translate each word, I feel there is yet a light glimmering at the end of the tunnel.

Exercise 5.4 Transcribe the following passage, including all the processes seen so far, with special attention to syllabicity.

As soon as Colette Little saw the technician pull up, she ran out. 'Please hurry up. It's fallen all the way down to the bottom.' The technician rushed through the door of the huge old folks home following Mrs Little. 'We have to hurry. I have nurses stationed at all doors but still...' They got to the elevator just in time, it seemed, as an old lady shuffled towards it and, clearly, no one was stopping her. 'Oh, no, the nurse must have taken a break or something', Mrs Little muttered under her breath. 'No, Hazel, you can't use the elevator today. Go back to your room now, dear' and she gave the old woman a little push towards the corridor. By this time the technician had opened the elevator doors. 'The buttons still work the doors, madam. By the looks of things, with the compartment at the bottom and half the cables shot, I can't do anything right now. I didn't bring the right tools for this and I'll certainly need somebody else to help me. You will have to wait.' 'Oh, no,' Mrs Little said, 'couldn't you at least disable the doors?' 'No, I can't, but I'll block all doors with the cones so that everybody knows there's something going on, if you like. We wouldn't want anybody falling down the shaft, would we?' 'No, no. Yes, all right, sir. That would be very helpful.' After dinner Colette went up to her room, which was on the top floor. It was late and everyone was asleep except for her. She undressed and got into bed. All the elevator doors had been blocked except for hers. She had thought it was silly. She would certainly remember, she kept telling the technician, who looked at her disbelievingly. 'Are you absolutely sure, madam.' 'Yes, I'll be fine,' she reassured him. She was quite stubborn and it was hard to change her mind once it had been set. She couldn't sleep that night. All she could think about was Charlie, her dead husband, and all they had together until that day in May last year. He had told her then about the other woman. She hadn't known how to react at first, but then, it seemed like the right thing to do. Colette shuddered. She remembered picking up the nearest heavy object, a lamp, and hitting him over the head with it. It was a metal lamp and it had killed him on the spot. She hadn't meant to kill him. It just happened. She shivered again, looked at the clock and fell back on her pillow. Half past three. 'I'll never get back to sleep' she thought and rolled over. Suddenly, she heard a noise. It sounded like water running. Was it the tap in the bathroom? 'It can't be. I didn't leave it on,' she muttered. Then it stopped. 'I'm hearing things. I must be getting old.' Then she heard someone softly calling her name: 'Collie.' Her muscles tightened. Who was it that used to call her that? Collie. It was Charlie. He had always called her that and she hated it. She wasn't a dog. But he was dead. She got up and headed towards the noise. It was coming from the landing. She opened the door: 'Who's there? Answer immediately or I'll call the police.' 'Collie' the voice said again. 'Charlie! No, it can't be you. You're dead,' she screamed to the empty corridor and, turning away from the sound, ran dazed to the elevator. She had to get out of this place. She pushed the button and as soon as the doors opened, she stepped inside.

Exercise 5.5 Transcribe the following passage, including all the processes seen so far, with special attention to syllabicity.

My favourite time of the year has got to be the autumn. Most people, in my experience, when asked to choose a preferred season, will pick spring or summer, listing sunshine, warmth, new growth, flowers, holidays and outdoor activities as reasons. Those people find autumn an odd choice, as they associate it with oncoming winter, worsening weather, short days, light deprivation and depression. While I enjoy the advantages of every season and wouldn't do without any of them, I do, on the other hand, find autumn the cosiest time of the year, the time when I love to nest and I revel in every shortening day. Sitting here as I write, I'm conjuring up pictures of long country walks, autumn leaves, wellington boots and puddles, mushrooms, cobwebs glittering with dew, a deliciously musky damp smell outdoors, a low sun, long shadows, a hint of red to the light and sharp contrasts. I imagine warm fires, home crafts, pumpkins, hot soup, warm baths and apple cinnamon scented candles. There's nothing more uplifting and inspirational in my opinion than a long trek through the woods accompanied by my dog, with frequent stops along the way for him to enjoy the various delicious smells and me to fill my pockets with treasures, until they sag, damp and fragrant, laden with precious spoils stolen from mother nature. I collect pine cones, seed pods, grasses, pretty leaves, pieces of bark and perhaps, a handful of berries to use in various ways at home. I used to get carried away, greedy, bringing home far more than I could ever use, because it was all so beautiful and I wanted to save it forever somehow. Then, later, when I would remove my haul from my pockets, I would find that all would have lost its splendour now that it was removed from its natural surroundings and I'd be left with a handful of sad, wet, brown objects, displaying little evidence of their previous glory. I have learned that it's better to arrive home with a head full of exquisite memories than to attempt to capture it all and trap it in a box. I lived in California for a few years and this may help to explain my particular affection for the autumn. Being Irish, I grew up taking rain, bad weather and the changing of the seasons for granted. I used to grumble along with everyone else about the continually grey skies and the so often unrelenting rain and wind. I never expected to see a day when I would long for rain or a day when I would wish to see some real winter weather and, indeed, would have laughed in your face had you then suggested such a thing. However, that's exactly what happened. For the first nine months that I lived in California, I saw day after day of glorious sunshine, marred only by the occasional patch of fog and after five or six months of this, I was gasping, just like a fish out of water, for a change. I discovered that a wet, raw climate, at least for part of the year, is as essential to me as breathing, that, just like a plant, I begin to dry up if I don't get rained on regularly. Perhaps it's there in my Irish genes, although I have met many a fellow patriot who does not share this problem. But I love the changing of the seasons, the rhythm of the year, all of it, and I can't do without it even when change sometimes arrives blown in on a bitterly cold winter wind. In fact, my true response to the question posed above is that I don't have a favourite season. It's impossible for me to choose just one. I need them all. Each one complements the others. Each has its own advantages and disadvantages, but each is as vital to me in one way or another as the others.

Lesson 6

Elision

Many **phonological processes** present in connected speech are designed to ease the articulation of sequences of sounds. One of the most radical things that we can do to make a string of sounds easier to articulate is to omit one of them. This is known as **elision** or **deletion**. Obviously, the elision of sounds is not random, that is to say, we do not just drop any sound anywhere. In different languages there are different sounds which tend to be elided. And of course, they are not dropped always, otherwise they would disappear from the language altogether.

We have already seen some sounds which are elided in English such as schwa /ə/ in triphthongs (Lesson 2) and in syllabicity (Lesson 5) and /h/ in weak forms (Lesson 3). We will now look at two other cases: alveolar plosive elision and schwa elision without syllabicity.

Alveolar plosive elision

It will be noted throughout this course that the alveolar plosives are quite unstable in English, that is to say, they often undergo phonological processes (see lessons 7 and 8). One example of their instability is the fact that they are the only obstruents which can be elided. As we said above, elision does not occur across the board. It happens under certain conditions. The environments for alveolar plosive elision are the following:

(I)   The alveolar plosive must be in the coda of the syllable, not in the onset.
(II)   It must be preceded by a consonant of the same voicing. Thus /t/ must be preceded by a voiceless consonant and /d/ by a voiced consonant.
(III) The following sound must be a consonant other than /h/.

Therefore, the alveolar plosives may be elided when in the middle of a sequence of three consonants. For example:

last night /ˈlɑːst ˈnaɪt/ → /ˈlɑːs ˈnaɪt/
locked door /ˈlɒkt ˈdɔː/ → /ˈlɒk ˈdɔː/

send them /ˈsend ðəm/ → /ˈsen ðəm/
bold man /ˈbəʊld ˈmæn/ → /ˈbəʊl ˈmæn/
exactly /ɪgˈzæktli/ → /ɪgˈzækli/

but not in:

built them /ˈbɪlt ðəm/ because the consonant preceding /t/ is voiced whilst /t/ is voiceless
send it /ˈsend ɪt/ because the sound following /d/ is a vowel
bad thing /ˈbæd ˈθɪŋ/ because the sound preceding /d/ is a vowel
most horrible /məʊst hɒrɪbl̩/ because the consonant following the /t/ is /h/

Notice, too, that alveolar plosive elision may be word-internal and that it often affects the regular past tense suffix which means that tense is often indicated by context. So, for example: /ðeɪ ˈlʊk ˈbæd/ could mean *They look bad* or *They looked bad*.

There are some exceptions to the conditions for deletion mentioned above:

- We have seen before (Lesson 3) that /d/ in the weak form of 'and' may be elided whatever the following sound. This is a special case of alveolar plosive elision which we will not highlight again in this lesson.
- Another special case is the following. There is one type of sequence in which /t/ deletion is possible even though it goes against the second condition above. In negative contractions, such as, 'don't', 'didn't' and 'can't', /t/ may be elided, although the preceding sound /n/ is voiced. In fact, elision can take place in these words even if the next word begins with a vowel or /h/, though not if the negative contraction is followed by a pause. Here, you can see some examples of this exception:

don't shout /ˈdəʊnt ˈʃaʊt/ → /ˈdəʊn ˈʃaʊt/
didn't dare /ˈdɪdn̩t ˈdeə/ → /ˈdɪdn̩ ˈdeə/
can't think /ˈkɑːnt ˈθɪŋk / → /ˈkɑːn ˈθɪŋk/
wouldn't answer /ˈwʊdn̩t ˈɑːnsə/ → /ˈwʊdn̩ ˈɑːnsə/
needn't hurry /ˈniːdn̩t ˈhʌri/ → /ˈniːdn̩ ˈhʌri/

but not in:

I don't /aɪ ˈdəʊnt/

because /t/ is followed by a pause.

Schwa elision

We saw in Lesson 5 that in syllabicity /ə/ disappears making the following consonant, /n/ or /l/, syllabic. To a certain extent we may see the disappearance of schwa in syllabicity as a kind of elision. However, in syllabicity schwa does not disappear without leaving any trace since it transfers to the following consonant its ability of being the nucleus of a syllable. That is why syllabicity is more a kind of fusion between two sounds (schwa and the following consonant) than an elision process.

However, there are other cases in which we can talk properly of schwa deletion. In words such as *history* or *travelling*, schwa may be elided, without making the following consonant syllabic. It is simply dropped. For this process to happen, schwa must be followed by /n/ or by a liquid, /r/or /l/, after which there must be an unstressed syllable in the same word. Schwa must be preceded by a consonant which should not be an approximant. For example:

history /ˈhɪstəri/ → /ˈhɪstri /
travelling /ˈtrævəlɪŋ/ → /ˈtrævlɪŋ/
federal /ˈfedərəl/ → /ˈfedrəl/
counsellor /ˈkaʊnsələ/ → /ˈkaʊnslə/
gardening /ɡɑːdənɪŋ/ → /ɡɑːdnɪŋ/

Notice that in all of these cases, the elision of schwa results in the *loss of one syllable*, which was not the case in syllabicity:

history /ˈhɪstəri/ three syllables   /ˈhɪstri / two syllables

But in syllabicity:

cotton /ˈkɒtən/ two syllables   /ˈkɒtn̩/ two syllables

Exceptional schwa elisions

In some cases /ə/ elision may happen when schwa precedes the stressed syllable as in:

police /pəˈliːs/ /pliːs/

but this is not generally possible. For example, the word *polite* cannot lose its schwa and is pronounced /pəˈlaɪt/ not /plaɪt/.

Occasionally, schwa may be elided when the following consonant is something other than /r l n/. This quite often happens in a word such as *suppose* /səˈpəʊz/ → /spəʊz/. Again, this is not generally possible. For instance, the initial schwa in *apart* can never be elided.

Cases such as /ɡɑːdnɪŋ/ and /ˈtrævlɪŋ/ above may be seen as /ə/ elision or as desyllabicity, as we saw in Lesson 5. The conditions for /ə/ elision in /ən/ sequences are similar to the ones mentioned in Lesson 5 for nasal syllabicity. Therefore, we will not mention them again in the transcription comments.

Another thing to notice is that /ə/ may only be elided if it is an independent vowel. The /ə/ component of diphthongs such as /ɪə eə ʊə/ cannot be elided.

Here is a transcribed passage with many cases of elision in it. You can find its orthographic version at the end of the book. Remember there are several explanations and comments we made in previous lessons but which will not be repeated here.

Sample transcription

|*ˈmɑːdʒri ˈpɪk ðə ˈbæg ʌp | ɪt siːmd[1] ɪkˈstrɔːdnrəli[2] ˈhevi fər[3] ɪts ˈsaɪz | ˈʃɔːli[4] ðə məs bi ˈsʌmθɪŋ ˈɪn ɪt wɪtʃ wʊd aɪˈdentɪfaɪ ɪts ˈəʊnə | ʃi kʊd ˈðen meɪk ə ˈkwɪk

---

NB. *In the transcriptions for this lesson, we will mark elision by shading the sounds before and after the one that has been deleted. Special cases of elision which do not follow the conditions laid out above will be indicated in the transcription comments.*

'kɔːl | ən 'meɪbi 'iːvn̩ prɪ'vent[5] hər 'ɑːftənuːn biːɪŋ 'ruːɪn baɪ ə 'lɪtl̩ waɪt 'laɪ |
'nəʊwʌn wʊd 'nəʊ ʃi əd 'lʊkt[1] ɪnsaɪd ðə 'bæg | ʃi kʊd dʒəs 'seɪ ðət ʃi 'rekəgnaɪzd[6]
huːz ɪt 'wɒz[7] | ənd əd 'fəʊn 'raɪt ɑːftə 'faɪndɪŋ ɪt | ʃi 'spəʊz[8] ʃi kʊd dʒəs 'fəʊn ðəm
'ɔːl wʌn baɪ 'wʌn | ən 'faɪn ði 'əʊnə 'ðæt[9] weɪ | bət *'mɑːdʒri 'felt[10] tuː 'wɪəri fər 'ɔːl
ðæt[9] 'rɪgmərəʊl[11] | 'nəʊ | ɪf 'sʌmwʌn 'kʊdn̩[12] bi 'keəfl̩ i'nʌf tə 'lʊk ɑːftə ðeə 'bæg |
ðen ðeɪd 'betə stɑːt 'sʌfrɪŋ ðə 'kɒnsəkwensɪz | ʃi 'əʊpn̩ ðə 'bæg | ðə 'fɜːs θɪŋ ʃi 'sɔː
wəz ə 'smɔːl jeləʊ 'daəri[13] | ənd 'ʌndəniːθ 'ðæt[9] | 'sʌmθɪŋ 'sɪlvri ən 'ʃaɪnɪŋ | ʃi 'lɪftɪd
aʊt ðə 'daəri[13]| ən 'ðeə[14] | 'laɪɪŋ 'kʌmftəbli[15] ət ðə 'bɒtəm əv ðə 'bæg | wəz ə
rɪ'vɒlvə | *'mɑːdʒri 'steəd ət ɪt 'fæsɪneɪtɪd | 'hɑːdli ʌndə'stændɪŋ 'wɒt ʃi wəz
'lʊkɪŋ æt[16] | ðen ʃi 'snæp ðə bæg 'ʃʌt ən 'kləʊzd[6] hər 'aɪz | həd ʃi 'drʌŋk tuː
'mʌtʃ | ʃi 'sɜːtn̩li 'dɪdn̩[12] 'fiːl ɪn ðə 'liːs bi'fʌdl̩ naʊ | ʃi felt[10] 'pænɪk 'raɪzɪŋ ɪn ə |
'ʃɔːli[4] 'nʌn əv hə 'frenz | hə 'feləʊ kə'mɪti 'membəz | wʊd 'kæri sʌtʃ ə 'θɪŋ | ʃi
'əʊpnd[1] ɪt ə'gen 'keəfli[17] | əz ʃi 'wʊd ə 'bæg ɪn wɪtʃ ʃi 'njuː ðə 'leɪ ə 'pɔɪznəs[17]
'sneɪk | 'ðeə[14] wəz ðə 'gʌn | 'ʃʌdrɪŋ | ʃi 'pʊt ɪn hə 'hænd[1] ən 'tʊk ɪt 'aʊt | 'wɒt
kʊd ʃi 'duː[18] | ðə 'θɪŋ felt[5] 'hɑːd ən 'kəʊl tə ðə 'tʌtʃ | 'haʊ kʊd ʃi kən'frʌnt[10] ðə
'pɜːsn̩ ɪt bi'lɒŋ tu[16] | ʃʊd ʃi dʒəs pri'ten ðət ɪt 'wɒzn̩[12] ðeə[14] | 'wɒt wʊd 'eni əv
hə 'leɪdiz 'wɒnt[10] wɪð sʌtʃ ə 'θɪŋ | ʃi 'drɒp ðə rɪ'vɒlvə 'bæk ɪntə ðə 'bæg əz ɪf ɪt
'bɜːnt[10-19] | ʃi wʊd dʒəs 'weɪt ən 'siː hu 'kɔːl fər[3] ɪt | ən 'ðen gɪv ɪt 'bæk ən 'traɪ
tə fə'get | bət ʃi 'sɔː ðiːz 'wɪmɪn 'regjʊləli[2] | 'sʌm[20] əv ðəm 'præktɪkli[17] 'evri 'deɪ
| 'haʊ kʊd ʃi 'kæri ɒn 'triːtɪŋ ðə 'wʌn hu 'əʊn ðə 'bæg ɪn ðə 'seɪm 'fæʃn̩ | ʃi
'kʊdn̩[12] 'θɪŋk əv ə 'suːtəbl̩ 'wɜːd tə dɪ'skraɪb ə 'wʊmən hu wʊd 'kiːp sʌtʃ ən
'ɒbdʒɪk 'wɪð ə |

Comments on sample passage

1. The alveolar plosive may not be deleted because it is followed by a vowel.
2. /ə/ may not be deleted because it is preceded by an approximant.
3. /ə/ is not usually deleted if it is not followed by an unstressed syllable in the same word. However, in very rapid, informal speech the words *for its* can be pronounced /frɪts/.
4. Monophthonging (see Lesson 2). ***
5. /t/ may not be deleted because it is preceded by a consonant of different voicing and because it is followed by /h/.
6. The alveolar plosive may not be deleted because it is followed by /h/.
7. Strong form because the grammatical word is stranded and stressed.
8. The word /sə'pəʊz/ is one of a number of special cases in which /ə/ may be deleted even though it is not followed by a liquid or nasal and even though it precedes the stressed syllable.
9. Strong form because *that* is used as a demonstrative.
10. /t/ cannot be deleted because it is preceded by a voiced consonant.
11. /ə/ is unlikely to be deleted because it would result in a sequence of consonants /gmr/ which is not possible in English.
12. /t/ may be deleted even though the previous consonant is voiced because the word is a negative contraction.
13. Smoothing (see Lesson 2). ***
14. Strong form because *there* is used as a locative adverb. ***

15. /'kʌmfətəbli/ is the citation form for this word. The only /ə/ which can be deleted is the first one.
16. Strong form because the grammatical form is stranded
17. Syllabicity could be an alternative to /ə/ elision here.
18. Strong form because the verb is not an auxiliary here.
19. The alveolar plosive cannot be deleted because it is followed by a potential pause.
20. Strong form because *some* is used as a pronoun (see Lesson 3).

Exercise 6.1 Look at the following passage which is given in orthography. Try to identify all the possible instances of elision in it and check your version with the one provided in the answers section, where you can also find a commented transcription.

Overhearing conversations on trains can be amusing, sometimes even alarming. Some years ago I used to travel on the London Underground to get to work. Quite often I used to spend the journey marking students' work, especially phonetic transcriptions of English. One morning in summer a group of tourists got into the carriage where I was sitting. It was an Italian family who were going into the centre of the city to see the sights. One of them sat next to me. After a few minutes he said to his family, in Italian of course, that he didn't know what I was doing. Apparently, I seemed to be reading things in a very peculiar language. I said nothing, but just carried on with my work. The odd thing is that exactly the same thing happened the next morning. This time the man said, 'It's him! He's doing it again! I wonder what that funny lettering is.' They all collected around me, peering over my shoulder. I couldn't resist the challenge. When I got off the train, I said in Italian, 'I hope you all have a pleasant day.' I wish I had had a camera to take a picture of the expressions on their faces. Another time, I was really puzzled by an exchange I overheard. Two men sitting opposite me were talking. One of them I could understand perfectly. He was talking about a police raid. The trouble was I couldn't make out a word of what the other was answering. It was after about ten minutes that I finally realised the reason. He wasn't speaking in English at all, but in Welsh. Why they chose to have a conversation in two different languages at the same time I don't know.

Exercise 6.2 The following transcribed passage contains cases where elisions are possible, but they have not been done. Retranscribe the passage showing the occurrence of elisions. There is an orthographic version and an annotated transcription in the answers section.

| wel 'wʌn əv ðə 'wɜːst θɪŋz ðət 'hæpənd tə 'miː | wəz 'wen aɪ æksɪ'dentəli dɪ'strɔɪd ði 'evɪdəns ðət wəz 'gəʊɪŋ tə bi 'juːzd fər ə 'kɔːt keɪs | ɪt 'hæpənd ten 'jɪəz əgəʊ | ət ðə 'taɪm | aɪ ə'keɪʒənəli dɪd bɪts əv 'wɜːk fə sə'lɪsɪtəz | wen ðeɪ 'niːdɪd 'ekspɜːt ə'pɪnjən ɒn 'teɪp ri'kɔːdɪŋz | ðə 'keɪs kən'sɜːnd ə dɪ'vɔːs | aɪ 'dəʊnt ri'membər ɔːl ðə 'diːteɪlz | bət 'wʌn əv ðə 'pɑːtiz əd ri'kɔːdɪd ə kɒnvə'seɪʃən wɪð ði 'ʌðə | 'juːzɪŋ ə 'dɪktəfəʊn mə'ʃiːn | ðə wəz ə dɪs'pjuːt əz tə wɒt wəz 'æktʃəli sed | bɪkɒz ðə ri'kɔːdɪŋ 'wɒzənt ə pə'tɪkjuləli 'klɪə wʌn | səʊ ðə sə'lɪsɪtə 'sent ɪt tə 'miː | ʌn'fɔːtʃənətli ðə ri'kɔːdɪŋ wəz ɒn ə 'mɪni kə'set | ənd aɪ 'dɪdənt hæv ə mə'ʃiːn ðət aɪ kʊd 'pleɪ ɪt ɒn | səʊ aɪ 'hæd tə 'get ðə sə'lɪsɪtə tu 'ɑːsk ɪz 'klaənt tə 'send mi ðə mə'ʃiːn əz 'wel | aɪ 'lɪsənd tə ðə 'θɪŋ ə 'kʌpəl əv 'taɪmz | ənd 'ðen dɪ'saɪdɪd tə 'teɪk ɪt 'həʊm | ənd 'wɜːk ɒn ɪt 'əʊvə ðə |

wiːkˈend | ˈwen aɪ ˈtraɪd tə ˈlɪsən tu ɪt ðə ˈnekst ˈdeɪ | aɪ ˈfaʊnd ðət ðə riˈkɔːdɪŋ əd
biːn ˈwaɪpt ˈkliːn | ðə məˈʃiːn məst əv ˈswɪtʃt ɪtself ˈɒn ɪn maɪ ˈbriːfkeɪs ˈsʌmhaʊ |
ˈɔːl ðət wəz ˈleft wəz ðə ˈsaʊnd frəm ði ˈʌndəɡraʊnd ˈtreɪn ðət ˈtʊk mi ˈhəʊm | aɪ
ˈdɪdənt nəʊ ˈwɒt tə ˈduː | aɪ ˈθɔːt ðət ˈwen aɪ ˈtəʊld ðə səˈlɪsɪtə | hi wʊd ɪˈmiːdjətli
ˈsuː mi fə ˈneɡlɪdʒəns ɔː ˈsʌmθɪŋ | aɪ wəz ɪn ˈsʌtʃ ə ˈsteɪt | ðət aɪ ˈpɔːd maɪself ə
ˈɡlɑːs əv ˈwɪski | tə ˈtraɪ ənd ˈkɑːm maɪself ˈdaʊn | wen maɪ ˈwaɪf əraɪvd ˈhəʊm
frəm ə ˈʃɒpɪŋ ˈtrɪp | ʃi ˈfaʊnd mi ˈslʌmpt ɪn ə ˈtʃeə | wɪð ə ˈbɒtəl ɪn ˈwʌn hænd |
ənd ə ˈɡlɑːs ɪn ði ˈʌðə | aɪ ˈfaɪnəli ˈɡɒt ʌp iˈnʌf ˈkʌrɪdʒ tə ˈfəʊn ðə səˈlɪsɪtə | ənd i
dʒəst ˈsed | əʊ ˈdɪə | wɒt ə ˈpɪti | wel ðəz ˈnʌθɪŋ wi kən ˈduː əbaʊt ɪt | ˈɪz ðeə | jud
ˈbetə ˈsend mi ðə məˈʃiːn ˈbæk | ˈɑːftə ˈðæt | əz ju kən ɪˈmædʒɪn | aɪ ˈɔːlweɪz
ɪnˈsɪstɪd ɒn ˈwɜːkɪŋ frəm ˈkɒpiz əv ði əˈrɪdʒɪnəl riˈkɔːdɪŋz |

Here, there are three passages for you to transcribe You can check your transcriptions against the ones provided in the answers section at the end of the book. Make
sure you understand all the comments before moving on to Lesson 7. If you are not
sure you do understand, you might need to revise previous lessons before starting
the next one.

Exercise 6.3 Transcribe this passage doing as many elisions as you can and including
all the processes that we have seen in the previous lessons too (weak forms, sandhi r,
syllabicity).

My first real day in Stratford. After breakfast we went off to find the summer school.
Every where you looked you saw foreign students and we were all heading towards
the same place, a local college. When my friend and I got there, we couldn't find the
group for ages in the big crowd of noisy and milling students, but at last they came
bounding towards us. Soon we had to go inside though and we were split up into
groups, so we postponed telling our stories until later. The classes weren't that
bad really, although I hadn't looked forward to the idea of going on holiday and
having lectures thrown in, but I suppose that a school trip isn't the same as a
holiday. It has to be more cultural, doesn't it? Our first teacher was a very nice
guy and his lecture was quite interesting. He told us about the things that we
were going to see and do over the next week. After lunch we went to the town
centre to do some exploring. We were shown a few landmarks and then we visited
a church, which was where Shakespeare was both baptized and buried. It was
hard to realise that you were standing in the same place as he did when he was
little. Well, I suppose he wasn't really standing at his christening. His grave had
beautiful engravings and inscriptions on it, but it was difficult to see it properly,
because there was a fence in front of it. In the evening we were booked for the
theatre. Earlier, we had managed to get tickets which included an amazing back-
stage tour and we thought the set was fantastic, so we were really looking forward
to seeing the production. The curtain went up and I forgot about everything else
until the last bows and curtsies were over. It was brilliant. The cast was very
good, the story fabulous, and the ending spectacular. I thoroughly enjoyed it despite
a few difficult words and jokes I didn't get. All of the characters were funny,
although my favourites were the womaniser and basket carriers. I thought their
facial expressions were hilarious. After seeing the play I finally realise why everyone
thinks he's such a grand playwright. I had never really read any of his work before or

seen any of his plays, so this one was an eye-opener for me. Even though his stories are over 300 years old, they seem to me still quite modern, which is supposed to be the mark of a true genius.

Exercise 6.4 Transcribe this passage doing as many elisions as you can and including all the processes that we have seen in the previous lessons too (weak forms, sandhi r, syllabicity).

Last time I was in Ireland, my mother gave me some letters to read. They were written to her parents in England when we were children. My grandparents had saved them for her and returned them neatly filed in folders and dated. When we left home, it was a sort of mother's eye-view record of our childhood and since my parents were both prolific and witty letter writers, they made wonderfully entertaining reading. I was absorbed in them for hours, transported back to marvellous afternoons imaginatively whiled away in our playroom with my siblings and friends. There we invented many of our own games and acted out all sorts of dramas for whatever audience we could entrap, usually my poor mother of course. She writes, for example, about us being inspired for months by a Christmas trip to the operetta *The Mikado*. We put on an excellent show, which included costumes and props. Our mother made sure we always had plenty of things that with a little skill and imagination could be turned into nearly anything. She passed on to us old bedspreads and blankets, odd ear-rings, gloves and socks, pieces of leftover materials and jumble sale acquisitions. This particular show became a classic with our drama company, so much so that the next door neighbour presented us with a recording of *The Pirates of Penzance*, hoping it, too, would catch our fancy and give him a break from 'Three Little Maids from School are We' floating melodically but all too frequently through his wall. It was fun reading their version of an event which I remember happening, also interesting to note how different my memories are from their descriptions. On a more solemn note, I found there were many things going on that we as children were unaware of, since my parents wanted to protect us from whatever we might find worrying or unpleasant. It was only by reading those letters that I realised how many problems my parents had to deal with and appreciated the amount of thinking and care they put into our upbringing. Through the letters I also discovered interesting views on some people which I only knew as a child, but never saw much of when I grew up. For instance, we used to look forward to visits from a specially eccentric family friend, because we found him very odd and entertaining. My mother used to dread them. Apparently, with an adult's perspective, his oddities were somewhat less amusing. As a result of this experience I am freshly converted to the advantages of letter writing. I too live abroad and have children. I do write to my mother every now and then, but I must say that I give in all too frequently to the immediacy of a quick telephone call. My mother saves my letters as hers did and my children could enjoy a nostalgic afternoon, buried in childhood memories one day. As my mother says, a phone call is over as soon as you hang up, but you can read a letter over and over again.

Exercise 6.5 Transcribe this passage doing as many elisions as you can and including all the processes that we have seen in the previous lessons too (weak forms, sandhi r, syllabicity).

When the men appeared at the door brandishing a warrant to search her house, she didn't think to check that it was a genuine one. It was because she was still half asleep and couldn't react properly. She had only got back yesterday after a holiday abroad. The long flight home had been very tiring and she went to bed as soon as she had organised some of her stuff. She decided to leave most things in the suitcases till the next day. Then shortly after seven in the morning the doorbell rang, followed by loud knocking. The men wore dark suits and told Linda that they were police detectives, narcotics division. Everything was so unreal. She kept wondering if it was a dream, a nightmare or some kind of practical joke. But the idea of it being a game soon left her mind when the detectives got to work. They went straight up to her bedroom and she could hear loud noises as drawers were emptied and dropped carelessly. One of them remained downstairs and examined her desk. He said that it wouldn't take them long. She needn't worry. They must be trying to find drugs if they were in narcotics, but why in her house? She'd never dealt with that kind of stuff, not even as a user, let alone as a dealer. She asked the detective, but got no coherent answer out of him. 'We have a warrant,' was all she managed to understand once again. She heard a voice upstairs asking the others if they had checked the suitcases. Linda realised that there must have been some mistake. Maybe they got the wrong address. She picked the phone up to call the police station nearest to the house. The detective stopped what he was doing, walked towards her and grabbed the receiver from her hand, whilst cutting off the call with his other hand. 'I'm sure you don't need to phone anybody,' he said. It was then that she became suspicious. Why shouldn't she use the phone? She only meant to call the station to clarify the situation. He wouldn't let her see the warrant again when she asked him. They had already shown it to her, hadn't they? How many times did she want to see it? The man said she should sit down and try to be patient for a bit longer. Linda did as she was told, whilst an idea dawned on her. This must be linked to yesterday's mess up with the luggage. She had picked the wrong bag up, but fortunately she'd noticed before leaving the airport. She'd gone back and explained to one of the ground staff. They were very relieved to see her. The owner of the bag had been there before her. He was extremely angry and had filed his complaint against the airline in rather strong terms. She apologised for her blunder and since her own luggage was right there, she put it on a trolley and walked towards the taxi rank. She had been slightly concerned that her foolishness had upset a fellow passenger so much, but as soon as she arrived back home, she forgot the whole episode until now. Whose bag had she mistakenly yanked from the luggage belt? What had it contained that these so-called detectives were looking for in such a thorough manner? And who were they anyway? Surely not who they pretended to be.

Lesson 7

Assimilation

Assimilation is a process by which two (or more) sounds become more similar to each other. This similarity is achieved by one of the sounds taking characteristics from the other one. Assimilations may be classified according to the direction in which the borrowing of characteristics is effected. Thus, for two adjacent sounds, if a sound takes features from the sound following it we talk about **regressive** or **anticipatory assimilation** since the features 'move' backwards or are anticipated, as it were: A ← B. When a sound takes features from the sound preceding it, we talk about **progressive** or **perseverative assimilation** since the features move forward A → B, they persevere into the following sound.

There is a related process known as **coalescence** which is often described as a type of assimilation. In coalescence two sounds merge into one sound which shares characteristics from the two original ones. In this sense it is a kind of bi-directional assimilation (see *Coalesence* below).

Assimilations may also be classified according to the type of feature which is borrowed. In English most connected speech assimilations involve place of articulation features, although there are also a few cases of voice assimilations (see *Voice assimilation* below).

Place assimilation in English involves alveolar stops which change their place of articulation to bilabial or velar depending on the surrounding sounds, or alveolar fricatives which may change their place of articulation to post-alveolar when followed by a post-alveolar or palatal consonant. We will study three different types of place assimilation in English which are classified according to the type of sounds which undergo the process: alveolar stops, alveolar fricatives and alveolar syllabic nasals.

Alveolar stop regressive place assimilation

The alveolar stops /t d n/ may become bilabial when followed by bilabial consonants (/p b m/) or they may become velar stops when followed by velars (/k g/) without altering their voicing. Thus /t/ may become /p/ or /k/, /d/ may become /b/ or /g/ and /n/ may become /m/ or /ŋ/.

Examples:

that man	/ðæt mæn/ → /ðæp mæn/
that car	/ðæt kɑː/ → /ðæk kɑː/
bad boy	/bæd bɔɪ/ → /bæb bɔɪ/
bad girl	/bæd gɜːl/ → /bæg gɜːl/
ten pens	/ten penz/ → /tem penz/
ten keys	/ten kiːz/ → /teŋ kiːz/

This process can also affect an entire sequence of two or three alveolar stops, so that /nt/, for example, can become /mp/ or /ŋk/. It is extremely unlikely that only the last of a sequence of alveolar stops will be assimilated. If one is affected, they all will be affected.

Examples:

front garden	/frʌnt gɑːdn̩/ → /frʌŋk gɑːdn̩/
couldn't be	/kʊdn̩t biː/ → /kʊbmp biː/

Notice that since the alveolar plosives may often be deleted, as we saw in the previous lesson, there will be quite a lot of instances in which an alveolar plosive may either be deleted or it may assimilate to the following sound, for example:

couldn't be	/kʊdn̩t biː/ → /kʊbm̩ biː/ or → /kʊbmp biː/
cold cream	/kəʊld kriːm/ → /kəʊl kriːm/ or → /kəʊlg kriːm/

As you can see, in 'couldn't be', previous alveolars assimilate both when /t/ is deleted and when it suffers assimilation too. We will mention these cases with alternative possible processes in the transcription comments.

Alveolar fricative regressive place assimilation

The alveolar fricatives /s z/ may become post-alveolar fricatives without altering their voicing when followed by a palatal approximant (/j/) or a post-alveolar fricative (/ʃ ʒ/). Thus /s/ may become /ʃ/ and /z/ may become /ʒ/.

Examples:

Is she	/ɪz ʃi/ → /ɪʒ ʃi/
dress shop	/dres ʃɒp/ → /dreʃ ʃɒp/

In RP English, the alveolar fricatives do not become post-alveolars by assimilation when the following sound is a post-alveolar affricate (/tʃ dʒ/), but in other accents of English such assimilations are possible.

Alveolar syllabic nasal progressive place assimilation

The alveolar syllabic nasal /n̩/ may become bilabial (/m̩/) or velar (/ŋ̍/) when **preceded** by a bilabial or velar plosive in the same word and followed by a consonant in the same or the next word or by a pause.

Examples:

open   /əʊpən/ → /əʊpn̩/ → /əʊpm̩/
bacon /beɪkən/ → /beɪkn̩/ → /beɪkŋ/

Coalescence

The alveolar plosives /t/ and /d/ may merge with a following palatal approximant /j/ to become post-alveolar affricates (/tʃ/ and /dʒ/ respectively). This type of coalescence, although historically found within a word, is only common in current RP English when the plosive and the approximant are in different words and the approximant is in a grammatical word.
   Examples:

don't you   /dəʊnt ju/ → /dəʊntʃu/
would you   /wʊd ju/ → /wʊdʒu/

Voice assimilation

In current English, voice assimilation is not very common as a connected speech process and is restricted to some close-knit structures, such as *have to* and *of course*. In these cases assimilation is regressive and the feature which is borrowed is voicelessness. Thus /v/ becomes /f/ because the following sound, /t/or /k/, is voiceless. This sort of voicing assimilation only affects /v/ and /z/. Assimilation of voiceless to voiced sounds does not occur in present day RP English.
   Examples:

have to   /hæv tu/ → /hæf tu/
of course /əv kɔːs/ → /əf kɔːs/
newspaper /njuːzpeɪpə/ → /njuːspeɪpə/

Study the following transcribed passage which has many examples of assimilation in it which have been highlighted. You can find its orthographic version in the answers section. Remember that we will include elision, syllabicity and other processes we have seen in previous lessons without commenting or highlighting them again, so you need to be extra careful when you read the transcriptions.

Sample transcription

| maɪ ˈhɒlɪdeɪ[1] ɪn ði ˈaɪləndz wəʒ ˈʃɪə ˈblɪs | ði ˈəʊnli ˈbæb pɔɪmp[2] biːɪŋ ˈhævɪŋ tə ˈteɪk səʊ meni ˈflaɪts | ˈfɔːr ɪn ˈɔːl | wɪtʃ dʒəst əbaʊt ˈdɪb maɪ ˈnɜːvz ɪn | ðə ˈweðər əraʊn ðə ˈkəʊs wəz veri ˈɒd | ɪt wəz ˈdʒenjuɪnli ˈkəʊl fər ə ˈkʌpl̩ əv ˈdeɪz | ˈwɔːm əŋ[3] ˈklaʊdi ðə ˈθɜːd | ən ðen ˈskɔːtʃɪŋ ˈhɒt ðə ˈneks ˈfɔː | əˈpærəntli ðə ˈwɪntər ən ˈsprɪŋ ðeər əb biːŋ ˈkwaɪk ˈkəʊld | wɪtʃ aɪ ˈθɪŋk səˈpraɪz ðə ˈstɑːf | hu əb ˈplæn tə spen ðə ˈwɪntə mʌnθs ˈwɜːkɪŋ ɪm ˈbetər ən ˈwɔːmə ˈklaɪmz | aə ˈfrenz əg ˈkleɪmd tə hæv[4] səm mɪsˈɡɪvɪŋz əbaʊk ˈɡəʊɪŋ ɒn ə ˈseɪlɪŋ ˈhɒlɪdeɪ[1] | sɪns ðeɪ hæd[4] ˈnəʊ ɪkˈspɪərɪəns

əbaʊp ˈbəʊts | ˈaɪ əf[5] ˈkɔːs | wəz ɔːlˈredi ən ˈəʊld ˈhænd | əˈpɑːt frəm ðə ˈjuːʒʊəl ˈtiːneɪdʒ ˈlesənz əm[3] ˈbəʊt trɪps wɪð ðə ˈgɜːl ˈskaʊts | aɪ əb biːn ˈaʊt wɪð *ˈdʒɒn ˈsevrəl ˈtaɪmz | sɪns wɪg gɒp ˈmærɪd tuː ˈjɪəz əgəʊ | ˈniːdləs tə ˈseɪ | ˈɔːl maɪ səˈpəʊz ˈnɒlɪdʒ | wəz ˈæbsəluːtli[6] ˈnəʊ ˈjuːs | səʊ ðət *ˈheðər ənd ˈaɪ | ˈmænɪdʒ tə kæpˈsaɪz ðə ˈbəʊt | ˈevri ˈtaɪm wi went ˈaʊt ɒn ɑər ˈəʊn | wi ˈsuːŋ gɒt θruː ə ˈlɒt əv ˈaʊtfɪts | ðəʊz ˈfɜːs fjuː ˈdeɪz | aɪ ˈiːvn fel ˈɪn | ˈweərɪŋ maɪ ˈdaʊm pædɪg ˈkəʊt | wɪtʃ ˈment nɒt ˈəʊnli ðət aɪ ˈdɪdn hæv[4] ˈeniθɪŋ ˈwɔːm tə ˈweə fə ðə ˈrest əv ðə ˈhɒlɪdeɪ[1] | bət ˈɔːlsəʊ ðət aɪ wəz ˈsʌk daʊn ˈʌndə ðə ˈwɔːtə | baɪ ðə ˈweɪt əv ðə ˈkəʊt wen ɪk gɒt ˈwet | ˈfɔːtʃnətli ðə ˈlaɪfdʒækɪts wə ˈrɪəli ˈgʊd | ənd aɪ ˈsuːŋ keɪm ˈʌp əgen[7] | bət ɪt ˈfraɪpm[2–3] mi səʊ ˈmʌtʃ | ðət aɪ ˈstɑːtɪd haɪpəˈventɪleɪtɪŋ wɪð ˈʃɒk | ət ˈðæp pɔɪnt | ði ˈʌðə ˈbəʊt əd ɔːlˈredi ˈrəʊd ɪm maɪ daɪˈrekʃn[8] | *ˈdʒɒn liːnd ˈəʊvər ən ˈhelb[9] mi əˈfləʊt | waɪlʃ[10] ˈʃeɪkɪŋ mi ən ˈtelɪŋ mi tə ˈstɒp ɪt | əŋ[3] ˈkɑːm ˈdaʊn | ˈðen aɪ wəz ˈfɪʃt ˈaʊt | ən wemp[2] ˈbæk tə ðə həʊˈtel fiːlɪŋ ˈtəʊtli ˈmɪzrəbl̩ | ˈwʌn ˈdeɪ | *ˈdʒɒn ˈtʃɑːtəd ə ˈjɒt | wɪð ðə ˈrest əv əs əz ɪz ˈkruː | ən wi went ˈɒf raʊn *ˈdʒæki *əʊˈnæsɪsəz ˈpraɪvət ˈaɪlənd | wi gɒt ˈɒf fə ˈlʌntʃ ɒn əˈnʌðər ˈaɪlənd | ə ˈbɪt ˈfɜːðər ˈɒn ˈstɪl | ɪts ə ˈrɪəli ˈbjuːtɪfl̩ ˈeərɪə | ɔːlðəʊ *ˈheðər əm[3] *ˈpɔːl wə səˈpraɪzd ət haʊ rʌnˈdaʊn ɔːl ðə lɪtl̩ ˈtaʊnz wɜː[11] | ˈveri ˈpɔː | əŋ[3] ˈkwaɪk ˈgrʌbi | aɪ ˈæktʃuəli priˈfɜːr ɪt laɪk ˈðæt[7–12] | bɪkɒz ɪt ˈsiːmz mɔː ˈrɪəl tə mi | ˈeniθɪŋ ˈels wʊd ˈlʊk laɪk səm ˈkaɪnd əv ˈglɔːrɪfaɪd ˈθiːm pɑːk | əz ə ˈfɔːsəm | wi ˈgɒt ɒn ˈwʌndəfli ˈwel | *ˈdʒɒn əm[3] *ˈpɔːl hɪt ɪt ˈɒf raɪt əˈweɪ | əz *ˈpɔːl wəz ɪˈmiːdɪətli[13] ˈbɪpm[2] baɪ ðə ˈseɪlɪŋ ˈbʌg | ən ˈsəʊ hi kʊd ˈʃeər ɪz ɪnˈθjuːzɪæzəm wɪð *ˈdʒɒn | ɒn ðə ˈlɑːs ˈdeɪ | ðə ˈseɪlɪŋ ˈklʌb ˈmænədʒə | ənd ˈəʊnər ˈəv ðə ˈbɪznɪs | priˈzentɪb *ˈpɔːl wɪð ə ˈspeʃl̩ ˈpraɪz | hi sed ðət ˈnevər ɪn ˈɔːl ðə ˈjɪəz hi əb ˈbiːn ət ðə ˈklʌb | əd i siːn ˈeniwʌn ˈtraɪ səʊ ˈhɑːd | ɔː ˈpʊt ɪn ˈsəʊ meni ˈɑəz ˈpræktɪs | əˈspeʃli əz ɪt wəz ɪz ˈfɜːs taɪm ˈevər əbɔːd ə ˈbəʊt | ɒn ðə ˈweɪ ˈbæk | ət *ˈhiːθrəʊ[14] ˈeəpɔːp *ˈpɔːl ˈbɔːt ɪmself ə ˈkʌpl̩ əv ˈjɒtɪŋ mægəˈziːnz | ən ˈsed ðət i ɪz ˈgəʊɪŋ tə stɑːt ˈlʊkɪŋ ˈaʊt fər ə ˈsekŋd hæm[3] ˈbəʊt ɔːlˈredi | səʊ *ˈheðər ɪz ˈnaʊ riˈzaɪnd | tu ə ˈfjuːtʃər ɪŋkluːdɪŋ ə ˈbəʊp mæd ˈhʌzbənd | əʒ ju kn̩[15] ɪˈmædʒɪn | ɑːftər ˈɔːl ðə ˈfʌn wi hæd[4–7] | ˈgəʊɪŋ bæk ˈhəʊm wəz ə ˈterɪbl̩ ˈletdaʊn | əˈspeʃli bɪkɒz *ˈdʒɒn ənd ˈaɪ | ˈwəʊm bi ˈeɪbl̩ tə spen ˈtaɪm təˈgeðər əˈgen | ʌntɪl ðə ˈsʌmər əˈraɪvz | aɪ ˈnəʊ ðət ɪk ˈkɑːm[3] bi əˈvɔɪdɪd | səʊ ɪts ˈpɔɪntləs ˈgetɪŋ ɪntu ə ˈsteɪt əˈbaʊt ɪt[7] | bət aɪ ˈkɑːn help ˈwɪʃɪŋ wi kʊd əv steɪd ˈɒn fər ə ˈhəʊl ˈmʌnθ | ɪnˈsted əv dʒəst ə fjuː ˈdeɪz | ɔːr ˈiːvn ðət ɪt wəz ˈpɒsɪbl̩ | tu ɪkˈsten ðə ˈseɪlɪŋ ˈhɒlɪdeɪ ɪntu ə ˈlaɪfstaɪl | ɪt ˈdʌzn̩ saʊn ˈsensɪbl̩ | bət ðər ə ˈpiːpl̩ ˈaʊt ðeə | hu əv ˈteɪkŋ sʌtʃ diˈsɪʒnz | əˈbændənɪŋ kəˈrɪər əŋ[3] ˈkʌntri | ɪn ˈsɜːtʃ əv ə mɔːr ɪnˈdʒɔɪəbl̩ | hjuːˈmeɪn | ɔː fʊlˈfɪlɪŋ ˈlaɪfstaɪl |

Comments on sample transcription

1. /hɒlɪdeɪ/ and /hɒlɪdi/ are alternative pronunciations. We could also have used /ə/ instead of /ɪ/.
2. Double assimilation.
3. The alveolar plosive could have been assimilated instead of elided.
4. Strong form because the verb is not an auxiliary here.
5. This is one of the few cases in which voice assimilation is possible in current RP English.

6. /æbsəljuːtli/ is an alternative pronunciation.
7. Assimilation may be inhibited by the potential pause.
8. /dɪrekʃn̩/ and /dərekʃn̩/ are alternative pronunciations.
9. The alveolar plosive could have been elided here instead of assimilated.
10. Assimilation is possible if we elide /t/ so that /s/ is followed by palatal or post-alveolar.
11. Strong form because the grammatical word is stranded.
12. Strong form because *that* is used as a demonstrative here. ***
13. In unstressed positions, the first element of the diphthongs /ɪə/, and /ʊə/, may lose its prominence and become /jə/ or /wə/ respectively. This is a common process which we will use consistently in the last lesson of the book. Meanwhile, don't worry if you use /ɪə/ and our version is /jə/. You can regard them as alternative pronunciations.
14. Heathrow is one of the airports in London.
15. Progressive assimilation of the syllabic nasal is not possible because /n̩/ is followed by a vowel sound.

Exercise 7.1 Transcribe each of the following phrases, including any possible assimilations. Be careful! Not all of the phrases can have an assimilation.

(a) red book	(b) does she	(c) back part
(d) won't go	(e) one by one	(f) has to
(g) had to	(h) shouldn't come	(i) this year

Exercise 7.2 The following passage is given in orthography. Try to identify all the places where an assimilation might occur. You can find an edited version and a transcription with comments in the answers section at the end of the book.

I've just been told a tragic story. A friend of mine's recently been on a trip abroad. He was doing some lectures at a couple of universities in South America. I think he went to Chile, Argentina and Brazil. He had a wonderful time. Apparently, while he was there, he had quite a lot of free time for sightseeing and he bought masses of souvenirs to bring back with him. He and his wife are very keen collectors of pottery and paintings and rugs and things like that. He was a bit concerned while he was over there that some of this stuff would get damaged, because some of the trips he did were in really rough country and the transport you have to use is often quite primitive. He told me that once he had to do a 40-mile journey sitting on the roof of a bus. Anyway, he managed to get back to England with everything in one piece. He landed back at Heathrow airport at some really uncivilised hour and decided to get a taxi back home, rather than struggle with all this stuff on public transport. He had all his clothes in one case and all these beautiful things he'd bought in another. The taxi dropped him at his front door and he got out with his suitcases and put them down while he paid the taxi driver. The taxi then started off, but for some reason in reverse, ran over his suitcase and ruined everything he'd bought.

Exercise 7.3 The transcription below contains no examples of assimilation, but it could do. Change the transcription to include all possible examples of assimilation. Check your version with the one provided in the answers section.

| aɪ ˈflʌŋkt ˈaʊt ɪn maɪ ˈfɜːst ˈjɪə | aɪ ˈdəʊn nəʊ ˈwaɪ | aɪ ˈθɔːt aɪ wəz ˈduːɪŋ ɔːˈlraɪt |
bət wen ɪt ˈkeɪm tə ðɪ ˈend əv ˈjɪər ɪgˈzæmz | aɪ dʒəst ˈpænɪkt | ən ˈfeɪld ˈevrɪθɪŋ |
ˈeniweɪ ðeɪ ˈsed aɪ kəd ˈteɪk ə jɪər ˈaʊt | ən riːˈsɪt ˈevrɪθɪŋ ðə ˈneks ˈsʌmə | ən ɪf aɪ
ˈpɑːst | aɪ kʊd ˈðen gəʊ ɒn tə ðə ˈseknd ˈpɑːt əv ðə ˈkɔːs | maɪ ˈdæd wəz
ˈfjʊərɪəs | hi ˈiːvn̩ ˈθretn̩ tə ˈθrəʊ mi ˈaʊt əv ðə ˈhaʊs | ɪn ðɪ ˈend | ˈmʌm ən ˈaɪ
ˈmænɪdʒ tə ˈkɑːm ɪm ˈdaʊn | bət i ˈstɪl ɪnˈsɪstəd ðət aɪ ʃəd ˈgəʊ aʊt ən ˈfaɪnd
ə ˈdʒɒb ɪˈmiːdjətli | hi ˈgeɪv mi ˈtuː ˈwiːks | ɪt ˈwɒzn̩ ˈiːzi | ðɪ ˈəʊnli ˈdʒɒb aɪ kəd
ˈget | wəz ˈstækɪŋ ˈʃelvz ɪn ə ˈsuːpəmɑːkɪt | ɪf ˈeniwʌn səˈdʒests ðət ju ˈstæk
ˈʃelvz ɪn ə ˈsuːpəmɑːkɪt | ˈdʒʌs ˈdəʊnt | ðə ˈwɜːk ɪz ɪnˈkredəbli ˈdʌl | ən ðə ˈpeɪ
ɪz dʒəs ˈluːdɪkrəs | aɪ ˈθɪŋk aɪ gɒt peɪd ˈtuː paʊnz ˈfɪfti ən ˈɑə | ən ðə ˈpiːpl̩
ðeə wər ʌnbiˈliːvəbl̩ | ðə ˈmænɪdʒər ɪn pəˈtɪkjulə wəz ə ˈrɪəli ʌnˈplezənt ˈpɜːsn̩|
hi ˈθɔːt ˈhiː wəz ðɪ ˈəʊnli ˈwʌn ɪn ðə ˈhəʊl ˈpleɪs | hu hæd ˈmɔː ɒn ə ˈbaʊt ˈtuː ˈbreɪn
ˈselz | ən ðə ˈkʌstəməz wər ˈɔːfl̩ ˈtuː | aɪ ˈdaʊn nəʊ ˈwaɪ ˈpiːpl̩ hæv tə ˈtriːt jə laɪk
ˈdɜːt | ˈdʒʌst bɪkəz jɔː ˈduːɪŋ ə ˈstjuːpɪd ˈdʒɒb | ðə wər ə ˈnʌmbər əv ˈtaɪmz | wen
aɪ ˈnɪəli ˈlɒst maɪ ˈtempə | ən ˈtəʊl ˈsʌmwʌn wɒt aɪ ˈrɪəli ˈθɔːt əv ðəm | bət ˈðen aɪ
wʊd əv ˈgɒt ðə ˈsæk | ən maɪ ˈdæd wʊd əv ˈhɪt ðə ˈruːf | aɪ ˈdaʊn nəʊ ˈhaʊ aɪ
ˈstʊd ˈgəʊɪŋ tə ðə ˈpleɪs fər əz ˈlɒŋ əz aɪ ˈdɪd | aɪ kn̩ ˈtel ju ɪt ˈteɪks ə ˈlɒt tə
ˈget mi tə ˈgəʊ ɪntu ə ˈsuːpəmɑːkɪt ˈðiːz ˈdeɪz | aɪ fiːl ˈkwaɪt ˈsɪk dʒəs ˈθɪŋkɪŋ
əˈbaʊt ɪt |

Exercise 7.4 Here is a passage for you to transcribe. Include as many assimilations as you can plus all the other processes we have seen so far. Make sure you understand the transcription we provide for these passages in the answers section and all their comments before you move on to the next lesson.

The first time Joan saw the house she knew it was where she had been born. It wasn't as though Joan could remember anybody describing it. Her parents had passed away when she was only three years old, so she retained no clear memory of them. Her grandparents had been forbidden to set foot on the property, both before the tragedy and after. It wasn't because the name of the house – Fourways – (which was her uncle's favourite jazz song) stirred her memory, even though her uncle played it constantly. For some reason she'd always hated it with a rare violence not at all in character with her otherwise mild personality. It might be the trellis with the poison ivy twined round it. Then again that could be her aunt's influence. No. In her heart she knew as surely as she could see the blacked out panes in the conservatory windows that this was the house in which she had been born. The asking price was more than she had planned to spend. In fact if she spent this much, there would be no money left for furniture or anything which needed doing. She'd gone in with the agent and within seconds her mind was made up. She must have it. 'And after all,' said the agent, 'everything is in pretty good condition – at least the important things. And it is fully furnished. Should you take it, all you'd have to spend is time giving it a thorough cleaning. And the owner will let you keep all the contents.' And he was right. In fact, once the linen covers were taken off, it could look as if it was still lived in: rugs and cushions, ornaments on the mantlepiece and on side-tables. The kitchen was equipped to the last saucepan and plate. As she stopped at the doorway an image took over her mind completely. A young woman was standing with her back to the door, bending over the stove and getting something out of the oven. Joan felt dizzy. She leaned against the door frame for stability. As soon as it had come, the vision was just gone. The kitchen was uninhabited once more. It must have been a mixture of lack of food and overactive imagination. She went out to the hallway. The agent was nowhere in sight. Cautiously Joan proceeded with her inspection. She went towards the back of the house and into a large room overlooking the garden. For some reason she knew it had been called the sunroom. There were several wicker armchairs with flowery cotton covers, two glass-topped coffee tables and potted plants everywhere. There was an atmosphere of comfortable lived-in tidiness. At the right end by the french windows stood a grand piano with several frames on top of it. Joan went in to have a closer look – black and white photographs in all of them. The same people appeared in different scenarios and postures – the woman she'd imagined in the kitchen, a man in his late thirties and a little blonde girl. The room reeled around Joan and she got the same nauseous feeling again. When she was able to open her eyes she saw it all in a flash. The man was at the piano with the little girl sitting by him, her fingers small and chubby beside his on the keys. It was her and the man was her father. The melody was being poorly played because of her contribution, but still recognisable. It was 'Fourways'. While she was staring at them, some instinct told her to look out of the window. The woman, Joan's mother, had come out into the garden. She was just about to pick some herbs when suddenly she stood up and looked around, obviously alerted by some sound. From the bottom of the garden a man came, walking with fast long strides. He carried a huge shotgun. Joan tried to scream, but couldn't make a sound. Her head started spinning and she fainted.

Exercise 7.5 Here is a passage for you to transcribe. Include as many assimilations as you can plus all the other processes we have seen so far.

- What did you do with the newspaper? You haven't thrown it away, have you?

- Newspaper? What newspaper?

- The newspaper I was reading. Which one do you think?

- Oh, it's on the table in the kitchen, isn't it?

- That's yesterday's newspaper. I don't want to read that, do I?

- Oh, dear. I've just used a newspaper to wrap up the ashes from the fire.

- Have you thrown my newspaper away again? You're always doing that.

- Look. I'm not always doing it. I've done it once or twice. That's all.

- Once or twice? You did it on Sunday, didn't you? And one day last week.

- Did I? Well, that's only twice.

- Yes, but today makes it three times, doesn't it?

- Yes. I suppose it does. Sorry. But you still can't claim that I'm always doing it, can you?

- Oh, all right. You always have to be right, don't you? I mean. You throw out my newspaper yet again and you still have to have the last word. It's really annoying.

- Come on! I did say I was sorry. What else do you want me to do? I'll go out and get you another one, shall I?

- No. Don't bother. I'll go myself. I was actually thinking about going for a walk anyway.

- Well, there you are then. You could get some bread and milk too.

- Now I didn't say I was planning to do the weekly shopping, did I?

- For goodness' sake! You're in a foul mood. What's the matter with you? Have you got toothache or something. Maybe rabies?

- Very funny. Just because I dislike having my plans for spending a quiet Sunday afternoon disturbed, it turns out I'm bad-tempered.

- Oh, I beg your pardon for interrupting your rest. I wouldn't mind having some time to relax too, but it so happens I've been doing things all the time, like cleaning the fireplace – my favourite pastime for a weekend. It beats doing the bathrooms anyway, which is what I did before lunch.

- You're not going to start on that again. I've heard it several thousand times before.

- You have? Well, maybe I should start putting it in writing then. Slip it inside your precious paper. That would make you notice it. And by the way, next time you can sweep the fireplace yourself. That will surely stop me from throwing your newspaper out again.

- Oh, lord! Why did I ever mention it?

Exercise 7.6 Here is another passage for you to transcribe. Include as many assimilations as you can plus all the other processes we have seen so far.

There was once a spider called Kell who lived by a river in the woods. He had built quite a cosy little nest at the top of a tree. The spider was well known for his extraordinary weaving. There was just nobody who could make better or stronger webs in the whole forest. Kell felt proud of his craft and devoted most of his time to it. All day long he worked, weaving and weaving, hardly stopping to eat or drink. At night he dreamt of all the new designs he would create, of how to make them hold and shine wonderfully. One day his friend the robin came around to visit, but Kell was struggling with a specially difficult knot. 'Sorry, Robin. I'm very busy,' said Kell. 'Oh! you can surely take a break and talk to me for a while,' replied the robin. 'Well, not now. Spider webs are more difficult than most people think. They should be strong as well as light and that means a lot of serious thinking and hard work. Right now I'm trying to work out this knot, so I can't stop to chat every time somebody turns up.' The robin went away feeling very upset, because she had particularly wanted to spend some time with her friend. Next morning the spider woke up feeling restless. It was a sunny spring day and he didn't care to do any work. He would go to see one of his friends. Then he remembered his words to the robin and realised how unfair he had been. Now that he thought about it, he had done the same to several of his friends. No wonder that most of them had given him up. Well, something had to be done and he had an idea. He would give a party. The spider started working on it straight away. He chose a clearing in the forest, surrounded by tall ash trees and started weaving from one to the other and across them. He wove and wove non-stop, day and night pushing all his skills to the limit. After seven days the canopy was finished. It covered the whole clearing like a dome and glowed in the sun with millions of dew drops that Kell had captured in his knots. Underneath the awning he had made curtains of webs hanging all around. There were also web streamers and at least a hundred balloons in colours taken from the rainbow. When Kell felt satisfied with the result, he went to the forest orchards and gathered masses of fruits and seeds which he then carried to the tent and placed carefully on many little leaves for everybody to eat. After finishing these arrangements, he went to find the robin. Luckily she was at home and Kell, after apologising for his behaviour, asked her to fly at all speed and call all their friends. The robin was delighted to see the spider was feeling more sociable and rushed to do as she was requested. Within a short time everybody had gathered around robin's house. Then the spider said, 'I'm very sorry to have ignored you all for so long. I sometimes worry too much about my weaving and get carried away with it, but it doesn't mean I forget my friends. So I have done something special for you. Follow me and I'll show you.' When the animals arrived at the clearing, they were all so amazed by the dazzling sight before their eyes that they couldn't move or speak. After a while some of them started gasping, sighing and cheering at the spider's work of art. Then everyone went inside the wonderful tent and celebrated Kell's return to his friends. However, it was the spider himself who was happiest, because his efforts had for once given pleasure to others and made them forgive him for his lack of consideration for them.

Lesson 8

Glottaling

In Lesson 7 we saw that alveolar sounds, especially /t d n/, are very unstable in English and may change their place of articulation to agree with sounds in their environment. One of these sounds, namely /t/, is alternatively affected by a process known as **glottaling** (some textbooks call it *glottal replacement*). Glottaling involves the replacement of a sound by a **glottal stop**, which is symbolised /ʔ/. A glottal stop is formed by a brief closure of the vocal folds which blocks the air coming up from the lungs. Its chief auditory characteristic is a brief period of silence. Glottal stops are common in many languages in emphatic speech. If one were to shout the word *Out!* loudly and angrily, it is extremely likely that there would be an initial glottal stop in this utterance – /ʔaʊt/.

There are various uses for a glottal stop in English: it may reinforce the articulation of a vowel as we saw in the above example; a glottal stop may also be introduced before a voiceless plosive to reinforce its articulation as in *right* /raɪʔt/; voiceless plosives may also be replaced by a glottal stop under certain circumstances as we shall see below.

Among all the possible uses of /ʔ/, we shall deal in this lesson with the one in which it replaces a voiceless alveolar plosive. The reasons for limiting the discussion to this instance are that the use of glottal stop as a reinforcement of articulation is more clearly allophonic and therefore belongs to narrow transcriptions. Amongst the cases where /ʔ/ may replace a sound, we shall not go into the replacement of the voiceless stops /p/ and /k/, since this is not usual in RP. On the other hand, the replacement of /t/ with /ʔ/ is very frequent. In this book to keep the typography as simple as possible, the glottal stop is written between slanted bars as with any phoneme. However, this does not mean that we are considering it a phoneme.

Many accents of English frequently replace /t/ with /ʔ/. It is common in London speech and in New York speech, for instance. In RP it is becoming increasingly common to glottal /t/, but only in specific environments. In London speech, for instance, one may hear glottal stop in the middle of words such as *water, butter, city*. Glottaling of /t/ is not possible in RP in these circumstances. Before /t/ can be glottaled in RP, a number of conditions must be satisfied. These are:

- /t/ must be followed by a consonant other than /h/;
- /t/ must be preceded by a sonorant sound;
- /t/ must be in the coda of the syllable, not in the onset.

In the following examples, all the conditions are met, so /t/ can be glottaled:

not now	ˈnɒʔ ˈnaʊ
at last	əʔ ˈlɑːst
eight books	ˈeɪʔ ˈbʊks
tent pole	ˈtenʔ ˈpəʊl
atlas	ˈæʔləs
don't delay	ˈdəʊnʔ diˈleɪ
what reason	ˈwɒʔ ˈriːzən
button	ˈbʌʔn̩

The last of the above examples shows that glottaling often interacts with syllabic consonant formation. If the final consonant of *button* is syllabic then glottaling can take place. If the sequence /ən/ is not merged into a syllabic consonant then glottaling is impossible, because the /t/ is followed by a vowel. Nevertheless, glottaling is not usual in RP before a syllabic /l/, so we shall not glottal /t/ in words such as *bottle* /bɒtl̩/ or *settle* /setl̩/.

For many RP speakers, there are further restrictions on glottaling. These usually involve word-internal /t/. A good example is the word *mattress*. Many speakers would not glottal the /t/ here, because it is followed by /r/. Our advice is to avoid /t/ glottaling in the middle of a word when the next consonant is /r/. Glottaling is all right across a word boundary before /r/, however. In non-RP accents, such as London, glottaling is common in such words.

Notice that when /t/ is followed by a bilabial or velar consonant, there is a choice of pronunciation. One may perform an assimilation and change the /t/ into a /p/ or a /k/, or one may glottal the /t/. Examples:

hot potato	ˈhɒp pəˈteɪtəʊ	or	ˈhɒʔ pəˈteɪtəʊ
right kind	ˈraɪk ˈkaɪnd	or	ˈraɪʔ ˈkaɪnd

Notice also that in negative contractions the speaker may choose to glottal the /t/ of the *n't* ending or to elide it. However, elsewhere the conditions for glottaling and those for alveolar plosive elision are mutually exclusive – where one can do glottaling, elision is impossible and vice versa.

Glottaling is becoming more common in modern RP English. However, like assimilation and other connected speech processes, glottaling is not obligatory and one can never guarantee that a particular speaker will glottal /t/ on a given occasion, even though all the conditions for glottaling are met. RP speech with no glottaling at all would sound very formal and over-careful. If you are a non-native speaker of English, it is up to you to what extent you adopt /t/ glottaling as part of your speech patterns. However, it is important to get it right and not to glottal /t/ where native speakers would not. Another warning: /d/ is *never* glottaled in RP English.

If you look at the following passage you will find many examples of glottaling. There is an orthographic version for it in the answers section. Remember, the comments will not refer to processes dealt with in previous lessons.

Sample transcription

| fə ˈsevrəl ˈjɪəz naʊ | aɪ əv ˈdrɪvn̩ tə ðə ˈsteɪʃn̩ məʊs[1-2] ˈmɔːnɪŋz əv ðə ˈwiːk | əm ˈpɑːk[1-2] maɪ ˈkɑːr ɪm ˈmɔːr ɔː ˈles ðə seɪm ˈpleɪs ɪn ðə ˈkɑː pɑːk | aɪ əv ˈðeŋ kɔːʔ ðə ˈtreɪn tə *ˈlʌndən | ən ˈdʌm maɪ ˈdeɪz ˈwɜːk | ɪn ði ˈiːvnɪŋ aɪ əv riˈtɜːnd | ˈfaʊm maɪ ˈkɑːr ən ˈdrɪvn̩ ˈhəʊm | ɪʔ[2] ˈprɒbbli[3] dʌznʔ[4] ˈsaʊn laɪk ə veri ˈɪntrəstɪŋ ruːˈtiːn | aɪ əbˈmɪʔ ðæt[5-6] | bəʔ wʌŋ ˈkɑːn[4-7] hæv[8] ɪkˈsaɪʔ[2]mənt[9] evri ˈdeɪ | ˈwʌn iːvnɪŋ lɑːs[1] ˈwiːk | aɪ gɒʔ[2] ˈbæk tə ðə ˈsteɪʃn ət[7] ˈhɑːf pɑːst[9-10] ˈeɪt[6] | ɪʔ wəz ə ˈmʌndeɪ ˈiːvnɪŋ | ənd aɪ əd hæg[8] ˈkwaɪt[9] ə ˈhɑːd ˈdeɪ | aɪ wɔːk[1] ˈwɪərəli tə ðə ˈkɑː pɑːk | lʊkɪŋ ˈfɔːwəd tə maɪ ˈiːvnɪŋ ət[7] ˈhəʊm | aɪd geʔ ˈsʌmθɪŋ tə ˈdrɪŋk | ˈiːʔ ˈdɪnə | əm ˈmeɪbi duː[8] səm ˈwɜːk ɒn ə ˈbʊkeɪs aɪ əb ˈbɔːʔ sekn̩ˈhænd[5] | bəʔ tə maɪ ˈʌtər[9] əˈmeɪzmənt[6] | ˈðeə | weə ˈmaɪ kɑː ʃʊd[11] əv ˈbiːn | wəz ə ˈstreɪndʒ ˈkɑː | aɪ ˈkʊbm̩[4-2-12] biˈliːv maɪ ˈaɪz | aɪ ˈlʊkt[9-10] ʌp ən ˈdaʊn ði ɪnˈtaə ˈrəʊ əv ˈkɑːz | bəʔ[2] ˈmaɪn wəz ˈnɒʔ tə bi ˈsiːn ˈeniweə | ɪʔ wəz ˈsevrəl ˈmɪnɪʔs biˈfɔːr aɪ kəg[11] kənˈsɪdə ðə pɒsəˈbɪləti[9] | ðəʔ ðə ˈkɑːr əb biːn ˈstəʊlən | fər ə ˈwaɪl | aɪ ˈθɔːʔ ðəʔ[2] maɪ ˈmaɪn wəz ˈgəʊɪŋ | həd aɪ ˈpɑːkt[9-10] ɪn ə ˈdɪfrəmʔ[13-2] ˈpleɪs ðəʔ[2] ˈmɔːnɪŋ | aɪ ˈsɪmpli ˈkʊdn̩[4-9] əkˈsep ðə ˈfæk[1] ðət[9] ɪʔ wəz ˈgɒn | ˈnaʊ ɪʔs ˈklɪər aɪl ˈnevə geʔ[2] maɪ ˈkɑː ˈbæk | maɪ ˈfiːlɪŋz əv ˈpʌzl̩mənt[9] ən kənˈfjuːʒn̩ | həv ˈtɜːnd ɪntuː[9] ˈæŋgə | ði ɪnˈʃɔːrəns ˈkʌmpni tʊk ˈkeər əv ˈevriθɪŋ | aɪ dʒəst[1-7] ˈhəʊp ðəʔ ðeɪ ˈleʔ[2] mi hæv[8] ə ˈnjuː kɑː ˈsuːn | ən ðəʔ[2] maɪ ˈəʊl wʌm breɪks ˈdaʊn ɒn huˈevər əz gɒʔ ðə ˈjuːs əv ɪʔ ˈnaʊ | ˈkɔːl ɪʔ ˈsɪli | bət[9] aɪ hæv[8] ə ˈraɪʔ tu ə ˈlɪtl̩[14] ˈhɑːmləs riˈvendʒ aɪ ˈθɪŋk | ˈðæʔ wəz nɒʔ ði ˈəʊnli mɪsˈfɔːtʃn̩ aɪ əv ˈriːsn̩ʔli ɪkˈspɪərɪəns[1] wɪð ˈkɑːz | maɪ ˈwaɪfs wəz brəʊkn̩ ˈɪntuː ə ˈfjuː mʌnθs əˈgəʊ | ðeɪ ˈsmæʃt[9-10] ə ˈwɪndəʊ | ən ˈtraɪd tə geʔ ðə ˈsteriəʊ | bəʔ wɪð ˈnəʊ ˈlʌk | ˈɔːl əv ˈðɪs went[9] ˈɒn | waɪl wi ˈsæt[7] hævɪŋ ˈdɪnər ɪn ðə ˈhaʊs | nɒt[9] ˈeɪʔ[15] ˈjɑːdz əˈweɪ frəm ðə ˈbæk ˈgɑːdn̩ | weə maɪ ˈwaɪf əb ˈpɑːkt[6-10] | ɑːftər ˈɔːl ˈðɪs[5] | ju kn̩ ɪˈmædʒɪn wɒʔ[2] maɪ ˈætɪtjuːd[9] tə ˈkɑː kraɪm ɪz | ˈwʌns aɪv ˈbɔːʔ[2] maɪ ˈnjuː wʌn | aɪm ˈgəʊɪŋ tə pʊʔ ˈsəʊ meni ˈlɒks | əˈlɑːm ˈsɪstəmz[9-10] | ənd sɪˈkjɔːrəti[9] diˈvaɪsɪz ɒn ɪt[6] | ðəʔ ðə məʊs[1] diˈtɜːmɪnd ən diˈvəʊtɪd[9] əv ˈθiːvz | wɪl ˈnɒʔ səˈksiːd ɪn ˈteɪkɪŋ ɪʔ frɒm[16] mi |

Comments on sample transcription

1. /t/ has been elided and not glottaled because glottaling is not possible since /t/ is not preceded by a sonorant.
2. Alternatively, /t/ could have been assimilated.
3. This is a special case of /ə/ elision since it is not followed by a liquid or /n/. An alternative, quite rapid, pronunciation to the one shown in the exercise would be /prɒbli/ in which one of the /b/ sounds is elided as well.
4. In negative contractions /t/ may be elided or, if followed by a consonant other than /h/, it may be glottaled instead.
5. Remember that assimilation may be inhibited by a potential pause (see Lesson 7).
6. Glottaling is not possible because /t/ is followed by a potential pause.
7. /t/ cannot be glottaled because it is followed by /h/.
8. Strong form because the verb is not used as an auxiliary here.
9. Glottaling is not possible because /t/ is followed by a vowel.

10. Glottaling is not possible because /t/ is not preceded by a sonorant.
11. Remember that grammatical words which have the vowel /ʊ/ in their citation form, such as *would*, *should* and *could*, may remain unchanged even if they are unstressed but they may be further weakened to /ə/ in a quicker pronunciation.
12. If glottaling had been applied in place of deletion, assimilation would still have been possible since glottal stop does not prevent assimilation.
13. Assimilation is possible despite the intervening glottal stop because glottaling does not prevent assimilation.
14. Glottaling is not usual in RP before a syllabic /l/.
15. /t/ could not have coalesced with the following /j/ because the palatal is in a lexical word (see Lesson 7).
16. A preposition preceding an unstressed pronoun may be used in strong form (see Lesson 3).

Exercise 8.1 Each of the following phrases contains a /t/. Say whether the /t/ can be affected by (a) assimilation, (b) elision, (c) glottaling, (d) none of these.

(1) first class (2) salt solution (3) hit parade (4) white shoes (5) most important

Exercise 8.2 Look at the following passage which is given in orthography. Try to identify all the possible instances of glottaling in it. Check your version with that at the end of the book, where you can also find this text transcribed and commented.

I've had some terrible car journeys in my time, but I think the very worst one was in Athens. We'd booked a holiday on a small island not far away from Athens and had to catch a ferry to get there. Well, of course the plane was late and we landed at the airport about three-quarters of an hour before the ferry was due to leave. Fortunately we found a taxi driver who spoke a bit of English and managed to make him understand what our problem was. It was the middle of the day and all the roads in the city were jammed solid. The driver didn't let this put him off. He drove most of the way to the port on the pavement. My wife and I sat in the back with our hands over our eyes, while he narrowly missed trees and pedestrians. Every time he came to a traffic light he simply drove onto the pavement and shot forward until he was level with the front of the queue. When the light changed to green, he cut in front of the first vehicle and drove on. We got to the ferry with about five minutes to spare and sat there shaking. Finally, the ship's hooter sounded to signal that we were about to sail. All the Greek passengers around us crossed themselves and muttered a prayer for a safe journey. I strongly advise you to do the same if ever you take a taxi from Athens airport.

Exercise 8.3 Now we ask you to look at the following transcription and insert all the possible instances of glottaling that you can find. You will find an edited version with explanations and comments as well as the orthographic version at the end of the book.

| fər əz ˈlɒŋ əʒ ʃi kʊd riˈmembə | ˈðɪs əd ˈɔːlweɪz biːn ˈwʌn əv hə ˈfeɪvrɪt ˈpleɪsɪz |
ʃi ˈsɔː *ˈdeɪzi kwaɪt ˈklɪəli ˈkʌmɪŋ təˈwɔːdz ðə ˈfænlaɪt wɪð ə ˈlʊk əv ˈpɜːpəs |
ˈmædəm sez ˈmɪʃ ʃʊg get ˈbæk tə hə ˈniːdl̩ wɜːk | ən ˈstɒp ˈweɪstɪŋ hə ˈtaɪm |
ɪt wəz nəʊ ˈwʌndə ðət hə ˈmʌðə ˈnjuː wɒt *ˈhærɪət wəz ˈæktʃuəli ˈduːɪŋ |
ˈwɒt wʊd əv biːn səˈpraɪzɪŋ | wəz ˈfaɪndɪŋ ðət ʃi wəz ˈduːɪŋ sʌmθɪŋ ˈʌðə ðn̩

ˈsteərɪŋ ət ðə ˈwɜːld bijɒn ðəuz ˈwɪndəuz | ˈevribɒdi ˈθɔːt ʃi wəz ən ʌnˈɪntrəstɪŋ
ən ˈkwaət ˈtʃaɪld | ə ˈlɪtl̩ ˈleɪzi ˈiːvn̩ | sɪns ɪt ˈtuk ə ˈlɒt tə ˈmeɪk ə ˈliːv ðə ˈwɪndəu
ˈsiːt | weə ʃi ˈsiːm tə ˈspen səu mʌtʃ ˈtaɪm ɪn ði ˈiːvnɪŋz | ˈlukɪŋ ˈaut θruː ðə
ˈwɪndəu peɪnz ət ðə ˈɡɑːdn̩ | *ˈhærɪət ˈnjuː wɒt ðeɪ ˈθɔːt | bət ʃi ˈdɪdnt let
ðəm ˈbɒðər ə | ðeɪ ˈrɪəli ʃud ˈnɒt bi ˈbleɪmd | bikɒz ðeɪ ˈkudnt ˈiːvn̩ ˈɡes |
dʒəst ə ˈʃɔːt luk ɪntə hə ˈwɜːl wud əv ˈʃəun ðəm | hau ˈrestləs ən ˈlaɪvli hə
ˈmaɪn wɒz | bət ðeɪ wud ˈnevə ˈtraɪ tə ˈsiː | ˈeniθɪŋ ðət ˈkudnt bi ˈtʌtʃt ɔːr ɪkˈspleɪn
saənˈtɪfɪkli | ˈdɪdn̩t ɪɡˈzɪst fə ðəm | ən ðəu ðeɪ ˈlukt θruː ðə ˈseɪm ˈwɪndəu | ən
ˈθɔːt ðeɪ ˈsɔː ðə ˈseɪm ˈθɪŋz | ˈnəubɒdi ɪn hə ˈfæmli əd ˈevə kɔːt ðə ˈslaɪtɪst
ˈɡlɪmps | ən ðeɪ wud ˈnevər əv ˈɡest wɒt wəz ˈhæpnɪŋ evri ˈnaɪt bihaɪn ðəuz
ˈbuʃɪz | ʃi ˈhɜːd ðə ˈmeɪɡ kləuz ðə ˈɡeɪt biˈhaɪnd ər əʒ ʃi ˈwent əˈweɪ | ɪt wəz
ˈkwaɪt ˈseɪf ˈnau | ðeɪ kud ˈstɑːt ˈkʌmɪŋ | ʃi sæt ˈstɪl ən ˈredi tə ˈweɪt fə ðə
ˈmɪrəkl̩ | hau ˈkud ʃi let hə ˈfæmli ˈnəu əbaut ðə ˈɡrɑːs ˈkɪŋdəm | ən ðə ˈkɔːt
hu ˈmet daun ət ði ˈəuk ˈkɑːsl̩ | ɔːr əbaut ðə ˈtreʒə ˈhɪdn̩ ʌndə ðə ˈθɜːd ˈstəun
| ɪt wəz ˈprɒbli ˈbetə ðət ðeɪ ˈdɪdn̩t ˈnəu | *ˈhærɪət ˈkudn̩t fəˈɡet ðə ˈsiːɡʌl
ˈprɪns ənd ɪz ˈprɒmɪs | ðət ˈwʌn naɪt wud ˈkʌm wen i wud ˈteɪk ə tu ɪz
ˈkɪŋdəm | ˈfɑːr əˈweɪ | biˈhaɪnd ðəuz ˈbuʃɪz |

Here there are three passages for you to transcribe, including glottaling whenever
you can, as well as all the processes covered in the previous lessons. After completing
each one, compare it to the version at the end of the book and study the comments carefully. We suggest you do not start a new transcription until you have fully understood
the last one you have done. It may be a good idea to revise the explanations given in this
lesson and previous ones if you find you don't understand the transcription comments
or that you are making many mistakes.

Exercise 8.4 Transcribe the following passage, including all we have seen so far, with
special attention to glottaling.

It was Saturday morning when I woke up to the sound of the alarm ringing in my
ears. I quickly jumped out of bed, remembering that we were going off to Wales
in less than an hour's time. I ran upstairs to the spare bedroom to wake my sister
up. I shook her vigorously and shouted, 'Come on, Madeleine! Get up or we'll
miss the train.' As I rushed into the bathroom, I heard her mumbling, 'What
train?' She had obviously forgotten what we had planned the night before. I shouted
at the top of my voice, 'The train to Wales! We are supposed to be catching a train at
eight thirty to go home to see Mum. Remember?' It all went quiet for a while, until
she realized she wasn't dreaming. She almost flew out of the bedroom and started to
panic as usual. 'What time is it now? Why didn't you wake me earlier? I must have a
cup of coffee first, otherwise I'll never make it through the day,' she said desperately.
This was a typical reaction from my sister, who doesn't have a care in the world.
'Never mind the coffee,' I screamed. 'Phone for a taxi.' I left her to it and went downstairs to put the kettle on. By this time I was also feeling anxious and wished we
hadn't decided to go on this trip at all. 'The taxi will be here in five minutes.
Forget about the coffee. Where's my handbag?' she yelled. The doorbell rang. 'Oh
no. It must be the taxi driver.' Even I wasn't ready just yet. I rushed to answer
the door to discover it was the postman asking me to accept a delivery on behalf
of my neighbour as she wasn't in. I took the parcel and signed for it. The doorbell

rang again. This time it was the taxi driver. 'Are you ready?' I asked my sister. 'The taxi is here.' She was running around like a headless chicken, but she grabbed her coat as I clutched my handbag and we both hurried out to the car. At last we were on our way, or so I thought then. We had only got to the bottom of the street when I had a sinking feeling. 'Turn back. I haven't locked the door.' The driver quickly made a diversion and headed back to our house. Time was ticking away and we were both wondering if it was a sensible idea to continue with our plan or not. However, I held the keys in my hand as we approached the house. I was out of the car even before it came to a total stop. Within seconds we were back on our journey to the station, but this time the taxi driver picked up his speed. There were only a few minutes left before the train was due to leave the platform. I realized we must be getting very near the station, as I could hear the station master mumbling something over the tannoy system. We finally arrived, paid the driver, collected the tickets from the office and dashed to the platform to find that there wasn't a train there. We had missed it despite doing what felt like a marathon. Suddenly a voice repeated the earlier message. 'The eight thirty Swansea train departing from platform two has been delayed until eight fifty seven. We apologise for the inconvenience.' 'What a relief!' we both sighed. We could now enjoy some coffee at last and something more substantial too after all the energy we had spent to get there.

Exercise 8.5 Transcribe the following passage, including all we have seen so far, with special attention to glottaling.

I really hate flying. It's not that I'm afraid or anything, though I do get a bit nervous if the flight's bumpy. The thing I really object to is that flying is so boring and so uncomfortable. The last long flight that we did was from Los Angeles to New Zealand. It took about twelve and a half hours overnight. Of course I was seated next to someone who dropped off to sleep immediately after we had taken off and spent most of the night snoring. I find it really difficult to sleep on planes. It's just totally impossible to get comfortable enough. When I did manage to get to sleep, the person sitting next to me woke up and wanted to get out to go to the toilet. Then the stewards kept coming round every half hour and offering us tea or water or orange juice. They were making sure nobody arrived dehydrated, but they also prevented me from getting any rest. On another occasion, I was on an eight-hour flight to North America. This was before I had given up smoking. As luck would have it, my travel agent booked me with one of the few companies who had a non-smoking policy on all their flights. I didn't find out about this until I checked in. Therefore I was completely unprepared for the experience. The first few hours were not too bad. I ate and drank everything I was offered, even though I wasn't hungry in the slightest. After the second main meal and coffee I started feeling edgy, so I went for the sweets. I ate so many that it's a wonder my teeth didn't fall out there and then. With only one hour to go according to schedule we were informed by the pilot that we'd be running about an hour late. That did it for me. I got really angry and was seriously tempted to hide somewhere and light up a cigarette. A stewardess, noticing my agitation, offered me some nicotine chewing gum. She was a smoker herself and always had a terrible time when she was working on one of the transatlantic flights. We finally landed and I rushed to the airport's smoking area. For my return journey I made sure I was very very tired, so that I spent most of the time asleep.

Exercise 8.6 Transcribe the following passage, including all we have seen so far, with special attention to glottaling.

When I woke up, I knew that day would be one of the most important days in my life. And it was, but for very different reasons to what was planned. It seemed like I had made it at last. I had been offered a part in a film. That night the producers, director and I were to meet to sign the contract. Even the weather was on my side. It started as a great day, much better than one would expect at that time of the year, but towards evening the atmosphere began showing signs of change. It became heavy and electric. I didn't have any premonition as such, but I do remember a kind of tickling on my skin, a feeling that put me on edge, as if my body was trying to warn me. I started getting ready very early. I wanted to be on time and I wasn't the most confident of drivers at night. At a quarter to seven I was already on the road. The restaurant wasn't all that far from my house, but the road I had to take was only a country lane and it would take me at least half an hour to get there. Night fell and I turned on the headlights. Suddenly the car stopped. I got out to see what was wrong with it, cursing it mildly under my breath. I would hate to be late for this appointment. 'You can break down any other time, but not today, please,' I pleaded. Then I found I was unable to walk, that my legs wouldn't move. A terrible light blinded me for a few seconds. Then it lessened and huge metal globe appeared in front of me. It was coming down and, as it did so, a big cloud of dust and steam rose off the ground. I heard some whistling kind of sound. It was beautiful and it made me start walking towards the globe. Perhaps I got close, maybe even went inside, but nothing else was registered in my mind. After what seemed seconds I was back in the car. The light globe had disappeared. I sat there while a dreamlike feeling overwhelmed me. It wouldn't let me think. At last I made my body start the car. My watch wasn't working, so I had no way of telling what the time was. When I got to the restaurant, it was empty. I thought it must be quite late for them to be closing. I asked the man who was putting out the bins. 'It's past midnight, madam,' he said. Really late then. There was no point hanging around, so I went back home. When I walked in I realised there was dust everywhere, as if the place hadn't been cleaned for ages. That was not possible. I had given the house a thorough cleaning the day before. I went to my answering machine. Maybe they had tried to let me know where they would be. The computerlike voice said, 'Wednesday September the eighth. You have twenty messages.' No, that could not be right, surely. It was March. I turned on the television to check the Ceefax pages. The same date came up on the screen. I had been away for six months. I felt very dizzy, so I sat down and put my head in my hands. What was I going to do? Where had I been?

Lesson 9

Further practice

This last lesson does not introduce new phonological processes because its aim is to provide you with further practice on the features we have covered in the rest of the book. It is therefore very important that these transcriptions should not be attempted before you are satisfied that you have mastered the points in lessons 1–8. We will refer to a couple of additional features of connected speech which we have mentioned before without discussing them, but they should be easily understood with the explanations given in the annotations to the transcribed passages.

Lesson 9 consists of six transcription exercises, for which you can find the answers at the end of the book. Your transcriptions of the passages should include all the processes that have been explained during the course. The answers will not include explanations on particular processes, since they have all been dealt with in their corresponding lessons. Nevertheless, a few reminder comments are occasionally made on some of the features which have already been discussed in previous lessons. You will also find three other types of comments. There will be annotations wherever different processes could have been applied so that you can check whether your version is a possible one. There will also be some explanations on a couple of features which were only mentioned in passing in previous lessons. Additionally, we will take the opportunity in this last lesson to introduce alternative pronunciations for some more words.

Remember that all the processes are optional, so the fact that you do not use them does not imply that the transcription is wrong. However, in a course such as this it is a good idea to take every opportunity to include the processes so that you get plenty of practice at using them. You should also bear in mind that it is unlikely that you will hear somebody speak making as constant and extensive a use of connected speech processes as we do in the transcriptions. This is true for any of the lessons in this book: whichever process we can think of, a speaker is not likely to apply consistently wherever it is possible to do so. But we try to include them all consistently in our versions so that you know where they can be used, should you choose to do so.

By this stage, you should be fairly confident about transcribing English. If you feel that you need even more practice, there are a number of ways of going about this. If you have a friend or colleague who is also learning to transcribe, you could swap short transcriptions and comment on each other's work. Almost any passage of modern English prose could serve as an exercise: a piece from a modern novel, a passage from a newspaper or magazine, even this paragraph. We would advise you not to attempt to transcribe prose written centuries ago and also to avoid poetry. Both of these might present special problems which have not been covered in this course.

Another way of providing yourself with further practice is to find passages which have already been transcribed. A number of textbooks on the phonetics of English and phonetic readers are available. Make sure you use fairly up-to-date ones. You can then turn the phonetic transcriptions into orthographic versions. This is good practice in itself. Then put away the work for a couple of days. Next, without looking again at the phonetic transcription, make your own transcription. Finally, compare your version with the original.

Phonetic transcription is a skill which needs practice. If you do not do any for a while, it is easy to become rusty. So if it is important for you to be proficient, keep transcribing. A short passage of, say, 100 words per week should be enough to keep you efficient.

We hope you have enjoyed this course and feel that your ability to transcribe has improved. It is not easy to produce perfect transcriptions. Indeed, the very concept of a perfect transcription is rather doubtful. If sometimes you have despaired, don't worry. That is perfectly normal. You are up against a formidable opponent called the English spelling system.

As a final demonstration of this, if any more demonstration is needed, here is an extract of a poem (by G. N. Trenite 1870–1946), which is full of words whose spelling defies logic. If you have the odd day to spare, you might try looking up the pronunciation of all these.

English is Tough Stuff

Dearest creature in creation,
Study English pronunciation.
I will teach you in my verse
Sounds like corpse, corps, horse, and worse.
I will keep you, Suzy, busy,
Make your head with heat grow dizzy.
Now I surely will not plague you
With such words as plaque and ague.
But be careful how you speak:
Say break and steak, but bleak and streak;
Cloven, oven, how and low,
Script, receipt, show, poem, and toe.
Hear me say, devoid of trickery,
Daughter, laughter, and Terpsichore,
Typhoid, measles, topsails, aisles,
Exiles, similes, and reviles,
Scholar, vicar, and cigar,
Solar, mica, war and far;

Tear in eye, your dress will tear.
So shall I! Oh hear my prayer.
Just compare heart, beard, and heard,
Dies and diet, lord and word,
Sword and sward, retain and Britain.
(Mind the latter, how it's written.)
One, anemone, Balmoral,
Kitchen, lichen, laundry, laurel;
Gertrude, German, wind and mind,
Scene, Melpomene, mankind.
Billet does not rhyme with ballet,
Bouquet, wallet, mallet, chalet.
Blood and flood are not like food,
Nor is mould like should and would.
Viscous, viscount, load and broad,
Toward, to forward, to reward.

Exercise 9.1 Transcribe the following passage, including all we have seen in previous lessons (weak forms, sandhi r, syllabicity, elision, assimilation, glottaling).

I used to visit this elderly neighbour of mine to wash and set her hair. One particular evening, I was there when her daughter Anita arrived. She'd just returned from the town's top-class hairdresser and she approached me with what I thought was an incredible opportunity. She asked me if I would consider being one of her hair-dresser's apprentices. He had been complaining about how short-staffed he was since two of his assistants had left. Anita had remembered me and thought that I might be interested, so she mentioned my name to him. Naturally I was delighted with this idea, so she called him at the salon and within fifteen minutes they had arranged for me to start work the following weekend. I was only fourteen at the time and being offered a Saturday job in one of the top establishments in town seemed liked the chance of a lifetime. It meant that I would have the opportunity to work with professional stylists and earn some pocket money which was desperately needed at the time. I have fond memories of my first day there, despite the fact that it didn't begin very promisingly. I was supposed start promptly at half past eight. I had never met the owner of the salon before and I was very nervous. I knew he was called Aldo, of Italian nationality, about forty years old and very well off, but I didn't know much about what he was like as an employer. I found my way to the place and arrived right on time, but the front door was locked. I waited nervously for a while and as the minutes ticked by I started wondering if I was in the right place, whilst I paced up and down the pavement waiting for someone to arrive, constantly checking my watch. I was feeling most anxious, as it was now a quarter to nine and still no-one in sight. Then from the bottom of the street a car came speeding towards me. With a screech of brakes the car halted and out jumped this tall, dark-haired man with a beard. 'This must be him,' I thought to myself. 'Good morning,' he said, fumbling with the keys as he tried to open the door. 'Sorry I'm late. Come on in.' I followed him upstairs. He asked me to take off my coat, took it from me and after putting it on a hanger he carried it to the cloakroom upstairs. I was really impressed by his good manners. He escorted me into the salon and asked me to take a seat whilst he switched on the lights. The rest of the staff and several clients started to arrive. I couldn't help noticing how posh everyone looked and how big and clean the room was. It was also very smartly decorated, with lots of fancy mirrors and plush, padded chairs. As I sat by the backwash, he offered me a gown to put on whilst he gently lowered my head. My long hair dangled into the back of the basin. I could hear water running from the tap behind me and got very worried, especially when he said to me, 'What time is the wedding?' I mumbled nervously, 'What wedding?' 'Your wedding,' he replied. 'Aren't you getting married today?' You can imagine how embarrassed I was when I answered 'No. I've come to work here.' By this time the salon was quite crowded. I couldn't stop blushing as I was taken to the back room where I was introduced to Helen, the supervisor. She gave me a towel to rub over the wet ends of my hair and tried to comfort me a little until I felt more relaxed. She took me around, showing me things I was expected to do. I was given a uniform to wear and went to work in the reception area. At the end of the day I got paid, and more than I had dreamed of, since many of the clients were very generous and I ended up with a lot of extra money from tips. Despite the long hours that I worked and the disastrous start to the day it all proved to be really challenging and enjoyable. I continued to work there every weekend and later on full time, until I completed the three-year apprenticeship and became a qualified stylist.

Exercise 9.2 Transcribe the following passage, including all we have seen in previous lessons (weak forms, sandhi r, syllabicity, elision, assimilation, glottaling).

It was a Thursday afternoon. I was on my way home from work on the underground. The train carriage was empty, because I was going home early. I hadn't got much sleep the night before, because a terrible cold kept making me cough and the cough kept waking me up. The whole morning in the office had gone in a daze. I felt tired and dizzy. It seemed I was going down with 'flu, so I packed up around three o'clock and told my secretary that I might not be in the following day at all if I wasn't feeling any better. So I sat in the train, thinking of a hot cup of tea and the lovely fire I would get going as soon as I arrived home. I avoided all thoughts of the twenty minute walk from the station. I would take a taxi if there was one, but that was unlikely in my village, so it would have to be the old trek home. I didn't usually mind it much, but the paths would be muddy from yesterday's rain and I wanted to be home as soon as possible. All this was going through my mind, when I realised I wasn't alone in the carriage any more. Someone was sitting opposite me. It was a blond chap in his early thirties. He must have got on while I was musing about my fire, because I hadn't noticed him before. I looked at him briefly, as one does, but then my eyes lingered on his face. 'I know this man,' I thought. Before making a fool of myself by greeting a total stranger, I tried to think where I knew him from – not the village. Because it was so small, we all knew each other very well, even too well for my liking. It must be from work then. I spent a few minutes mentally reviewing all the departments, but he didn't fit in any of them. I glanced in his direction again, trying to be subtle. His clothes should have told me that he wasn't from my firm. We have quite a strict dress code and he was wearing old faded sweat pants, trainers and a jacket of indefinite colour. Was it a friend of a friend? No, I didn't think so. Suddenly it dawned on me. I knew where I had seen his face before. It was on television, in a police programme. His photograph had been shown as that of a wanted criminal. As I looked at him again from beneath my eyebrows, all the details of the programme came back to me. He was wanted for questioning (which in other words meant arrest) over a brutal murder. He had previously done time in prison for manslaughter. The police warned anybody who might come across him to be extremely careful, because he was known for his violent, unstable temper. Then I realised I'd been staring at him and he was looking back. I felt so frightened that I started shaking, but at the same time was unable to get up and do something like pull the alarm. 'Is there something the matter?' he said suddenly, scaring the life out of me. 'What's the matter with you?' he repeated. I tried to say something, but found that my lip movements were not accompanied by any sound. I felt cold and hot and was trying hard for a scream. 'Look,' he said, 'Are you all right? You look as pale as a ghost. Can I help you at all?' Well, you can imagine the shock I got at that – a hardened criminal offering me assistance. I couldn't take any more. My head started feeling light and I knew I was going to faint. I managed to say totally the wrong thing before passing out: 'I know you.'

Sometime later I woke up to somebody slapping me. I remembered my last words and realised I was surely done for when I saw him leaning over me. 'Do you feel better?' he asked me. I nodded. God knows why. 'I wasn't sure you'd remember me,' he said. My face must have showed my total bewilderment, because he enlightened me. 'The gym, you know?' 'The gym,' I croaked. 'Yes,' he replied cheerfully. 'We go to the same gym in town. Are you on your way home to Chelnham? It's funny you should live out here. I've just moved, you know? I could give you a lift home when we get there. You don't look as if you should try to make it on your own.' As he talked, everything fell into place. Of course I knew him from the gym. We often worked out at the same time. I felt terribly foolish. 'I think I've got the 'flu,' I told him. 'Yes. That's what I thought myself. Don't worry. I'll get you home soon enough.'

Exercise 9.3 Transcribe the following passage, including all we have seen in previous lessons (weak forms, sandhi r, syllabicity, elision, assimilation, glottalling).

Some people have a special natural talent that makes all the difference. They may look like normal humans, who go to work, eat, sleep – nothing out of the ordinary, until you find out about their ability. Then they shine in their own domain with a kind of luminous radiance which makes them unique. In our house everybody seemed to have a distinct flare. My father was a gifted story-teller. He could make any anecdote come to life. We would sit for hours listening to him telling us about the past, about the history of our country. What would have been dry chronicles coming from anybody else were transformed by his telling into romantic tales of kings and queens, lords and peasants, blood enemies and broken vows. My sister inherited his skills, because she owned a powerful imagination which she used in various ways. At school it served her well, because she excelled in fiction writing. When I was little, at times she would get me mesmerised or scared out of my wits, depending on the story she was recounting, and she always did so as if she were speaking of pure facts. Other times she would concoct the most entrancing games for us play. Our dolls would acquire a life of their own, full of adventures in which we also would become characters. The only times I can remember ever being bored were those when she wasn't at hand. Our mother had a flare for making everyone comfortable. In an unobtrusive way she would get you feeling at home within minutes of arriving at the house. It was partly the fact that she was always genuinely interested in people which made her a sympathetic and appreciative listener, but there was something else more difficult to pin down – maybe a heartfelt gladness about having that person around. Whatever it was, it invariably worked, so that all our friends felt immediately welcome and never failed to return. Our grandmother had a gift for animals. It was quite amazing how they would take to her instantly. This was especially true of the sick ones. There was one occasion that particularly impressed everyone. Our uncle's alsatian had eaten some rat poison left lying in the streets. The vet prescribed certain tablets that might just work and give him a chance to pull through. The problem was that he wouldn't eat at all, so there was no point mixing the medicine with his food. My uncle tried feeding him the tablets, but the poor dog wouldn't let anyone near him either. It got to a stage where he was so sick and emaciated that we were sure he'd die within a few days. That was when my grandmother arrived. Very frail and unstable on her feet, she went up to the dog, opened his mouth with one hand and popped in a tablet with the other one, pushing it right down his throat, so that he wouldn't spit it out. After that she fed him, still by hand, some milksops. This went on for several days until the dog was fully recovered and he was at her beck and call ever after. Of course there are people who possess truly extraordinary abilities like a perfect ear for music, so that they can tell what a note is exactly, even when they hear it in isolation. Others have photographic memories. I used to envy them, specially when studying for exams. Have you ever thought what an advantage it must be to be capable of remembering something just by looking at it a couple of times? But if I was given the opportunity to choose, I would settle for musical talent – having a good singing voice or playing an instrument really well. Of course those skills come with practice too, but no doubt a natural gift for it gives you a head start.

Exercise 9.4 Transcribe the following passage, including all we have seen in previous lessons (weak forms, sandhi r, syllabicity, elision, assimilation, glottaling).

Margaret stood holding the neatly wrapped present tight. The small box fitted nicely into the palms of her hands and she felt quite content standing there on the platform of the tube station. The bow on the box rippled gently in the warm air that came from inside the tunnel. Waiting for the northbound train to take her away and with nothing to distract her attention (all the posters were old and advertised holidays or exotic drinks, things she could not get interested in) Margaret's mind wandered. She knew she did not have long to wait now. The strength of the wind told of the imminent arrival of the train. She hoped for a seat to be free, so that the twenty-minute journey would at least pass in comfort for once. Daydreaming was difficult when one was uncomfortable. She pondered on the nature of her favourite pastime. Daydreaming certainly wasn't something that could be done just anywhere. Or could it? The surroundings had to be sympathetic. I wonder what would be the best kinds of places for daydreaming – the ones that would let a small lingering thought develop into a full-scale drama involving love and intrigue. What if the surroundings had an influence on the type of dream? Maybe different kinds of places produced different kinds of daydreams. Her mind was working hard. This was an avenue of exploration that seemed so obvious, yet in all her years of daydreaming never had it occurred to her. When people are asleep and they smell smoke, they dream of fire. She remembered someone telling her. Sometimes daydreams could be really unpleasant. Was there such a thing as a day nightmare? She closed her eyes and took a deep breath. After a second or two her mind felt clear and calm. She opened her eyes again and was greeted by the sight of the tube train slowing down as it passed along the platform. Gradually it came to a stop and luckily enough the doors opened directly opposite her. A smile grew on her lips.

Exercise 9.5 Transcribe the following passage, including all we have seen in previous lessons (weak forms, sandhi r, syllabicity, elision, assimilation, glottaling).

It was over a year ago that Mary last went to church. However, nobody dared criticize her for it. Not even the most inveterate gossips talked about it. Mary didn't go to church any more, and the whole village respected her decision. That is, everyone except for the vicar. He couldn't approve of her resolve, which went against all established customs, and she did not respect the vicar's attitude. Their last so-called argument took place months ago, on All Souls' day. Mary had gone to the service, as she always did, to pray for the souls of those departed: her father, then her brother and then her mother. Either the sea or sorrow, which sometimes were one and the same thing, had taken them one by one. 'The sea gives, but it takes away more, much more,' her mother used to say, and she would stare out, her eyes lost in the vastness of the sea, from where all her joys and sorrows had always sprung. Her eyes, murky now, had often held their own, challenging the sea. A sigh broke out of Mary when she came back to the real world at the end of the mass that All Souls' day. A sigh that brought to the altar as an offering, all her memories: father, mother, brother, Tony. 'No! Not Tony!' she heard herself shout, as the vicar said a prayer for the sailors lost with the fishing boat *Mounty*, naming each one of them and last of all Tony. 'Not Tony! Not him!' she kept on shouting whilst she strode out of the church. 'Tony is alive and you won't be the ones to kill him. Tony will come back to me soon and you won't be able to take him away from me.' And that day she left the church never to return. As she walked past the cemetery gates, she turned her head the other way, so that she wouldn't have to heed the call from behind the gates, the call which beckoned her to stop and give up her firm belief. Mary sat on a stone bench, facing the misty sea. She refused to go back, not even for her family would she do it. The flowers she had prepared to put by their graves were left behind on the church pew. They had been married for a few months that day when Tony came back in the evening, bursting to share his news. He had been given a job on the *Mounty*, the best and most modern boat in the whole area, it was any fisherman's dream ship he beamed. An imperceptible shadow crossed Mary's brow as he spoke. She decided to ignore it and bring her smile back to the surface. She wouldn't dwell on phantoms, not when Tony was so happy. However, maybe sensing her mood, he reassured her. It was the safest boat in the whole fleet. He'd be away for a few weeks only, three months at the most. The pay would be very good and when he returned, they could think of starting up a family. Mary got up from the bench and started walking home, her jaws clenched with determination. That was a debt destiny owed her, and she had no intention of giving up on it. A year went by, a year since the *Mounty* disappeared. Mary kept on waiting. Every day without fail she would go down to the harbour. With hurried steps she would skip the nets which the women were mending. They would look up and shake their heads sadly. One or two would greet her, getting in return the flicker of a smile or a murmur from Mary. She continued on her way, the same every single day, to the very end of the pier. There, by the light house, she'd stand for a long time, staring hard out towards the horizon, screening the seas. Then she would turn back and retrace her steps, slowly now, as if she had done a ritual duty. She'd go up the hill little by little, delaying her return to the cottage. Nobody would see her until the following morning, back at the pier. One dark rainy day in November on which the wind blew like an omen, Mary left the house, her face flushed and glowing with excitement. She wore the gold brooch her mother had given her on her best coat and a few drops of that really good perfume Tony had brought her from one of his trips. She opened an umbrella against the rain and started walking, light and quick, towards the pier. Only old Tom saw her go by. Mary smiled and waved at him cheerfully without stopping. When she reached the lighthouse, she closed the umbrella and placed it carefully against one of the stone walls. She took a mirror out of her handbag and touched up her hair. Very slowly, as slowly as one who believes she's walking on water, Mary went into the foam, smiling like a cherub, looking fearlessly at the dark turbulent sea. Then a big wave, sudden and rough, lashed at her waist, took her in its embrace and carried her away.

Exercise 9.6 Transcribe the following passage, including all we have seen in previous lessons (weak forms, sandhi r, syllabicity, elision, assimilation, glottaling).

Travelling is what I like doing best. It is wonderful to find yourself suddenly, after a few hours' plane journey, in a totally different culture and atmosphere unlike yours, where everything surprises you, everything is new, and you can detach yourself from your everyday life. When we go abroad, we like to make our own arrangements which is certainly harder, because you face many more problems and difficulties and you have more contact with the often cruel reality of the places you visit, but that is just why I like travelling like that. You get to know other ways of life. When travelling, you have to have an open mind and be able to adjust to all sorts of situations and, even when you're having a bad time, enjoy it as part of the experience. A lot of people find strange foods and smells unpleasant or they can't bear seeing poverty. And some people are not prepared to be uncomfortable, sleep anywhere, put up with insects or face danger. I don't get scared easily and don't mind going off the beaten track, even if it's supposed to be dangerous. Once we went to visit a Masai village away from the safari circuits. We were taken there by a man from the village who worked for a friend of ours and who was bringing some presents for the girl he was engaged to. He introduced us to all his family and we were welcomed as friends. We visited some of the huts belonging to his father's wives. The huts were made of pressed cow dung. Although a man can have several wives, each woman must have her own dwelling. Everywhere we went we were offered tea and they killed a goat in our honour. They do so by slitting its throat so that it bleeds to death. They drink the blood, because the Masai believe that animal blood gives them the strength to make them the good warriors they are. While they were filling jars with the blood, we thought we were going to be offered some. Fortunately they cooked the animal's meat on an open fire for us. There is no single place I wouldn't want to go to. Hand me a plane ticket and I'm on my way. I don't care. The simple fact of crossing the border, and listening to the radio or looking at petrol station signs in a foreign language is something I adore. I love airports, walking down the streets of foreign towns, watching people. And that's something you can do in Third World countries or in developed ones. In developed countries you have a better chance of enjoying man-made works: architecture, paintings, the history of cities and civilizations. Perhaps in other parts of the world, like central Africa, which is my favourite, what you can enjoy is nature, which is superb, and the people and their way of life, but there aren't great museums to go to. Those are two different kinds of trip. I like them both, but perhaps as a better way of breaking away from everything I prefer the more adventurous type. My latest trip, last winter, was to Zimbabwe. One of the things that impressed me most was flying over the Victoria Falls. It was an indescribably magnificent scene. We were still many miles away from the falls when we saw what seemed to be the smoke from a huge forest fire rising incredibly high. As we got closer, we realised it was the steam coming up from the falls. We were luckily given permission to fly over the falls, which is usually forbidden. To crown it all, we saw two totally circular rainbows over the water. That was a really moving experience. Facing such splendid natural phenomena puts you in a reflective mood. It makes you stop and think about your-self. It's as if you were sent into a trance. Travelling for me is a chance to know more. Our immediate environment is so restricted, like a grain of sand. Knowing other situations makes you a much richer person. You realise that people's views and habits vary a lot from one place to another and that there is no absolute truth, that anything may be valid, any type of behaviour, any religion. That is why we can't judge from where we are news we get about things happening in another part of the world if we haven't been and haven't seen what things are like there. Travelling is my passion. It's as if one could live several different lives. I like having that store of memories to delve into every now and then. I hope my children feel this way too. It will teach them to appreciate and value other cultures and not to despise anything just because it is not what they are used to.

Appendix: Answers to exercises

Answers to Lesson 1: symbols and terminology

Exercise 1.1 The voiceless consonants in the passage are in bold type.

I **haven't** got a **car** at the moment. My **car** was **stolen** last **Friday**. I le**ft** it at the **station** all day and when I got ba**ck** in the evening it **had** vani**shed**. I **hope** the insurance **company** will **send** me a **cheque soon**, **so that** I **can** go and buy another one.

Here is the whole passage in transcription:

/aɪ hævənt gɒt ə kɑːr ət ðə məʊmənt | maɪ kɑː wəz stəʊlən lɑːst fraɪdeɪ | aɪ left ɪt ət ðə steɪʃən ɔːl deɪ | ənd wen aɪ gɒt bæk ɪn ði iːvnɪŋ | ɪt həd vænɪʃt | aɪ həʊp ði ɪnʃɔːrəns kʌmpəni wɪl send mi ə tʃek suːn | səʊ ðət aɪ kən gəʊ ənd baɪ ənʌðə wʌn/

Exercise 1.2 The words which contain only voiced consonants are marked with a ✓ All the words are transcribed for you.

much	/mʌtʃ/	moody ✓	/muːdi/	number ✓	/nʌmbə/
yellow ✓	/jeləʊ/	roses ✓	/rəʊzəz/	knees ✓	/niːz/
youth	/juːθ/	loses ✓	/luːzəz/	doses	/dəʊsəz/
dozes ✓	/dəʊzəz/	wishing	/wɪʃɪŋ/	leisure ✓	/leʒə/
those ✓	/ðəʊz/	under ✓	/ʌndə/	jeans ✓	/dʒiːnz/
this	/ðis/	his	/hɪz/	wins ✓	/wɪnz/
garage ✓	/gærɑːdʒ/	universal	/juːnivɜːsəl/		
	/gærɑːʒ/				
	/gærɪdʒ/				

Exercise 1.3 Each word which begins with a consonant is followed by an indication of the place of articulation of that consonant: (a) = alveolar, (b) = bilabial, (d) = dental, (g) = glottal, (l) = labiodental, (lv) = labial-velar, (p) = palatal, (pa) = postalveolar, (v) = velar.

Last (a) Tuesday (a) my (b) brother (b) came (v) to (a) see (a) me (b). He (g) wanted (lv) to (a) borrow (b) my (b) videorecorder (l) because (b) his (g) is not (a) very (l) reliable (pa). My (b) nephew's (a) birthday (b) is next (a) Thursday (d). They (d) are going (v) to (a) have (g) a party (b) for (l) some (a) friends (l) and they (d) want (lv) to show (pa) some (a) films (l).

Exercise 1.4

plosive:	doubt /daʊt/ give /gɪv/ quite /kwaɪt/ chemist /kemɪst/
fricative:	sixty /sɪksti/ five /faɪv/ xylophone /zaɪləfəʊn/ thrown /θrəʊn/ then /ðen/ hope /həʊp/ physics /fɪzɪks/
affricate:	generous /dʒenərəs/ cherry /tʃeri/
approximant:	lesson /lesən/ usual /juːʒwəl/ yacht /jɒt/ wrong /rɒŋ/ rubber /rʌbə/
nasal:	monster /mɒnstə/ knot /nɒt/

Exercise 1.5

- Words beginning with an obstruent: choose, soap, coast, told, friend, thought, boast, purple, gate, violet, quiet
- Words beginning with a sonorant: metal, ripe, white, youth, lorry, nasty
- Words beginning with a stop: choose, metal, coast, told, boast, purple, gate, nasty, quiet

Exercise 1.6 The close and close–mid monophthongs are shown in bold type.

There are three reasons I should give if anyone asked why it is a good idea to learn English transcription. First, it helps you to realise what you say as opposed to what you think you say. Second, it teaches you that written language is not the same as spoken language. Third, it can be quite a lot of fun.

Exercise 1.7

bænd	hɔːl	dʒʌmp	wiːp	lʌv	kwɪt
ɑːsk	tɒp	mɪs	dʒuːs	aʊt	taɪm
bles	klɪf	drɒp	huːp	biːd	tɜːn
træp	daɪv	fɪə	grəʊ	ləʊd	feə
bɔɪl	wɜːk	wɒnt	luːz	kləʊs[1]	buːt
				kləʊz	
kʊk	pʊl	dəʊm	waɪ	krɒs	tʃeə

Answers to Lesson 2: transcription hints

Exercise 2.1

weights	/weɪts/	lambs	/læmz/	views	/vjuːz/
doves	/dʌvz/	ideas	/aɪdɪəz/	myths	/mɪθs/
towns	/taʊnz/	songs	/sɒŋz/		
rods	/rɒdz/	tracks	/træks/		

[1]close = /kləʊs/ if it is an adjective, but /kləʊz/ if it is a verb

Exercise 2.2

- He missed it   /hi mɪst ɪt/
- She repairs watches   /ʃi rɪpeəz wɒtʃəz/
- Bill's brother's passed   /bɪlz brʌðəz pɑːst/
- Jack's started school   /dʒæks stɑːtəd skuːl/
- He makes badges   /hi meɪks bædʒəz/
- He misses his friends' company   /hi mɪsəz hɪz frendz kʌmpəni/

Exercise 2.3

- hours   /aəz/
- wiring   /waərɪŋ/
- showered   /ʃaəd/
- grower   /grɜː/

Exercise 2.4

Why do you want to leave so early? I'd have thought that we could get there on time if we left at about half past ten. If we leave at nine, we'll arrive far too early and we'll have to stand around in the cold, waiting for the others to show up.

Answers to Lesson 3: stress, rhythm and weak forms

Orthographic version for the sample transcription passage

When I think of my years at university, one of the things I regret is the fact that I did not take some subjects seriously and I only did enough work to scrape by. Somehow they have all contrived to come back hauntingly, since I have ended up needing to know about them for my work. What a lot of wasted opportunities! At the time, for whatever reason, I couldn't see any interest in them. A lot of it was my own fault for spending my time in other pursuits, such as playing cards with my classmates, or going to the cafeteria for long chats and numerous coffees, but I must also point out that it often was the lecturer's fault. Now I am throwing stones in my own glasshouse, but it has to be said. There was this course which went totally over my head and to this day I don't know how I passed it. The lecturer was a very nice man, a bit shy and with a monotonous voice quality, which meant that you were easily sent to sleep. But the worst was that he knew too much, or rather he didn't know how to pitch things low enough for students to follow. He finally gave up teaching and became a full-time researcher, which I think is what he was cut out for. I'm not trying to shift all the blame for the courses I wasted. Like I said, it was also due to my interests leaning towards other things. Still, socialising is another skill that has to be learnt, and is important for your future, don't you think?

Exercise 3.1 Edited orthographic version (*You will find some words highlighted. They are grammatical words which are likely to be used in the weak form.*)

A group of people were sitting having a drink in a bar and onc man was boasting about how tough he was. After a while, everyone else got fed up with listening to this, so someone said, 'All right. You say you're so tough, but I bet you can't spend the night alone on the top of the mountain without a coat or anything to keep you warm.' The man took on the bet and the next night he climbed the mountain alone. He found a sheltered spot and sat down. He had brought a book with him and he lit a candle so that he was able to read. He spent the coldest, most miserable night of his life. In the morning, he staggered down the mountain half dead and went to find his friends and to claim his winnings. 'Are you sure you didn't have a coat?' they asked him. 'I was dressed just as I am now,' he said. 'And you didn't light a fire? Not even a candle?' 'Oh, yes. I had a candle, but only in order to read my book.' 'The bet's off,' they said and went away laughing. The man was very annoyed, but he didn't say anything. A few weeks later, he invited them all to dinner at his house. They all arrived on time and sat waiting for the meal to be served. An hour went by, two hours, but still no food appeared. Finally, they began to lose patience and asked the man what he was playing at. 'All right,' he said. 'Let's go into the kitchen and see if the food's ready.' They all followed him into the other room where they saw a huge pot of water on a stand and underneath was a single lighted candle. The man put his finger into the water. 'No. It's not ready yet. I can't under-stand it. The candle's been there since yesterday.' His friends laughed and took him out for an expensive meal at the nearest restaurant.

Transcription

| ə ˈgruːp əv ˈpiːpəl wə ˈsɪtɪŋ hævɪŋ[1] ə ˈdrɪŋk ɪn ə ˈbɑː | ənd[2] ˈwʌn mæn wəz ˈbəʊstɪŋ əbaut hau ˈtʌf i[3] wɒz[4] | ˈɑːftər[5] ə ˈwaɪl | ˈevriwʌn ˈels gɒt fed ˈʌp wɪð ˈlɪsənɪŋ tə ˈðɪs | səu ˈsʌmwʌn ˈsed | ɔːlˈraɪt | ju ˈseɪ jɔː[6] səu ˈtʌf | bət aɪ ˈbet ju ˈkɑːnt[7] spend ðə ˈnaɪt əˈləʊn ɒn ðə ˈtɒp əv ðə ˈmauntən | wɪðaut ə ˈkəut ɔːr[5] ˈeniθɪŋ tə ˈkiːp ju ˈwɔːm | ðə ˈmæn tuk ˈɒn ðə ˈbet | ənd[2] ðə ˈnekst ˈnaɪt i[3] ˈklaɪmd[8] ðə ˈmauntən əˈləun | hi[9] ˈfaund ə ˈʃeltəd[8] ˈspɒt ənd[2] sæt ˈdaun | hi[9] əd[3] ˈbrɔːt ə ˈbuk wɪð ɪm[3] | ənd[2] i[3] ˈlɪt ə ˈkændəl səu ðət i[3] wəz eɪbəl tə ˈriːd | hi[9] ˈspent ðə ˈkəuldɪst | ˈməust ˈmɪzərəbəl ˈnaɪt əv ɪz[3] ˈlaɪf | ɪn ðə ˈmɔːnɪŋ i[3] ˈstægəd[8] ˈdaun ðə ˈmauntən hɑːf ˈded | ənd[2] ˈwent tə ˈfaɪnd ɪz[3] ˈfrendz[10] | ənd[2] tə ˈkleɪm ɪz[3] ˈwɪnɪŋz[10] | ə ju ˈʃɔː[6] ju ˈdɪdənt hæv[11] ə ˈkəut ðeɪ ˈɑːskt[12] ɪm[3] | aɪ wəz ˈdrest[12] ˈdʒʌst[13] əz aɪ ˈæm[4] ˈnau i[3] ˈsed | ənd[2] ju ˈdɪdənt laɪt ə ˈfaə[14] | nɒt ˈiːvən ə ˈkændəl | əu ˈjes | aɪ ˈhæd[11] ə ˈkændəl | bət ˈəunli ɪn ˈɔːdə tə ˈriːd maɪ ˈbuk | ðə ˈbets[15] ˈɒf ðeɪ ˈsed | ənd[2] ˈwent əweɪ ˈlɑːfɪŋ | ðə ˈmæn wəz ˈveri əˈnɔɪd[8] | bət i[3] ˈdɪdənt seɪ ˈeniθɪŋ | ə ˈfjuː wiːks[15] ˈleɪtə | hi[9] ɪnˈvaɪtɪd[16] ðəm ˈɔːl tə ˈdɪnər[5] ət ɪz[3] ˈhaus | ðeɪ ˈɔːl əˈraɪvd[8] ɒn ˈtaɪm | ənd[2] sæt ˈweɪtɪŋ fə ðə ˈmiːl tə bi ˈsɜːvd[8] | ən ˈaə[14] went ˈbaɪ | ˈtuː ˈaəz[10-14] | bət ˈstɪl nəu ˈfuːd əˈpɪəd[8] | ˈfaɪnəli ðeɪ bɪˈgæn tə ˈluːz ˈpeɪʃəns | ənd[2] ˈɑːskt[12] ðə ˈmæn wɒt i[3] wəz ˈpleɪɪŋ æt[4] | ɔːl ˈraɪt i[3] ˈsed | ˈlets gəu ɪntə ðə ˈkɪtʃən ənd[2] ˈsiː ɪf ðə ˈfuːdz[10] ˈredi | ðeɪ ˈɔːl ˈfɒləud[8] ɪm[3] ɪntə ðiː[17] ˈʌðə ˈruːm | weə ðeɪ ˈsɔː ə ˈhjuːdʒ pɒt əv ˈwɔːtər[5] ɒn ə ˈstænd | ənd[2] ˈʌndəniːθ ðə wəz ə ˈsɪŋgəl ˈlaɪtɪd[16] ˈkændəl | ðə ˈmæn put ɪz[3] ˈfɪŋgər[5] ɪntə ðə ˈwɔːtə | ˈnəu | ɪts[15] ˈnɒt redi ˈjet | aɪ ˈkɑːnt[7] ʌndəˈstænd ɪt | ðə ˈkændəlz[10] biːn ˈðeə[18] sɪns ˈjestədeɪ[19] | hɪz[9] ˈfrendz[10] ˈlɑːft[12] | ənd[2] ˈtuk ɪm[3] ˈaut fər[5] ən ɪkˈspensɪv ˈmiːl ət ðə ˈnɪərɪst ˈrestərɒnt[20] |

Comments to transcription (*Remember that *** after a comment means that it won't be repeated in future lessons.*)

1. Only monosyllabic grammatical words have weak forms.***

2. /ənd/ and /ən/ are alternative weak forms for *and*.***
3. /h/ can be deleted because it is not following a potential pause.***
4. Use of strong form because the grammatical word is stranded.
5. /r/ is pronounced here because the next word begins with a vowel sound (see Lesson 4).***
6. Monophthonging (see Lesson 2).
7. Notice this is the form for the negative contraction *can't*.***
8. The regular past tense morpheme agrees in voicing with the previous sound. In this case the previous sound is voiced so the morpheme is pronounced /d/.***
9. /h/ cannot be deleted because the word is following a potential pause.***
10. When it is a morpheme or contraction, 's' agrees in voicing with the previous sound. In this case the previous sound is voiced so the morpheme is pronounced /z/.***
11. The strong form is used because the verb does not function as an auxiliary here.
12. The regular past tense morpheme agrees in voicing with the previous sound. In this case the previous sound is voiceless so the morpheme is pronounced /t/.***
13. When *just* is used in the sense of *exactly*, *precisely* it tends to be stressed and therefore pronounced in strong form. On the other hand, when it means *only* it tends to be in weak form (see Lesson 3, note 5).
14. Smoothing (see Lesson 2).
15. When it is a morpheme or contraction, 's' agrees in voicing with the previous sound. In this case the previous sound is voiceless so the morpheme is pronounced /s/.***
16. The regular past tense morpheme is pronounced /ɪd/ or /əd/ when the previous sound is either /t/ or /d/.***
17. /ði/ is the form used when the next word begins with a vowel sound.***
18. Strong form because *there* is being used as a location adverb.
19. /ˈjestədi/ is an alternative pronunciation.
20. /ˈrestərɑːnt/ and /ˈrestərənt/ are alternative pronunciations.

Exercise 3.2: transcription

| ˈhaʊ dɪd ju ˈget ˈhɪə ðɪs ˈmɔːnɪŋ | aɪ ˈdɪdənt ˈsiː ju ət ðə ˈsteɪʃən | aɪ ˈkeɪm baɪ ˈkɑː | bət aɪ ˈwʊdənt[1] ˈduː[2] ɪt əˈgen | ˈwaɪ ˈnɒt | ðə ˈtræfɪk ˈɪzənt tuː ˈbæd | ˈɪz ɪt | ɪt ˈwɒz[3] ðɪs ˈmɔːnɪŋ | ðər[4] ər[4] ə ˈlɒt əv ˈrəʊd wɜːks[5] ˈdʒʌst[6] ði[7] ˈʌðə ˈsaɪd əv ðə ˈrɪvə | əʊ ˈjes | aɪd kəmˈpliːtli fəˈgɒtən əbaʊt ˈðəʊz | səʊ ˈwaɪ dɪdənt ju ˈkætʃ ðə ˈtreɪn | ði[7] əˈlɑːm klɒk ˈdɪdənt gəʊ ˈɒf | ðə ˈmʌst[8] əv[9] biːn ə ˈpɑə[10] kʌt ˈlɑːst naɪt | bɪkɒz ðə ˈnʌmbəz[11] wə ˈblɪŋkɪŋ | ənd[12] ˈðen ðə ˈtræfɪk ˈmeɪd mi ˈtwenti ˈmɪnɪts[5] ˈleɪt | əʊ ˈdɪə | ˈmɪstə *ˈdʒeŋkɪnz ˈwʊdənt[1] ˈlaɪk ˈðæt[13] | hi[14] ˈsɜːtənli ˈdɪdənt ˈlaɪk ɪt | hi[14] gɒt ˈrɑːðər[4] ʌnˈpleZənt əˈbaʊt ɪt | aɪm ˈnɒt səˈpraɪzd[15] | hiz[11-14] biːn ˈgetɪŋ ˈmɔːr[4] ənd[12] ˈmɔː ˈbæd ˈtempəd[15] ˈleɪtli | ˈevribɒdiz[11] ˈnəʊtɪst[16] ɪt | ˈevə sɪns i[9] ˈhæd[2] ðæt[13] ˈmiːtɪŋ ət ðə ˈhed ˈɒfɪs | hi[14] əz[9] biːn ˈkwaɪt ʌnˈbeərəbəl | ˈjes | aɪ ˈnəʊ iz[9-11] ˈgɒt ə ˈlɒt ɒn ɪz[9] ˈpleɪt ət ðə ˈməʊmənt | bət ðəz[11] ˈrɪəli ˈnəʊ ˈniːd tə bi ˈruːd tə ˈsʌmwən ɪn ˈfrʌnt əv ˈevribɒdi ˈels | hi[14] ˈmeɪd mi ˈfiːl əz ɪf aɪ əd[9] dʒəst ˈkɪld[15] sʌmbədi[17] | aɪ ˈtel ju | aɪ ˈθɪŋk i[9] ˈmiːnz[11] tə ˈmeɪk mi ˈpeɪ fə ˈðɪs | əʊ aɪ ˈʃudənt[1] ˈwʌri ˈtuː ˈmʌtʃ əˈbaʊt ɪt | hil[14] əv[9] fəˈgɒtən ˈɔːl əˈbaʊt ɪt baɪ təˈmɒrəʊ | hi[14] ˈɔːlweɪz ˈdʌz[3] | ɪts[5] ˈwʌn əv ɪz[9] ˈfjuː ˈgʊd ˈkwɒlətiz[11]

| hi[14] 'wɪl ɪf aɪm 'nɒt 'leɪt ə'gen | bət 'ðɪs ɪz ðə 'fɔ:θ 'taɪm | aɪv bi:n 'leɪt ðɪs 'mʌnθ | wen ɪts[5] 'nɒt 'rəud wɜːks[5] | ɪts[5] ə 'brəukən daun 'bʌs | aɪ 'rɪəli 'mʌst[8] 'mænɪdʒ tə get 'hɪər[4] ɒn 'taɪm frəm 'nau 'ɒn | aɪd 'du:[2] maɪ 'veri 'best ɪf 'aɪ wə 'ju:[8] | ju 'mʌsənt[1] ʌndər'estɪmeɪt ɪm[9] | 'nɒt wɪð 'ɔ:l ði:z 'gəul ə'tʃi:vɪŋ 'pɒlɪsiz[11] | hɪz[11–14] 'ɔ:lweɪz 'ræntɪŋ əbaut | bi'saɪdz | ðər[4]ə 'kwaɪt ə 'fju: 'pi:pəl ə'raund | ðət wud[18] 'lʌv tə 'hæv[2] ə 'gəu ət 'jɔ: 'dʒɒb | 'nʌθɪŋ 'pɜːsənəl ju ʌndə'stænd | ɪts[5] 'dʒʌst[6] 'pjɔ:[19] 'klaɪmɪŋ | əu aɪ 'du:[8] 'nəu | ənd[12] aɪ 'wɪl 'traɪ | 'laɪk ju 'sed | 'ðɪs pleɪs ɪz 'ti:mɪŋ wɪð kəm'petɪtəz[11] | ənd[12] 'getɪŋ ɒn ðə 'rɒŋ saɪd əv *'dʒeŋkɪnz | ɪz 'nɒt ðə 'best weɪ tə 'ki:p ðəm ət 'beɪ | aɪv ɔ:l'redi 'tʃeɪndʒd[15] 'dʒɒbz[11] 'twaɪs ɪn ðə 'lɑːst θri: 'jɪəz[11] | aɪ 'dəunt[20] 'wɒnt tə 'gəu θru: 'ɔ:l 'ðæt[13] ə'gen |

Comments to transcription

1. The strong form must be used because it is a negative contraction. Additionally, words of more than one syllable do not have weak forms.
2. The strong form is used because the verb is not being used as an auxiliary.
3. The strong form is used because the grammatical word is stranded.
4. /r/ is pronounced here because the next word begins with a vowel sound and there is no pause in between (see Lesson 4). ***
5. When it is a morpheme or contraction, 's' agrees in voicing with the previous sound. In this case the previous sound is voiceless so the morpheme is pronounced /s/. ***
6. When *just* is used in the sense of *exactly*, *precisely* it tends to be stressed and therefore pronounced in strong form. On the other hand, when it means *only* it tends to be in weak form unless it is stressed for emphatic reasons (see Lesson 3, note 5).
7. /ði/ is the weak form used when the next word begins with a vowel sound. ***
8. The strong form is used because the grammatical word is being emphasised and therefore stressed.
9. /h/ can be deleted here because it is not preceded by a potential pause. ***
10. Smoothing (see Lesson 2).
11. When it is a morpheme or contraction, 's' agrees in voicing with the previous sound. In this case the previous sound is voiced so the morpheme is pronounced /z/. ***
12. /ənd/ and /ən/ are alternative weak forms for *and*. ***
13. *that* is used in the strong form here because it is a demonstrative.
14. /h/ cannot be deleted here because it is preceded by a potential pause.***
15. The regular past tense morpheme agrees in voicing with the previous sound. In this case the previous sound is voiced so the morpheme is pronounced /d/. ***
16. The regular past tense morpheme agrees in voicing with the previous sound. In this case the previous sound is voiceless so the morpheme is pronounced /t/. ***
17. /sʌmbɒdi/ is an alternative pronunciation.
18. Grammatical words which have the vowel /ʊ/ in their citation form, such as *would*, *should* and *could*, may remain unchanged even if they are unstressed because /ʊ/ is already a weak vowel, but in a faster pronunciation they may be further weakened to /ə/. ***
19. Monophthonging (see Lesson 2).
20. Notice this is the form for the negative contraction *don't*.***

Exercise 3.3

| aɪ əv[1] 'lɪvd[2] ɪn *'lʌndən fə 'ten 'jɪəz[3] naʊ | ɪt 'siːmz[3] sʌtʃ ə 'lɒŋ 'taɪm wen aɪ 'æktʃuəli 'stɒp ənd[4] 'θɪŋk ə'baʊt ɪt | 'ten 'jɪəz[3] | 'mɔː ðən ə 'θɜːd əv maɪ 'laɪf | wen aɪ 'θɪŋk əv 'həʊm | haʊ'evə | *'ʃeldən 'ɔːlweɪz 'kʌmz[3] tə 'maɪnd | ə 'taɪni 'vɪlɪdʒ ɪn ðə 'haːt əv ðə *'blækdaʊn 'hɪlz[3] | 'hɪdən ɪn ðə 'depθs[5] əv *'devən | aɪ 'lʌv gəʊɪŋ 'həʊm ət 'ðɪs taɪm əv 'jɪə | 'sprɪŋ ɪz mə'tʃuərɪŋ laɪk ən 'ædəlesənt 'gɜːl | ðə 'liːvz[3] ʌn'fɜːlɪŋ | 'mɒdəstli ɪk'stendɪŋ ðeə 'freʃ griːn 'grəʊθ | ðə 'fiːldz[3] riˈvɜːbəreɪt wɪð ðə 'hezɪtənt 'bliːtɪŋ əv 'njuːbɔːn 'læmz[3] | ənd[4] ðə 'hedʒɪz[6] ənd[4] 'triːz[3] | ə 'fɪld[2] wɪð ði[7] ɪk'spektənt 'rʌsəl əv 'njuː 'laɪf ɪn kri'eɪʃən| *'lʌndən haʊ'evə ri'meɪnz[3] ə'blɪvɪəs tə ðə fɜːˈtɪləti əv 'sprɪŋ | wi ə 'berɪd[2] ɪn ɑə[8]'selvz[3] | ðər[9] ə di'leɪz[3] ɒn ðə 'nɔːðən laɪn ə'gen | ə 'sɪgnəl 'feɪljər[9-10] ət sʌm[11] 'steɪʃən | meɪks[5] 'ɔːl treɪnz[3] 'leɪt | ðə *'bɪg *'ɪʃuː[12] 'vendər[9] ət ði[7] 'ʌndəgraʊnd 'tɪkɪt 'ɒfɪs | 'ʃaʊts[5] ɪn jɔː 'feɪs | ðə 'kraʊdz[3] 'puʃ ənd[4] 'ʃʌv ɪn ðə daɪ'rekʃən əv ðə 'suːpəmaːkɪt | 'maʊðz[3] 'wɔːtərɪŋ ɪn æntɪsɪ 'peɪʃən əv ðeər[9] 'iːvnɪŋ 'miːl | aɪ 'teɪk ə 'wɔːk daʊn ðə 'rəʊd tə 'pəʊst ə 'letə | *'lʌndən 'kɪlz[3] mi | 'red 'bʌsɪz[6] 'ʃʌdərɪŋ 'paːst mi | 'beltʃɪŋ 'θɪk 'sməʊk | wɪtʃ 'klɪŋz[3] tə ðə 'bæk əv maɪ 'θrəʊt| ɪn 'ðɪs 'sɪti | ju 'lɜːn tə 'wɔːk 'faːst | ə'vɔɪd ɔːl 'aɪ kɒntækt | ənd[4] meɪn'teɪn ði[7] 'eər[9] əv 'sʌmwʌn ɒn ən 'erənd | ɪts[5] 'kɔːld[2] 'self prezə'veɪʃən | ɪf ju 'sləʊ 'daʊn | ɔː 'kæts ə 'streɪndʒəz[3] 'aɪ | ðen huː[13] 'nəʊz[3] wɒt maɪt 'hæpən | ɪt ɪz 'seɪfə tə ri'meɪn wɪð'ɪn ðə 'bʌbəl əv ænə'nɪməti | aɪ 'wɒnt tə gəʊ 'həʊm | 'maɪ 'həʊm | weər[9] aɪ kən 'sɪt ʌndə ðə juːkə'lɪptəs 'triː ɪn ðə 'dʌsk | ən[4] 'wɒtʃ ðə hə'raɪzən 'daːkən əz ðə 'sʌn 'sets[5] | ənd[4] ðə 'bæts[5] staːt ðeə 'naɪtli 'hʌnt fə 'dʒuːsi 'ɪnsekts[5] |

Comments to transcription

1. /h/ can be deleted here because it is not following a potential pause. ***
2. The regular past tense morpheme agrees in voicing with the previous sound, so in this case, because the previous sound is voiced, it is pronounced /d/. ***
3. When it is a morpheme or contraction, 's' agrees in voicing with the previous sound, in this case the previous sound is voiced so 's' is pronounced /z/. ***
4. /ənd/ or /ən/ are alternative weak forms for *and*. ***
5. When it is a morpheme or contraction, 's' agrees in voicing with the previous sound, in this case the previous sound is voiceless so 's' is pronounced /s/. ***
6. The morpheme 's' is pronounced /ɪz/ or /əz/ after sibilants (/s/, /z/, /ʃ/, /ʒ/, /tʃ/ and /dʒ/).***
7. /ði/ is the weak form used when the next word begins with a vowel sound. ***
8. Smoothing (see Lesson 2).
9. /r/ is pronounced because it is immediately followed by a word beginning with a vowel sound (see Lesson 4). ***
10. In unstressed positions, the first element of the diphthongs /ɪə/ and /ʊə/ may lose its prominence and become /jə/ or /wə/ respectively. This is a common process which we will use consistently in the last lesson of the book. Meanwhile, don't worry if you use /ɪə/ and our version is /jə/. You can regard them as alternative pronunciations.
11. The strong form is used because *some* modifies a countable noun in the singular (see Lesson 3 note 5).

12. The *Big Issue* is a weekly magazine sold by and for the homeless in London.
13. Strong form because *who* is used as an interrogative pronoun.

Exercise 3.4

| aɪ ˈhævənt[1] ˈgɒt ə ˈkɑːr[2] əv maɪ ˈəʊn | bət ˈsʌmtaɪmz[3] aɪ ˈbɒrəʊ wʌn frəm ə ˈfrend | ənd[4] ˈdraɪv tə ˈsiː maɪ ˈbrʌðər[2] ənd[4] ˈsɪstər[2] ɪn ˈlɔː | huː[5] ˈlɪv əˈbaʊt ˈsɪksti ˈmaɪlz[3] frəm *ˈlʌndən | aɪ əv[6] ˈdʌn ðə ˈdʒɜːni ɪn ˈɔːl ˈkaɪndz[3] əv ˈweðə | bət ðə ˈwɜːst ˈtaɪm aɪ ˈevə ˈhæd[7] | wəz ɒn ə ˈveri ˈfɒgi ˈdeɪ ɪn ðə ˈmɪdəl əv nəʊˈvembə | wen aɪ ˈstɑːtɪd[8] ðə ˈdraɪv | ðə ˈweðə wəz ə ˈbɪt ˈmɪsti | bət aɪ ˈdɪdənt ˈθɪŋk ɪt wəz ˈbæd iˈnʌf tə pəsˈpəʊn maɪ ˈtrɪp ɔː tə ˈgəʊ baɪ ˈtreɪn | ˈwɪtʃ | ɔːlˈðəʊ ɪt wəz ˈpɒsɪbəl ət ˈðæt[9] ˈtaɪm | ˈwɒzənt[1] ˈveri ˈiːzi ɔː kənˈviːnɪənt | ˈeniweɪ | aɪ ˈgɒt əˈbaʊt ˈtwenti ˈmaɪlz[3] ˈaʊtsaɪd *ˈlʌndən | ənd[4] ðə ˈmɪst ˈstɑːtɪd[8] ˈgetɪŋ ˈθɪkər[2] ən[4] ˈθɪkə | aɪ wəz ˈgetɪŋ ˈmɔːr[2] ən[4] ˈmɔː ˈnɜːvəs | bɪˈkɒz aɪ əm ˈnɒt ə ˈveri ˈkɒnfɪdənt ˈdraɪvər[2] ət ðə ˈbest əv ˈtaɪmz[3] | aɪ səˈpəʊz aɪ ˈdəʊnt[10] ˈget iˈnʌf ˈpræktɪs | aɪ ˈrɪəli ˈheɪt ˈfɒg | ˈiːvən wen aɪm ˈnɒt ˈdraɪvɪŋ | bət wen jɔː[11] bɪˈhaɪnd ðə ˈwiːl əv ə ˈkɑːr[2] ɪt ˈsiːmz[3] ˈten ˈtaɪmz[3] ˈwɜːs | ˈdʌzənt[1] ɪt | aɪ ˈhæd[7] tə ˈdraɪv ɪksˈtriːmli ˈsləʊli | ənd[4] ðə ˈdʒɜːni ˈtʊk mi ˈɔːlməʊst ən ˈaʊə[12] ˈlɒŋgə[13] ðən ɪt ˈnɔːməli ˈdʌz[14] | ˈfaɪnəli aɪ ˈgɒt tə ðə ˈpleɪs weər[2] aɪ ˈhæd[7] tə ˈtɜːn ˈɒf ðə ˈmeɪn ˈrəʊd | ɪntə ðə ˈsmɔːl ˈkʌntri ˈleɪn | wɪtʃ ˈliːdz[3] tə ðə ˈvɪlɪdʒ weə maɪ ˈbrʌðə ˈlɪvz[3] | ət ˈliːst aɪ ˈθɔːt aɪ əd[6] ˈgɒt tə ðə ˈraɪt ˈleɪn | ˈɑːftər[2] əˈbaʊt ə ˈmaɪl | aɪ ˈpɑːst[15] ə ˈhaʊs wɪtʃ aɪ kʊd[16] ˈdʒʌst[17] meɪk ˈaʊt ɪn ðə ˈfɒg | bət wɪtʃ aɪ ˈdɪdənt ˈrekəgnaɪz ət ˈɔːl | aɪ ˈdɪdənt ˈfænsi ˈtɜːnɪŋ ˈraʊnd | ənd[4] ˈgəʊɪŋ ˈbæk tə ðə ˈmeɪn ˈrəʊd | bɪkɒz aɪ ˈθɔːt ɪt wʊd[16] bi ˈveri ˈdeɪndʒərəs ˈgetɪŋ ˈbæk ɪntə ðə ˈfləʊ əv ˈtræfɪk | ɪn ˈsʌtʃ ˈpɔː[11] vɪzɪˈbɪləti | aɪ dɪˈsaɪdɪd[8] tə ˈpres ˈɒn | ənd[4] ˈsiː ɪf aɪ ˈkeɪm tu[18] ˈeni ˈsaɪnpəʊsts[19] | wɪtʃ wʊd[16] ˈpʊt mi ˈbæk ɒn ðə ˈraɪt ˈtræk | ˈðæt[9] wəz maɪ ˈsɪliəst mɪˈsteɪk | ðə ˈnekst ˈaʊə[12] wəz laɪk ə ˈnaɪtmeə | aɪ ˈgɒt ˈdiːpər[2] ɪntə ðə ˈkʌntrisaɪd | ən[4] ðə ˈfɒg gɒt ˈiːvən ˈθɪkə | ət ˈwʌn ˈpɔɪnt aɪ ˈlɒst ðə ˈrəʊd ɔːltəˈgeðə | ən[4] ˈfaʊnd maɪˈself ˈdraɪvɪŋ əˈkrɒs ə ˈfiːld | ˈθruː ə ˈhɜːd əv ˈrɑːðə səˈpraɪzd[20] ˈkaʊz[3] | ˈwʌns aɪ ˈmɪst[15] baɪ ˈɪntʃɪz[21] ˈgəʊɪŋ ɪntu[18] ə ˈrɑːðə ˈdiːp ˈdɪtʃ | ˈfaɪnəli aɪ ˈkeɪm tu[18] ə ˈsaɪnpəʊst wɪð ðə ˈneɪm əv maɪ ˈbrʌðəz[3] ˈvɪlɪdʒ ˈɒn ɪt | ɪt wəz ˈten ˈmaɪlz[3] ˈbæk ɪn ðə daɪˈrekʃən aɪ əd[6] ˈdʒʌst[16] ˈkʌm | ðə ˈnekst taɪm aɪ ˈvɪzɪt maɪ ˈbrʌðər[2] ɪn nəʊˈvembə | aɪ ʃəl ˈlɪsən veri ˈkeəfəli tə ðə ˈweðə ˈfɔːkɑːst | bɪˈfɔːr[2] aɪ set ˈaʊt | ˈbetə ˈstɪl | aɪ ʃəl ˈget ɪm[6] tə ˈvɪzɪt ˈmiː[22] |

Comments to transcription

1. Strong form is used because it is a negative contraction and disyllabic.
2. /r/ is pronounced here because it is followed by a word which begins with a vowel sound and there is no pause between them (see Lesson 4). ***
3. When it is a morpheme or a contraction, 's' agrees in voicing with the previous sound, In this case the previous sound is voiced so 's' is pronounced /z/.***
4. /ənd/ and /ən/ are alternative weak forms for *and*.***
5. Weak form because it is the relative pronoun, not the interrogative one.***
6. /h/ can be deleted here because it is not preceded by a potential pause.***
7. Strong form because the verb is not used as an auxiliary here.
8. The regular past tense morpheme is pronounced /ɪd/ or /əd/ when the previous sound is either /t/ or /d/. ***

9. *that* is used in the strong form because here it is a demonstrative.
10. The strong form must be used because it is a negative contraction.
11. Monophthonging (see Lesson 2).
12. Smoothing (see Lesson 2).
13. *long* (/lɒŋ/) is an exception in that, when forming the comparative and superlative forms, /g/ is added after the velar nasal /ŋ/. Other such exceptions are the words *strong* and *young*.
14. The strong form is used because the grammatical word is stranded.
15. The regular past tense morpheme agrees in voicing with the previous sound. In this case the previous sound is voiceless so the morpheme is pronounced /t/. ***
16. Grammatical words which have the vowel /ʊ/ in their citation form, such as *would, should* and *could*, may remain unchanged even if they are unstressed because /ʊ/ is already a weak vowel, but in a faster pronunciation they may be further weakened to /ə/. ***
17. When *just* means *exactly, precisely* or *barely, hardly*, it tends to be stressed and therefore pronounced in strong form. When it means 'a short time before/ago' it is pronounced in the strong form if it is stressed for emphatic reasons (see Lesson 3, note 5).
18. /tu/ is the weak form used when the next word begins with a vowel sound. ***
19. When it is a morpheme or a contraction, 's' agrees in voicing with the previous sound. In this case the previous sound is voiceless so 's' is pronounced /s/. ***
20. The regular past tense morpheme agrees in voicing with the previous sound. In this case the previous sound is voiced so the morpheme is pronounced /d/. ***
21. The morpheme or contraction 's' is pronounced /əz/ or /ɪz/ when it follows a sibilant (/s/, /z/, /ʃ/, /ʒ/, /tʃ/ and /dʒ/). ***
22. The strong form is used because the grammatical word is emphasised and therefore stressed.

Exercise 3.5

| ðə 'geɪmz¹ 'sʌmθɪŋ laɪk 'beɪsbɔːl | 'sʌmθɪŋ laɪk 'fʊtbɔːl | bət 'let mi 'tel ju | ɪts² 'mʌtʃ 'betə ðən 'aɪðə³ | ɪts² 'pleɪd⁴ ɒn ə 'flæt 'pɑːk | wɪtʃ hæz⁵ ə 'skweə mɑːkt⁶ ɪn ðə 'mɪdəl | ənd⁷ ə 'lɪmɪt raʊnd ði⁸ aʊt'saɪd | ðə 'skweər⁹ ɪz weə ðə 'bætmən¹⁰ 'stændz¹ | hi¹¹ hæz⁵ ə 'bæt meɪd əv 'wʊd | ən⁷ 'ʃeɪpt⁶ sʌmθɪŋ laɪk ə 'gɑːdən 'speɪd | ðə 'bætmən¹⁰ kænɒt 'liːv ði⁸ 'eərɪə wɪtʃ ɪz mɑːkt⁶ 'ɒf | ət 'eni taɪm 'djɔːrɪŋ¹² ɪz¹³ 'raʊnd ɒn ðə 'pɪtʃ | ɪf i¹³ 'dʌz¹⁴ | hi¹¹ 'luːzɪz¹⁵ 'wʌn əv ɪz¹³ 'θriː 'laɪvz¹ | ðə 'bɔːlmən¹⁰ stændz¹ 'eniweər⁹ i¹³ 'wɒnts² | 'aʊtsaɪd ðə 'skweə | ənd⁷ 'θrəʊz⁶ ðə 'bɔːl tə ðə 'bætmən¹⁰ | ðə 'bɔːl məst 'lænd wɪðɪn ðə 'skweə | ɪf ɪt 'dʌzənt¹⁶ | ðə 'bætmən¹⁰ gets² ə 'pɔɪnt | 'ʌðəwaɪz i¹³ hæz⁵ tə 'hɪt ðə 'bɔːl bɪfɔːr⁹ ɪt 'baʊnsɪz¹⁵ ə 'sekənd 'taɪm | bət i¹³ 'kɑːnt¹⁷ 'hɪt ɪt bɪfɔːr⁹ ɪt 'baʊnsɪz¹⁵ ət 'ɔːl | ɪf ðə 'bɔːl 'baʊnsɪz¹⁵ ə 'sekənd taɪm ɪn'saɪd ðə 'skweə | ðə 'bætmən¹⁰ 'luːzɪz¹⁵ 'tuː əv ɪz¹³ 'laɪvz¹ | 'lets ə'sjuːm ðət ðə 'bætmən¹⁰ 'hɪts² ðə 'bɔːl | hi¹¹ kən get 'tuː 'pɔɪnts² ɪf ðə 'bɔːl gəʊz¹ 'əʊvə ðə 'lɪmɪt wɪðaʊt 'tʌtʃɪŋ ðə 'graʊnd | ənd⁷ 'wʌn 'pɔɪnt ɪf ɪt 'dʌz¹⁸ tʌtʃ 'daʊn | bəʊθ ðə 'bætmənz¹⁰⁻¹ 'tiːm ənd⁷ ðə 'bɔːlmənz¹⁰⁻¹ 'tiːm hæv⁵ 'fiːldmən¹⁰ ɒn ðə 'pɑːk | ɪg'zæktli haʊ 'meni ɪz dɪ'saɪdɪd¹⁹ baɪ ðə 'bɔːlmən¹⁰ | fər⁹ 'iːtʃ njuː 'raʊnd | 'sʌmtaɪmz¹ ðər⁹ ə 'twenti ɔː 'mɔː | ðə 'bætmənz¹⁰⁻¹ 'tiːm məst 'ɔːlweɪz 'hæv⁵ əz 'meni əz ðə 'bɔːlmənz¹⁰⁻¹ 'tiːm | ɪf ə 'fiːldmən¹⁰ əv ðə 'bɔːlmənz¹⁰⁻¹

'tiːm gets[2] ðə 'bɔːl | hi[11] məst 'traɪ tə 'get ɪt 'bæk tə ðə 'skweər[9] ənd[7] 'drɒp ɪt 'ɪn | hi[11] kən 'duː[5] ðɪs baɪ 'rʌnɪŋ wɪð ðə 'bɔːl | ɔː 'θrəʊɪŋ ɪt tuː[20] əˈnʌðə 'fiːldmən[10] ɒn ɪz[13] 'tiːm | ɪf i[13] səkˈsiːdz[1] | ðə 'bætmən[10] 'dʌzənt[16] skɔːr[9] 'eniθɪŋ | ðə 'bætmənz[10-1] 'tiːmz[1] 'fiːldmən[10] hæv[5] tə 'traɪ tə 'stɒp ðɪs 'hæpənɪŋ | ən[7] tə 'get ðə 'bɔːl əkrɒs ðə 'lɪmɪt | əˈgen baɪ 'θrəʊɪŋ ɪt ɔː baɪ 'rʌnɪŋ wɪð ɪt | 'ðɪs 'feɪz əv ðə 'geɪm ɪz 'mɔː laɪk 'wɔː ðən 'eniθɪŋ | əbaʊt ðiː[8] 'əʊnli 'θɪŋ ðət 'fiːldmən[10] aːnt[17] əˈlaʊd[4] tə 'duː[5] | ɪz tə 'hɪt ən əˈpəʊnənt wɪð ðeə 'fɪsts[2] | 'ɔːlməʊst 'eniθɪŋ 'els 'gəʊz[1] | 'fiːldmən[10] 'niːd tə bi 'rɪəli 'tʌf | 'aɪ kən 'tel ju | 'məʊst əv ðəm ər[9] əbaʊt 'eɪt fiːt 'tɔːl | ənd[7] ju 'wʊdənt[16] wɒnt tə 'miːt 'eni əv ðəm ɪn ən 'æli ɒn ə 'daːk 'naɪt | ə 'fjuː 'jɪəz[1] əˈgəʊ | ðə 'geɪm wəz 'pleɪd[4] wɪðaʊt 'eni prəˈtektɪv 'gɪə | bət ðə wə 'meni 'æksɪdənts[2] | ənd[7] 'ɒftən[21] 'pleəz[1-22] gɒt 'sɪərɪəsli 'ɪndʒəd[4] | 'naədeɪz[22] ɪf ju 'sɔː ðə 'pleəz[1-22] fə ðə 'fɜːst 'taɪm | ju wʊd[23] 'θɪŋk ðeɪ biˈlɒŋd[4] tuː[20] ə kəˈmaːndəʊ 'juːnɪt | ɔː tuː[20] ə 'saəns[22] 'fɪkʃən 'fɪlm | ðeɪ ə 'pædɪd[19] frəm 'hed tə 'təʊ | ðeɪ weə 'kræʃ 'helmɪts[2] | ən[7] prəˈtekʃənz[1] ɒn 'ɔːl ðeə 'dʒɔɪnts[2] ənd[7] 'sɒft 'paːts[2] | 'speʃəli ðə 'fiːldmən[10] | bət ðeɪ 'dəʊnt[17] weə 'glʌvz[1] | 'ðæt[24] ɪz bikɒz ju kən 'get ə 'betə 'grɪp wɪð jɔː 'beə 'hændz[1] | 'bætmən[10] 'duː[18] juːz 'glʌvz[1] | səʊ ðət ðə 'bæt dəz nɒt 'slɪp | 'əʊld 'taɪməz[1] 'θɪŋk ðiːz 'njuː 'aʊtfɪts[2] meɪk ɪt ə 'sɒftə 'geɪm | səʊ ðeɪ ə 'nɒt ɪn 'feɪvər[9] əv 'pleəz[1-22] 'juːzɪŋ ðəm | bət aɪm 'ʃɔː[12] ðə 'pleəz[1-22] aː[14] |

Comments to transcription

1. When it is a morpheme or a contraction, 's' agrees in voicing with the previous sound. In this case the previous sound is voiced so 's' is pronounced /z/.***
2. When it is a morpheme or a contraction, 's' agrees in voicing with the previous sound. In this case the previous sound is voiceless so 's' is pronounced /s/.***
3. /iːðə/ is an alternative pronunciation.
4. The regular past tense morpheme agrees in voicing with the previous sound. In this case the previous sound is voiced so the morpheme is pronounced /d/. ***
5. The strong form is used because the verb is not an auxiliary here.
6. The regular past tense morpheme agrees in voicing with the previous sound. In this case the previous sound is voiceless so the morpheme is pronounced /t/. ***
7. /ənd/ and /ən/ are alternative weak forms for *and*. ***
8. /ði/ is the weak form used when the next word begins with a vowel sound. ***
9. /r/ is pronounced here because the next word begins with a vowel sound and there isn't a pause in between (see Lesson 4).***
10. When the word *man* becomes a suffix, it is unstressed and pronounced /mən/. In such cases the singular and plural forms ('-man' '-men') may both be pronounced /mən/.
11. /h/ cannot be deleted here because it is preceded by a potential pause. ***
12. Monophthonging (see Lesson 2).
13. /h/ may be deleted here because it is not preceded by a potential pause. ***
14. The strong form is used because the grammatical word is stranded.
15. The morpheme or contraction 's' is pronounced /ɪz/ or /əz/ when it follows a sibilant.***
16. The strong form is used because it is a negative contraction and it is also a disyllabic word.
17. The strong form is used because it is a negative contraction.

18. The strong form is used because the grammatical word is emphasised and therefore stressed.

19. The regular past tense morpheme is pronounced /ɪd/ or /əd/ when the previous sound is either /t/ or /d/. ***

20. /tu/ is the weak form used when the next word begins with a vowel sound.***

21. /ɒfən/ is an alternative pronunciation.

22. Smoothing (see Lesson 2).

23. Grammatical words which have the vowel /ʊ/ in their citation form, such as *would*, *should* and *could*, may remain unchanged even if they are unstressed because /ʊ/ is already a weak vowel, but in a faster pronunciation they may be further weakened to /ə/. ***

24. Strong form because *that* is used as a demonstrative.

Exercise 3.6

| aɪ ˈriːsəntli went tə *ˈlʌndən tə ˈmiːt ə ˈfrend aɪ əd[1] ˈnɒt siːn fə ˈsʌm[2] ˈtaɪm | aɪ əˈreɪndʒd[3] tə ˈmiːt ər[4] ət *vɪkˈtɔːrɪə ˈsteɪʃən | ənd[5] ˈtrævəld[3] baɪ ˈtreɪn | ɪnˈsted əv ˈdraɪvɪŋ əz ˈjuːʒuəl | ðə ˈtreɪn wəz ə ˈfjuː mɪnɪts[6] ˈleɪt | djuː tə ˈmeɪntənəns ˈwɜːk ɒn ðə ˈlaɪn | ɪt wəz ˈnɒt ˈkraʊdɪd[7] | əz ɪt wəz tuː ˈleɪt fə kəˈmjuːtəz[8] tə bi ˈjuːzɪŋ ɪt | ən[5] wi hæd[9] ə ˈkʌmfətəbəl ˈdʒɜːni | maɪ ˈfrend wəz ˈweɪtɪŋ fə mi baɪ ðə əˈraɪvəlz[8] ənd[5] diˈpaːtʃəz[8] ˈbɔːd | ənd[5] əz wi əd[1] ˈbəʊθ ˈbrekfəstɪd[7] ˈɜːlɪə ðən ˈjuːʒuəl | wi ˈwent ɪntə ðə ˈsteɪʃən ˈkæfeɪ | ənd[5] ˈhæd[9] ə ˈkʌp əv ˈkɒfi | wen wi əd[1] ˈfɪnɪʃt[10] aə[11] ˈdrɪŋk | wi ˈwent baɪ ˈtjuːb tə *ˈsaʊθ ˈkenzɪŋtən[12] | tə ðə *vɪkˈtɔːrɪə ənd[5] *ˈælbət mjuːˈziːəm | ɪt wəz ˈdɪfɪkəlt tə diˈsaɪd ˈweə tə gəʊ ˈfɜːst | əz ðə wəz ˈsəʊ mʌtʃ əv ˈɪntərəst tə ˈsiː | bət wi ˈfaɪnəli ˈtʃəʊz ən eksiˈbɪʃən ɒn ˈdres | weə wi sɔː ˈkɒstjuːmz[8] frəm ðiˈ[13] ˈeɪtiːnθ ˈsentʃəri ˈɒnwədz | ˈsʌm[14] əv ðəm fə ˈdeɪweə | bət ˈməʊstli fər[4] ˈiːvnɪŋweə | ən[5] ˈɔːl fə ˈwel ɒf ˈpiːpəl | ˈsʌm[14] əv ðə ˈbɔːlgaʊnz wə mægˈnɪfɪsənt | wi ðen ˈlʊkt[10] ət ɪzˈlæmɪk[15] ˈaːt | ˈməʊstli ˈpɒtəri | səˈræmɪks[6] ən[5] ˈkaːpɪts[6] | ðə ˈleɪtə wə ˈveri ˈbjuːtɪfəl | wɪð ˈɪntrɪkət ˈpætənz[8] ənd[5] ˈrɪtʃ ˈkʌləz[8] | ðə wər[4] ˈɔːlsəʊ ˈlʌvli ˈpleɪts[6] ən[5] ˈjuːəz[5] | ən[5] ˈkaːvd[3] ˈwʊd ɪnˈleɪd wɪð ˈaɪvəri | wi ˈɔːlsəʊ ənˈdʒɔɪd[3] ˈlʊkɪŋ ət *ˈjɔːrəˈpiːən[16] mediˈiːvəl ˈkaːvɪŋz[8] ənd[5] ˈsɪlvə ˈkʌps[6] | wi hæd[9] ˈlʌntʃ ɪn ðə kæfɪˈtɪərɪə ɪn ðə mjuːˈziːəm | ən[5] hævɪŋ ədˈmaːd[3-11] səm ˈsteɪnd[3] ˈglaːs ənd[5] ˈtʃɜːtʃ ɪmˈbrɔɪdəriz[8] | wi ˈleft ðə mjuːˈziːəm | ənd[5] ˈwent tə ˈlʊk ət mɔː ˈriːsənt ˈwɜːk ɪn *ˈhærədz[8-17] diˈpaːtmənt ˈstɔː | wi spent ˈməʊst əv aə[11] ˈtaɪm ðeər[18-4] ɪn ðə ˈfuːd hɔːlz[8] | weər[4] aə[11] ˈmaʊðz[8] ˈwɔːtəd[3] | əz wi paːst[10] ˈpaɪlz[8] əv ˈfruːt ənd[5] ˈvedʒətəbəlz[8] | frəm ˈɔːl paːts[6] əv ðə ˈwɜːld | ˈlʌʃəs ˈtʃɒkələts[6] | ˈspaɪst[10] ˈsməʊkt[10] ənd[5] ˈfreʃ ˈmiːts[6] | ðə wər[4] ˈɔːlsəʊ ˈpaɪz[8] | ˈpæteɪz[8] | ˈtʃiːzɪz[19] ˈpɪkəlz[8] ən[5] priˈzɜːvz[8] | maɪ ˈfrend sed ɪt məst bi ˈpɒsɪbəl tə baɪ ˈeniθɪŋ ju ˈwɪʃt[10] fɔː[20] | əz ˈlɒŋ əz ju hæd[9] ɪnʌf ˈmʌni | ˈɔːl tuː ˈsuːn ɪt wəz ˈtaɪm tə ˈkætʃ maɪ treɪn ˈhəʊm | ˈðɪs taɪm ɪt wəz ˈfɪld[3] wɪð kəˈmjuːtəz[8] | ən[5] ˈsʌm[21] piːpəl kʊdənt ˈfaɪnd ə ˈsiːt | ənd[5] ˈhæd[9] tə ˈstænd fər[4] ə ˈlɒŋ ˈtaɪm | ʌntɪl ˈʌðəz[8] ˈriːtʃt[10] ðeə destɪˈneɪʃən ən[5] gɒt ˈaʊt | ðiˈ[13] ˈɜːli ˈpaːt əv ðə ˈdʒɜːni wəz ˈθruː ðə *ˈlʌndən ˈsʌbɜːbz[8] | ˈwen wi wə ˈweɪtɪŋ fə ðə ˈsɪgnəlz[8] tə ˈtʃeɪndʒ ɪn aə[11] ˈfeɪvə nɪə *ˈklæpəm ˈdʒʌŋkʃən | aɪ ˈsɔː ə ˈfɒks | ˈwɔːkɪŋ əˈlɒŋ biˈsaɪd ðə ˈtræk | weə ðə wəz ə ˈgraːsi ˈspeɪs biˈtwiːn ðə ˈreɪlz[8] | hl[22] ˈsliːmd[3] kwaɪt ʌŋkənˈsɜːnd[3] əbaʊt ðə ˈtreɪn | hi[22] ˈkɔɪm tu[23] ə ˈpleɪɜ weə ðə wəz ə ˈskætər[4] əv ˈfeðəz[8] | ən[5] aɪ ˈwʌndəd[3] ɪf iˈ[1] əd[1] ˈkɔːt ə ˈpɪdʒən ðə ˈpriːvɪəs

ˈiːvnɪŋ | ən[5] əd[1] kʌm ˈbæk tə ˈsiː ɪf i[1] kəd[24] kætʃ əˈnʌðə fər[4] ɪz[1] ˈdɪnə | ðə wəz ˈnəu mɔːr[4] ɪkˈsaɪtmənt[25] ɑːftə ˈðæt[26] | ðəu ði[13] ɪmˈbæŋkmənts[6] wə lukɪŋ ˈbjuːtifəl | wɪð ˈtʃeri blɒsəm ən[5] ˈlaɪlək ɪn ðə ˈgɑːdənz[8] | ˈfreʃ griːn ˈfəuliɪdʒ ənd[5] ˈwaɪld ˈflɑəz[8–11] | aɪ hæd[9] ə ˈveri ɪnˈdʒɔɪəbəl ˈdeɪ | ðəu aɪ felt ˈplezəntli ˈtaəd[3–11] ət ði[13] ˈend əv ɪt |

Comments to transcription

1. /h/ may be deleted here because it is not preceded by a potential pause. ***
2. When it means 'a considerable amount of' the strong form /sʌm/ tends to be used (see Lesson 3, note 5).
3. The regular past tense morpheme agrees in voicing with the previous sound. In this case the previous sound is voiced so the morpheme is pronounced /d/. ***
4. /r/ is pronounced here because the next word begins with a vowel sound and there is no pause between the two words (see Lesson 4). ***
5. /ənd/ and /ən/ are alternative weak forms for *and*. ***
6. When it is a morpheme or a contraction, 's' agrees in voicing with the previous sound. In this case the previous sound is voiceless so 's' is pronounced /s/. ***
7. The regular past tense morpheme is pronounced /ɪd/ or /əd/ when the previous sound is either /t/ or /d/. ***
8. When it is a morpheme or a contraction, 's' agrees in voicing with the previous sound. In this case the previous sound is voiced so 's' is pronounced /z/. ***
9. The strong form is used because the verb is not an auxiliary here.
10. The regular past tense morpheme agrees in voicing with the previous sound. In this case the previous sound is voiceless so the morpheme is pronounced /t/. ***
11. Smoothing (see Lesson 2).
12. South Kensington is an area of London where there are many important museums.
13. /ði/ is the weak form used when the next word begins with a vowel sound. ***
14. *some* is pronounced in strong form when it is used as a pronoun (see Lesson 3, note 5).
15. The first syllable of this word may also be pronounced /ɪs/ and the remainder may also be pronounced /lɑːmɪk/.
16. Monophthonging (see Lesson 2).
17. Harrod's is a famous department store in London.
18. Strong form because *there* is used as a location adverb here.
19. The morpheme or contraction 's' is pronounced /ɪz/ or /əz/ when it follows a sibilant. ***
20. The strong form is used because the grammatical word is stranded.
21. *some* tends to be used in strong form when it means 'a portion of the whole' (see Lesson 3, note 5).
22. /h/ cannot be deleted here because it is preceded by a potential pause. ***
23. /tu/ is the weak form used when the next word begins with a vowel sound. ***
24. Grammatical words which have the vowel /ʊ/ in their citation form, such as *would*, *should* and *could*, may remain unchanged even if they are unstressed because /ʊ/ is already a weak vowel, but in a faster pronunciation they may be further weakened to /ə/. ***
25. The first syllable of this word may be pronounced /ɪk/ or /ək/.
26. *that* is used in the strong form here because it is a demonstrative.

Exercise 3.7

| maɪ 'frend ən[1] 'aɪ | 'bəʊθ hæv[2] 'veri enə'dʒetɪk 'dɒgz[3] | səʊ 'fɜːst θɪŋ ɪn ðə 'mɔːnɪŋ | wi 'laɪk tə 'teɪk ðəm fər[4] ə 'wɔːk | tə 'bɜːn ʌp ə lɪtəl 'bɪt əv ðeər[4] 'enədʒi | ən[1] 'kiːp 'fɪt əə'selvz[5–3] ət ðə 'seɪm 'taɪm | wi ə 'lʌki tə hæv[2] ə 'pɑːk nɪə'baɪ | 'juːʒuəli 'nəʊn əz ðə *'hɪl | ɪt ɪz 'rɪəli 'tuː 'hɪlz[3] | 'wʌn 'əʊpən ənd[1] 'rɒki | wɪð 'waɪld pleɪsɪz[6] 'kʌvəd[7] ɪn 'brækən ən[1] 'gɔːs | ðər[4] ɪz ə 'sɪstəm əv 'pɑːθs[8] | ðət əv[9] biːn 'sɜːfɪst[10] wɪð 'tɑːmæk | səʊ ðət wi kən 'kiːp əə[5] 'ʃuːz[3] 'draɪ | 'iːvən ɒn 'veri 'reɪni 'deɪz[3] | wi 'dəʊnt[11] juːʒuəli 'siː mʌtʃ 'waɪldlaɪf | 'bɜːdz[3] | 'skwɪrəlz[3] ənd[1] ə 'ræbɪt ɔː 'tuː | bət aɪm 'təʊld ðət ət ðə 'les dɪ'stɜːbd[7] 'taɪmz[3] əv 'ɜːli 'mɔːnɪŋ | 'leɪt 'iːvnɪŋ ən[1] 'naɪt taɪm | 'bædʒəz[3] | 'fɒksɪz[6] | 'hedʒhɒgz[3] | 'lɪzədz[3] | 'ɔːl ɪn'dʒɔɪ ðə 'hɪl | 'ædɪŋ tə ðə 'fʌn fə ðə 'dɒgz[3] | bɪkɒz ðər[4] ər[4] 'ɪntərəstɪŋ 'sents[8] tə pɪk 'ʌp | ənd[1] 'treɪlz[3] tə 'fɒləʊ | ðə 'sekənd 'hɪl hæz[2] ə 'kɒnɪfə 'wʊd | wɪð ə 'sɒft 'flɔːr[4] əv 'paɪn 'niːdəlz[3] | ən[1] ə dɪ'sɪdjuəs 'wʊd | weə 'tʃɪldrən dɪ'laɪt tə 'sɜːtʃ fə 'hɔːs 'tʃesnʌts[8] | wɪtʃ ə 'nəʊn əz 'kɒŋkəz[3] | ɪn ðɪ[12⁵]'ɔːtəm | fə ðə 'rest əv əs | ðər[4] ə 'bjuːtɪfəl 'vjuːz[3] tu[13] ɪn'dʒɔɪ | tə ðə 'saʊθ ənd[1] 'west | ju kən siː ðə *'dʌblɪn 'maʊntənz[3] | 'iːtʃ 'siːzən hæz[2] ɪts dɪ'laɪts[8] | ðə 'griːn əv 'sprɪŋ | wɪð ðə 'waɪt 'blækθɔːn 'blɒsəm | ɪz 'fɒləʊd[7] baɪ ðə 'hɔːθɔːn ənd[1] 'ɔːldə 'blɒsəm | 'hevi wɪð 'sent wɪtʃ ə'trækts[8] ðə 'biːz[3] | ðə 'gɔːs 'bluːmz[3] ɪn 'spæzəmz[3] frəm 'sprɪŋ 'ɒn | bət 'pʊts[8] ɒn ɪts 'rɪəl 'ʃəʊ əv 'gəʊld ɪn 'leɪt 'sʌmə | tə 'kɒmplɪmənt ðə 'pɜːpəl əv ðə 'heðə | ənd[1] 'grædjuəli ðə 'brækən 'tɜːnz[3] ɪts 'lʌvli 'red 'braʊn 'kʌlə | 'iːvən ɪn 'wɪntə ðə 'maʊntənz[3] lʊk 'lʌvli | 'sʌmtaɪmz[3] 'mɪsti | 'ʌðə 'taɪmz[3] 'paʊdəd[7] wɪð 'snəʊfɔːlz[3] ðət wi 'mɪs | əz wi ə 'nɪə ðə 'siː | ðə 'snəʊ ɪz 'nɒt ɒfən[14] 'diːp | bət ɪt 'aʊtlaɪnz[3] ðə 'fɑːmz[3] | 'hedʒɪz[6] ənd[1] 'fiːldz[3] | ən[1] 'ɔːlsəʊ ðə 'rɒki 'aʊtkrɒps[8] ən[1] 'siːmz[3] | ɪf wi 'tɜːn tə feɪs 'iːst | wi kən 'siː ðə 'siː | 'ɔːlweɪz[15] wɪð ə 'leɪs əv 'waɪt 'fəʊm ɒn ðə 'dɪstənt 'biːtʃ | ɪn 'faɪn 'weðə | ðər[4] ə 'lɪtəl 'fɪʃɪŋ 'bəʊts[8] | ən[1] 'men 'hɔːlɪŋ ʌp 'lɒbstər[4] ən[1] 'kræb 'pɒts[8] | 'tæŋkəz[3] ənd[1] 'kɑːgəʊ ʃɪps[8] seɪl 'ʌp tə 'dɒk | ʌp'rɪvər[4] ɪn *'dʌblɪn 'pɔːt | ənd[1] ðə 'feri frəm *'weɪlz kən bi 'siːn | 'meɪkɪŋ fə 'wʌn əv ðə 'tuː 'hɑːbəz[3] nɪə'baɪ | bɪ'ləʊ əs | ðər[4] ə 'bjuːtɪfəl 'haʊzɪz[16] 'skɜːtɪŋ ðə 'kəʊstlaɪn | 'məʊst əv ðəm ə 'kwaɪt 'əʊld | bət ðeɪ lʊk 'splendɪd | sɪns ðeɪ bɪ'lɒŋ tə 'piːpəl hu ə 'veri wel 'ɒf | ə 'fjuː 'feɪməs 'ɑːtɪsts[8] ə'mʌŋst ðəm | ənd[1] hu kən ə'fɔːd tə 'kiːp ðəm ɪn 'eksələnt kən'dɪʃən | tə ðə 'nɔːθ | ju kən 'siː ðə 'sɪti | wɪð 'ɜːli 'sʌnʃaɪn 'glɪntɪŋ ɒn 'kɑːz[3] | əz 'piːpəl meɪk ðeə 'weɪ tə 'wɜːk | ə'krɒs ðə 'beɪ ɪz ðə 'nɔːθsaɪd ɪ'kwɪvələnt tu[13] əə[5] 'hɪl | ɪts[8] ə 'feɪvərɪt 'pleɪs tə 'gəʊ ɒn 'aʊtɪŋz[3] | ɪf ɪts[8] nɒt 'reɪnɪŋ | wi 'laɪk tə 'teɪk ə 'pɪknɪk 'bɑːskɪt 'wɪð əs | ənd[1] 'spend ðɪ[12] ɑːftə'nuːn ðeə[17] | 'sɪpɪŋ 'tiː ɔː 'kɒfi | ənd[1] 'iːtɪŋ ə fjuː 'sændwɪdʒɪz[6] ənd[1] 'keɪks[8] | waɪlst wi 'wɒtʃ ðə 'gʌlz[3] 'dɪpɪŋ ɪntə ðə 'siː | ðə 'treɪn spiːdz[3] baɪ bɪ'ləʊ əs | təwɔːdz ðə 'sɪti ən[1] ðɪ[12] 'ʌðə saɪd əv ðə 'beɪ | ət 'lɑːst aɪ 'tɜːn daʊn'hɪl | ɪn'vɪgəreɪtɪd[18] bət ri'lʌktənt tə 'liːv | ɔːlðəʊ aɪm lʊkɪŋ 'fɔːwəd tə 'tiː ən[1] 'təʊst | bɪfɔː 'stɑːtɪŋ ɒn 'haʊswɜːk ənd[1] 'ʃɒpɪŋ |

Comments to transcription

1. /ənd/ and /ən/ are alternative weak forms for *and*. ***
2. The strong form is used because the verb is not an auxiliary here.
3. When it is a morpheme or a contraction, 's' agrees in voicing with the previous sound. In this case the previous sound is voiced so 's' is pronounced /z/. ***

4. /r/ is pronounced here because it is immediately followed by a word which begins with a vowel sound (see Lesson 4).***

5. Smoothing (see Lesson 2).

6. The morpheme or contraction 's' is pronounced /ɪz/ or /əz/ when it follows a sibilant.***

7. The regular past tense morpheme agrees in voicing with the previous sound. In this case the previous sound is voiced so the morpheme is pronounced /d/. ***

8. When it is a morpheme or a contraction, 's' agrees in voicing with the previous sound. In this case the previous sound is voiceless so 's' is pronounced /s/.***

9. /h/ may be deleted here because it is not preceded by a potential pause. ***

10. The regular past tense morpheme agrees in voicing with the previous sound. In this case the previous sound is voiceless so the morpheme is pronounced /t/. ***

11. The strong form is used because it is a negative contraction.

12. /ði/ is the weak form used when the next word begins with a vowel sound. ***

13. /tu/ is the weak form used when the next word begins with a vowel sound.***

14. /ɒftən/ is an alternative pronunciation.

15. /ɔ:lwɪz/ is an alternative pronunciation.

16. Irregular plural (see Lesson 2).

17. Strong form because *there* is used as a location adverb.

18. The regular past tense morpheme is pronounced /ɪd/ or /əd/ when the previous sound is either /t/ or /d/. ***

Exercise 3.8

| maɪ 'fɑ:ðə wəz ə 'seɪlər[1] ənd[2] aɪ wəz bɔ:n 'fɑ: frəm 'həʊm | ɪn ðə 'saʊθ | sɪns maɪ 'fɑ:ðə hæd[3] tə 'trævəl 'ɒfən[4] tə 'ðæt[5] pɑ:t əv ðə 'kʌntri | maɪ 'fæmɪli went tə 'lɪv ðeə[6] | ən[2] 'ðæt[5] wəz 'weər[1] aɪ wəz 'bɔ:n | wen aɪ wəz dʒəst 'sɪks mʌnθs[7] 'əʊld | wi 'ɔ:l keɪm bæk 'nɔ:θ | tə ðə 'taʊn weə maɪ 'peərənts[7] hæd[3] ðeə 'haʊs | 'ðeər[1-6] aɪ gru: 'ʌp | ən[2] hæd[3] ə 'veri 'hæpi 'tʃaɪldhʊd | 'laɪf wəz 'sɪmpəl ənd[2] 'seɪf | aɪ 'jʊst[8] tə mi:t 'ʌðə 'tʃɪldrən ɪn ðə 'stri:t | tə 'pleɪ ɑ:ftə 'sku:l | aɪ rɪ'membə wʌn ᵊdeɪ wen maɪ 'brʌðə gɒt 'veri 'æŋgri | bɪ'kɒz aɪ əd[9] 'lɒst ɪn ə 'geɪm əv 'mɑ:bəlz[10] | ənd[2] i[9] 'hæd[3] tə 'gəʊ ən[2] 'wɪn ðəm ɔ:l 'bæk | 'θɪŋz[10] kærɪd[11] 'ɒn 'pi:sfəli ʌntɪl ðə 'wɔ: | aɪ wəz 'əʊnli 'sevən wen ɑə[12] 'taʊn wəz 'bɒmd[11] | ənd[2] wi wə 'left wɪð ðə 'kləʊðz[10] wi wə 'stændɪŋ ɪn | 'nʌθɪŋ 'els | aɪ wəz 'veri ʌp'set əbaʊt 'lu:zɪŋ ə 'veri prɪti 'dɒl aɪ 'hæd[3] | ənd[2] ə 'taɪtən 'dres wɪð 'mætʃɪŋ velvɪt 'dʒækɪt | maɪ 'mʌðər[1] əd[9] hæd[3] ðəm 'meɪd | fə mi tə 'weər[1] ɑ:ftə maɪ 'fɜ:st kə'mju:nɪən | 'ðæt[5] wəz ðə 'naɪnti:nθ əv 'eɪprəl ət ðə 'kɒnvənt nɪə'baɪ | ɪt wəz ə 'bju:tɪfəl 'deɪ | ən[2] 'veri 'speʃəl | bɪkɒz ɪt 'meɪd mi 'fi:l veri ɪm'pɔ:tənt | 'ɑ:ftə ðə 'wɔ: wi 'went tə 'lɪv ɪn ə ju:nɪ'vɜ:sɪti 'taʊn ɪn ðə 'west | waɪlst maɪ 'brʌðə stʌdɪd[11] 'lɔ: | ðeɪ wə 'rɪəli hɑ:d 'taɪmz[10] | wi 'ɔ:l hæd[3] tə meɪk 'du:[3] wɪð wɒt'evə wəz ə'veɪləbəl | aɪ rɪ'membə haʊ 'kəʊld ɪt wɒz[13] ɪn ðə 'wɪntə | maɪ 'mʌðə meɪd mi ə 'kəʊt aʊt əv ə 'blæŋkɪt | ʃi 'daɪd[11] ɪt 'blu: | bət ðə 'straɪps[7] gəʊɪŋ ə'krɒs stɪl ʃəʊd[11] | wen 'fɑ:ðə keɪm tə 'vɪzɪt | hi[14] 'brɔ:t əs 'wʌndəfəl 'θɪŋz[10] | ðət wə 'nɒt tə bi faʊnd 'eniweər[1] ət 'həʊm | 'sɔ:ltɪd[15] 'bʌtə | 'tɪnd[11] 'mi:t frəm *ɑ:dʒən'ti:nə | 'tʃɒkələt ən[2] 'kɒfi | ɪt 'meɪd əs fi:l 'prɪvɪlɪdʒd[11] | aɪl 'nevə fə'get haʊ ʌp'set aɪ wɒz[13] | wen aɪ faʊnd 'aʊt əbaʊt 'fɑ:ðə 'krɪsməs | ɪt 'hæpənd[11] wʌn ɑ:ftə'nu:n | maɪ 'mʌðər[1] ən[2] 'brʌðə

went aʊt ˈʃɒpɪŋ | ənd[2] tʊk ə ˈlɒŋ taɪm tə kʌm ˈbæk | wen ðeɪ əˈraɪvd[11] | aɪ ˈhɜːd ðə ˈkriːkɪŋ frəm ðə ˈlɪd əv ə ˈbɪg wɪkə ˈtrʌŋk wi ˈhæd[3] ɪn ə ˈkʌbəd | aɪ ˈweɪtɪd[15] ʌntɪl ðeɪ wɜːnt[16] ˈlʊkɪŋ | ən[2] ˈðen went veri ˈkeəfəli tə ðə ˈkʌbəd | ˈlɪftɪd[15] ðə ˈlɪd ə lɪtəl ˈbɪt | ənd[2] ˈðeə[6] ðeɪ ˈwɜː[13] | ðə ˈtɔɪz[10] | aɪ ˈθɔːt ɪf aɪ ˈget ðiːz ˈtɔɪz[10] əz ˈprezənts[7] təˈmɒrəʊ | aɪl ˈnəʊ hu ˈfɑːðə ˈkrɪsməs ɪz | ən[2] ˈsəʊ ɪt ˈwɒz[13] | ðə ˈfɒləʊɪŋ ˈmɔːnɪŋ | aɪ ˈəʊpənd[11] ðə ˈprezənts[7] aɪ əd[9] ˈsiːn ðə ˈdeɪ biˈfɔː | wen maɪ ˈbrʌðə ˈfɪnɪʃt[17] ɪz[9] ˈstʌdiz[10] | wi ˈmuːvd[11] tu[18] ə ˈsɪti nɒt ˈfɑː frəm aər[12] ˈəʊld ˈhəʊm | maɪ ˈpeərənts[7] ˈwɒntɪd[15] tə gəʊ ˈbæk tə ðeə ˈpɑːt əv ðə ˈkʌntri | bət ˈsɪns ðeɪ hæd[3] tə ˈstɑːt frəm ˈskrætʃ | ðeɪ ˈtʃəʊz ə ˈsɪti | səʊ ðət wi hæd[3] ˈmɔːr[1] ɒpəˈtjuːnɪtiz[10] tə ˈstʌdi ənd[2] faɪnd ˈdʒɒbz[10] | aɪ ˈwent tə ˈsekəndəri ˈskuːl | ən[2] ðen ˈtreɪnd[11] tə bi ə ˈtiːtʃə | aɪ ˈwɜːkt[17] ət ə ˈpraɪməri ˈskuːl fə ˈnaɪn ˈjɪəz[10] | ˈtiːtʃɪŋ smɔːl ˈtʃɪldrən haʊ tə ˈriːd ən[2] ˈraɪt | ɪt əˈmjuːzɪz[19] mi ˈnaʊədeɪz[12] | wen aɪ ˈfaɪnd ðət sʌm[20] əv ˈðəʊz jʌŋ ˈpjuːpəlz[10] əv ˈmaɪn | həv[14] biˈkʌm ɪmˈpɔːtənt ˈpiːpəl | ɔː ˈhaɪli ˈkwɒlɪfaɪd[11] prəˈfeʃənəlz[10] | ɪt ˈɔːlsəʊ ˈfɪlz[10] mi wɪð ˈpraɪd | ˈiːvən ɪf ˈmaɪ kɒntrɪˈbjuːʃən tə ðeə kəˈrɪəz[10] | wəz ˈəʊnli ə ˈmaɪnə wʌn | laɪk ˈevriwʌn aɪ əv[9] hæd[3] ˈgʊd ənd[2] ˈbæd taɪmz[10] ɪn maɪ ˈlaɪf | maɪ ˈmærɪdʒ əz[9] biːn ə ˈveri ˈhæpi wʌn | ən[2] wi hæd[3] ˈθri: ˈgreɪt ˈtʃɪldrən | ˈmeni ˈjɪəz[10] əv[9] gɒn ˈbaɪ | bət aɪ fiːl ˈfɔːtʃənət | bikɒz aɪ ˈhæv[3] ə ˈfæmɪli hu ˈlʌvz[10] mi | ən[2] teɪks[7] ˈkeər[1] əv mi | ən[2] ˈtuː ˈgrænddɔːtəz[10] | aɪ ˈlʌv spendɪŋ ˈtaɪm wɪð ðəm | ənd[2] ˈwɒtʃɪŋ ðəm grəʊ ˈʌp | ˈlɑːst ˈkrɪsməs | aɪ ˈsɔː ðə ˈwʌndər[1] ɪn ðeər[1] ˈaɪz[10] | wen ðeɪ ˈkeɪm ɪntə ðə ˈruːm ənd[2] ˈsɔː ðeə ˈprezənts[7] | ðeə ˈflʌʃt[17] ˈfeɪsɪz[19] ənd[2] ˈɪnəsəns | brɔːt ə ˈlɒt əv ˈmeməriz[10] ˈbæk | aɪ ˈhəʊp ðeɪ dəʊnt[16] ˈhɪə ðə ˈsaʊnd əv ə ˈkriːkɪŋ ˈlɪd fər[1] ə ˈlɒŋ taɪm ˈjet |

Comments to transcription

1. /r/ is pronounced here because the next word begins with a vowel sound and there is no pause in between (see Lesson 4).***
2. /ənd/ and /ən/ are alternative weak forms for *and*. ***
3. The strong form is used because the verb is not an auxiliary here.
4. /ɒftən/ is an alternative pronunciation.
5. *that* is in strong form here because it is used as a demonstrative.
6. *there* is used in the strong form because it functions as a location adverb.
7. When it is a morpheme or a contraction, 's' agrees in voicing with the previous sound. In this case the previous sound is voiceless so 's' is pronounced /s/.***
8. *used* is pronounced /juːzd/ when it means *employed* or *utilised* but is pronounced /juːst/ when it means *accustomed*.
9. /h/ may be deleted here because it is not preceded by a potential pause. ***
10. When it is a morpheme or a contraction, 's' agrees in voicing with the previous sound. In this case the previous sound is voiced so 's' is pronounced /z/.***
11. The regular past tense morpheme agrees in voicing with the previous sound. In this case the previous sound is voiced so the morpheme is pronounced /d/. ***
12. Smoothing (see Lesson 2).
13. The strong form is used because the grammatical word is stranded.
14. /h/ cannot be deleted here because it is preceded by a potential pause. ***
15. The regular past tense morpheme is pronounced /ɪd/ or /əd/ when the previous sound is either /t/ or /d/. ***
16. The strong form is used because it is a negative contraction.

17. The regular past tense morpheme agrees in voicing with the previous sound. In this case the previous sound is voiceless so the morpheme is pronounced /t/. ***
18. /tu/ is the weak form used when the next word begins with a vowel sound.***
19. The morpheme or contraction 's' is pronounced /ɪz/ or /əz/ when it follows a sibilant.***
20. *some* is used in strong form when it is a pronoun (see Lesson 3 note 5).

Exercise 3.9

| ðə ˈjʌŋ ˈwumən ˈwɔːkt[1] daʊn ði ˈeɪtiːnθ ˈsentʃəri *ˈlʌndən ˈhaɪ striːt | wɪð hə[2] ˈlɒŋ ˈskɜːt ˈbɪləʊɪŋ ɪn ðə ˈwɪnd | ənd[3] ðə ˈhem ˈtæpɪŋ ət hər[2-4] ˈæŋkəlz[5] | ʃi wəz ˈlɒst ɪn ˈθɔːt | ənd[3] wəz ˈteɪkən əˈbæk wen hə[2] ˈdeɪdriːmɪŋ wəz dɪˈstɜːbd[6] baɪ ə jʌŋ ˈdʒentəlmən[7] | gʊd ˈmɔːnɪŋ leɪdi *ˈhelən sed ðə ˈmæn | ðə ˈwumən wəz kənˈfjuːzd[6] | hævɪŋ ˈəʊnli ˈriːsəntli əˈraɪvd[6] | ʃi njuː ˈnəʊwʌn ɪn ðə ˈkæpɪtəl | ən[3] ˈdɪd nɒt ˈɑːnsə tə ðə ˈneɪm əv *ˈhelən | bət *ˈdʒeɪn | ˈrekəgnaɪzɪŋ ðə mɪˈsteɪk | ðə ˈmæn əˈpɒlədʒaɪzd[6] fər[4] ɪz[8] ˈerə | ʃi wəz əˈbaʊt tə ˈtɜːn əˈweɪ frəm ðə jʌŋ ˈmæn | hu wəz ɪkˈstriːmli wel ˈdrest[1] | ən[3] ˈsiːmd[6] tə bi ˈveri wel ˈɒf | wen i[8] ˈkɒməntɪd[9] ɒn ðə ˈkʌlər[4] əv hər[2-4] ˈaɪz[5] | ən[3] ðə ˈbjuːti əv hər[2-4] ɪkˈspreʃən | ðə kɒnvəˈseɪʃən kənˈtɪnjuːd[6] | ʌntɪl ɪˈventʃuəli ðə ˈmæn | hu ɪntrəˈdjuːst[1] ɪmself[8] əz ˈlɔːd *ˈtʃɑːlz | ɪnˈsɪstɪd[9] ðət ʃi ˈdʒɔɪn ɪm[8] fə ˈtiː ət ɪz[8] əˈpɑːtmənt nɪəˈbaɪ | ðɪ[10] əˈpɑːtmənt | ɔːlðəʊ ˈmɒdəst | wəz ˈfɑː mɔː ˈglæmərəs ðən ˈeniθɪŋ ʃi əd[8] ˈevə siːn bɪˈfɔː | ðə ˈmeɪd sɜːvd[6] ðəm ˈtiː | ənd[3] ˈkjuːkʌmbə ˈsændwɪdʒəz[11] | ənd[3] ðə ˈlɔːd dɪˈskʌst[1] ɪz[8] ˈkɒntækts[12] | ənd[3] ɪz[8] ˈɪmɪnənt ˈtrɪp tə ðə ˈkɒntɪnənt | sɪns ʃi əd[8] ˈtəʊld ɪm[8] ðət ʃi wəz ˈfluənt ɪn *ˈfrentʃ | *ˈdʒɜːmən ənd *ˈspænɪʃ | hi[13] səˈdʒestɪd[9] ðət ʃi əˈkʌmpəni ɪm[8] ɒn ɪz[8] ˈdʒɜːni ðə ˈveri nekst ˈwiːk | *ˈdʒeɪn wəz ət fɜːst ˈspiːtʃləs | bət wɪð ˈəʊnli ə ˈlɪtəl mɔː pəˈsweɪʒən | ʃi əˈgriːd[6] | ðə ˈlɔːd felt ðət ɪt wəz ˈnesəsəri fə ðə ˈwumən tuː[14] əbˈteɪn ə njuː ˈwɔːdrəʊb | səʊ ðət ʃi wʊd[15] hæv[16] mɔːr[4] ˈædɪkwət ˈkləʊðz[5] fə ðə ˈweðər[4] ənd[3] ˈkʌmpəni ðət ðeɪ wəd[15] ˈmiːt | fə ˈðɪs ðə ˈlɔːd ˈgeɪv ər[4-8] ə ˈlɪst əv ˈʃɒps[12] ɒn *ˈbɒnd striːt | weə ˈhiː[17] ˈhæd[16] ən əˈkaʊnt | ðə ˈnekst ˈkwestʃən wəz ˈðæt[18] əv ˈdʒuəlri[19] | lɔːd *ˈtʃɑːlz wəz ˈmiːtɪŋ ə ˈdʒuələ[19] ˈfrend əv ɪz[20] | ˈleɪtə ðæt[18] ˈdeɪ | ən[3] kʊd[15] ˈbaɪ ˈwɒtʃɪz[11] | ˈɪərɪŋz[5] ənd[3] ˈrɪŋz[5] | ðət wʊd[15] bi ˈsuːtəbəl[21] fə ðə ˈtrɪp | ðə ˈprɒbləm wɒz[22] | ðət ðə ˈlɔːd maɪt nɒt ˈget ðə kəˈrekt ˈsaɪz | ðen i[8] əˈpɪəd[6] tə ˈstʌmbəl əkrɒs ə səˈluːʃən[23] | *ˈdʒeɪn wəz ˈweərɪŋ ə səˈlekʃən əv ˈdʒuəlz[5-19] | pəˈhæps ɪf i[8] kəd[15] ˈbɒrəʊ ðəm fə ðə ˈdeɪ | hi[13] kəd[15] ˈʃəʊ ðəm tə ðə ˈdʒuələ[19] | hu wʊd[15] ˈðen bi ˈeɪbəl tuː[14] əbˈteɪn ə ˈpɜːfɪkt ˈmætʃ | rɪˈlʌktəntli | *ˈdʒeɪn əˈgriːd[6] | hævɪŋ ɪˈstæblɪʃt[1] ðət ʃi wəz tə rɪˈtɜːn ðə ˈfɒləʊɪŋ ˈdeɪ | ən[3] hæv[15] ðɪ[10] ˈaɪtəmz[5] rɪˈtɜːnd[6] tuː[14] ə[8] | ðə ˈnekst deɪ *ˈdʒeɪn went ˈbæk tə ðə ˈflæt | ən[3] wəz əˈlɑːmd[6] tə dɪˈskʌvə ðə ˈpleɪs kəmˈpliːtli ˈempti | wɪð ˈtaɪm ʃi ˈrɪəlaɪzd[6] ðət ðə ˈmæn ʃi əd[8] ˈtrʌstɪd[9] wəz ə ˈfrɔːd | ən[3] ˈvaʊd[6] ðət ʃi wəd[15] hæv[16] ˈdʒʌstɪs ˈsɜːvd[6] əˈpɒn ɪm[8] | fə ˈwiːks[12] ʃi ˈwɔːkt[1] ðə ˈstriːts[12] əv *ˈlʌndən | ˈlʊkɪŋ fə lɔːd *ˈtʃɑːlz| ðen ˈwʌn deɪ ʃi ˈsɔː ɪm[8] | ʃi əˈprəʊtʃt[1] ɪm[8] daɪˈrektli[24] ənd[3] dɪˈmɑːndɪd[9] ðət i[8] rɪˈtɜːn wɒt wəz ˈhɜːz[25] | ˈteɪkən əˈbæk | ðə mæn ˈblʌndəd[6] | ˈkleɪmɪŋ ðət i[8] ˈdɪdənt nəʊ ˈhu ðə wumən ˈwɒz[22] | hi[13] kənˈtɪnjuːd[6] tə ˈmeɪk ɪz[8] ˈweɪ daʊn ðə ˈstriːt | *ˈdʒeɪn ˈfɒləʊd[6] ɪm[8] | ʌntɪl ʃi ˈsɔː ə pəˈliːsmən[7] | ðen ʃi ɪnˈsɪstɪd[9] ðət ðə ˈmæn bi əˈrestɪd[9] fə ðə ˈθeft əv hə[2] ˈdʒuəlri[19] |

Comments to transcription

1. The regular past tense morpheme agrees in voicing with the previous sound. In this case the previous sound is voiceless so the morpheme is pronounced /t/. ***
2. /h/ is not deleted when *her* is a possessive adjective (see Lesson 3, note 5).
3. /ənd/ and /ən/ are alternative weak forms for *and.* ***
4. /r/ is pronounced here because the next word begins with a vowel sound (see Lesson 4). ***
5. When it is a morpheme or a contraction, 's' agrees in voicing with the previous sound. In this case the previous sound is voiced so 's' is pronounced /z/.***
6. The regular past tense morpheme agrees in voicing with the previous sound. In this case the previous sound is voiced so the morpheme is pronounced /d/. ***
7. When the word 'man' becomes a suffix, it is unstressed and pronounced /mən/. In such cases the singular and plural forms ('-man' '-men') may both be pronounced the same, i.e., /mən/.
8. /h/ may be deleted here because it is not preceded by a potential pause. ***
9. The regular past tense morpheme is pronounced /ɪd/ or /əd/ when the previous sound is either /t/ or /d/. ***
10. /ði/ is the weak form used when the next word begins with a vowel sound. ***
11. The morpheme or contraction 's' is pronounced /ɪz/ or /əz/ when it follows a sibilant.***
12. When it is a morpheme or a contraction, 's' agrees in voicing with the previous sound. In this case the previous sound is voiceless so 's' is pronounced /s/.***
13. /h/ cannot be deleted here because it is preceded by a potential pause. ***
14. /tu/ is the weak form used when the next word begins with a vowel sound.***
15. Grammatical words which have the vowel /ʊ/ in their citation form, such as *would, should* and *could*, may remain unchanged even if they are unstressed because /ʊ/ is already a weak vowel, but they may be further weakened to /ə/.***
16. The strong form is used because the verb is not an auxiliary here.
17. The strong form is used because the grammatical word is emphasised.
18. *that* is used in the strong form here because it is a demonstrative.
19. /dʒuːəl/ and /dʒuːl/ are alternative pronunciations for the word *jewel* and its derivatives.
20. This construction (noun phrase + of + personal pronoun) is exceptional in that /h/ may be deleted, although *his* is a personal pronoun. Note, however, that other personal pronouns in the same construction may not be weakened, for instance 'A friend of hers' must be pronounced /hɜːz/.
21. /sjuːtəbəl/ is an alternative pronunciation.
22. Strong form because the grammatical word is stranded.
23. /səˈljuːʃən/ is an alternative pronunciation.
24. /dɪˈrektli/ is an alternative pronunciation.
25. Possessive pronouns tend to be used in strong form apart from some constructions such as the one mentioned above.

Exercise 3.10

| ðə ˈmæn hu wəz əˈrestɪd¹ | wəz ˈnəun əz *ˈhærəld *ˈtɒks | ənd² ɪt wəz əˈsjuːmd³ ðət ðə ˈneɪm lɔːd *ˈtʃɑːlz | həd⁴ biːn ən ˈeɪliəs tə ˈhaɪd ɪz⁵ ˈtruː aɪˈdentɪti | ən əˈnaunsmənt wəz ˈmeɪd ɪn ðə ˈnjuːzpeɪpəz⁶ | ən² ˈfɪftiːn

'wɪmɪn[7] keɪm 'fɔːwəd | tuː[8] əd'mɪt ðət ðeɪ 'tuː əd[5] biːn 'vɪktɪmz[6] əv sʌtʃ ə 'kraɪm
| ɪt ə'pɪəd[3] ðət mɪstə *'fɒks əd[5] juːzd[9] ə sə'lekʃən əv 'neɪmz[6] | ən[2] ðət 'ɔːl əv ɪz[5]
'kærəktəz[6] hæd[10] 'sɪmɪlə 'hɪstəriz[6] | di'spaɪt mɪstə *'fɒksɪz[11] 'ædəmənt
di'naəl[12] əv ði[13] ə'fens | ən aɪ'dentɪti pə'reɪd wəz ə'reɪndʒd[3] | ənd[2] 'eɪt əv ðə
'vɪktɪmz[6] 'pɒzɪtɪvəli aɪ'dəntɪfaɪd[3] ɪm[5] | əz ðə 'pɜːsən hu əd[5] 'trɪkt[14] ðəm 'aut
əv ðeə pə'zeʃənz[6] | θruː'aut ðə həʊl 'traəl[12] | mɪstə *'fɒks meɪn'teɪnd[3] ɪz[5]
'ɪnəsəns | 'kleɪmɪŋ ðət i[5] wəz eɪbəl tə 'pruːv ðət i[5] wəz 'nɒt ðə 'pɜːsən hu əd[5]
kə'mɪtɪd[1] ðəʊz 'kraɪmz[6] | ri'gɑːdləs əv 'wɪtʃ | hi[4] wəz faund 'gɪlti ɒn 'sevərəl
'kaunts[15] əv dɪs'ɒnəsti | dɪ'strɔːt ənd[2] ɪn dɪsbɪ'liːf | mɪstə *'fɒks wəz 'teɪkən
tə ðə 'selz[6] | weər[16] i[5] kən'tɪnjuːd[3] tə 'kleɪm | ðət ðə wəz ə mɪs'kærɪdʒ əv
'dʒʌstɪs | ənd[2] ðət hɪz[4] 'ɪnəsəns kud[17] bi 'pruːvən | hi[4] 'rəʊt tə ðə 'həʊm ɒfɪs
| ðə 'prɪzən 'gʌvənər[16] ən[2] ðə 'tʃiːf əv pə'liːs | fə ði[13] ən'taə[12] 'fɔːtiːn 'jɪəz[6] əv
ɪz[5] 'sentəns | bət tə 'nəʊ ə'veɪl | i'ventʃuəli i[5] wəz ri'liːst[14] frəm 'dʒeɪl | ən[2]
riː'entəd[3] ðə 'wɜːld | ən 'əʊldər[16] ən[2] mʌtʃ 'wiːkə 'mæn | nevəðə'les i[5]
pɜːsə'vɪəd[3] ɪn ɪz[5] 'mɪʃən tə 'klɪər[16] ɪz[5] 'neɪm | ən[2] meɪd 'evri 'efət tə 'kɒntækt
ði[13] ɔː'θɒrətiz[6] | ə'gen | 'nəʊwʌn 'lɪsənd[3] | 'sevərəl 'mʌnθs[15] ɑːftər[16] ɪz[5] ri'liːs
frəm 'prɪzən | hi[4] wəz ə'prəʊtʃt[14] baɪ ə jʌŋ 'wumən i[5] əd[5] 'nevə siːn bi'fɔː | ʃi
bi'gæn ə'kjuːzɪŋ ɪm[5] əv hævɪŋ 'teɪkən hə[18] 'dʒuəlri[19] | hi[4] wəz ə'restɪd[1]
ɪ'miːdɪətli | ən[2] 'ðɪs taɪm i[5] wəz 'sentənst[14] tə 'twenti 'jɪəz[6] | əz ðə 'deɪz[6]
tɜːnd[3] ɪntə 'wiːks[15] | ən[2] ðə 'wiːks[15] ɪntə 'mʌnθs[15] | mɪstə *'fɒks 'grædʒuəli
geɪv 'ʌp ɪz[5] 'faɪt | ənd[2] bi'gæn tuː[8] ək'sept ðət ɪt wəz *'gɒdz[6] 'wɪl | ðət i[5]
ʃəd[17] 'sʌfə fə 'wɒt i[5] 'hædənt[20] 'dʌn | 'ðen | 'aut əv ðə 'bluː | ɪt wəz ri'pɔːtɪd[1]
ɪn ə 'njuːzpeɪpə | ðət ə 'mæn əd[5] biːn ə'restɪd[1] fə 'stiːlɪŋ 'dʒuəlri[19] frəm jʌŋ
'wɪmɪn[7] | ðɪs 'mæn əd[5] əd'mɪtɪd[1] tuː[8] ə'sjuːmɪŋ ðə 'neɪm əv lɔːd *'tʃɑːlz ən[2]
'ʌðəz[6] | ðʌs 'pruːvɪŋ ðət mɪstə *'fɒks əd[5] biːn 'ɪnəsənt ɔːl ðə 'taɪm | ri'sɜːtʃ
ɪntə ðə 'keɪs 'ʃɔːtli 'ɑːftə | ʃəʊd[3] ðət mɪstə *'fɒks əd[5] biːn ɪn *pə'ruː ət
ðə 'taɪm əv ði[13] ə'rɪdʒɪnəl ə'fensɪz[11] | ən[2] kəd[17] 'nɒt | baɪ 'eni 'stretʃ əv ði[13]
ɪmædʒɪ'neɪʃən | həv[4] biːn ri'spɒnsɪbəl fə ðə 'kraɪmz[6] i[5] əd[5] biːn 'pʌnɪʃt[14] fɔː[21]
| mɪstə *'fɒks ri'siːvd[3] səm kɒmpən'seɪʃən fə ðə mɪs'kærɪdʒ əv 'dʒʌstɪs | bət
pəhæps 'mɔːr[16] ɪm'pɔːtəntli | ə 'kɔːt əv ə'piːl wəz ɪ'stæblɪʃt[14] ɪn *'brɪtən fə
ðə 'fɜːst 'taɪm |

Comments to transcription

1. The regular past tense morpheme is pronounced /ɪd/ or /əd/ when the previous sound is either /t/ or /d/. ***
2. /ənd/ and /ən/ are alternative weak forms for *and*. ***
3. The regular past tense morpheme agrees in voicing with the previous sound. In this case the previous sound is voiced so the morpheme is pronounced /d/. ***
4. /h/ cannot be deleted here because it is preceded by a potential pause. ***
5. /h/ may be deleted here because it is not preceded by a potential pause. ***
6. When it is a morpheme or a contraction, 's' agrees in voicing with the previous sound. In this case the previous sound is voiced so 's' is pronounced /z/. ***
7. Notice the irregular pronunciation of the plural *women*.
8. /tu/ is the weak form used when the next word begins with a vowel sound. ***
9. *used* is pronounced /juːzd/ when it means *employed* or *utilised* but may be pronounced /juːst/ when it means *accustomed*.
10. The strong form is used because the verb is not an auxiliary here.

11. The morpheme or contraction 's' is pronounced /ɪz/ or /əz/ when it follows a sibilant.***
12. Smoothing (see Lesson 2).
13. /ði/ is the weak form used when the next word begins with a vowel sound. ***
14. The regular past tense morpheme agrees in voicing with the previous sound. In this case the previous sound is voiceless so the morpheme is pronounced /t/. ***
15. When it is a morpheme or a contraction, 's' agrees in voicing with the previous sound. In this case the previous sound is voiceless so 's' is pronounced /s/.***
16. /r/ is pronounced here because the next word begins with a vowel sound and there is no potential pause between the two vowels (see Lesson 4). ***
17. Grammatical words which have the vowel /ʊ/ in their citation form, such as *would*, *should* and *could*, may remain unchanged even if they are unstressed because /ʊ/ is already a weak vowel, but they may be further weakened to /ə/. ***
18. /h/ is not deleted when *her* is used as a possessive adjective.
19. /dʒuːəl/ and /dʒuːl/ are alternative pronunciations for the word *jewel* and its derivations.
20. The strong form is used because it is a negative contraction and a two-syllable word.
21. Strong form because the grammatical word is stranded.

Answers to Lesson 4: Sandhi r

Orthographic version for the sample transcription passage

I never imagined that I would move away from the tiny little village where I grew up to settle down in such a big city as London. It's only now that I understand why my family were not so keen on the idea of us leaving. Now I have two young kids, Linda and Paul, and a husband to care about, I realise the disadvantages a child has in a city. Looking back to the days when I was a small girl, I remember above all how independent we all were and how much freedom we had. We used to go to school on our own, ride bicycles, play hide-and-seek in the park, hopscotch in the street, swim in the stream and ride on the swing which we used to make from a tree in the woods. We would literally play for hours, having great fun. It would be almost dark before I got home, yet I never saw either my mother or my father concerned about it, since they knew we were all safe and we would come home when we felt hungry. I would like my children to have plenty of fun too and do outdoor activities, but it's impossible for a child here in the city to have the kind of freedom I enjoyed. They certainly cannot go out on their own. Cars are a danger I'm very aware of, not to mention motorbikes. The rush hour is particularly bad, with everyone speeding and driving like maniacs. Then there is the violence. It's not even safe for an adult to walk around without the fear of getting mugged or assaulted. Anyway, I try to take my son and daughter out to play as much as I can. On summer evenings we go to the park and take picnics with us. There is an adventure area in the park where a lot of children get together and play, but they don't have the opportunity of doing very many things on their own, nor of running around, or cycling all over the place as we did. Sometimes I wonder whether, after all, I should have moved away. I just hope the kids don't feel they are actually missing out. Maybe, as they say, you don't miss what you have never experienced.

Exercise 4.1: Edited orthographic version (*linking r is indicated in bold type; intrusive r is indicated by bold type on the letters before and after it*)

My exams are over and I have some breathing space now for a few months, before I have to start thinking about revising again. I was very insecure about my ability to study again when the course began. I felt as though my brain had been atrophied for all those years since I left college. And to make the matter even worse, most of the students in my class were much younger than me. However, I'm happy to report that I did very well, so now I'm more at ease and can relax and really enjoy the lessons. My class is made up of a very diverse group of people, coming from a variety of countries, cultures, religions and economic backgrounds. It is interesting to discover all the various reasons that brought all these students to this particular area of the world and I have learnt a lot more in this place than a new language by listening to their sometimes harrowing stories. Many of them are refugees and were faced with the dilemma of leaving it all behind or risking prison or worse. It is once more evident to me how easily things come to a western European and how very much we take for granted things like fair law and justice. Over a few months all of us in the class have become a close-knit group, since we share a common problem that crosses all barriers. We are all struggling to understand the same new culture and settle into the same new country. And everyone has funny things to relate about the lack of progress we sometimes find. There is no one who understands better about the difficulties we face than a fellow foreigner in the same boat. It doesn't matter if they come from the other end of the world. We are all far away from home and missing those we left behind, so we console, cajole, and encourage each other along frequently.

Transcription

| maɪ[1] ɪgˈzæmz[2] əɾ ˈəʊvəɾ ənd aɪ ˈhæv[3] səm ˈbriːðɪŋ speɪs ˈnaʊ | fəɾ ə ˈfjuː ˈmʌnθs | biˈfɔːɾ aɪ ˈhæv[3] tə ˈstɑːt ˈθɪŋkɪŋ əbaʊt riˈvaɪzɪŋ əˈgen | aɪ wəz ˈveri[1] ɪnsɪˈkjɔːɾ[4] əbaʊt maɪ[1] əˈbɪlɪti tə ˈstʌdi[1] əˈgen | wen ðə ˈkɔːs biˈgæn | aɪ ˈfelt əz ˈðəʊ maɪ ˈbreɪn əd biːn ˈætrəfid fəɾ ˈɔːl ðəʊz ˈjɪəz | sɪns aɪ ˈleft ˈkɒlɪdʒ | ən tə ˈmeɪk ðə ˈmætəɾ iːvən ˈwɜːs | ˈməʊst əv ðə ˈstjuːdənts ɪn maɪ ˈklɑːs wə mʌtʃ ˈjʌŋgə[5] ðən ˈmiː[6] | haʊˈevəɾ aɪm ˈhæpi tə riˈpɔːt ðət aɪ ˈdɪd veri ˈwel | səʊ[1] aɪm ˈnaʊ mɔːɾ ət ˈiːz ən kən riˈlæks | ənd ˈrɪəli[1] ɪnˈdʒɔɪ ðə ˈlesənz | maɪ ˈklɑːs ɪz meɪd ˈʌp əv ə ˈveri ˈdaɪvɜːs ˈgruːp əv ˈpiːpəl | ˈkʌmɪŋ frəm ə vəˈraəti[1–7] əv ˈkʌntriz | ˈkʌltʃəz ri'lɪdʒənz ənd ˈiːkənɒmɪk ˈbækgraʊndz | ɪt ɪz ˈɪntərəstɪŋ tə ˈdɪskʌvəɾ ɔːl ðə ˈveərɪəs ˈriːzənz | ðət ˈbrɔːt ðiːz ˈstjuːdənts tə ˈðɪs pəˈtɪkjʊləɾ ˈeərɪəɾ[8] əv ðə ˈwɜːld | ənd aɪ[1] əv ˈlɜːnt ə ˈlɒt ˈmɔːɾ ɪn ˈðɪs ˈpleɪs | ðən ə ˈnjuː ˈlæŋgwɪdʒ | baɪ ˈlɪsənɪŋ tə ðeə ˈsʌmtaɪmz ˈhærəʊɪŋ ˈstɔːriz | ˈmeni[1] əv ðəm ə refjuˈdʒiːz | ənd wə ˈfeɪst wɪð ðə daɪˈləməɾ[8] əv ˈliːvɪŋ ɪt ɔːl biˈhaɪnd | ɔː ˈrɪskɪŋ ˈprɪzən ɔː ˈwɜːs | ɪt ɪz ˈwʌns mɔːɾ ˈevɪdənt tə mi | haʊ[1] ˈiːzɪli θɪŋz ˈkʌm tuː[1] ə ˈwestən jɔːrəˈpɪən[4] | ən haʊ ˈveri ˈmʌtʃ wi ˈteɪk fə ˈgrɑːntɪd θɪŋz laɪk ˈfeə ˈlɔːɾ[8] ən ˈdʒʌstɪs | ˈəʊvər ə ˈfjuː ˈmʌnθs | ˈɔːl əv əs ɪn ðə ˈklɑːs əv biˈkʌm ə ˈkləʊsnɪt ˈgruːp | sɪns wi ˈʃeəɾ ə ˈkɒmən ˈprɒbləm | ðət ˈkrɒsɪz ɔːl ˈbærɪəz | wi[1] əɾ ˈɔːl ˈstrʌglɪŋ tuː[1] ʌndəstænd ðə ˈseɪm njuː ˈkʌltʃə[9] | ənd ˈsetəl ɪntə ðə ˈseɪm njuː ˈkʌntri[1–9] | ənd ˈevriwʌn hæz[3] ˈfʌni ˈθɪŋz tə riˈleɪt | əbaʊt ðə ˈlæk əv ˈprəʊgres wi ˈsʌmtaɪmz ˈfaɪnd | ðəɾ ɪz ˈnəʊ wʌn huː[1] ʌndəstændz

ˈbetər əbaut ðə ˈdɪfɪkəltɪz wi ˈfeɪs | ðən ə ˈfeləu ˈfɒrɪnər ɪn ðə ˈseɪm ˈbəut | ɪt ˈdʌzənt[10] ˈmætər ɪf ðeɪ ˈkʌm frəm ðiˈ ˈʌðər ˈend əv ðə ˈwɜːld | wiˈ ər ˈɔːl fɑːr əˈweɪ frəm ˈhəum | ənd ˈmɪsɪŋ ˈðəuz wi ˈleft biˈhaɪnd | səu wi kənˈsəul | kəˈdʒəul ənd ɪŋˈkʌrɪdʒ iːtʃ ˈʌðər ələŋ ˈfriːkwəntli |

Comments to transcription

1. Sandhi r is not possible because the preceding vowel is a high one.
2. The unstressed syllable /ɪg/ can also be pronounced /eg/, /əg/, or with /k/ instead of /g/.
3. The strong form is used because here the verb is not an auxiliary.
4. Monophthonging (see Lesson 2).
5. The word *young* /jʌŋ/ is an exception in that it adds the voiced velar plosive after the nasal when forming the comparative and superlative. Other such words are *strong* and *long*.
6. The strong form is used because the grammatical word is emphasised and therefore stressed.
7. Smoothing (see Lesson 2).
8. Notice this is an intrusive r.
9. Sandhi r is not possible when the two vowels are separated by a boundary.
10. The strong form is used because it is a negative contraction and disyllabic.

Exercise 4.2: Transcription

| *ˈemər[1] ənd hə[2] ˈjʌŋgə[3] ˈsɪstər *ˈænθɪər[1] ə ˈkʌmɪŋ tə ˈsteɪ | maɪ ˈbrʌðər ənd ɪz ˈwaɪf ə ˈgəuɪŋ əˈweɪ fər ə ˈlɒŋ wiːkˈend ɒn ðeər ˈəun | səu ðeə ˈdɔːtəz wɪl bi ˈleft wɪð ˈʌs | əv ˈkɔːs | aɪ[4] əv ˈnəun ðɪs fər ə ˈwaɪl | ənd əv ˈgɒn əbaut maɪ ˈdeɪli ˈbɪznɪs wɪð maɪ ˈjuːʒuəl ˈtʃɪəri[4] ˈætɪtjuːd | ɪt ɪz ˈəunli[4] ɪn ðə ˈlɑːst fjuː ˈdeɪz | ˈnau ðət ðeər əˈraɪvəl ɪz ˈɔːlməust əˈpɒn əs | ðət aɪ[4] əv ˈnəutɪst ˈklɪər ɪndɪˈkeɪʃənz əv ˈstres ɪn mi | maɪ ˈhændz ʃeɪk ˈslaɪtli frəm ˈtaɪm tə ˈtaɪm | ənd maɪ ˈθrəu[4]əweɪ riˈmɑːks əbaut hau ˈgɑːstli[4] ɪt wɪl ɔːl ˈbiː | həv biˈgʌn tə siːm ˈkʌləd wɪð ðə ˈtaɪniəst ˈtʌtʃ əv ˈhɪstɪəriər[1] ən ˈsaund ə lɪtəl ˈstreɪnd | aɪ ˈdəunt wɒnt ju tə ˈget mi ˈrɒŋ | aɪ ˈlʌv ðəm bəuθ ˈdɪəli | ˈteɪkən ɪndɪˈvɪdʒəli[5] maɪ ˈniːsɪz ər əˈfekʃənət | ˈɪntərəstɪŋ ən diˈlaɪtfəl | ðə ˈtrʌbəl ˈɪz | ðeɪ[4] ə ˈnɒt ˈkʌmɪŋ ɪndɪˈvɪdʒəli[5] | ðeɪ[4] ə tə bi ˈwɪð əs təˈgeðər ənd fər ət ˈliːst ˈfɔː həul ˈdeɪz | *ˈænθɪər[1] ɪz nɒt ˈəunli[4] *ˈeməz jʌŋgə[3] ˈsɪstə | ʃi[4] ɪz ˈɔːlsəu hər[2] ˈenəmi[4–6] | ənd ðə ˈfiːlɪŋ ɪz ˈmjuːtʃuəl | ˈhau ˈtuː sʌtʃ ˈwel brɔːt ʌp ˈtʃɪldrən kən ˈmænɪdʒ tə gəu[4] ɒn ˈfaɪtɪŋ iːtʃ ˈʌðər ɪn sʌtʃ ə kənˈsɪstənt ˈmænə[6] | ɪz ˈhɑːd tu[4] ɪkˈspleɪn | ðeər ænɪˈmɒsəti dɪd ˈnɒt ˈgrəu[4] əuvər ˈeniθɪŋ ɪn pəˈtɪkjulər aɪ maɪt ˈæd | ɪt wəz ˈðeə[7] frəm ðə biˈgɪnɪŋ | ðə ˈdeɪ[4] *ˈemə wəz ɪntrəˈdjuːst tə hə[2] ˈnjuːbɔːn ˈsɪblɪŋ | wəz wʌn əv ˈɒmɪnəs fəˈbəudɪŋ | *ˈemər[1] ət ðə ˈtaɪm wəz ˈəunli ˈtuː | ʃi wəz ˈbrɔːt ɪn tə ˈsiː ðə ˈbeɪbi[4–6] | ənd ɑːftər ə ˈkwɪk ˈluk ət ðə ˈtaɪni ˈbʌndəl | ʃi ˈsnɒːtɪd ˈlaudli | ˈtɜːnd ɒn hə[2] ˈhiːl ənd ˈleft | ʃi riˈfjuːzd tə ˈtɔːk tu[4] ˈenibɒdi fər ə ˈnʌmbər əv ˈdeɪz | ənd ɪt wəz ˈnɪər ə ˈmʌnθ | bifɔːr ˈeniwʌn kud pəˈsweɪd ə tə ˈspiːk tə hə[2] ˈmʌðər əˈgen | ðiˈ[4] aɪˈdɪər[1] əv ˈtraɪɪŋ tu[4] entəˈteɪn ðiːz ˈtuː lɪtəl ˈgɜːlz | fər ˈeniθɪŋ ˈəuvər ən ˈɑʊ[8]r ɪz ˈfɪlɪŋ mi wɪð ˈpænɪk | aɪ[4] əv ˈtraɪd tə priˈpeər əz ˈmʌtʃ əz aɪ ˈkæn[9] | aɪ[4] əv ˈbɔːt ðə ˈdʒeli[4–6] | əbaut ˈten ˈpækɪts əv ɪt | ɪn ˈevri ˈfleɪvər aɪ kud ˈfaɪnd | aɪ ˈnəu ðət wɒtˈevər ɪz *ˈeməz ˈfleɪvər əv ðə ˈmʌnθ | *ˈænθɪər[1] ɪz ˈbaund tə ˈheɪt ɪt | ðə ˈlɑːst taɪm ðeɪ ˈkeɪm

tə ˈvɪzɪt | aɪ meɪd ˈbrɪndʒ ˈdʒeli⁴⁻⁶ | *ˈeməɹ[1] əˈdɔːd ɪt | *ˈænθɪə tʊk ˈwʌn smɔːl ˈspuːnfʊl[10] | ˈskruːd ʌp hə² ˈfeɪs ənd ˈsed ðət ɪt ˈteɪstɪd ˈnɑːsti⁴⁻⁶ | aɪ wɪl ˈtraɪ ˈteɪkɪŋ ðəm fəɹ ə ˈwɔːk tə ˈfiːd ðə ˈdʌks ɒn ðə ˈvɪlɪdʒ ˈpɒnd | bət aɪm ˈʃɔː[11]ɹ ɪt wɪl bi ðə ˈbest aɪˈdɪəɹ[1] ɪn ðə ˈwɜːld fə ˈwʌn əv ðəm | ənd ðiː⁴ ˈʌðə wʌn wɪl ˈstɪk aʊt hə² ˈləʊə ˈlɪp | ˈstæmp hə² ˈfʊt ənd ˈseɪ ðət ʃi ˈheɪts sɪli ˈdʌks | aɪ ˈwʌndəɹ ɪf ɪt wɪl bi ðiː⁴ ˈeldəst hu wɪl ˈflætli riˈfjuːz tə hæv[12] ˈbɔɪld ˈeg fə ˈbrekfəst | ɔː ˈgəʊ fəɹ ə ˈsaɪkəl ˈraɪd | ɔːɹ ˈiːvən wɒtʃ ə ˈvɪdɪəʊ⁴ ət ˈhəʊm | ˈhaʊ kən ˈtuː ˈtʃɪldrən əv ˈfɔːɹ ənd ˈsɪks ˈmænɪdʒ tə ˈsʌmən ðiː⁴ ˈenədʒi tə dɪsəˈgriː⁴ ɒn ˈæbsəluːtli⁴ ˈevriθɪŋ | aɪ ˈsʌmtaɪmz səˈspekt ðət ðeɪ ˈkʌm tə ˈsiːkrət əˈgriːmənts wen ˈnəʊwʌn ɪz ˈprezənt | əz tə ˈwɪtʃ ˈsaɪd əv ðeəɹ ɪnˈevɪtəbəl dɪsəˈgriːmənt ɒn ˈevri ˈsʌbdʒɪkt | ˈiːtʃ wɪl ˈteɪk | ˈmeɪbi⁴ ɪts ˈɔːl ə ˈplɔɪ tə draɪv ˈædʌlts ʌp ðə ˈwɔːl |

Comments to transcription

1. Notice the intrusive r.
2. /h/ elision is not recommended for the adjectival use of *her*.
3. The word *young*, like other adjectives ending in /ŋ/ such as *long* and *strong*, adds the voiced velar plosive /g/ when forming the comparative and superlative.
4. Sandhi r is not possible because the preceding sound is a high vowel.
5. An alternative pronunciation would be /ɪndɪˈvɪdʒʊəli/.
6. Sandhi r is not possible because the two vowels are separated by a potential pause.
7. The strong form is used because *there* is used as a location adverb.
8. Smoothing (see Lesson 2).
9. Strong form because the grammatical word is stranded.
10. The suffix '-ful' is pronounced /fʊl/ when, like in this word, it still means 'full of …'. On the other hand, in words such as *awful, beautiful* where it has lost its original meaning, it is usually pronounced /fəl/.
11. Monophthonging (see Lesson 2).
12. The verb is in the strong form because here it is not an auxiliary.

Orthographic version

Emma and her younger sister Anthea are coming to stay. My brother and his wife are going away for a long weekend on their own, so their daughters will be left with us. Of course, I have known this for a while, and have gone about my daily business with my usual cheery attitude. It is only in the last few days, now that their arrival is almost upon us, that I have noticed clear indications of stress in me. My hands shake slightly from time to time and my throwaway remarks about how ghastly it will all be have begun to seem coloured with the tiniest touch of hysteria and sound a little strained. I don't want you to get me wrong: I love them both dearly. Taken individually, my nieces are affectionate, interesting and delightful. The trouble is they are not coming individually. They are to be with us together and for at least four whole days. Anthea is not only Emma's younger sister, she is also her enemy and the feeling is mutual. How two such well brought up children can manage to go on fighting each other in such a consistent manner is hard to explain. Their animosity did not grow over anything in particular, I might add. It was there from the beginning. The day Emma was introduced to her newborn sibling, was one of ominous foreboding. Emma at the time was only two. She was brought in to see the baby, and after a quick look at the tiny bundle, she snorted loudly, turned on her heel and left. She refused to talk to anybody for a number of days, and it was near a month before anyone could persuade her to speak to her mother again. The idea of trying to entertain these two little girls for anything over an hour, is filling me with panic. I have tried to prepare as much as I can. I have bought jelly, about ten packets of it, in every flavour I could find. I know that whatever is Emma's flavour of the month, Anthea is bound to hate it. The last time they came to visit, I made orange jelly. Emma adored it. Anthea took one small spoonful, screwed up her face and said that it tasted nasty. I will try taking them for a walk to feed the ducks on the village pond, but I'm sure that it will be the best idea in the world for one of them , and the other one will stick her lower lip, stamp her foot and say that she hates silly ducks. I wonder if it will be the eldest who will flatly refuse to have boiled egg for breakfast or go for a cycle ride, or even watch a video at home. How can two children of four and six manage to summon the energy to disagree on absolutely everything? I sometimes suspect that they come to secret agreements when no one is present as to which side of their inevitable disagreement on every subject, each will take. Maybe it's all a ploy to drive adults up the wall.

Exercise 4.3

| wen i ˈhɜːd əv ðiˈ ˈɒfər əv ə ˈhaʊs ɒn ə ˈsmɔːl ˈaɪlənd | hi ˈwent fər ɪt | hiˈ əd ˈleɪtli biːn ˈfiːlɪŋ ʌnˈhæpiˈ ɪn ðə ˈbɪg ˈsɪti | hɪz ˈwɜːk ˈwɒzənt² ˈgəʊɪŋ ˈeniweər ət ˈɔːl | hi ˈsæt ɪn ˈfrʌnt əv ðə kəmˈpjuːtər evri ˈmɔːnɪŋ | ˈstiːmɪŋ ˈkʌp əv ˈkɒfiˈ ɪn ɪz ˈhænd | hi wʊd ˈsteər ət ðə ˈblæŋk ˈskriːn | ˈdeərɪŋ ɪt tə diˈfiːt ɪm | ˈɑːftər əbaʊt ən ˈɑə³r əv ˈreslɪŋ | hi wʊd səˈrendər ənd ˈstɑːt tə ˈwɒndər ˈendləsliˈ əˈraʊnd ðə ˈflæt | ðen ˈlɑːst wenzdeɪ | hi ˈgɒt ə ˈbreɪk | ðə ˈdeɪ bɪˈfɔːr iˈ əd ˈbʌmpt ɪntuˈ *ˈænər⁴ ɪn ðə ˈpʌb | ʃiˈ əd ˈriːsəntliˈ ɪnˈherɪtɪd ə ˈhaʊs ɒf ðə ˈwest ˈkəʊst | ˈwel | ˈrɑːðər ən ˈəʊld ˈkɒtɪdʒ ʃi ˈsed | ʃid ˈθɔːt əbaʊt ˈselɪŋ ɪt | haʊˈevə | hər ˈeɪdʒənt ˈsed ɪt ˈwʊdənt² ˈfetʃ ə ˈgʊd ˈpraɪs | bɪkɒz əv ɪts riˈməʊt ləʊˈkeɪʃən | biˈsaɪdz | ɪt wʊd biˈ ə ˈnaɪs ˈpleɪs fər *ˈænə tə ˈspend ðə ˈsʌmər æt⁵ | ɪn ðə ˈwɪntər ɪt kʊd bi ˈrentɪd ˈaʊt | bət ʃi ˈhæd⁶ tə ˈfaɪnd sʌm⁷ ˈtaɪm tə ˈtrævəl aʊt ˈðeə⁸r ənd ˈsɔːt ɪt ˈaʊt | ðə wər ə ˈkʌpəl əv ˈθɪŋz ðət ˈhæd⁶ tə bi ˈdʌn tuˈ ɪt | bɪˈfɔːr eni diˈsɪʒənz wə ˈteɪkən | ə ˈkaʊt əv ˈpeɪnt | ˈmeɪbiˈ ə ˈwɪndəʊ ˈʃʌtər ɪn ˈniːd əv əˈdʒʌstɪŋ | ənd ə ˈfjuː ˈtaɪlz ˈhɪər ənd ˈðeə⁸r ˈɔːt tə bi riˈpleɪst | əˈpɑːt frəm ˈðæt⁹ | ðə wəz ˈnʌθɪŋ ðə ˈmætər *ˈænə ˈsed | hi wəz ˈriəli ˈteɪkən wɪð ðiˈaɪˈdɪər⁴ əv ɪt | ənd ˈiːvən ˈhɪntɪd ðət ˈhiːˈ⁰ ɪnˈdʒɔɪd ˈwɜːkɪŋ wɪð ɪz ˈhændz | *ˈænə ˈræŋ ðə ˈfɒləʊɪŋ ˈmɔːnɪŋ | ʃiˈ əd biːn ˈθɪŋkɪŋ əbaʊt ðə ˈhaʊs | ənd ɪz ɪnˈθjuːzɪæzəm ˈəʊvər ɪt | ˈwʊd i biˈ ˈɪntərəstɪd ɪn ˈmuːvɪŋ ɪn ˈrent ˈfriːˈ¹⁻¹| ɪn ɪksˈtʃeɪndʒ i wʊd ˈdʒʌst¹² hæv⁶ tə ˈfɪks ʌp wɒtˈevər i ˈθɔːt ˈnesəsəri | hi kʊd ˈsteɪˈ ʌntɪl ðə ˈsʌmər ɪf i ˈwɒntɪd tuːˈ⁵⁻¹⁻¹¹ | *ˈænər⁴ əv ˈkɔːs wʊd ˈpeɪ fər ˈɔːl ðə məˈtɪərɪəlz ðət wə ˈjuːzd | ʃiˈ əd ˈhɑːdli ˈfɪnɪʃt ˈspiːkɪŋ wen iˈ əkˈseptɪd | ˈwɒt ə ˈwʌndəfəl ˈaɪdɪər⁴ ɪt wɒz⁵ | ənd ɪt wəz ˈpɜːfɪkt ˈtaɪmɪŋ ˈtuː | hi ˈriəli ˈwɒntɪd tə ˈget aʊt ˈðeə⁸r ənd ɪnˈdʒɔɪ ðə ˈlæk əv dɪˈstrækʃənz | ˈʌðə ðən ˈneɪtʃər ənd ˈhelθi ˈwɜːk | hi wəz ˈnaʊ ˈstændɪŋ ɪn ðə ˈkɪtʃən əv ðə ˈhaʊs | ˈfeər iˈnʌf | ʃi ˈhæd¹⁰ sed ˈkɒtɪdʒ | ənd ˈfiːlɪŋ ðə ˈweɪt əv ðə ˈwɜːld ɒn ɪz ˈʃəʊldəz | wen i ˈfɜːst ˈsɔːr⁴ ɪt | ɪt ˈhædənt² ˈlʊkt tuː ˈbæd | ə ˈfjuː ˈsleɪts ˈmɪsɪŋ frəm ðə ˈruːt | ənd ˈəʊnli ˈwʌn ˈʃʌtər ɪn ɪts ˈraɪt ˈpleɪs | ˈnʌθɪŋ ˈmeɪdʒər ɪt ˈsiːmd | bət ˈwen i wɔːkt ˈɪn | hi ˈstɑːtɪd ˈrɪəlaɪzɪŋ ˈwɒt iˈ əd ˈlet ɪmself ˈɪn fɔːⁱ⁵ | ˈðɪs wəz ˈʃɔːliˈ¹³ nɒt ə ˈmætər əv ˈfɪksɪŋ | bət əv ˈgʌtɪŋ ˈaʊt ənd ˈbɪldɪŋ

frəm ˈskræt∫ | ˈnʌn əv ðə ˈlaɪts ˈwɜːkt | ˈhaʊ ˈkʊd ðeɪ | wen ðiˡ ilekˈtrɪsɪti ˈdɪdənt ˈaɪðəˡ⁴ | ðə ˈfjuːz bɒks wəz ˈbɜːnt tuˡ ə ˈsɪndəˡˡ | ənd ˈnʌθɪŋ ˈ∫ɔːt əv ˈnjuː ˈwaərɪŋ³ wʊd ˈsɒlv ˈðætˡ⁹ | ˈtɜːnɪŋ ɒn ə ˈtæp meɪd ðə ˈpaɪps ˈrætəl | əz ɪf ðeɪ wəˡ əˈbaʊt tə ˈteɪk ˈɒf | bət ˈnəʊ ˈwɔːtəˡ ˈækt∫ʊəli keɪm ˈaʊt | ðə ˈsiːlɪŋ ˈbiːmz əd biːn ˈiːtən baɪˡ ən ˈɑːmiˡ əv ˈtɜːmaɪts | ˈɔːl ˈflɔː bɔːdz ˈkriːkt wen ˈstept ɒn | ənd ˈsevərəl ∫əʊd ðeə ˈtruː ˈneɪt∫əˡ ənd ˈbrəʊk ʌndəˡ ɪz ˈprəʊbɪŋ ˈfʊt | hi hædˡ⁶ ə ˈfʌni ˈfiːlɪŋ ðət ðə ˈhaʊs ment tə kəˈlæps | ənd ˈberiˡ ɪm fərˈevəˡ ʌndəˡ ɪts ˈweɪt |

Comments to transcription

1. Sandhi r is not possible because the preceding sound is a high vowel.
2. Strong form because it is a negative contraction and disyllabic.
3. Smoothing (see Lesson 2).
4. Intrusive r.
5. Strong form because the grammatical word is stranded.
6. Strong form because here the verb is not an auxiliary.
7. When it means 'a considerable amount of . . .', *some* tends to be stressed and there-fore in strong form (see Lesson 3, note 5).
8. Strong form because *there* is used as a location adverb.
9. Strong form because *that* is a demonstrative.
10. Strong form because the grammatical word is being emphasised and therefore stressed.
11. Sandhi r is not possible because there is a potential pause between the two vowels.
12. *just* is used in the strong form although it means *only* (see Lesson 3, note 5) because it is emphasised and therefore stressed.
13. Monophthonging (see Lesson 2).
14. /iːðə/ is an alternative pronunciation.

Exercise 4.4

| *ˈfredi gruːˡ ˈʌp ɪn ðə ˈsɪti wɪð ɪz ˈbrʌðəˡ *ˈæləks ənd ðeə ˈpeərənts | bət ɪz ˈfɒndɪst ˈmeməriz | ðə ˈwʌnz i ˈtelz ɒv² | ˈtaɪm ənd ˈtaɪm əˈgen | əˡ əv ðeə ˈhɒlideɪz ɪn ðə ˈkʌntri | ðeɪˡ ˈəʊnd ə ˈbjuːtifəl ˈhaʊs | ɪts ˈstɪl ˈðeə³⁻⁴ | ən ˈnaʊˡ ɪt biˈlɒŋz tə *ˈfredi | sɪns i ˈbɔːt ɪz ˈbrʌðəˡ ˈaʊt | *ˈæləks əz ˈlɪvd əˈbrɔːd fəˡ ˈəʊvə ˈθɜːti ˈjɪəz | ənd ɪz ˈnɒt laɪkli tə ˈkʌm bæk ˈnaʊ | ðə ˈhaʊs ɪz ˈwaɪt wɪð ˈdɑːk griːn ˈwɪndəʊz | ə ˈvərændəˡ⁵ ənd ˈbælkəniz | ðeə ɪz ə ˈpɔːt∫ daʊnˈsteəz | ˈruːft baɪ ə ˈvaɪn ˈtrelɪs | ðə ˈwɔːlz ɪn ðə ˈpɔːt∫ ə ˈkʌvəd | tə ˈweɪst ˈhaɪt | wɪð ˈmɔːrɪ∫⁶ lʊkɪŋ ˈtaɪlz ɪn ˈɔːl ˈkʌləz | ðeəˡ ɪz ˈkwaɪt ə ˈlɒt əv ˈlænd səˈraʊndɪŋ ðə ˈmeɪn ˈbɪldɪŋ | ˈməʊstli ˈteɪkən ʌp baɪˡ ə ˈwaɪld lʊkɪŋ ˈgɑːdən | wɪð ˈfruːt ˈtriːz | ˈbʊ∫ɪz ənd ˈflaəz⁷ | *ˈfredi ˈsteɪz ðeəˡ ˈɔːl θruː ðə ˈsʌməˡ ənd ˈɜːliˡ ˈɔːtəm | ən ˈgəʊz fəˡ ən ɑːftəˈnuːn | djɔːrɪŋ⁶⁻⁸ ðə ˈrest əv ðə ˈjɪəˡ ət ˈliːst ˈwʌns ə ˈwiːk | ɪts ˈtuː ˈkəʊld tə ˈsteɪ ðeə³ˡ əʊvəˈnaɪt ɪn ðə ˈwɪntə⁴ | əz ðiˡ ˈəʊnliˡ əˈveɪləbəl ˈhiːtɪŋ | ɪz ðæt⁹ prəˈvaɪdɪd baɪ ðə ˈfaəpleɪs⁷ ɪn ðə ˈsɪtɪŋruːm¹⁰ | ənd ðiˡ ˈɑːgəˡ⁵ ɪn ðə ˈkɪt∫ɪn | ðə ˈgɑːdən sləʊps ˈdaʊn təwɔːdz ðə ˈvɪlɪdʒ | sɪns ðə ˈhaʊs ɪz kənˈviːnɪəntli ˈsɪtjʊeɪtɪd | ˈslaɪtli riˈmuːvd ˈfrɒm² | ənd əˈbʌv ɔːl ðiˡ ˈʌðəz | *ˈfrediz ˈfɑːðəˡ *ˈælbət | ˈbɔːt ðə ˈhaʊs ɪn ðə ˈnaɪntiːn ˈtwentiz | hiˡ əd ˈgɒn tə *ˈkjuːbəˡ⁵ ət ðə biˈgɪnɪŋ əv ðə ˈsent∫əri wɪð ɪz ˈtuː ˈbrʌðəz | ðeɪ ˈwɜːkt veri ˈhɑːd | laɪk ˈməʊst ˈemɪgrənts | ˈænd¹¹ | laɪk ˈsʌm¹² əv ðəm | *ˈælbət

meɪd ˈkwaɪt ə ˈlɒt əv ˈmʌni[1⁻4] | ənd ˈkeɪm bæk ˈhəʊm tə biˈ ə ˈdʒentəlmən əv
ˈleʒər ənd ˈfaʊnd ə ˈfæməli | biˈfɔːr̥ ɪmˈbɑːkɪŋ ɒn ðə ˈlætər ˈeɪm | hi ˈbɔːt ðə
ˈhaʊs ənd səˈraʊndɪŋ ˈlænd | ənd ɪnˈvestɪd ðə ˈrest əv ɪz ˈfɔːtʃuːn[13] ˈwaɪzli[1⁻4] |
ˈɑːftər ə ˈwaɪl | ə ˈjʌŋ ˈɡɜːl ɪn ðə ˈvɪlɪdʒ ˈkɔːt ɪz ˈaɪ | hi lɒst ˈnəʊ ˈtaɪm ɪn ˈsetɪŋ
θɪŋz ɪn ˈməʊʃən | hi ˈspəʊk tə ðə ˈvɪlɪdʒ ˈpriːst | ənd wəz əˈʃɔːd[6] əv ðə ˈɡɜːlz
ˈkærəktər ənd ˈfæməli ˈbækɡraʊnd | ɑːftər əbˈteɪnɪŋ ˈsɪmɪlər ʌnɪmˈpiːtʃəbəl
krəˈdenʃəlz fər *ˈælbət | ðə ˈpriːst ˈpʊt ɪn ə ˈɡʊd ˈwɜːd wɪð ðə ˈɡɜːlz ˈpeərənts
| ənd wɪðɪn ə ˈfjuː ˈmʌnθs ðeɪ wə ˈmærɪd | *ˈfredi ənd *ˈæləks hæd[14] ə ˈveri
ˈstrɪkt ənd riˈlɪdʒəs ˈʌpbrɪŋɪŋ | *ˈælbət hæd[14] ˈɔːl ðə ˈtaɪm ɪn ðə ˈwɜːld tə ˈkiːp
ən ˈaɪ[1] ɒn ðə ˈrʌnɪŋ əv ðə ˈhaʊshəʊld ənd ɪz ˈtʃɪldrən | nevəðəˈles | ðə ˈtuː
ˈbɔɪz wər ˈɔːlweɪz ˈnəʊn fə ðeər ɪˈmædʒɪnətɪv ˈpræŋks | ðeɪ wər əˈweər əv ðə
ˈkɒnsəkwənt ˈpʌnɪʃmənts | bət ðeɪ[1] əkˈseptɪd ðə ˈpenənsɪz | əz ðə ˈnætʃərəl
ˈpraɪs ðət ˈhæd[14] tə bi ˈpeɪd fər əˈtʃiːvɪŋ ðeər ˈendz | ðeə ˈmʌðə wʊd ˈtraɪ tə
ˈkʌvər ʌp əz ˈmʌtʃ əz ʃi ˈkʊd fə ðəm | bət ʃi ˈnevər ʌndəˈstʊd wɒt ɪt ˈwɒz[2] ðət
ˈmeɪd ðəm səʊ[1] ʌnˈruːli | ˈwen | ənd ˈðɪs wəz ˈevɪdənt tuˈ ˈɔːl | ðeɪ wə sʌtʃ
ˈɡʊd ənd ˈkaɪndhɑːtɪd ˈbɔɪz | ˈwʌn ˈwɪntər ɪn ðə ˈsɪti[1⁻4] | *ˈæləks spent ə ˈfjuː
ˈpleʒərəbəl ˈɑəz[7] | ˈθrəʊɪŋ ˈeɡz daʊn frəm ɪz ˈwɪndəʊ[1⁻4] | ət ˈɔːl ðə ˈpɑːsəz
ˈbaɪ hu ˈkɔːt ɪz ˈfænsi | hiˈ ˈɔːlsəʊ ˈkærɪd ə ˈlɪtəl ˈnəʊtbʊk | weər i ˈkept ə
ˈrekɔːd əv ˈɔːl ðə ˈstriːt ˈlaɪts iˈ əd ˈbrəʊkən | ɔː ˈrɑːðə ˈstəʊnd | *ˈfredi wəz ə
ˈkiːn ɡɪˈtɑːˈpleə[7⁻4] | ənd ˈkɒnsəkwəntli | hɪz ˈprezəns wəz ˈmʌtʃ riˈkwæəd[7] ət
ˈɔːl ˈpɑːtiz ənd ˈgæðərɪŋz | sɪns ˈnəʊwʌn ˈəʊnd ə ˈrekɔːd ˈpleə[7] ət ðə ˈtaɪm |
ˈbiːɪŋ səʊ ˈpɒpjʊlər ə ˈfeləʊ[1⁻4] | ɪt wəz ˈiːzi fər ɪm tə fəˈɡet pəˈrentəl ˈkɜːfjuːz |
ɒn ˈwʌn əˈkeɪʒən | hi ˈgɒt bæk ˈhəʊm ɑːftər ˈeɪt eɪˈ ˈem | tə ˈfaɪnd ɪz ˈfɑːðər
ɒn ðə ˈpɔːtʃ ˈweɪtɪŋ fər ɪm | ˈdaʊnt[15] iːvən ˈθɪŋk əv ˈɡəʊɪŋ tə ˈbed *ˈælbət
ˈsed | biˈfɔːr̥ ɔːl ˈðəʊz ˈsæks ər ˈæbsəluːtli ˈfʊl əv pəˈteɪtəʊz | ðen i riˈzjuːmd ɪz
ˈnjuːzpeɪpə ˈriːdɪŋ ɒn ðə ˈpɔːtʃ ˈsiːt | ðə ˈwɜːkmən tʊk ˈpɪtiˈ ɒn *ˈfredi[1⁻4] | ən
ˈhelpt ɪm baɪ ˈsniːkɪŋ ə ˈfjuː pəˈteɪtəʊz ɪntuˈ ɪz ˈsæks | wen *ˈælbət ˈwɒzənt[15]
ˈlʊkɪŋ | ˈstɪl i wəz ˈdɪɡɪŋ ɪn ðə ˈɡɑːdən ʌntɪl ˈlʌntʃ taɪm | ˈɔːl θruː ðə ˈsʌməz |
ˈbəʊθ ˈbrʌðəz wʊd ˈɒftən[16] get ðə ˈləʊkəl ˈkæbi | tə ˈɡɪv ðəm ˈraɪdz tə ðə
ˈveərɪəs ˈpɑːtiz ɪn səˈraʊndɪŋ ˈvɪlɪdʒɪz | sɪns ðeɪ ˈdɪdənt hæv[14] eni ˈmʌni |
ðeər əˈkaʊnt wɪð ðə ˈdraɪvər ˈendɪd ʌp ət ˈsʌtʃ ə haɪ ˈfɪɡə | ðeɪ wə ˈfɔːst tə
ˈɡəʊ tuˈ ˈɑːnt *ˈsæli fə ˈfʌndz | ʃi wəz ðeə ˈfɑːðəz ˈsɪstə[4] | ənd ˈwʌn əv ðə
ˈməʊst ˈɪnəsənt | ˈkaɪndɪst ˈpɜːsənz ju wʊd ˈevər ɪŋkaʊntər ɪn ðɪs ˈwɜːld | ʃi
wəz ʌnˈmærɪd ənd ˈlɪvd ɒn həˈ[17]r̥ ˈəʊn | ət ðiˈ ˈʌðər ˈend əv ðə ˈvɪlɪdʒ | *ˈfredi[1]
ənd *ˈæləks | wʊd ˈɔːlweɪz ˈtɜːn tuˈ ər ɪn ə ˈskreɪp | ˈkwaɪt ə ˈnʌmbər əv
ˈtaɪmz | ðeɪ riˈtɜːnd lʊkɪŋ ˈhɒrəbli ˈskrʌfi[1⁻4] | ɑːftər ə pəˈtɪkjʊləli ˈfʌn ˈaʊtɪŋ |
ˈɡəʊɪŋ ˈhəʊm ɪn ˈsʌtʃ ə ˈsteɪt | wʊd əv biːn ˈlʊkɪŋ fər ʌnˈnesəsəri ˈtrʌbəl | səʊ
ðeɪ wʊd ˈpɒp ɪntə *ˈsæliz haʊs ˈfɜːst | ˈspɪn ər ən ɪŋˈkredɪbəl ˈjɑːn | ənd ˈget
ə ˈfʊl ˈmiːl | waɪlst ðeə ˈkləʊðz wə biːɪŋ ˈkliːnd ən ˈɑːnd[7] | ˈðen ðeɪ wʊd ɡəʊ
ˈhəʊm | lʊkɪŋ əz ˈniːt əz tuː ˈpɪnz | ɪt ɪz ʌnɪˈmædʒɪnəbəl ˈwɒt ðə ˈtuːˈ əv ðəm
wʊd əv ɡɒt ˈɪntuː[2] | hæd[2] *ˈælbət biːn ə ˈfɑːðər əv ə ˈles ˈstrɪkt ˈkaɪnd | ənd
ˈjet | wɪðˈaʊt səʊ meni ˈruːlz tə bi ˈbrəʊkən | ənd ə ˈles ˈfɔːmɪdəbəl əˈpəʊnənt
| ðeɪ ˈmaɪt əv ˈθɔːt ðət ɪt ˈwɒzənt[15] ˈwɜːθ ðeə ˈwaɪl | ˈprɒbəbli fə ˈðem | ˈhɑːf
ðə ˈfʌn wəz ˈbestɪŋ *ˈælbət |

Comments to transcription

1.   Sandhi r is not possible because the preceding vowel is a high one.

2. The strong form is used because the grammatical word is stranded.
3. *there* is used in the strong form because it functions as a locative adverb.
4. Sandhi r is not used because the two vowels are separated by a boundary.
5. Intrusive r.
6. Monophthonging (see Lesson 2).
7. Smoothing (see Lesson 2).
8. The sequence /dj/ can also be pronounced /dʒ/ in this word.
9. *that* is used in the strong form here because it functions as a demonstrative.
10. When part of a compound, *room* can also be pronounced /rʊm/.
11. The strong form is used because the word is emphasised and therefore stressed.
12. *some* is used in the strong form when it is a pronoun (see Lesson 3, note 5).
13. /fɔːtʃən/ is an alternative pronunciation.
14. The verb is in the strong form because here it is not an auxiliary.
15. The strong form is used because it is a negative contraction.
16. /ɒfən/ is an alternative pronunciation.
17. /h/ is not deleted because it is the adjectival use of *her*.

Exercise 4.5

| ðeɪ 'wɔːkt ɪntə ðə 'restərɒnt | bət *kɔːˈdiːlɪəz 'hɑːt dʒest 'wɒzənt¹ 'ɪn ɪt | ʃʊd ʃi 'liːv ɪt fə təˈnaɪt | ɑːftər 'ɔːl ɪt 'wɒz² ðeər ænɪˈvɜːsəri³ | ɔː 'ʃʊd² ʃi kʌm 'aʊt wɪð ɪt | raɪt 'ðeər⁴ ənd 'ðen ɪn 'frʌnt əv ə 'ruːm fʊl əv 'piːpəl | wʊd ju 'laɪk ə 'teɪbəl nekst tə ðə 'wɪndəʊ 'mædəm | ɔːr 'aʊt ɪn ðə kənˈsɜːvətri | hər⁵ ʌnˈiːzi 'θɔːts wər ɪntəˈrʌptɪd | ənd kwaɪt 'ɒnəstli | ʃi 'dɪd nɒt 'keər ɪn ðə 'liːst 'weə ðeɪ 'sæt | ʃi hæd⁶ mɔːr ɪmˈpɔːtənt 'θɪŋz ɒn hə⁷ 'maɪnd | lets 'sɪt nekst tə ðə 'wɪndəʊ ʃi riˈplaɪd | 'θɪŋkɪŋ ðət ɪf ðɪs 'dɪd get ə 'bɪt tuː 'hɒt tə 'beə | ʃi kʊd 'ɔːlweɪz meɪk ə 'kwɪk 'getəweɪ | θruː ðə 'nɪərɪst 'dɔːr ɔːr 'iːvən əkrɒs ðə 'pætiəʊ | ðeɪ 'tʊk ðeər 'æləkeɪtɪd 'siːts | *ˈdʒɔːdʒ əz 'juːʒʊəl pʊld ðə 'tʃeər aʊt | ənd meɪd 'ʃɔːr əv hə⁷ 'kʌmfət | biˈfɔːr i sæt 'daʊn ɪmˈself | hi 'gɒt ðə 'waɪn menju | wɪl hæv⁶ ʃæmˈpeɪn i diˈsaɪdɪd | ɪt wəz 'əʊnli 'prɒpər ɒn ðeər ænɪˈvɜːsəri | *kɔːdiːlɪər⁸ əkˈnɒlɪdʒd ðə 'dʒestʃər ɔːlˈðəʊ ʃi 'wɒzənt¹ əbaʊt tə 'fɔːl fər ɪt | hə⁵ 'maɪnd wəz elsˈweər ət ðə 'taɪm | ʃi wəz 'traɪɪŋ tə riˈmembər ɪgˈzæktli 'wen əd ʃi bikʌm səˈspɪʃəs | ðə wəz 'nʌθɪŋ 'klɪər ət 'fɜːst | dʒest ðət i 'wɒzənt¹ əˈraʊnd əz 'mʌtʃ əz i 'juːst tə biː⁹ | bət i 'wɒz² ə 'bɪzi 'mæn | ənd ət 'dɪfrənt 'taɪmz əv ðə 'jɪər ɪz 'dʒɒb dɪd meɪk diˈmɑːndz ɒn ɪm | *kɔːˈdiːlɪər⁸ əd 'juːzd ðiːz ɪkˈskjuːsɪz 'əʊvər ənd 'əʊvər əˈgen | bət ʃi 'njuː ɪn hə⁷ 'hɑːt ðət hər⁷ 'ɪnstɪŋkts wər 'ɔːlweɪz 'raɪt | ɪt əd biːn 'pruːvd 'meni¹⁰ ə 'taɪm | 'iːvən wen ðə 'dredfəl 'mɪsɪz *ˈʃɔːr⁸ əˈnaʊnst ðət ʃi¹⁰ əd 'siːn *ˈdʒɔːdʒ | hər⁵ 'əʊn *ˈdʒɔːdʒ | ət ðə mjuːˈzɪəm kæfɪˈtɪərɪər⁸ ɪn ðə 'kʌmpəni¹⁰ əv əˈnʌðə 'wʊmən | ʃi¹⁰ əd diˈnaɪd ðət ðə wəz 'eniθɪŋ ʌntəˈwɔːd 'hæpənɪŋ | ɪt əd biːn ə 'priːvɪəsli¹⁰ əˈreɪndʒd 'bɪznɪs 'dɪnə | ənd 'jes |*kɔːˈdiːlɪər⁸ əd 'nəʊn ɔːl əˈbaʊt ɪt | ʌnˈfɔːtʃənətli ʃi 'tuː əd biːn ɪnˈgeɪdʒd ðæt¹¹ 'iːvnɪŋ | ənd 'ðeəfɔːr ʌnˈeɪbəl tuː¹⁰ əˈtend | wen ʃi 'gɒt həʊm ðæt¹¹ 'naɪt | ʃi 'dɪdənt brɪŋ ʌp ðə 'sʌbdʒɪkt wɪð hə⁷ 'hʌzbənd | ənd wɪð 'taɪm | ʃi¹⁰ əd 'mænɪdʒd tə kənˈvɪns əself ðət 'meɪbi wɒt ʃi 'təʊld mɪsɪz *ˈʃɔː wəz 'truː | hɪz 'æbsənsɪz bikeɪm 'mɔːr ən mɔː 'friːkwənt | hi 'stɑːtɪd gəʊɪŋ əˈweɪ fər ə 'lɒŋ wiːkˈend evri 'naʊ¹⁰ ənd 'ðen | ənd 'ɑːftər ə 'waɪl | 'evri 'θɜːd 'wiːk | 'kleɪmɪŋ ðət i hæd⁶ ə 'wiːkend 'kɒnfrəns¹² | ɪt wəz 'sʌtʃ ə 'bɔːr i kleɪmd | 'haʊ¹⁰ i wʊd əv 'lʌvd dʒest tə 'steɪ¹⁰ ət 'həʊm | ənd 'spend ðə 'taɪm

wɪð ˈhɜːr² ɪnˈsted | bət ðə ˈmɔːgɪdʒ ˈniːdɪd tə bi ˈpeɪd | ənd ˈmʌni ˈhæd⁶ tə biˈ¹⁰ ˈɜːnd | wen i keɪm ˈbæk | hi wəz dɪˈstræktɪd | ə ˈdɪfɪkəlt ˈmiːtɪŋ i ˈsed | ɪt əd ˈbrɔːt ʌp ˈmʌtʃ tə ˈθɪŋk əbaut | *kɔːˈdiːlɪər⁸ ˈɔːlweɪz ʃəud ˈsɪmpəθi | bət ʃi ˈnjuː wen i wəz ˈlaɪɪŋ | ənd wəz ɪnˈsʌltɪd ðət i ˈθɔːt i kʊd ˈpʊl ðə ˈwʊl ˈəuvə hər⁷ ˈaɪz | həd i ˈlɜːnt ˈnʌθɪŋ əˈbaut ər ɪn ˈɔːl ðeə ˈjɪəz təˈgeðər ʌndə ðə ˈseɪm ˈruːf | ɪn hər⁷ aɪsəˈleɪʃən ən ˈləunlinəs | ʃiˈ¹⁰ əd bɪˈgʌn tə lʊk ˈɪntuˈ¹⁰ əˈself fər ə səˈluːʃən | fər ə ˈriːzən waɪ *ˈdʒɔːdʒ nəu lɒŋgəˈ¹³ ˈlʌvd ə | ʃi ˈfaund nəuˈ¹⁰ ˈaːnsər ɪnˈsaɪd | hər⁵ ɪntjuˈɪʃən ˈtəuld ər ɪt wəz ən ˈautsaɪd ˈkɔːz | ɪn ðə ˈkɔːs əv ðɪs ˈɪnər əˈpreɪzəl | *kɔːˈdiːlɪər⁸ ədˈmɪtɪd ðə ˈfækt ðət wɒtˈevər ʌŋˈkɒnʃəs mɪˈsteɪks ʃi ˈmaɪt əv ˈmeɪd | ʃi dɪˈzɜːvd ˈbetər əz ə ˈhjuːmən ˈbiːɪŋ | ənd wʊd ˈhæv⁶ tə gəuˈ¹⁰ ˈaːftər ɪt | ʃi wʊd ˈtel ɪm təˈnaɪt | hi ˈhæd⁶ tə ˈtʃuːz | ɪt wəz ˈhɜːr²ɔː ðiˈ¹⁰ ˈʌðə wʌn | hɪz dɪˈsiːt wʊd ˈnɒt bi ˈtɒləreɪtɪd frəm ˈnauˈ¹⁰ ˈɒn | ɪt ˈhæd⁶ tuˈ¹⁰ ˈend | kwaɪt ˈɒnəstli | ʃi ˈdɪdənt maɪnd ˈwɒt ɪz dɪˈsɪʒən wɒz⁹ | ˈnɒt eni ˈlɒŋgərˈ¹³ ˈæktʃuəli | ˈwɒt ə səˈpraɪzɪŋ ənd ˈkʌmfətɪŋ ˈθɔːt | aɪ ˈdəunt¹ ˈkeər eni ˈmɔː |

Comments to transcription

1. The strong form is used because it is a negative contraction.
2. The strong form is used because the word is being emphasised and therefore stressed.
3. Sandhi r is not possible because the preceding vowel is a high one and because there is a potential pause between the two vowel sounds.
4. The strong form is used because *there* is being used as a location adverb.
5. /h/ cannot be dropped here because it is the adjectival use of *her* and because there is a boundary preceding it.
6. The verb is used in the strong form because it is not being used as an auxiliary.
7. /h/ cannot be dropped because 'her' is used as an adjective.
8. Intrusive r.
9. The strong form is used because the grammatical word is stranded.
10. Sandhi r is not possible because the preceding vowel is a high one.
11. *that* is in the strong form because it is being used as a demonstrative.
12. /ˈkɒnfərəns/ is an alternative pronunciation.
13. *long* is an exception in that it adds the voice velar plosive /g/ after the nasal in the formation of superlatives and comparatives. Other such exceptions are *strong* and *young*.

Answers to Lesson 5: consonant syllabicity

Orthographic version for the sample transcription passage

Many countries have introduced juries. This is done in an attempt to bring justice closer to ordinary people, so that we all take part in the application of the law. In such countries jurors are randomly selected from the electoral census and whoever is chosen has the obligation to act as a juror in any case that goes up for trial in the local courts. This is known as jury service. Fifteen persons are appointed, from whom twelve will have to take part in a trial. The defence can reject up to three candidates on different grounds, such as being prejudiced against the defendant. Once you've been chosen, there's little chance of being able to get out of it. Jury service is considered a right but also a duty, an obligation. Why should anybody want to avoid it? Well, many people would be honoured to be asked to form part of a jury, but others have strong reservations. Not everybody feels capable of bearing the responsibility that it involves. I recently watched a television programme in which various people who had been jurors told of their experiences. All of them had tried murder cases. There was a lady who had been threatened, she and her family, by friends of the accused. The police could only suggest that she call 999 if anything should happen. Another man was so devastated by the whole thing that he still had tears in his eyes when he talked about it. For him, it wasn't only the burden of having to decide whether someone was guilty or not, it was the whole trial – listening to awful details about the victim's death, looking at the photographs, the weapons. The thing that came across as hardest on the jurors was the fact that they were not allowed to talk to anybody about what was happening every day in court. Their family lives had been disrupted, because they were unable to say why they were feeling low or upset, and therefore no one could help them cope with it. I suppose these were to a certain extent exceptional cases. Most people only attend minor trials, things like theft, forgery or burglary. Still there is always the chance that one of us will get called for a capital case.

Exercise 5.1: Edited orthographic version (*Syllabic consonants are marked in bold type.*)

It is a widely held belief that whenever two English people meet, they will start talking about the weather. I am not sure that is entirely true but I can see the reaso**n** why the English should be so interested in this subject. For one thing, English society is one which, unlike some others, doesn't easily tolerate total silence, eve**n** between strangers. The exceptio**n** to this is, of course, when the English are on trains. It is another supposed typical trait of the national character that the English never speak to one another on a train. Apart from this, the weather makes a nice neutral topic of conversatio**n** for a few minutes. One cannot blame anybody for the weather, so talking about it is unlikely to cause any ill feeling. You *can*, of course, blame the weather forecasters for getting their predictio**n**s wrong and the English frequently do this. The other thing about the weather in England is that it is certai**n**ly worth talking about. Things change so rapidly here. You ca**n** experience three of more different types of weather in a singl**e** day. Quite recently I left home early in the morning and drove to the statio**n** in terrible fog and frost. By the middl**e** of the morning it was sunny and warm, but I came home in the evening and had to drive through an awful storm with wind, rain, thunder and lightning. Give**n** this uncertainty, it is hardly surprising that we comment on the weather so often. I find it difficult to envisage what it is like living in a completely predictable climate. It must be so boring to wake up every day and know for certai**n** what the temperature is going to be within a few degrees and whether there will be any rain or not. It is hard to imagine two people who live in an oasis on the edge of a desert saying things like 'it's turned out nice again, hasn't it?', but for the English such a remark has some meaning.

Transcription

| ɪt ɪz ə ˈwaɪdli held biˈliːf | ðət wenˈevə tuː *ˈɪŋglɪʃ ˈpiːp| ˈmiːt | ðeɪ wɪl ˈstɑːt ˈtɔːkɪŋ əbaʊt ðə ˈweðə | aɪ əm ˈnɒt ˈʃɔː[1] ˈðæt[2] ɪz ɪnˈtɑəli[3] ˈtruː | bət aɪ kn̩ ˈsiː ðə ˈriːzn̩ waɪ ði *ˈɪŋglɪʃ ʃʊd bi ˈsəʊ ˈɪntərəstɪd ɪn ðɪs ˈsʌbdʒɪkt | fə ˈwʌn θɪŋ | *ˈɪŋglɪʃ səˈsaɪəti[3] ɪz ˈwʌn wɪtʃ | ʌnˈlaɪk səm ˈʌðəz | ˈdʌznt̩[4] ˈiːzili ˈtɒləreɪt ˈtəʊt| ˈsaɪləns[5] | ˈiːvn̩ bɪtwiːn ˈstreɪndʒəz | ði ɪkˈsepʃn̩ tə ˈðɪs ɪz | əv ˈkɔːs | wen ði *ˈɪŋglɪʃ ər ɒn ˈtreɪnz | ɪt ɪz əˈnʌðə səpəʊzd ˈtɪpɪk| ˈtreɪt əv ðə ˈnæʃn̩l ˈkærəktə | ðət ði *ˈɪŋglɪʃ ˈnevə ˈspiːk tə wʌn əˈnʌðər ɒn ə ˈtreɪn | əˈpɑːt frəm ˈðɪs | ðə ˈweðə meɪks ə ˈnaɪs ˈnjuːtrəl[6] ˈtɒpɪk əv kɒnvəˈseɪʃn̩ fər ə ˈfjuː ˈmɪnɪts | wʌn ˈkænɒt ˈbleɪm ˈenibɒdi fə ðə ˈweðə | səʊ ˈtɔːkɪŋ əˈbaʊt ɪt ɪz ʌnˈlaɪkli tə ˈkɔːz eni ˈɪl ˈfiːlɪŋ | ju ˈkæn[7] əv ˈkɔːs ˈbleɪm ðə weðə ˈfɔːkɑːstəz | fə ˈgetɪŋ ðeə priˈdɪkʃn̩z ˈrɒŋ | ənd ði *ˈɪŋglɪʃ ˈfriːkwəntli[5] ˈduː[8] ðɪs | ði ˈʌðə θɪŋ əbaʊt ðə ˈweðər ɪn *ˈɪŋglənd[9] | ɪz ðət ɪt ɪz ˈsɜːtnli ˈwɜːθ ˈtɔːkɪŋ əbaʊt | ˈθɪŋz ˈtʃeɪndʒ səʊ ˈræpɪdli ˈhɪə | ju kn̩ ɪkˈspɪərɪəns ˈθriː ɔː ˈmɔː ˈdɪfərənt[5] ˈtaɪps əv ˈweðər ɪn ə ˈsɪŋg| ˈdeɪ | kwaɪt ˈriːsn̩tli aɪ ˈleft həʊm ˈɜːli ɪn ðə ˈmɔːnɪŋ | ənd ˈdrəʊv tə ðə ˈsteɪʃn̩ ɪn ˈterɪb| ˈfɒg ənd ˈfrɒst | baɪ ðə ˈmɪd| əv ðə ˈmɔːnɪŋ | ɪt wəz ˈsʌni ənd ˈwɔːm | bət aɪ ˈkeɪm həʊm ɪn ði ˈiːvnɪŋ | ənd ˈhæd[8] tə ˈdraɪv ˈθruː ən ˈɔːf| ˈstɔːm | wɪð ˈwɪnd | ˈreɪn | ˈθʌndər ən ˈlaɪtnɪŋ | ˈgɪvn̩ ðɪs ʌnˈsɜːtn̩ti | ɪt ɪz ˈhɑːdli səˈpraɪzɪŋ ðət wi ˈkɒment ɒn ðə ˈweðə səʊ ˈɒfn̩ | aɪ ˈfaɪnd ɪt ˈdɪfɪk|t tu ɪnˈvɪzɪdʒ wɒt ɪt ɪz ˈlaɪk | ˈlɪvɪŋ ɪn ə kəmˈpliːtli priˈdɪktəb| ˈklaɪmət | ɪt məst bi ˈsəʊ ˈbɔːrɪŋ tə ˈweɪk ʌp evri ˈdeɪ | ənd tə ˈnəʊ fə ˈsɜːtn̩ | wɒt ðə ˈtempərətʃər ɪz ˈgəʊɪŋ tə bi | wɪðɪn ə ˈfjuː dɪˈgriːz | ənd ˈweðə ðə wɪl bi eni ˈreɪn ɔː ˈnɒt | ɪt ɪz ˈhɑːd tu ɪˈmædʒɪn ˈtuː ˈpiːp| hu ˈlɪv ɪn ən əʊˈeɪsɪs ɒn ði ˈedʒ əv ə ˈdezət | seɪɪŋ ˈθɪŋz laɪk ɪts ˈtɜːnd aʊt ˈnaɪs əgen | ˈhæznt̩[4] ɪt | bət fə ði *ˈɪŋglɪʃ | ˈsʌtʃ ə riˈmɑːk hæz[8]ˈsʌm[10] ˈmiːnɪŋ |

Comments to transcription

1. Monophthonging (see Lesson 2).
2. Strong form because it is used as a demonstrative.
3. Smoothing (see Lesson 2).
4. Strong form because it is a negative contraction. ***
5. Syllabicity for the alveolar nasal is not possible here because the sound preceding schwa is a sonorant.
6. Syllabicity for /l/ is not possible because schwa is preceded by an approximant.
7. The strong form is used because the word is being emphasised.
8. Strong form because here the verb is not an auxiliary.
9. Syllabicity for /n/ is not possible for several reasons: the sound preceding schwa is a sonorant, there is more than one consonant preceding schwa and one of them is a nasal.
10. *some* is used in the strong form with countable nouns in the singular when it means 'a certain' or 'a considerable amount of' (see Lesson 3).

Exercise 5.2: Transcription

| *ˈneɪθn̩ ˈlʌvd ˈmiːt | ʌnˈfɔːtʃnətli[1] ˈhiː[2] ənd ɪz ˈwaɪf wə ˈveri ˈpɔːr[3] ən ðeɪ ˈkʊdn̩t[4] ˈjuːʒuəli əˈfɔːd ɪt | ðeɪ ˈhædn̩t[4] iːtn̩ ˈmiːt fə ˈsevərəl[5] ˈwiːks | ən *ˈneɪθn̩ wəz ˈgetɪŋ ə ˈterɪb| ˈkreɪvɪŋ fər ɪt | ɪˈventʃuəli i ˈkʊdn̩t[4] ˈstænd ɪt eni ˈlɒŋgə[6] | səʊ i

ˈɡeɪv ɪz ˈwaɪf sʌm[7] əv ðə ˈmʌni i əd biːn ˈseɪvɪŋ tə ˈbaɪ səm ˈnjuː ˈʃuːz | ˈlɪʃn̩ | ju məst ˈɡəu ənd baɪ səm ˈmiːt təˈdeɪ | ðəz iˈnʌf ˈðeə[8] fər əbaut ˈsevn̩ ˈpaundz əv ˈstjuːɪŋ ˈbiːf | ˈmeɪk ə ˈhjuːdʒ ˈstjuː | aɪ dəunt ˈkeə wɒt ˈvedʒətəblz ju put ˈɪn ɪt | bət ɪt ˈmʌst[2] hæv[9] ˈmiːt | ðen *ˈneɪθn̩ went ˈɒf tə ˈwɜːk | ənd ˈɔːl ˈdeɪ i felt ˈhæpi ət ðə ˈθɔːt əv ðə ˈmɑːvləs[1] ˈstjuː i wəz ˈɡəuɪŋ tə ˈɡet ɪn ði ˈiːvnɪŋ | ˈmiːnwaɪl | *ˈneɪθnz ˈwaɪf set ˈɒf fə ðə ˈbutʃə tə ˈbaɪ ðə ˈmiːt | ʃi ˈwɒznt[4] əz ˈfɒnd əv ˈmiːt əz *ˈneɪθn̩ wɒz[10] | ˈhɜː[2] ɡreɪt ˈpæʃn wəz ˈtʃɒklət[1] | ənd ʃi ˈhædnt[4] ˈiːtn̩ ˈeni əv ˈðæt[11] fə ˈmʌnθs | ˈraɪt nekst tə ðə ˈbutʃəz ˈʃɒp | ðə wəz ə kənˈfekʃnə[1] | wɪð ə ˈwɪndəu dɪˈspleɪ | ˈful əv ðə ˈməust dɪˈlɪʃəs lukɪŋ ˈθɪŋz ʃi əd ˈsiːn fə ˈjɪəz | ʃi ˈkudnt[4] rɪˈzɪst ɪt | ʃi went ˈɪn ən ˈspent ɔːl əv ðə ˈmʌni *ˈneɪθn̩ əd ˈɡɪvn ə | ðæt[11] ˈiːvnɪŋ *ˈneɪθn̩ keɪm həum ˈbiːmɪŋ ɔːl ˈəuvə | hɪz ˈwaɪf put ə ˈpɒt əv ˈstjuː ɒn ðə ˈteɪbl | ən ˈsɜːvd ɪm ə ˈbɪɡ ˈpleɪtful[12] | ɪt wəz ə ˈwʌndəfl[12] ˈstjuː kənteɪnɪŋ ˈbiːnz | ənd pəˈteɪtəuz ənd ˈlentlz | ənd ˈɔːl sɔːts əv ˈʌðə ˈvedʒətəblz | bət *ˈneɪθn̩ ˈkudnt[4] ˈfaɪnd iːvn ə ˈlɪtl piːs əv ˈmiːt | hi ˈsɜːvd ɪmself ə ˈkʌpl əv ˈtaɪmz | ˈfɪʃɪŋ əˈraund ɪn ðə ˈpɒt | bət ˈstɪl i ˈfaund nəu ˈmiːt | ˈdɪdnt ju ˈbaɪ ðə ˈmiːt ɑːskt *ˈneɪθn̩ | əu aɪ ˈsɜːtnli ˈdɪd sed ɪz ˈwaɪf | bət ðə məust ˈhɒrɪbl ˈθɪŋ hæpnd | wen aɪ keɪm ˈhəum frəm ðə ˈbutʃər aɪ ˈrɪəlaɪzd aɪ əd fəˈɡɒtn tə ɡet ˈsɔːlt | səu aɪ ˈwent tə ðə ˈneɪbə tə ˈbɒrəu sʌm[10] | ˈwen aɪ ɡɒt ˈbæk | aɪ ˈəupnd ðə ˈdɔːr ənd sɔː ðə ˈkæt ˈnæpɪŋ ʌndə ðə ˈteɪbl | ɪt wəz ˈklɪər ɪt əd ˈiːtn ɔːl ðə ˈmiːt | *ˈneɪθn̩ ɡɒt ˈʌp ənd went ɪn ˈsɜːtʃ əv ðə ˈkæt wɪð ə ˈterɪbl ˈluk ɒn ɪz ˈfeɪs | hi keɪm ˈbæk ən ˈput ɪt ɪn ə ˈkɒtn ˈbæɡ | ənd put ðə ˈbæɡ ɒn ðə ˈkɪtʃn ˈskeɪlz | ðə ˈkæt weɪd ˈdʒʌst[13] əuvər ˈsevn̩ ˈpaundz | ɪf ˈðɪs ɪz ðə ˈkæt | ˈweər ɪz ðə ˈmiːt | ənd ɪf ˈðɪs ɪz ðə ˈmiːt | ˈweər ɪz ðə ˈkæt ɡrauld *ˈneɪθn̩ |

Comments to transcription

1. We could have de-syllabicity because the syllabic consonant is followed by a weak vowel in the same word so the consonant can become the onset of the following syllable. It could also be seen as /ə/ elision (see Lesson 6).

2. The strong form is used because the grammatical word is emphasised and therefore, stressed.

3. Smoothing (see Lesson 2).

4. Strong form because it is a negative contraction. ***

5. Syllabicity is not possible because /əl/ is preceded by an approximant.

6. The word *long* adds /ɡ/ after /ŋ/ when forming the comparative and superlative. Thus, /ˈlɒŋ/ but /ˈlɒŋɡə/. Other adjectives ending in /ŋ/, such as *strong* and *young* behave similarly.

7. When it acts as a pronoun, *some* is used in the strong form (see Lesson 3).

8. *there* is used in the strong form because it is used as a locative adverb.

9. The strong form is used because here the verb is not an auxiliary.

10. Strong form because the grammatical word is stranded.

11. Strong form because *that* is used as a demonstrative.

12. The suffix 'ful' is pronounced /ful/ when it still means 'full of...' as in the *plateful*. In words such as *wonderful* this meaning is no longer present and the usual pronunciation is /fəl/.

13. When it means *precisely*, *exactly* we tend to stress *just* and therefore use it in the strong form (see Lesson 3).

Orthographic version

Nathan loved meat. Unfortunately he and his wife were very poor and they couldn't usually afford it. They hadn't eaten meat for several weeks and Nathan was getting a terrible craving for it. Eventually he couldn't stand it any longer, so he gave his wife some of the money he had been saving to buy some new shoes. 'Listen. You must go and buy some meat today. There's enough there for about seven pounds of stewing beef. Make a huge stew. I don't care what vegetables you put in it, but it must have meat.' Then Nathan went off to work and all day he felt happy at the thought of the marvellous stew he was going to get in the evening. Meanwhile, Nathan's wife set off for the butcher to buy the meat. She wasn't as fond of meat as Nathan was. Her great passion was chocolate and she hadn't eaten any of that for months. Right next to the butcher's shop there was a confectioner with a window display full of the most delicious looking things she had seen for years. She couldn't resist it. She went in and spent all of the money Nathan had given her. That evening Nathan came home beaming all over. His wife put a pot of stew on the table and served him a big plateful. It was a wonderful stew containing beans and potatoes and lentils and all sorts of other vegetables, but Nathan couldn't find even a little piece of meat. He served himself a couple of times, fishing around in the pot, but still he found no meat. 'Didn't you buy the meat?' asked Nathan. 'Oh, I certainly did,' said his wife, 'but the most horrible thing happened. When I came home from the butcher, I realised I had forgotten to get salt, so I went to the neighbour to borrow some. When I got back, I opened the door and saw the cat napping under the table. It was clear it had eaten all the meat.' Nathan got up and went in search of the cat with a terrible look on his face. He came back and put it in a cotton bag and put the bag on the kitchen scales. The cat weighed just over seven pounds. 'If this is the cat, where is the meat? And if this is the meat, where is the cat?' growled Nathan.

Exercise 5.3

| sɪns wi 'muːvd hɪər ə 'jɪər əgəʊ | aɪ əv biːn 'veri frʌs'treɪtɪd baɪ maɪ ɪnə'bɪlɪti tə kə'mjuːnɪkeɪt 'flʊəntli | aɪ hæv[1] 'mʌtʃ | 'sʌm[2] wʊd seɪ 'tuː mʌtʃ | tə 'seɪ ɒn 'eni 'gɪvn̩ 'sʌbdʒɪkt | aɪ əv 'ɔːlweɪz biːn 'nəʊn əz 'sʌmwʌn hu ɪz 'wɪlɪŋ | iːvn̩ 'iːgə | tə 'ʃeə hər[3] ə'pɪnjənz ɒn 'ɔːlməʊst 'eni 'tɒpɪk | ənd 'sʌdn̩li əv 'faʊnd maɪself wɪð ðɪs 'kjɔːrɪəs[4] 'njuː dɪsə'bɪlɪti | ðət pri'vents mi frəm 'duːɪŋ səʊ | baɪ ðə 'taɪm aɪ əv 'fɔːmjuleɪtɪd maɪ 'vaɪtl̩ kɒntrɪ'bjuːʃn̩ tu ə dɪ'skʌʃn̩ ɪn 'prəʊgrəs | ðə kɒnvə'seɪʃn̩ əz muːvd 'ɒn | ən aɪ hæv[1] tə bɪ'gɪn 'prəʊsesɪŋ 'ɔːl 'əʊvər ə'gen | aɪ 'faɪnd maɪself 'regjʊləli[5] ənd 'lɪtərəli[5] ət ə 'lɒs fə 'wɜːdz | ən ʌnfə'mɪljə daɪ'lemə fə 'miː[6] | ðə 'məʊst ɪm'pɔːtn̩t 'benəfɪt əv ðiːz 'klaːsɪz 'ðeəfɔː | ɪz ðət ðeɪ əv 'staːtɪd ri'əʊpnɪŋ[7] ðəʊz 'vɜːbl̩ 'flʌd geɪts | aɪ kn̩ kən'vɜːs[8] ə'gen | ən səʊ 'naʊ aɪm 'bæk ɒn 'həʊm 'graʊnd | ɒn maɪ 'əʊld 'səʊpbɒks | pɒn'tɪfɪkeɪtɪŋ ə'gen tu 'eniwʌn hul 'lɪsn̩ | ði 'əʊnli 'dɪfərəns[9] ɪz ðət 'naʊ | aɪ 'həʊld 'fɔːθ ɪn ə'nʌðə 'læŋgwɪdʒ | ən ðət 'ʌðə 'piːpl̩ get 'mɔː 'tʃaːnsɪz tə 'spiːk | sɪns aɪ 'stɪl hæv[1] tə 'stɒp tə 'θɪŋk mɔː 'friːkwəntli ðn̩ ɪn maɪ 'neɪtɪv 'læŋgwɪdʒ | aɪ 'stɪl hæv[1] 'mʌtʃ tə 'lɜːn | ənd 'meɪk ðə 'sɪlɪəst mɪ'steɪks 'regjʊləli[5] | maɪ 'kaɪndə 'frendz seɪ ɪts 'paːt əv maɪ 'tʃaːm | ən ðeɪ məst hæv[1] 'sɔː 'tʌŋz | frəm 'baɪtɪŋ ðəm səʊ 'ɒfn̩[10] | tə ri'zɪst ðə təmp'teɪʃn̩ tə kə'rekt mi 'kɒnstəntli[11] | aɪ faɪnd

'hjuːmə ðə məust 'dɪfɪk|t 'æspəkt tə 'mɑːstə | ənd 'fɪər aɪ meɪ 'nevə 'get ɪt | aɪ əm 'stɪl træns'leɪtɪŋ 'seɪɪŋz 'lɪtərəli[5] | ənd biːɪŋ 'left ɪn kən[8]'fjuːʒn̩ əz ə rɪ'zʌlt | aɪ tend tə swɪtʃ 'ɒf ɪn ə kɒnvə'seɪʃn̩ | ɪf 'nəuwʌn ɪz 'spiːkɪŋ daɪ'rektli tə mi | əz aɪ hæv[1] tə 'kɒnsəntreɪt[12] səu 'hɑːd | səu 'sʌmtaɪmz aɪ 'sʌdn̩li 'rɪəlaɪz ðət 'evrɪwʌn ɪz 'lʊkɪŋ ət mi ɪk'spektəntli[13] | ə'weɪtɪŋ ə rɪ'spɔːns | 'ðen aɪ 'hæv[1] tu əd'mɪt ðət aɪ 'hævn̩t[14] gɒt ə 'kluː əz tə 'wɒt ðeɪv biːn 'tɔːkɪŋ əbaut | ənd 'kʊd aɪ 'get ə 'kwɪk 'riːkæp 'pliːz | aɪ 'æm[6] 'meɪkɪŋ 'prəugrəs hau'evə | 'evrɪtaɪm aɪm 'eɪb|l tu 'ɑːnsə 'sʌmwʌn wɪðaut 'kɒnʃəsli 'niːdɪŋ tə træns'leɪt iːtʃ 'wɜːd | aɪ 'fiːl ðər ɪz 'jet ə 'laɪt 'glɪmərɪŋ ət ðɪ 'end əv ðə 'tʌn|l |

Comments to transcription

1. The verb is in strong form because here it is not an auxiliary.
2. Strong form because *some* is used as a pronoun (see Lesson 3).
3. /h/ is not deleted because *her* is used as an adjective. ***
4. Monophthonging (see Lesson 2).
5. Syllabicity is not possible because /əl/ is preceded by an approximant.
6. Strong form because the grammatical word is emphasised and therefore stressed.
7. Syllabicity can be lost (de-syllabicity) because there is an unstressed vowel following and the nasal becomes the onset of the following syllable. That could also be seen as /ə/ elision (see Lesson 6).
8. Syllabicity in the syllable preceding the stress is not very frequent.
9. Syllabicity is not possible because /ən/ is preceded by a sonorant.
10. /ɒftən/ is an alternative pronunciation for which syllabicity is unlikely, because /ən/ is preceded by two consonants.
11. Syllabicity is not possible because /ən/ is preceded by three consonants, one of which is a nasal.
12. Syllabicity is not possible because the sequence /ən/ is preceded by two consonants, the first of which is a nasal.
13. Syllabicity is not possible because the sequence /ən/ is preceded by two plosive consonants.
14. The strong form is used because it is a negative contraction. ***

Exercise 5.4

| əz 'suːn əz *kə'let *'lɪt|l sɔː ðə tek'nɪʃn̩ pʊl 'ʌp | ʃi ræn 'aut | 'pliːz hʌri 'ʌp | ɪts 'fɔːlən[1] ɔːl ðə 'weɪ daun tə ðə 'bɒtəm | ðə tək'nɪʃn̩ 'rʌʃt θruː ðə 'dɔːr əv ðə 'hjuːdʒ 'əuld 'fəuks həum | 'fɒləuɪŋ mɪsɪz *'lɪt|l | wi 'hæv[2] tə 'hʌri | aɪ hæv[2] 'nɜːsɪz 'steɪʃn̩d ət ɔːl 'dɔːz | bət 'stɪl | ðeɪ 'gɒt tə ðɪ 'eləveɪtə dʒəst ɪn 'taɪm ɪt 'siːmd | əz ən əuld 'leɪdi 'ʃʌf|ld tə'wɔːdz ɪt | ən 'klɪəli 'nəuwʌn wəz 'stɒpɪŋ ə | əu 'nəu | ðə 'nɜːs məst əv 'teɪkn̩ ə 'breɪk ɔː 'sʌmθɪŋ mɪsɪz *'lɪt|l 'mʌtəd ʌndə hə 'breθ | 'nəu *'heɪz|l | ju 'kɑːnt[3] juːz ðɪ 'eləveɪtə tə'deɪ | 'gəu bæk tə jɔː 'ruːm nau 'dɪə | ənd ʃi 'geɪv ðɪ əuld 'wumən[1] ə 'lɪt|l 'pʊʃ təwɔːdz ðə 'kɒrɪdə | baɪ 'ðɪs taɪm ðə tek'nɪʃn̩ əd 'əupn̩d ðɪ 'eləveɪtə 'dɔːz | ðə 'bʌtn̩z stɪl 'wɜːk ðə 'dɔːz 'mædəm | baɪ ðə 'lʊks əv 'θɪŋz | wɪð ðə kəm'pɑːtmənt[4] ət ðə 'bɒtəm | ən 'hɑːf ðə 'keɪb|lz 'ʃɒt | aɪ 'kɑːnt[3] duː[2] 'eniθɪŋ raɪt 'nau | aɪ 'dɪdn̩t brɪŋ ðə raɪt 'tuːlz fə 'ðɪs | ənd aɪl 'sɜːtn̩li 'niːd sʌmbədi[5] 'els tə 'help mi | ju wɪl 'hæv[2] tə 'weɪt | əu 'nəu mɪsɪz *'lɪt|l sed | 'kʊdn̩t[3] ju ət 'liːst dɪs'eɪb|l ðə 'dɔːz | nəu aɪ 'kɑːnt[3] | bət aɪl 'blɒk ɔːl 'dɔːz wɪð ðə 'kəunz | səu ðət 'evrɪbɒdi 'nəuz ðəz

'sʌmθɪŋ gəʊɪŋ 'ɒn | ɪf ju 'laɪk | wi 'wʊdn̩t 'wɒnt enibɒdi 'fɔːlɪŋ daʊn ðə 'ʃɑːft | 'wʊd wi | 'nəu | 'nəʊ | 'jes | 'ɔːlraɪt sɜː | 'ðæt⁶ wʊd bi 'veri 'helpfl̩ | ɑːftə 'dɪnə | *kə'let went 'ʌp tə hə⁷ 'ruːm | wɪtʃ wəz 'ɒn ðə 'tɒp 'flɔː | ɪt wəz 'leɪt | ənd 'evriwʌn wəz ə'sliːp ɪk'sept fə 'hɜː⁸ | ʃi ʌn'drest ən 'gɒt ɪntə 'bed | 'ɔːl ði 'eləveɪtə 'dɔːz əd biːn 'blɒkt ɪksept fə 'hɜːz⁹ | ʃi əd 'θɔːt ɪt wəz 'sɪli | 'ʃiː⁸ wʊd 'sɜːtn̩li ri'membə | ʃi kept 'telɪŋ ðə tek'nɪʃn̩ | hu 'lʊkt ət ə dɪsbɪ'liːvɪŋli | ə ju 'æbsəluːtli 'ʃɔː¹⁰ mædəm | 'jes | aɪl bi 'faɪn ʃi rɪə'ʃɔːd¹⁰ ɪm | ʃi wəz 'kwaɪt 'stʌbn̩ | ənd ɪt wəz 'hɑːd tə 'tʃeɪndʒ hə⁷ 'maɪnd | 'wʌns ɪt əd biːn 'set | ʃi 'kʊdn̩t³ 'sliːp ðæt⁶ 'naɪt | 'ɔːl ʃi kʊd 'θɪŋk əbaʊt wəz *'tʃɑːli | hə 'ded 'hʌzbənd¹¹ | ənd 'ɔːl ðeɪ əd 'hæd² tə'geðə | ʌn'tɪl ðæt⁶ 'deɪ ɪn 'meɪ lɑːst 'jɪə | hi əd 'təʊld ə 'ðen əbaʊt ði 'ʌðə 'wʊmən | ʃi hæd n̩t³ 'nəʊn haʊ tə ri'ækt ət 'fɜːst | bət 'ðen | ɪt 'siːmd laɪk ðə 'raɪt θɪŋ tə 'duː² | *kə'let 'ʃʌdəd | ʃi ri'membəd 'pɪkɪŋ ʌp ðə 'nɪərɪst 'hevi 'ɒbdʒɪkt | ə 'læmp | ənd 'hɪtɪŋ ɪm 'əʊvə ðə 'hed wɪð ɪt | ɪt wəz ə 'metl̩ 'læmp | ənd ɪt əd 'kɪld ɪm ɒn ðə 'spɒt | ʃi 'hæd n̩t³ 'ment tə 'kɪl ɪm | ɪt dʒəst 'hæpn̩d | ʃi 'ʃɪvəd ə'gen | 'lʊkt ət ðə 'klɒk | ən fel 'bæk ɒn hə⁷ 'pɪləʊ | 'hɑːf pɑːst 'θriː | aɪl 'nevə get tə 'sliːp ʃi 'θɔːt | ən 'rəʊld 'əʊvə | 'sʌdn̩li ʃi 'hɜːd ə 'nɔɪz | ɪt 'saʊndɪd laɪk 'wɔːtə 'rʌnɪŋ | wəz ɪt ðə 'tæp ɪn ðə 'bɑːθrum¹² | ɪt 'kɑːnt³ bi | aɪ 'dɪdn̩t 'liːv ɪt 'ɒn ʃi 'mʌtəd | ðen ɪt 'stɒpt | aɪm 'hɪərɪŋ 'θɪŋz | aɪ məst bi 'getɪŋ 'əʊld | 'ðen ʃi hɜːd 'sʌmwʌn 'sɒftli 'kɔːlɪŋ hə⁷ 'neɪm | *'kɒli | hə 'mʌsl̩z 'taɪtn̩d | huː¹³ 'wɒz¹⁴ ɪt ðət 'juːst¹⁵ tə 'kɔːl ə 'ðæt⁶ | *'kɒli | ɪt wəz *'tʃɑːli | hi əd 'ɔːlweɪz 'kɔːld ə 'ðæt⁶ | ən ʃi 'heɪtɪd ɪt | ʃi 'wɒzn̩t³ ə 'dɒg | bət 'hiː⁸ wəz 'ded | ʃi 'gɒt ʌp ənd 'hedɪd təwɔːdz ðə 'nɔɪz | ɪt wəz 'kʌmɪŋ frəm ðə 'lændɪŋ | ʃi 'əʊpn̩d ðə 'dɔː | 'huːz¹³ 'ðeə¹⁶ | 'ɑːnsər ɪ'miːdjətli¹⁷ | ɔːr aɪl 'kɔːl ðə pə'liːs | *'kɒli ðə 'vɔɪs sed ə'gen | *'tʃɑːli | 'nəʊ | ɪt 'kɑːnt bi ju | jɔː¹⁰ 'ded ʃi 'skriːmd tə ði 'empti 'kɒrɪdə | ən 'tɜːnɪŋ ə'weɪ frəm ðə 'saʊnd | ræn 'deɪzd tə ði 'eləveɪtə | ʃi 'hæd² tə get 'aʊt əv ðɪs 'pleɪs | ʃi 'pʊʃt ðə 'bʌtn̩ | ənd əz 'suːn əz ðə 'dɔːz 'əʊpn̩d | ʃi 'stept ɪn'saɪd |

Comments to transcription

1. Syllabicity is not possible because /ən/ is preceded by a sonorant.
2. The strong form is used because here the verb is not an auxiliary.
3. Strong form because it is a negative contraction. ***
4. Syllabicity is not possible because /ən/ is preceded by two consonants, one of which is a nasal.
5. /sʌmbɒdi/ is an alternative pronunciation.
6. The strong form is used because *that* is used as a demonstrative.
7. /h/ is not deleted because it is the adjectival use of *her*. ***
8. Strong form because the grammatical word is emphasised, and therefore stressed.
9. Possessive pronouns tend not to have weak forms.
10. Monophthonging (see Lesson 2).
11. Syllabicity is unlikely here because /ən/ is preceded by two consonants.
12. *room* can be pronounced either /ruːm/ or /rʊm/ when it appears in compounds.
13. Strong form because here *who* is the interrogative pronoun.
14. Strong form because the grammatical word is stressed.
15. Notice this is the pronunciation for *used* when it means *accustomed*. ***
16. Strong form because *there* is used here as locative adverb.

17. In unstressed positions, the first element of the diphthongs /ɪə/ and /ʊə/ may lose
its prominence and become /jə/ or /wə/ respectively. This is a common process
which we will use consistently in the last lesson of the book. Meanwhile, don't
worry if you use /ɪə/ and our version is /jə/. You can regard them as alternative
pronunciations.

Exercise 5.5

| maɪ ˈfeɪvərɪt ˈtaɪm əv ðə ˈjɪər əz ˈɡɒt tə bi ði ˈɔːtəm | ˈməʊst ˈpiːpl̩ ɪn ˈmaɪ
ɪkˈspɪərɪəns | wen ˈɑːskt tə ˈtʃuːz ə prɪˈfɜːd ˈsiːzn̩ | wɪl pɪk ˈsprɪŋ ɔː ˈsʌmə | ˈlɪstɪŋ
ˈsʌnʃaɪn | ˈwɔːmθ | ˈnjuː ˈɡrəʊθ | ˈflaəz¹ | ˈhɒlɪdeɪz ən ˈaʊtdɔːr ækˈtɪvɪtiz əz
ˈriːzn̩z | ˈðəʊz piːpl̩ faɪnd ˈɔːtəm ən ˈɒd ˈtʃɔɪs | əz ðeɪ əˈsəʊʃɪeɪt ɪt wɪð ˈɒŋkʌmɪŋ
ˈwɪntə | ˈwɜːʃɪŋ² ˈweðə | ˈʃɔːt ˈdeɪz | ˈlaɪt deprɪˈveɪʃn̩ ənd dɪˈpreʃn̩ | waɪl aɪ
ɪnˈdʒɔɪ ði ədˈvɑːntədʒɪz əv ˈevri ˈsiːzn̩ | ən ˈwʊdn̩t duː³ wɪðaʊt ˈeni əv ðəm | aɪ
ˈduː⁴ | ɒn ði ˈʌðə ˈhænd | faɪnd ˈɔːtəm ðə ˈkəʊzɪəst ˈtaɪm əv ðə ˈjɪə | ðə ˈtaɪm
wen aɪ ˈlʌv tə ˈnest | ənd aɪ ˈrevl̩ ɪn ˈevri ˈʃɔːθɪŋ² ˈdeɪ | ˈsɪtɪŋ ˈhɪər əz aɪ ˈraɪt |
aɪm ˈkʌndʒərɪŋ ʌp ˈpɪktʃəz əv ˈlɒŋ kʌntri ˈwɔːks | ˈɔːtəm ˈliːvz | ˈwelɪŋtən⁵ ˈbuːts
| ən ˈpʌdl̩z | ˈmʌʃrumz | ˈkɒbwebz ˈɡlɪtərɪŋ wɪð ˈdjuː | ə dəˈlɪʃəsli ˈmʌski ˈdæmp
ˈsmel aʊtˈdɔːz | ə ˈləʊ ˈsʌn | ˈlɒŋ ˈʃædəʊz | ə ˈhɪnt əv ˈred tə ðə ˈlaɪt | ən ˈʃɑːp
ˈkɒntrɑːsts | aɪ ɪˈmædʒɪn ˈwɔːm ˈfaəz¹ | ˈhəʊm ˈkrɑːfts | ˈpʌmpkɪnz | ˈhɒt ˈsuːp |
ˈwɔːm ˈbɑːθs | ənd ˈæpl̩ ˈsɪnəmən⁶ ˈsentɪd ˈkændl̩z | ðəz ˈnʌθɪŋ mɔːr ʌpˈlɪftɪŋ
ənd ɪnsprɪˈreɪʃn̩ | ɪn ˈmaɪ əˈpɪnjən | ˈɒn ə ˈlɒŋ ˈtrek θruː ðə ˈwʊdz | əˈkʌmpənɪd⁵
baɪ maɪ ˈdɒɡ | wɪð ˈfriːkwənt⁶ ˈstɒps əlɒŋ ðə ˈweɪ | fər ɪm tu ənˈdʒɔɪ ðə ˈveərɪəs
dɪˈlɪʃəs ˈsmelz | ənd ˈmiː⁴ tə ˈfɪl maɪ ˈpɒkɪts wɪð ˈtrezəz | ʌntɪl ðeɪ ˈsæɡ | ˈdæmp
ənd ˈfreɪɡrənt⁶ | ˈleɪdn̩ wɪð ˈpreʃəs ˈspɔɪlz | ˈstəʊlən⁶ frəm ˈmʌðə ˈneɪtʃə | aɪ
kəˈlekt ˈpaɪn ˈkəʊnz | ˈsiːd ˈpɒdz | ˈɡrɑːsɪz | ˈprɪti ˈliːvz | ˈpiːsɪz əv ˈbɑːk | ənd
pəˈhæps ə ˈhændfl̩⁷ əv ˈberɪz | tə ˈjuːz ɪn ˈveərɪəs ˈweɪz ət ˈhəʊm | aɪ ˈjuːst⁸ tə
ɡet ˈkærɪd əˈweɪ | ˈɡriːdi | ˈbrɪŋɪŋ həʊm ˈfɑː mɔː ðə̩n aɪ kʊd ˈevə ˈjuːz⁸ | bɪkɒz ɪt
wəz ˈɔːl səʊ ˈbjuːtɪfl̩⁷ | ənd aɪ ˈwɒntɪd tə ˈseɪv ɪt fərˈevə sʌmhaʊ | ðen ˈleɪtə |
wen aɪ wʊd rɪˈmuːv maɪ ˈhɔːl frəm maɪ ˈpɒkɪts | aɪ wʊd ˈfaɪnd ðət ˈɔːl wʊd əv
ˈlɒst ɪts ˈsplendə | ˈnaʊ ðət ɪt wəz rɪˈmuːvd frəm ɪts ˈnætʃərəl⁹ səˈraʊndɪŋz | ənd
aɪd bi ˈleft wɪð ə ˈhændfl̩⁷ əv ˈsæd | ˈwet | ˈbraʊn ˈɒbdʒɪkts | dɪˈspleɪɪŋ ˈlɪtl̩
ˈevɪdn̩s əv ðeə ˈpriːvɪəs ˈɡlɔːri | aɪ əv ˈlɜːnd ðət ɪts ˈbetə tu əraɪv ˈhəʊm wɪð ə
ˈhed fʊl əv ɪkˈskwiːzɪt ˈmeməriz | ˈɒn tu əˈtempt tə ˈkæptʃər ɪt ˈɔːl | ən ˈtræp ɪt ɪn
ə ˈbɒks | aɪ ˈlɪvd ɪn *ˈkælɪˈfɔːnɪə fər ə fjuː ˈjɪəz | ən ˈðɪs meɪ ˈhelp tu ɪkˈspleɪn
maɪ pəˈtɪkjʊlər əˈfekʃn̩ fə ði ˈɔːtəm | ˈbiːɪŋ ˈaərɪʃ¹ | aɪ ɡruː ˈʌp teɪkɪŋ ˈreɪn | ˈbæd
ˈweðər ənd ðə ˈtʃeɪndʒɪŋ əv ˈsiːzn̩z fə ˈɡrɑːntɪd | aɪ ˈjuːst⁸ tə ˈɡrʌmbl̩ əlɒŋ wɪð
ˈevrɪwʌn ˈels əbaʊt ðə kənˈtɪnjʊəli¹⁰ ˈɡreɪ ˈskaɪz | ən ðə səʊ ˈɒfn̩¹¹ ʌnrɪˈlentɪŋ
ˈreɪn | ənd ˈwɪnd | aɪ ˈnevər ɪkˈspektɪd tə ˈsiː ə ˈdeɪ | wen aɪ wʊd ˈlɒŋ fə ˈreɪn |
ɔːr ə ˈdeɪ wen aɪ wʊd ˈwɪʃ tə ˈsiː səm ˈrɪəl ˈwɪntə ˈweðə | ən ɪnˈdiːd | wʊd əv
ˈlɑːft ɪn jɔː ˈfeɪs əd ju ðen səˈdʒestɪd sʌtʃ ə ˈθɪŋ | haʊˈevə | ðæts¹² ɪɡˈzæktli wɒt
ˈhæpn̩d | fə ðə ˈfɜːst ˈnaɪn ˈmʌnθs ðət aɪ ˈlɪvd ɪn *ˈkælɪˈfɔːnɪə | aɪ sɔː ˈdeɪ ɑːftə
ˈdeɪ əv ˈɡlɔːrɪəs ˈsʌnʃaɪn | mɑːd ˈəʊnli baɪ ði əˈkeɪʒn̩l̩ ˈpætʃ əv ˈfɒɡ | ənd ɑːftə
ˈfaɪv ɔː sɪks ˈmʌnθs əv ˈðɪs | aɪ wəz ˈɡɑːspɪŋ | ˈdʒʌst¹³ laɪk ə ˈfɪʃ aʊt əv ˈwɔːtə |
fər ə ˈtʃeɪndʒ | aɪ dɪsˈkʌvəd ðət ə ˈwet | ˈrɔː ˈklaɪmət ət ˈliːst fə ˈpɑːt əv ðə ˈjɪə |
ɪz əz iˈsenʃl̩ tə ˈmiː⁴ əz ˈbriːðɪŋ | ðət ˈdʒʌst¹³ laɪk ə ˈplɑːnt | aɪ bɪˈɡɪn tə draɪ ˈʌp |
ɪf aɪ ˈdəʊnt¹⁴ ɡet ˈreɪnd ɒn ˈreɡjʊləli⁹ | pəˈhæps ɪts ˈðeər ɪn maɪ *ˈaərɪʃ¹ ˈdʒiːnz |
ɔːlˈðəʊ aɪ əv met ˈmeni ə ˈfeləʊ ˈkʌntrimən | hu dəz ˈnɒt ʃeə ˈðɪs ˈprɒbləm | bət

aɪ ˈlʌv ðə ˈtʃeɪndʒɪŋ əv ðə ˈsiːzn̩z | ðə ˈrɪðəm əv ðə ˈjɪə | ˈɔːl əv ɪt | ənd aɪ ˈkɑːnt[14] duː[3] wɪðˈaʊt ɪt | ˈiːvn̩ wen ˈtʃeɪndʒ sʌmtaɪmz əˈraɪvz | ˈbləʊn ɪn ɒn ə ˈbɪtl̩i ˈkəʊld ˈwɪntə ˈwɪnd | ɪn ˈæktʃuəl ˈfækt | maɪ ˈtruː riˈspɒns tə ðə ˈkwestʃn̩ pəʊzd əˈbʌv | ɪz ðət aɪ dəʊnt[14] ˈhæv[3] ə ˈfeɪvərɪt ˈsiːzn̩ | ɪts ɪmˈpɒsɪbl̩ fə mi tə ˈtʃuːz dʒəst ˈwʌn | aɪ ˈniːd ðəm ˈɔːl | ˈiːtʃ wʌn ˈkɒmplɪments ði ˈʌðəz | ˈiːtʃ hæz[3] ɪts ˈəʊn ədˈvɑːntɪdʒɪz ənd ˈdɪsədvɑːntɪdʒɪz | bət ˈiːtʃ ɪz əz ˈvaɪtl̩ tə mi ɪn ˈwʌn weɪ ɔːr əˈnʌðə | əz ði ˈʌðəz |

Comments to transcription

1. Smoothing (see Lesson 2).
2. Syllabicity can be lost (de-syllabicity) because there is an unstressed vowel follow-ing the syllabic consonant. Thus the consonant may become the onset to the following syllable. This could also be seen as /ə/ elision (see Lesson 6).
3. Strong form because the verb is not an auxiliary here.
4. Strong form because the grammatical word is emphasised, and therefore stressed.
5. Syllabicity is not possible because /ən/ is preceded by two consonants, the first of which is a nasal.
6. Syllabicity is not possible because /ən/ is preceded by a sonorant.
7. The suffix 'ful' is pronounced /fʊl/ only when it retains its original meaning of 'full of...' but in words such as *beautiful* it is pronounced /fəl/ or /fl̩/.
8. *used* is pronounced /juːst/ when it means *accustomed*, otherwise it is pronounced /juːzd/. ***
9. Syllabicity is not possible because /əl/ is preceded by an approximant.
10. Syllabicity in the syllable preceding the stress is not very common.
11. /ɒftən/ is an alternative pronunciation for which syllabicity would be unlikely since schwa is preceded by two consonants. ***
12. Strong form because *that* is being used as a demonstrative.
13. When it means *exactly, precisely*, the word *just* tends to be used in strong form (see Lesson 3).
14. Strong form because it is a negative contraction. ***

Answers to Lesson 6: elision

Orthographic version for the sample transcription passage

Marjory picked the bag up. It seemed extraordinarily heavy for its size. Surely there must be something in it which would identify its owner. She could then make a quick call and maybe even prevent her afternoon being ruined by a little white lie. No one would know she had looked inside the bag. She could just say that she recognised whose it was and had phoned right after finding it. She supposed she could just phone them all one by one and find the owner that way, but Marjory felt too weary for all that rigmarole. No. If someone couldn't be careful enough to look after their bag, then they'd better start suffering the consequences. She opened the bag. The first thing she saw was a small yellow diary and, underneath that, some-thing silvery and shining. She lifted out the diary and there, lying comfortably at the bottom of the bag, was a revolver. Marjory stared at it, fascinated, hardly under-standing what she was looking at. Then she snapped the bag shut and closed her eyes. Had she drunk too much? She certainly didn't feel in the least befuddled now. She felt panic rising in her. Surely none of her friends, her fellow committee members, would carry such a thing. She opened it again carefully, as she would a bag in which she knew there lay a poisonous snake. There was the gun. Shuddering, she put in her hand and took it out. What could she do? The thing felt hard and cold to the touch. How could she confront the person it belonged to? Should she just pretend that it wasn't there? What would any of her ladies want with such a thing? She dropped the revolver back into the bag as if it burnt. She would just wait and see who called for it and then give it back and try to forget. But she saw these women regularly, some of them practically every day. How could she carry on treating the one who owned the bag in the same fashion? She couldn't think of a suitable word to describe a woman who would keep such an object with her.

Exercise 6.1: Edited orthographic version (*Elided sounds are marked in bold type.*)

Overhearing conversations on trains can be amusing, sometimes even alarming. Some years ago I use**d** to travel on the London underground to get to work. Quite often I use**d** to spen**d** the journey marking students' work, especially phonetic transcriptions of English. One morning in summer a group of tourists got into the carriage where I was sitting. It was an Italian family who were going into the centre of the city to see the sights. One of them sat next to me. After a few minutes he said to his family, in Italian of course, that he didn't know what I was doing. Apparently, I seeme**d** to be reading things in a very peculiar language. I said nothing, but jus**t** carried on with my work. The odd thing is that exactly the same thing happene**d** the next morning. This time the man said, 'It's him! He's doing it again! I wonder what that funny lettering is.' They all collected aroun**d** me, peering over my shoulder. I couldn't resist the challenge. When I got off the train, I said in Italian, 'I hope you all have a pleasant day.' I wish I had had a camera to take a picture of the expressions on their faces. Another time, I was really puzzle**d** by an exchange I overheard. Two men sitting opposite me were talking. One of them I could understan**d** perfectly. He was talking about a police raid. The trouble was I couldn't make out a word of what the other was answering. It was after about ten minutes that I finally realise**d** the reason. He wasn't speaking in English at all, but in Welsh. Why they chose to have a conversation in two different languages at the same time I don't know.

Transcription

| ˈəʊvəhɪərɪŋ kɒnvəˈseɪʃnz ɒn ˈtreɪnz kn̩ bi əˈmjuːzɪŋ | ˈsʌmtaɪmz ˈiːvn̩ əˈlɑːmɪŋ | səm ˈjɪəz əˈɡəʊ aɪ ˈjuːs tə ˈtrævl̩ ɒn ðə *ˈlʌndən ˈʌndəɡraʊn tə ˈɡet tə ˈwɜːk | kwaɪt ˈɒfn̩ aɪ juːs tə ˈspen ðə ˈdʒɜːni ˈmɑːkɪŋ ˈstjuːdn̩ts[1] ˈwɜːk | iˈspeʃli[2] fəˈnetɪk trænˈskrɪpʃnz əv *ˈɪŋglɪʃ | ˈwʌn ˈmɔːnɪŋ ɪn ˈsʌmə | ə ˈgruːp əv ˈtɔːrɪss[3] ɡɒt ɪntə ðə ˈkærɪdʒ weər aɪ wəz ˈsɪtɪŋ | ɪt wəz ən *ɪˈtæljən fæmli[2] | hu wə ˈɡəʊɪŋ ɪntə ðə ˈsentə tə ˈsiː ðə ˈsaɪts | ˈwʌn əv ðəm sæt ˈneks tə ˈmiː[4] | ˈɑːftər[5] ə ˈfjuː ˈmɪnɪts | hi ˈsed tu ɪz ˈfæmli[2] | ɪn *ɪˈtæljən əv ˈkɔːs | ðət i ˈdɪdn̩[6] ˈnəʊ ˈwɒt aɪ wəz ˈduːɪŋ | əˈpærəntli[1-7] aɪ ˈsiːm tə bi ˈriːdɪŋ ˈθɪŋz ɪn ə ˈveri prɪˈkjuːljə ˈlæŋgwɪdʒ | aɪ sed ˈnʌθɪŋ | bət dʒəs ˈkærid ɒn wɪð maɪ ˈwɜːk | ði ˈɒd θɪŋ ˈɪz | ðət ɪgˈzækli ðə ˈseɪm θɪŋ ˈhæpn̩ ðə ˈneks mɔːnɪŋ | ˈðɪs taɪm ðə ˈmæn sed | ɪts ˈhɪm[8] | hiz ˈduːɪŋ ɪt əˈgen | aɪ ˈwʌndə wɒt ðæt[9] ˈfʌni ˈletrɪŋ ɪz |

ðeɪ 'ɔːl kə'lektɪd[10] ə'raʊn mi | 'pɪərɪŋ 'əʊvə maɪ 'ʃəʊldə | aɪ 'kʊdn̩[6] ri'zɪs ðə 'tʃæləndʒ | wen aɪ 'gɒt ɒf ðə 'treɪn | aɪ 'sed ɪn *ɪ'tæljən | aɪ 'həʊp ju 'ɔːl hæv[11] ə 'pleznt̩[1] deɪ | aɪ 'wɪʃ aɪ əd 'hæd[11] ə 'kæmrə tə 'teɪk ə 'pɪktʃər[5] əv ðɪ ɪk'spreʃnz ɒn ðeə 'feɪsɪz | ə'nʌðə 'taɪm aɪ wəz 'rɪəli 'pʌzl̩ baɪ ən ɪks'tʃeɪndʒ aɪ əʊvə'hɜːd | 'tuː men sɪtɪŋ 'ɒpəzɪt mi wə 'tɔːkɪŋ | 'wʌn əv ðəm aɪ kʊd ʌndə'stæn 'pɜːfəkli | hi wəz 'tɔːkɪŋ əbaʊt ə 'pliːs[12] 'reɪd | ðə 'trʌbl̩ wɒz[13] | aɪ 'kʊdn̩[6] meɪk 'aʊt ə 'wɜːd əv 'wɒt ðɪ 'ʌðə wəz 'aːnsrɪŋ | ɪt wəz 'aːftər[5] əbaʊt 'ten 'mɪnɪts ðət aɪ 'faɪnli rɪəlaɪz ðə riːzn̩ | hi wɒzn̩[6] spiːkɪŋ ɪn *'ɪŋglɪʃ ət 'ɔːl | bət ɪn *'welʃ | 'waɪ ðeɪ 'tʃəʊz tə 'hæv[11] ə kɒnvə'seɪʃn ɪn 'tuː 'dɪfrənt[1] 'læŋgwɪdʒɪz ət ðə 'seɪm 'taɪm | aɪ 'dəʊn̩[6] nəʊ |

Comments to transcription

1. /t/ may not be deleted because it is preceded by a voiced consonant.
2. Syllabicity could be applied instead of /ə/ elision here.
3. Monophthonging (see Lesson 2). ***
4. Strong form because the grammatical form is being emphasised and therefore stressed.
5. /ə/ is unlikely to be deleted (except in very rapid and informal speech) because it is not followed by an unstressed syllable in the same word.
6. /t/ is deleted even though the previous consonant is voiced because it is a negative contraction.
7. /ə/ cannot be deleted because it is preceded by an approximant.
8. /h/ cannot be deleted because the pronoun is emphasised and thus stressed.
9. *that* is used in the strong form because it is used as a demonstrative.
10. /ə/ is not usually elided when it precedes the stressed syllable.
11. Strong form because the verb is not used as an auxiliary here.
12. Special case in which /ə/ is deleted when preceding the stressed syllable.
13. Strong form because the grammatical word is stranded.

Exercise 6.2: Transcription

| wel 'wʌn əv ðə 'wɜːs θɪŋz ðət 'hæpn̩ tə 'miː[1] | wəz 'wen aɪ æksɪ'dentli[2–3] dɪ'strɔɪd ðɪ 'evɪdn̩s ðət wəz 'gəʊɪŋ tə bi 'juːz fər[4] ə 'kɔːt keɪs | ɪt 'hæpn̩ ten 'jɪəz əgəʊ | ət ðə 'taɪm | aɪ ə'keɪʒn̩li[3] dɪd bɪts əv 'wɜːk fə sə'lɪsɪtəz[5] | wen ðeɪ 'niːdɪd 'ekspɜːt ə'pɪnjən ɒn 'teɪp ri'kɔːdɪŋz | ðə 'keɪs kən'sɜːnd[5–6] ə dɪ'vɔːs | aɪ 'dəʊn̩[7] ri'membər[4] ɔːl ðə 'diːteɪlz | bət 'wʌn əv ðə 'paːtiz əd ri'kɔːdɪd ə kɒnvə'seɪʃn wɪð ðɪ 'ʌðə | 'juːzɪŋ ə 'dɪktəfəʊn mə'ʃiːn | ðə wəz ə dɪs'pjuːt əz tə 'wɒt wəz 'æktʃli[3–8] sed | bɪkɒz ðə ri'kɔːdɪŋ 'wɒzn̩[7–9] ə pə'tɪkjuləli[10] 'klɪə wʌn | səʊ ðə sə'lɪsɪtə 'sent[2–6] ɪt tə 'miː[1] | ʌn'fɔːtʃnətli[3] ðə ri'kɔːdɪŋ wəz ɒn ə 'mɪni kə'set | ənd aɪ 'dɪdn̩[7–9] hæv[11] ə mə'ʃiːn ðət aɪ kʊd 'pleɪ ɪt ɒn | səʊ aɪ 'hæd[11] tə 'get ðə sə'lɪsɪtə[5] tu 'aːsk ɪz 'klaənt[2–12] tə 'sen mi ðə mə'ʃiːn əz 'wel | aɪ 'lɪsn̩ tə ðə 'θɪŋ ə 'kʌpl̩ əv 'taɪmz | ən 'ðen dɪ'saɪdɪd tə 'teɪk ɪt 'həʊm | ən 'wɜːk ɒn ɪt 'əʊvə ðə wiːk'end[13] | 'wen aɪ 'traɪd tə 'lɪsn̩ tu ɪt ðə 'neks 'deɪ | aɪ 'faʊn ðət ðə ri'kɔːdɪŋ əd biːn 'waɪp 'kliːn | ðə mə'ʃiːn məst[6] əv 'swɪtʃt[6] ɪtself 'ɒn ɪn maɪ 'briːfkeɪs 'sʌmhaʊ | 'ɔːl ðət wəz 'lef wəz ðə 'saʊn frəm ðɪ ʌndəgraʊn 'treɪn ðət 'tʊk mi 'həʊm | aɪ 'dɪdn̩[7] nəʊ 'wɒt tə 'duː[11] | aɪ 'θɔːt ðət 'wen aɪ 'təʊl ðə sə'lɪsɪtə[5] | hi wʊd ɪ'miːdjətli 'suː mi fə 'neglɪdʒn̩s ɔː 'sʌmθɪŋ | aɪ wəz ɪn 'sʌtʃ ə 'steɪt | ðət aɪ 'pɔːd[14] maɪself ə 'glaːs əv 'wɪski | tə 'traɪ ən 'kaːm maɪself

'daʊn | wen maɪ 'waɪf əraɪvd¹⁵ 'həʊm frəm ə 'ʃɒpɪŋ 'trɪp | ʃi 'faʊn mi 'slʌmpt⁶ ɪn
ə 'tʃeə | wɪð ə 'bɒtl̩ ɪn 'wʌn hænd¹³ | ən ə 'glɑːs ɪn ði 'ʌðə | aɪ 'faɪnli 'gɒt ʌp i'nʌf
'kʌrɪdʒ tə 'fəʊn ðə sə'lɪsɪtə⁵ | ən i dʒəs 'sed | əʊ 'dɪə | wɒt ə 'pɪti | wel ðəz 'nʌθɪŋ
wi kn̩ 'duː¹¹ əbaʊt ɪt | 'ɪz ðeə | jud 'betə 'sen mi ðə mə'ʃiːn 'bæk | 'ɑːftə 'ðæt¹⁶ |
əz ju kn̩ ɪ'mædʒɪn | aɪ 'ɔːlweɪz ɪn'sɪstɪd ɒn 'wɜːkɪŋ frəm 'kɒpiz əv ði ə'rɪdʒɪnl̩
ri'kɔːdɪŋz |

Comments to transcription

1. Strong form because the grammatical word is emphasised, and therefore stressed.
2. /t/ cannot be deleted because it is preceded by a voiced consonant.
3. Syllabicity could be applied instead of /ə/ deletion.
4. /ə/ cannot be deleted because it is not followed by an unstressed syllable in the same word.
5. /ə/ cannot be deleted because it is preceding the stressed syllable.
6. The alveolar plosive cannot be deleted because it is followed by a vowel.
7. /t/ is deleted even though the previous sound is voiced because it is a negative contraction.
8. /ækʃli/ is an altenative pronunciation.
9. /t/ can be deleted even when it is followed by a vowel or /h/ because it is a negative contraction.
10. /ə/ is not deleted because is preceded by an approximant.
11. The strong form is used because the verb is not used as an auxiliary here.
12. Smoothing (see Lesson 2). ***
13. The alveolar plosive cannot be deleted because it is followed by a potential pause.
14. Monophthonging (see Lesson 2). ***
15. The alveolar plosive cannot be deleted because it is followed by /h/.
16. Strong form because *that* is used as a demonstrative here.

Orthographic version

Well, one of the worst things that happened to me was when I accidentally destroyed the evidence that was going to be used for a court case. It happened ten years ago. At the time I occasionally did bits of work for solicitors, when they needed expert opinion on tape-recordings. The case concerned a divorce. I don't remember all the details, but one of the parties had recorded a conversation with the other using a dictaphone machine. There was a dispute as to what was actually said, because the recording wasn't a particularly clear one. So the solicitor sent it to me. Unfortunately the recording was on a mini-cassette and I didn't have a machine that I could play it on, so I had to get the solicitor to ask his client to send me the machine as well. I listened to the thing a couple of times and then decided to take it home and work on it over the weekend. When I tried to listen to it the next day, I found that the recording had been wiped clean. The machine must have switched itself on in my briefcase somehow. All that was left was the sound from the underground train that took me home. I didn't know what to do. I thought that when I told the solicitor, he would immediately sue me for negligence or something. I was in such a state that I poured myself a glass of whisky to try and calm myself down. When my wife arrived home from a shopping trip, she found me slumped in a chair with a bottle in one hand and a glass in the other. I finally got up enough courage to phone the solicitor and he just said, 'Oh dear. What a pity. Well, there's nothing we can do about it, is there? You'd better send me the machine back.' After that, as you can imagine, I always insisted on working from copies of the original recordings.

Exercise 6.3

| maɪ ˈfɜːs rɪəl[1] ˈdeɪ ɪn *ˈstrætfəd | ˈɑːftə ˈbrekfəs wi ˈwent[2-3] ɒf tə ˈfaɪn ðə ˈsʌmə skuːl | ˈevriweə ju ˈlʊk ju sɔː ˈfɒrɪn ˈstjuːdn̩ts[2] | ənd wi wər[4-5] ˈɔːl ˈhedɪŋ təwɔːdz ðə ˈseɪm ˈpleɪs | ə ˈləʊkl̩ ˈkɒlɪdʒ | wen maɪ ˈfrend[3] ən aɪ ˈgɒt ðeə[6] | wi ˈkʊdn̩[7] faɪn ðə ˈgruːp fər[4] ˈeɪdʒəz | ɪn ðə ˈbɪg ˈkraʊd əv ˈnɔɪzi ən ˈmɪlɪŋ stjuːdn̩ts[2] | bət ət ˈlɑːs ðeɪ keɪm ˈbaʊndɪŋ təˈwɔːdz əs | ˈsuːn wi ˈhæd[8] tə ˈgəʊ ɪnˈsaɪd ˈðəʊ | ən wi wə ˈsplɪt ʌp ɪntə ˈgruːps | səʊ wi pəˈspəʊn̩ ˈtelɪŋ ɑə[9] ˈstɔːriz ʌntɪl ˈleɪtə | ðə ˈklɑːsɪz ˈwɜːn[7] ðæt[10] ˈbæd ˈrɪəli | ɔːlˈðəʊ aɪ ˈhædn̩[7] lʊk ˈfɔːwəd tə ði aɪˈdɪər[11] əv ˈgəʊɪŋ ɒn ˈhɒlɪdeɪ | ən hævɪŋ ˈlektʃəz θrəʊn ˈɪn | bət aɪ ˈspəʊz[12] ðət ə ˈskuːl ˈtrɪp | ɪzn̩[7] ðə ˈseɪm əz ə ˈhɒlɪdeɪ | ɪt ˈhæz[8] tə bi mɔː ˈkʌltʃrəl[5] | ˈdʌzn̩[7-13] ɪt | ɑə[9] ˈfɜːs ˈtiːtʃə wəz ə ˈveri naɪs ˈgaɪ | ən ɪz ˈlektʃə wəz ˈkwaɪt ˈɪntrəstɪŋ | hi ˈtəʊld[3] əs əˈbaʊt ðə ˈθɪŋz ðət wi wə ˈgəʊɪŋ tə ˈsiː ən ˈduː[8] | əʊvə ðə ˈneks ˈwiːk | ˈɑːftə ˈlʌntʃ | wi ˈwent[2] tə ðə ˈtaʊn ˈsentə tə ˈduː[8] səm ɪkˈsplɔːrɪŋ | wi wə ˈʃəʊn ə fjuː ˈlænmɑːks | ən ðen wi ˈvɪzɪtɪd ə ˈtʃɜːtʃ | wɪtʃ wəz weə *ˈʃeɪkspɪə wəz bəʊθ bæpˈtaɪzd[3] ən ˈberid | ɪt wəz ˈhɑːd tə ˈrɪəlaɪz ðət ju wə ˈstændɪŋ ɪn ðə ˈseɪm pleɪs əz ˈhiː[14] dɪd wen i wəz ˈlɪtl̩ | ˈwel | aɪ ˈspəʊz[12] i ˈwɒzn̩[7] rɪəli ˈstændɪŋ ət ɪz ˈkrɪsn̩ɪŋ[15] | hɪz ˈgreɪv hæd[8] ˈbjuːtɪfl̩ ɪŋˈgreɪvɪŋz ən ɪnˈskrɪpʃn̩z ɒn ɪt | bət ɪt wəz ˈdɪfɪklt[2] tə ˈsiː ɪt ˈprɒpli[15] | bɪkɒz ðə wəz ə ˈfens ɪn ˈfrʌnt[2-3] əv ɪt | ɪn ði ˈiːvnɪŋ wi wə ˈbʊk fə ðə ˈθɪətə | ˈɜːlɪə | wi əd ˈmænɪdʒ tə get ˈtɪkɪts wɪtʃ ɪnˈkluːdɪd ən əˈmeɪzɪŋ ˈbæksteɪdʒ ˈtɔː[16] | ən wi ˈθɔːt ðə ˈset wəz fænˈtæstɪk | səʊ wi wə ˈrɪəli lʊkɪŋ ˈfɔːwəd tə ˈsiːɪŋ ðə prəˈdʌkʃn̩ | ðə ˈkɜːtn̩ went[2-3] ˈʌp | ən aɪ fəˈgɒt əbaʊt ˈevrɪθɪŋ ˈels | ʌntɪl ðə ˈlɑːs ˈbaʊz ən ˈkɜːtsɪz wər[4-5] ˈəʊvə | ɪt wəz ˈbrɪljənt[2-17] | ðə ˈkɑːs wəz ˈveri ˈgʊd | ðə ˈstɔːri ˈfæbjʊləs | ən ði ˈendɪŋ spekˈtækjʊlə | aɪ ˈθʌrəli[5] ɪnˈdʒɔɪd ɪt | diˈspaɪt ə fjuː ˈdɪfɪklt[2] ˈwɜːdz | ən ˈdʒəʊks aɪ ˈdɪdn̩[7] get | ˈɔːl əv ðə ˈkærəktəz wə ˈfʌni | ɔːlˈðəʊ maɪ ˈfeɪvrɪts | wə ðə ˈwʊmənaɪzər[4] ən ðə ˈbɑːskɪt ˈkærɪəz | aɪ ˈθɔːt ðeə ˈfeɪʃl̩ ɪkˈspreʃn̩z wə hɪˈleərɪəs | ɑːftə ˈsiːɪŋ ðə ˈpleɪ | aɪ ˈfaɪnli ˈrɪəlaɪz waɪ ˈevriwʌn ˈθɪŋks hɪz ˈsʌtʃ ə ˈgræn̩ ˈpleɪraɪt | aɪ əd ˈneve rɪəli ˈred eni əv ɪz ˈwɜːk bɪˈfɔː | ɔːr ˈsiːn ˈeni əv ɪz ˈpleɪz | səʊ ˈðɪs wʌn wəz ən ˈaɪəʊpn̩ə[15] fə mi | ˈiːvn̩ ðəʊ ɪz ˈstɔːriz ər əʊvə ˈθriː hʌndrəd jɪəz ˈəʊld[17] | ðeɪ ˈsiːm tə mi ˈstɪl kwaɪt ˈmɒdn̩ | wɪtʃ ɪz ˈspəʊz[12] tə bi ðə ˈmɑːk əv ə ˈtruː ˈdʒiːnɪəs |

Comments to transcription

1. /ə/ cannot be deleted because it is not preceded by consonant.
2. The alveolar plosive cannot be deleted because it is not preceded by a consonant with the same voicing.
3. The alveolar plosive cannot be deleted because it is followed by vowel.
4. /ə/ cannot be deleted because it is not followed by an unstressed vowel in the same word.
5. /ə/ cannot be deleted because it is preceded by an approximant.
6. Strong form because *there* is used as a locative adverb here. ***

7. /t/ can be deleted although it is preceded by a voiced consonant because it is a negative contraction.

8. Strong form because here the verb is not used as an auxiliary.

9. Smoothing (see Lesson 2). ***

10. Strong form because *that* is used as a demonstrative.

11. Intrusive-r (see Lesson 4).

12. /sə'pəʊz/ is one of a group of words which are exceptional in that /ə/ may be elided although it doesn't meet the general conditions for the process.

13. /t/ may be elided even though it is followed by a vowel because it is a negative contraction.

14. Strong form because the grammatical word is being emphasised and therefore stressed.

15. Syllabicity could be applied here instead of /ə/ elision.

16. Monophthonging (see Lesson 2). ***

17. The alveolar plosive cannot be deleted because it is followed by a potential pause.

Exercise 6.4

| ˈlaːs ˈtaɪm aɪ wəz ɪn *ˈəələnd¹⁻² | maɪ ˈmʌðə ˈgeɪv mi səm ˈletəz tə ˈriːd | ðeɪ wə ˈrɪtn̩ tə hə ˈpeərənts³ ɪn *ˈɪŋglən wen wi wə ˈtʃɪldrən | maɪ ˈgrænpeərənts³ əd ˈseɪv ðəm fər⁴ ə | ən riˈtɜːn ðəm ˈniːtli ˈfaɪld⁵ ɪn ˈfəʊldəz ən ˈdeɪtɪd | wen wi ˈleft⁶ ˈhəʊm | ɪt wəz ə ˈsɔːt əv ˈmʌðəz aɪ ˈvjuː ˈrekɔːd əv aə¹ ˈtʃaɪldhʊd⁶ | ən ˈsɪns maɪ ˈpeərənts³ wə ˈbəʊθ prəˈlɪfɪk⁷⁻⁸ ən ˈwɪti ˈletə ˈraɪtəz | ðeɪ meɪd ˈwʌndəfl̩⁹ entəˈteɪnɪŋ ˈriːdɪŋ | aɪ wəz əbˈzɔːbd⁵ ɪn ðəm fər ˈaəz¹ | trænˈspɔːtɪd ˈbæk tə ˈmaːvləs⁹ aːftəˈnuːnz | ɪˈmædʒɪnətɪvli ˈwaɪld⁵ əˈweɪ ɪn aə¹ ˈpleɪrum wɪð maɪ ˈsɪblɪŋz ən ˈfrenz | ˈðeə¹⁰ wi ɪnˈventɪd ˈmeni əv aə¹ ˈəʊn ˈgeɪmz | ən ˈæktɪd aʊt ˈɔːl sɔːts əv ˈdraːməz | fə wɒtˈevər⁴ ˈɔːdɪəns wi kʊd ɪnˈtræp | ˈjuːʒuəli maɪ ˈpɔː¹¹ ˈmʌðər⁴ əv ˈkɔːs | ʃi ˈraɪts | fər⁴ ɪgˈzaːmpl̩ | əbaʊt əs biːɪŋ ɪnsˈpaːd¹ fə ˈmʌnθs | baɪ ə ˈkrɪsməs ˈtrɪp tə ði ɒpəˈreɪtə⁸ ðə *mɪˈkaːdəʊ¹² | wi ˈpʊt ɒn ən ˈekslənt⁹⁻³ ˈʃəʊ | wɪtʃ ɪŋˈkluːdɪd ˈkɒstjuːmz ən ˈprɒps | aə¹ ˈmʌðə meɪd ˈʃɔː¹¹ wi ˈɔːlweɪz hæd¹³ ˈplenti əv ˈθɪŋz | ðət wɪð ə ˈlɪtl̩ ˈskɪl ən ɪmædʒɪˈneɪʃn̩ | kʊd bi ˈtɜːnd⁵ ɪntə ˈnɪəli ˈeniθɪŋ | ʃi ˈpaːst⁵ ɒn tu əs ˈəʊl̩ ˈbedspredz ən ˈblæŋkəts | ˈɒd ˈɪərɪŋz | ˈglʌvz ən ˈsɒks | ˈpiːsɪz əv ˈleftəʊvə məˈtɪərɪəlz ən ˈdʒʌmbl̩ seɪl ækwɪˈzɪʃn̩z | ðɪs pəˈtɪkjʊlə ˈʃəʊ bɪkeɪm ə ˈklæsɪk wɪð aə¹ ˈdraːmə ˈkʌmpni¹⁴ | ˈsəʊ mʌtʃ ˈsəʊ | ðət ðə ˈneks dɔː ˈneɪbə priˈzentɪd əs wɪð ə riˈkɔːdɪŋ əv ðə *ˈpaərəts¹ əv *penˈzæns¹⁵ | ˈhəʊpɪŋ ɪt ˈtuː wʊd ˈkætʃ aə¹ ˈfænsi | ən ˈgɪv ɪm ə ˈbreɪk frəm ˈθri: ˈlɪtl̩ ˈmeɪdz frəm ˈskuːl ə ˈwiː¹⁶⁻¹⁷ | fləʊtɪŋ məˈlɒdɪkli bət ˈɔːl tuː ˈfriːkwəntli⁷⁻³ θruː ɪz ˈwɔːl | ɪt wəz ˈfʌn ˈriːdɪŋ ðeə ˈvɜːʃn̩ əv ən iˈvent³ wɪtʃ aɪ riˈmembə ˈhæpnɪŋ⁹ | ˈɔːlsəʊ ˈɪntrəstɪŋ tə ˈnəʊt haʊ ˈdɪfrənt⁷⁻³ maɪ memrɪz aː¹⁸ | frəm ˈðeə dɪˈskrɪpʃn̩z | ɒn ə mɔː ˈsɒləm ˈnəʊt | aɪ ˈfaʊn ðə wə ˈmeni θɪŋz ˈgəʊɪŋ ˈɒn | ðət ˈwiː¹⁹ əz ˈtʃɪldrən⁷ wər⁴⁻⁷ ˈʌnəˈweər ɒv¹⁸ | sɪns maɪ ˈpeərənts³ ˈwɒntɪd tə prəˈtekt⁵ əs frəm wɒtˈevə wi maɪt ˈfaɪn ˈwʌriɪŋ ɔːr ʌnˈpleznt²⁻³ | ɪt wəz ˈəʊnli baɪ ˈriːdɪŋ ðəʊz ˈletəz | ðət aɪ ˈrɪəlaɪzd⁶ haʊ ˈmeni ˈprɒbləmz maɪ ˈpeərənts³ hæd¹³ tə ˈdiːl wɪð | ən əˈpriːʃieɪtɪd ði əˈmaʊnt³⁻⁵ əv ˈθɪŋkɪŋ ən ˈkeə ðeɪ pʊt ˈɪntu aə¹ ˈʌpbrɪŋɪŋ | θruː ðə ˈletəz | aɪ ˈɔːlsəʊ dɪˈskʌvəd ˈɪntrəstɪŋ ˈvjuːz ɒn səm ˈpiːpl̩ wɪtʃ aɪ ˈəʊnli ˈnjuː əz ə ˈtʃaɪld | bət ˈnevə sɔː ˈmʌtʃ ɒv¹⁸ wen aɪ ˈgruː ˈʌp | fər⁴ ˈɪnstəns | wi ˈjuːs tə lʊk ˈfɔːwəd tə ˈvɪzɪts frəm ə ˈspeʃli⁹ ɪkˈsentrɪk ˈfæmli⁹ ˈfrend² | bɪkɒz wi ˈfaʊnd⁵ ɪm veri ˈɒd ən entəˈteɪnɪŋ |

maɪ ˈmʌðə juːs tə ˈdred ðəm | əˈpærəntli[7] wɪð ən ˈædʌlts[3] pəˈspektɪv | hɪz ˈɒdɪtiz wə ˈsʌmwɒt les əˈmjuːzɪŋ | əz ə rɪˈzʌlt[3–5] əv ðɪs ɪkˈspɪərɪəns | aɪ əm ˈfreʃli kənˈvɜːtɪd[8] tə ði ədˈvɑːntədʒɪz əv ˈletə raɪtɪŋ | ˈaɪ ˈtuː lɪv əˈbrɔːd ən hæv[13] ˈtʃɪldrən[7] | aɪ ˈduː[19] ˈraɪt tə maɪ ˈmʌðər[4] evri ˈnaʊ ən ˈðen | bət aɪ ˈmʌs[19] seɪ ðət aɪ ˈgɪv ɪn ˈɔːl tuː ˈfriːkwəntli[7] | tə ði ɪˈmiːdɪəsi əv ə ˈkwɪk ˈtelifəʊn ˈkɔːl | maɪ ˈmʌðə ˈseɪvz ˈmaɪ ˈletəz əz ˈhɜːz[20] dɪd | ən maɪ ˈtʃɪldrən[7] kʊd ənˈdʒɔɪ ə nɒsˈtældʒɪk ɑːftəˈnuːn | ˈberɪd ɪn ˈtʃaɪldhʊd[6] ˈmemrɪz wʌn ˈdeɪ | əz maɪ ˈmʌðə ˈsez | ə ˈfəʊn kɔːl ɪz ˈəʊvər[4] əz ˈsuːn əz ju hæŋ ˈʌp | bət ju kn̩ ˈriːd ə ˈletər[4] ˈəʊvər[4] ən ˈəʊvər[4] əˈgen |

Comments to transcription

1. Smoothing (see Lesson 2). ***
2. Elision is not possible because the alveolar plosive is followed by a potential pause.
3. The alveolar plosive cannot be elided because it is preceded by a consonant with different voicing.
4. /ə/ is not usually deleted when it is not followed by an unstressed syllable in the same word.
5. The alveolar plosive may not be deleted because it is followed by a vowel.
6. The alveolar plosive may not be deleted because it is followed by /h/.
7. /ə/ deletion is not possible because it is preceded by an approximant.
8. /ə/ is not usually elided when it precedes the stressed syllable.
9. Syllabicity could be applied here instead of /ə/ elision.
10. *there* is used in the strong form because here it is a locative adverb. ***
11. Monophthonging (see Lesson 2). ***
12. *The Mikado*, operetta by Gilbert and Sullivan.
13. Strong form because the verb is not used as an auxiliary here.
14. Elision of /ə/ is possible even though it is preceded by two consonants one of which is a nasal. The general conditions for sounds which can precede /ən/ sequences for schwa elision are wider than those for nasal syllabicity (see Lesson 5).
15. *The Pirates of Penzance,* operetta by Gilbert and Sullivan.
16. Strong form because the word is stressed. The syllable is stressed because of rhythmic reasons since the phrase is a quotation from a song.
17. 'Three Little Maids Are We' is a song in *The Mikado*.
18. Strong form because the grammatical word is stranded.
19. Strong form because the grammatical word is emphasised and therefore stressed.
20. The possessive pronouns are not used in weak form.

Exercise 6.5

| wen ðə ˈmen əˈpɪəd ət ðə ˈdɔː | ˈbrændɪʃɪŋ ə ˈwɒrənt[1–2] tə ˈsɜːtʃ hə ˈhaʊs | ʃi ˈdɪdn̩[3] ˈθɪŋk tə ˈtʃek ðət ɪt wəz ə ˈdʒenjuɪn wʌn | ɪt wəz bɪkɒz ʃi wəz ˈstɪl hɑːf əˈsliːp | ən ˈkʊdn̩[3] ˈriˈæk prɒpli[4] | ʃi əd ˈəʊnli gɒt bæk ˈjestədeɪ | ɑːftər[5] ə ˈhɒlɪdeɪ əˈbrɔːd | ðə ˈlɒŋ ˈflaɪt ˈhəʊm | əd biːn ˈveri ˈtaərɪŋ[6] | ən ʃi ˈwent[2] tə ˈbed əz ˈsuːn əz ʃi əd ˈɔːgnaɪz[4] ˈsʌm[7] əv ə ˈstʌf | ʃi dɪˈsaɪdɪd tə ˈliːv ˈməʊs θɪŋz ɪn ðə ˈsuːtkeɪsɪz tɪl ðə ˈneks ˈdeɪ | ðen ˈʃɔːtli ɑːftə ˈsevn̩ ɪn ðə ˈmɔːnɪŋ | ðə ˈdɔːbel ˈræŋ | ˈfɒləʊd baɪ ˈlaʊd ˈnɒkɪŋ | ðə ˈmen wɔː ˈdɑːk ˈsuːts | ən ˈtəʊl* ˈɪndə ðət ðeɪ wə ˈpliːs[8] dɪˈtektɪvz | nɑːˈkɒtɪks dɪˈvɪʒn̩ | ˈevriθɪŋ wəz ˈsəʊ ʌnˈrɪəl | ʃi ˈkep ˈwʌndrɪŋ ɪf ɪt wəz ə ˈdriːm | ə ˈnaɪtmeər ɔː ˈsʌm[9] kaɪnd[10] əv ə ˈpræktɪkl̩ ˈdʒəʊk | bət ði aɪˈdɪər[11] əv ɪt ˈbiːɪŋ ə ˈgeɪm |

'suːn left[12] hə 'maɪnd[13] | wen ðə diˈtektɪvz gɒt tə 'wɜːk | ðeɪ went[2] 'streɪt ʌp tə hə
'bedrʊm | ən ʃi kʊd 'hɪə laʊd 'nɔɪzɪz əz 'drɔːz wər 'emptɪd | ən 'drɒp 'keələsli | 'wʌn
əv ðəm riˈmeɪn daʊn'steəz | ən ɪgˈzæmɪnd[12] hə 'desk | hi 'sed ðət ɪt 'wʊdn̩[3] teɪk
ðəm 'lɒŋ | ʃi 'niːdn̩[3] 'wʌri | ðeɪ 'mʌs[14] bi 'treɪɪŋ tə 'faɪn 'drʌgz | ɪf ðeɪ wər[1-5] 'ɪn
naːˈkɒtɪks | bət 'waɪ ɪn 'hɜː[14]'haʊs | ʃid 'nevə 'delt[2] wɪð 'ðæt[15] kaɪnd[10] əv 'stʌf |
nɒt 'iːvn̩ əz ə 'juːzə | 'let əˈləʊn əz ə 'diːlə | ʃi 'aːsk ðə diˈtektɪv | bət gɒt 'nəʊ
kəˈhɪərənt[2-10] 'aːnsər 'aʊt əv ɪm | wi 'hæv[16] ə 'wɒrənt[2-13] | wəz 'ɔːl ʃi 'mænɪdʒ
tu ʌndəˈstæn wʌns əˈgen | ʃi 'hɜːd ə 'vɔɪs ʌpˈsteəz | 'aːskɪŋ ði 'ʌðəz ɪf ðeɪ əd
'tʃek ðə 'suːtkeɪsɪz | *'lɪndə 'rɪəlaɪz ðət ðə 'mʌst[10-14] əv biːn sʌm[9] mɪˈsteɪk |
'meɪbi ðeɪ 'gɒt ðə 'rɒŋ əˈdres | ʃi 'pɪk ðə 'fəʊn ʌp | tə 'kɔːl ðə 'pliːs[8] steɪʃn̩ 'nɪərɪs
tə hə 'haʊs | ðə diˈtektɪv 'stɒp wɒt i wəz 'duːɪŋ | 'wɔːk təˈwɔːdz ər ən 'græb ðə
riˈsiːvə frəm hə 'hænd[13] | waɪls 'kʌtɪŋ ɒf ðə 'kɔːl wɪð ɪz 'ʌðə 'hænd[13] | aɪm 'ʃɔː[17]
ju dəʊn[3] 'niːd tə 'fəʊn enibɒdi i 'sed | ɪt wəz 'ðen ðət ʃi biˈkeɪm səˈspɪʃəs | 'waɪ
'ʃʊdn̩[3] ʃi 'juːz ðə 'fəʊn | ʃi 'əʊnli 'ment[2] tə 'kɔːl ðə 'steɪʃn̩ tə 'klærɪfaɪ ðə sɪtʃuˈeɪʃn̩
| hi 'wʊdn̩[3] let ə 'siː ðə 'wɒrənt[2-10] əˈgen wen ʃi 'aːskt[10] ɪm | ðeɪ əd ɔːlˈredi 'ʃəʊn
ɪt tu ə | 'hædn̩[3] ðeɪ | 'haʊ meni 'taɪmz dɪd ʃi 'wɒnt[2] tə 'siː ɪt | ðə 'mæn sed ʃi
ʃʊd 'sɪt 'daʊn | ən 'traɪ tə bi 'peɪʃn̩t[2] fər[5] ə 'bɪt 'lɒŋgə | *'lɪndə 'dɪd əz ʃi wəz
'təʊld[13] | waɪlst[10] ən aɪˈdɪə 'dɔːnd[10] ɒn ə | 'ðɪs məs bi 'lɪŋk tə 'jestədeɪz 'mes ʌp
wɪð ðə 'lʌgɪdʒ | ʃi əd 'pɪk ðə 'rɒŋ 'bæg ʌp | bət 'fɔːtʃn̩ətli[4] ʃid 'nəʊtɪs bifɔː 'liːvɪŋ
ði 'eəpɔːt | ʃid gɒn 'bæk ən ɪkˈspleɪn tə 'wʌn əv ðə 'graʊn staːf | ðeɪ wə 'veri
riˈliːv tə 'siː ə | ði 'əʊnər[5] əv ðə 'bæg əd biːn 'ðeə[18] biˈfɔːr ə | hi wəz ɪkˈstriːmli
'æŋgri | ən əd 'faɪld[10] ɪz kəmˈpleɪnt[2-10] əgens ði 'eəlaɪn ɪn 'raːðə 'strɒŋ 'tɜːmz |
ʃi əˈpɒlədʒaɪz fə hə 'blʌndə | ən 'sɪns hər[5] 'əʊn 'lʌgɪdʒ wəz 'raɪt 'ðeə[18] | ʃi 'pʊt ɪt
ɒn ðə 'trɒli | ən 'wɔːk təwɔːdz ðə 'tæksi ræŋk | ʃi əd biːn 'slaɪtli kənˈsɜːn̩[19] ðət
hə 'fuːlɪʃnəs əd ʌpˈset ə 'feləʊ 'pæsɪndʒə səʊ 'mʌtʃ | bət əz 'suːn əz ʃi əˈraɪv
bæk 'həʊm | ʃi fəˈgɒt ðə 'həʊl 'epɪsəʊd | ʌntɪl 'naʊ | 'huːz[20] 'bæg əd ʃi mɪˈsteɪkn̩li
'jæŋk frəm ðə 'lʌgɪdʒ 'belt[2-13] | 'wɒt əd ɪt kənˈteɪn[19] ðət ðiːz 'səʊkɔːl diˈtektɪvz | wə
'lʊkɪŋ fɔːr[21] ɪn 'sʌtʃ ə 'θʌrə 'mænə | ən 'huː[20] 'wɜː[14] ðeɪ | 'eniweɪ | 'ʃɔːli[17] nɒt hu ðeɪ
priˈtendɪd tə bi |

Comments to transcription

1. /ə/ elision is not possible because it is preceded by an approximant.
2. The alveolar plosive may not be deleted because it is preceded by a consonant of different voicing.
3. /t/ is deleted even though the previous consonant is voiced because it is a negative contraction.
4. Syllabicity could be applied here instead of /ə/ elision.
5. /ə/ is not usually deleted when it is not followed by an unstressed syllable in the same word.
6. Smoothing (see Lesson 2). ***
7. Strong form because *some* is used as a pronoun (see Lesson 3).
8. Special case of /ə/ elision when preceding a stressed syllable.
9. Strong form when *some* modifies a countable noun in the singular (see Lesson 3).
10. The alveolar plosive may not be deleted because it is followed by a vowel.
11. Intrusive-r (see Lesson 4).
12. The alveolar plosive may not be deleted because it is followed by /h/.
13. The alveolar plosive may not be deleted because it is followed by a potential pause.

14. Strong form because the grammatical word is emphasised and therefore stressed.
15. Strong form because *that* is used as a demonstrative here.
16. Strong form because the verb is not used as an auxiliary here.
17. Monophthonging (see Lesson 2). ***
18. Strong form because *there* is used as a locative adverb here. ***
19. /ə/ is not usually elided when it precedes the stressed syllable.
20. Strong form because it is an interrogative pronoun.
21. Strong form because the grammatical word is stranded.

Answers to Lesson 7: assimilation

Orthographic version for the sample transcription passage

My holiday in the islands was sheer bliss, the only bad point being having to take so many flights – four in all – which just about did my nerves in. The weather around the coast was very odd. It was genuinely cold for a couple of days, warm and cloudy the third, and then scorching hot the next four. Apparently the winter and spring there had been quite cold, which I think surprised the staff, who had planned to spend the winter months working in better and warmer climes. Our friends had claimed to have some misgivings about going on a sailing holiday, since they had no experience about boats. I, of course, was already an old hand. Apart from the usual teenage lessons and boat trips with the girl scouts, I had been out with John several times since we got married two years ago. Needless to say, all my supposed knowledge was absolutely no use, so that Heather and I managed to capsize the boat every time we went out on our own. We soon got through a lot of outfits those first few days. I even fell in wearing my down-padded coat, which meant not only that I didn't have anything warm to wear for the rest of the holiday, but also that I was sucked down under the water by the weight of the coat when it got wet. Fortunately, the life-jackets were really good and I soon came up again, but it frightened me so much that I started hyperventilating with shock. At that point the other boat had already rowed in my direction. John leaned over and held me afloat, whilst shaking me and telling me to stop it and calm down. Then I was fished out and went back to the hotel feeling totally miserable. One day John chartered a yacht with the rest of us as his crew and we went off round Jackie Onassis's private island. We got off for lunch on another island a bit further on still. It's a really beautiful area, although Heather and Paul were surprised at how rundown all the little towns were – very poor, and quite grubby. I actually prefer it like that, because it seems more real to me. Anything else would look like some kind of glorified theme park. As a foursome, we got on wonderfully well. John and Paul hit it off right away, as Paul was immediately bitten by the sailing bug, and so he could share his enthusiasm with John. On the last day the sailing club manager and owner of the business presented Paul with a special prize. He said that never in all the years he had been at the club had he seen anyone try so hard or put in so many hours' practice, especially as it was his first time ever aboard a boat. On the way back, at Heathrow airport Paul bought himself a couple of yachting magazines and said that he is going to start looking out for a secondhand boat already, so Heather is now resigned to a future including a boat-mad husband. As you can imagine, after all the fun we had, going back home was a terrible letdown, especially because John and I won't be able to spend time together again until the summer arrives. I know that it can't be avoided, so it's pointless getting into a state about it, but I can't help wishing we could have stayed on for a whole month instead of just a few days, or even that it was possible to extend the sailing holiday into a lifestyle. It doesn't sound sensible, but there are people out there who have taken such decisions, abandoning career and country in search of a more enjoyable, humane or fulfilling lifestyle.

Exercise 7.1

(a) /reb bʊk/   (b) /dʌʒ ʃi/   (c) /bæk pɑːt/
(d) /wəʊŋk gəʊ/   (e) /wʌm baɪ wʌn/   (f) /hæs tu/
(g) /hæd tu/   (h) /ʃʊgŋk kʌm/   (i) /ðɪʃ jɪə/

Exercise 7.2: Edited orthographic version (*Assimilation is marked in bold type.*)

I've just been told a tragic story. A friend of mine's recently been on a trip abroad. He was doing some lectures at a couple of universities in South America. I think he went to Chile, Argentina and Brazil. He had a wonderful time. Apparently, while he was there, he had quite a lot of free time for sightseeing and he bought masses of souvenirs to bring back with him. He and his wife are very keen collectors of pottery and paintings and rugs and things like that. He was a bit concerned while he was over there that some of this stuff would get damaged, because some of the trips he did were in really rough country and the transport you have to use is often quite primitive. He told me that once he had to do a forty mile journey sitting on the roof of a bus. Anyway, he managed to get back to England with everything in one piece. He landed back at Heathrow airport at some really uncivilised hour and decided to get a taxi back home, rather than struggle with all this stuff on public transport. He had all his clothes in one case and all these beautiful things he'd bought in another. The taxi dropped him at his front door and he got out with his suitcases and put them down while he paid the taxi driver. The taxi then started off, but for some reason in reverse, ran over his suitcase and ruined everything he'd bought.

Transcription

| aɪv dʒəsp[1] biːn ˈtəʊld ə ˈtrædʒɪk ˈstɔːri | ə ˈfrend əv ˈmaɪnz | ˈriːsəntli biːn ɒn ə ˈtrɪp əˈbrɔːd | hi wəz ˈduːɪŋ səm ˈlektʃəz | ət ə ˈkʌpl̩ əv juːniˈvɜːsətiz[2] ɪn *saʊθ *əˈmerɪkə | aɪ ˈθɪŋk i ˈwent tə *ˈtʃɪli | *ɑːdʒn̩ˈtiːnə | əm[3] *brəˈzɪl | hi hæd[4] ə ˈwʌndəfl̩ ˈtaɪm | əˈpærəntli | ˈwaɪl i wəz ˈðeə | hi hæg[4] ˈkwaɪt ə ˈlɒt əv ˈfriː ˈtaɪm fə ˈsaɪtsiːɪŋ | ən i ˈbɔːp ˈmæsəz əv suːvəˈnɪəz | tə ˈbrɪŋ ˈbæk wɪð ɪm | ˈhiː[5] ən ɪz ˈwaɪf | ə ˈveri kiːŋ kəˈlektəz əv ˈpɒtri | əm[3] ˈpeɪntɪŋz | ən ˈrʌgz | ən ˈθɪŋz laɪk ˈðæt[6] | hi wəz ə ˈbɪk kənˈsɜːnd | ˈwaɪl i wəz ˈəʊvə ˈðeə | ðət ˈsʌm[7] əv ðɪs ˈstʌf wʊg get ˈdæmɪdʒd[8] | bikəz[9] ˈsʌm[7] əv ðə ˈtrɪps i ˈdɪd | wər ɪn ˈrɪəli ˈrʌf ˈkʌntri | ən ðə ˈtrɑːnspɔːt ju ˈhæf[4–10] tə ˈjuːz | ɪz ˈɒfŋ̩ ˈkwaɪp ˈprɪmɪtɪv | hi ˈtəʊl[1] mi ðət ˈwʌns | hi ˈhæd[4] tə ˈduː[4] ə ˈfɔːti maɪl ˈdʒɜːni | ˈsɪtɪŋ ɒn ðə ˈruːf əv ə ˈbʌs | ˈeniweɪ | hi ˈmænɪdʒ tə ˈgep ˈbæk tu *ˈɪŋglən wɪð ˈevrɪθɪŋ ɪn ˈwʌm ˈpiːs | hi ˈlændəb[11] bæk ət *ˈhiːθrəʊ ˈeəpɔːt | ət sʌm[12] ˈrɪəli ʌnˈsɪvɪlaɪzd ˈaə | ən diˈsaɪdəd[11] tə ˈget ə ˈtæksi bæk ˈhəʊm | ˈrɑːðə ɒn ˈstrʌgl̩ wɪð ɔːl ðɪs ˈstʌf

ɒm ˈpʌblɪk ˈtraːnspɔːt | hi hæd[4] ˈɔːl ɪz ˈkləʊðz ɪn ˈwʌɳ ˈkeɪs | ən ˈɔːl ðiːz ˈbjuːtɪfl̩
ˈθɪŋz ɪb̬ ˈbɔːt | ɪn əˈnʌðə | ðə ˈtæksi ˈdrɒpt ɪm ət ɪz ˈfrʌnt ˈdɔː | ən i ˈgɒt ˈaʊt wɪð ɪz
ˈsuːk̬keɪsəz[11] | əm[3] ˈpʊt ðəm ˈdaʊn | waɪl i ˈpeɪd ðə ˈtæksi ˈdraɪvə | ðə ˈtæksi ðen
ˈstɑːtəd[11] ˈɒf | bət fə ˈsʌm[12] ˈriːzn̩ | ɪn riˈvɜːs | ˈræn ˈəʊvər ɪz ˈsuːk̬keɪs | ən ˈruːɪnd
ˈevriθɪŋ ɪb̬ ˈbɔːt |

Comments to transcription

1. In this case one can either delete the alveolar plosive or assimilate it.
2. Alternatively, /ə/ could be elided in which case the alveolar fricative would be made longer giving the pronunciation /juːnivɜːsstiz/. This is a special type of /ə/ elision since a trace of the presence of /ə/ is left behind, in this case the greater duration of the fricative sound. Some people call it 'pseudo-elision'. The term was introduced by J C Wells.
3. The alveolar plosive could have been assimilated instead of deleted, giving rise to a double assimilation.
4. Strong form because the verb is not an auxiliary here.
5. The strong form is used because the grammatical word is emphasised and therefore stressed.
6. Strong form because *that* is a demonstrative here. ***
7. Strong form because in this case *some* is used as a pronoun (see Lesson 3).
8. Assimilation is inhibited by the potential pause.
9. /bikəz/ and /bikɒz/ are alternative pronunciations. The first syllable may also be pronounced /bə/.
10. This is one of the few cases in which voice assimilation is possible in current RP English.
11. Remember that /ɪ/ and /ə/ are alternative pronunciations in many endings such as the regular past tense morpheme when the previous sound is /t/ or /d/, the morpheme 's' when it follows a sibilant consonant, the superlative morpheme 'est' or in the suffixes 'ness' and 'less' (see Lesson 3).
12. *some* is used in the strong form when it modifies a countable noun in singular (see Lesson 3).

Exercise 7.3: Transcription

/aɪ ˈflʌŋkt ˈaʊt ɪm̬ maɪ ˈfɜːs[1] ˈjɪə | aɪ ˈdəʊn nəʊ ˈwaɪ | aɪ ˈθɔːt aɪ wəz ˈduːɪŋ ɔːlˈraɪt
| bət wen ɪk̬ ˈkeɪm tə ði ˈend əv ˈjɪər ɪgˈzæmz | aɪ dʒəs[2] ˈpænɪkt | ən ˈfeɪld
ˈevriθɪŋ | ˈeniweɪ ðeɪ ˈsed aɪ kəd[3] ˈteɪk ə jɪər ˈaʊt | ən riːˈsɪt ˈevriθɪŋ ðə ˈneks
ˈsʌmə | ən ɪf aɪ ˈpɑːst | aɪ kʊd ˈðeɳ gəʊ ɒn tə ðə ˈsekɳ[4] ˈpɑːt əv ðə ˈkɔːs |
maɪ ˈdæd wəz ˈfjʊəriəs | hi ˈiːvn̩ ˈθretn̩ tə ˈθrəʊ mi ˈaʊt əv ðə ˈhaʊs | ɪn ði
ˈend[5] | ˈmʌm ən ˈaɪ ˈmænɪdʒ tə ˈkɑːm ɪm ˈdaʊn[5] | bət i ˈstɪl ɪnˈsɪstəd ðət aɪ
ʃəg[3] ˈgəʊ aʊt ən ˈfaɪnd ə ˈdʒɒb ɪˈmiːdjətli | hi ˈgeɪv mi ˈtuː ˈwiːks | ɪt ˈwɒzn̩ ˈiːzi
| ði ˈəʊnli ˈdʒɒb aɪ kəg[3] ˈget | wəz ˈstækɪŋ ˈʃelvz ɪn ə ˈsuːpəmɑːkɪt | ɪf ˈeniwʌn
səˈdʒests ðətʃu ˈstæk ˈʃelvz ɪn ə ˈsuːpəmɑːkɪt | ˈdʒʌs[6] ˈdəʊnt | ðə ˈwɜːk ɪz
ɪɳˈkredəbli ˈdʌl | ən ðə ˈpeɪ ɪz[7] dʒəs ˈluːdɪkrəs | aɪ ˈθɪŋk aɪ gɒp̬ peɪd ˈtuː
paʊnz[8] ˈfɪfti ən ˈɑə | ən ðə ˈpiːpl̩ ðeə wər ʌmbiˈliːvəbl̩ | ðə ˈmænɪdʒər ɪm̬
pətɪkjʊlə wəz ə ˈrɪəli ʌmˈplezm̬p[9] ˈpɜːsn̩ | hi ˈθɔːt ˈhiː[6] wəz ði ˈəʊnli ˈwʌn ɪn ðə
ˈhəʊl ˈpleɪs | hu hæb̬[10] ˈmɔː ɒ̃n əˈbaʊt ˈtuː ˈbreɪn ˈselz | ən ðə ˈkʌstəməz wər
ˈɔːfl̩ ˈtuː | aɪ ˈdəʊn nəʊ ˈwaɪ ˈpiːpl̩ hæf[11] tə ˈtriːtʃ̬ə[12] laɪk ˈdɜːt | ˈdʒʌs[2-6] bikəg̬[13]

jɔː ˈduːɪŋ ə ˈsɪmpl̩ ˈdʒɒb | ðə wər ə ˈnʌmbər əv ˈtaɪmz | wen aɪ ˈnɪəli ˈlɒs² maɪ ˈtempə | ən ˈtəʊl ˈsʌmwʌn wɒt aɪ ˈrɪəli ˈθɔːt əv ðəm | bət ˈðen aɪ wʊd əv ˈgɒt ðə ˈsæk | əm¹⁴ maɪ ˈdæd wʊd əv ˈhɪt ðə ˈruːf | aɪ ˈdəʊn nəʊ ˈhaʊ aɪ ˈstʊg ˈgəʊɪŋ tə ðə ˈpleɪs fər əz ˈlɒŋ əz aɪ ˈdɪd | aɪ kn̩ ˈtel ju ɪt ˈteɪks ə ˈlɒt tə ˈgep mi tə ˈgəʊ ɪntu ə ˈsuːpəmɑːkɪt ˈðiːz ˈdeɪz | aɪ fiːl ˈkwaɪt ˈsɪk dʒəs ˈθɪŋkɪŋ əˈbaʊt ɪt/

Comments to transcription

1. Even if the alveolar plosive had not been deleted, coalescence with the following /j/ would not have been usual in RP English because the approximant is not in a grammatical word.
2. The alveolar plosive could have been assimilated instead of elided.
3. Weaker, more colloquial, version (see Lesson 2).
4. Here there is an option between progressive assimilation (as in our version) or regressive bilabial assimilation. In the second case the alveolar /d/ could have been retained and assimilated rather than deleted. The retention of the plosive is also possible in the first case, but it cannot be assimilated. Accordingly, the following are alternative pronunciations for 'second part' in the exercise: /sekŋ pɑːt/ or /sekŋd pɑːt/(progressive assimilation with and without deletion of the alveolar); /sekm̩b pɑːt/ (double regressive assimilation); /sekm̩ pɑːt/ (regressive assimilation and alveolar deletion).
5. Assimilation can be blocked by a potential pause.
6. Strong form because the grammatical word is emphasised, and therefore stressed.
7. In other English accents, the alveolar fricatives can become post-alveolars by assimilation to a following post-alveolar affricate, as in the text here, but not in RP.
8. Notice the word-internal alveolar plosive deletion (see Lesson 6).
9. Double assimilation.
10. Strong form because the verb is not an auxiliary here.
11. This is one of the few cases in which voicing assimilation is possible in current RP.
12. The pronunciation /jə/ for *you* in *treat you* is a more colloquial alternative (see Lesson 3).
13. /bikəz/ and /bikɒz/ are alternative pronunciations. The first syllable may also be pronounced /bə/.
14. The alveolar plosive could have been assimilated rather than elided, giving rise to a double assimilation.

Orthographic version

I flunked out in my first year. I don't know why. I thought I was doing all right, but when it came to the end of year exams, I just panicked and failed everything. Anyway, they said I could take a year out and resit everything the next summer and if I passed I could then go on to the second part of the course. My dad was furious. He even threatened to throw me out of the house. In the end Mum and I managed to calm him down, but he still insisted that I should go out and find a job immediately. He gave me two weeks. It wasn't easy. The only job I could get was stacking shelves in a supermarket. If anyone suggests that you stack shelves in a supermarket, just don't. The work is incredibly dull and the pay is just ludicrous. I think I got paid two pounds fifty an hour. And the people there were unbelievable. The manager in particular was a really unpleasant person. He thought he was the only one in the whole place who had more than about two brain cells. And the customers were awful too. I don't know why people have to treat you like dirt just because you're doing a simple job. There were a number of times when I nearly lost my temper and told someone what I really thought of them. But then I would have got the sack and my dad would have hit the roof. I don't know how I stood going to the place for as long as I did. I can tell you it takes a lot to get me to go into a supermarket these days. I feel quite sick just thinking about it.

Exercise 7.4

| ðə ˈfɜːs taɪm *ˈdʒəʊn sɔː ðə ˈhaʊs | ʃi ˈnjuː ɪt wəz ˈweə ʃi əb biːm ˈbɔːn | ɪt ˈwɒzn̩ əz ðəʊ *ˈdʒəʊŋ kʊd riˈmembər ˈenibɒdi dɪˈskraɪbɪŋ ɪt | hə ˈpeərənts əb ˈpɑːst əˈweɪ wen ʃi wəz ˈəʊnli ˈθriː jɪəz ˈəʊld | səʊ ʃi riˈteɪn ˈnəʊ klɪə ˈmemri əv ðəm | hə ˈgræmpeərənts[1] əb biːn fəˈbɪdn̩ tə set ˈfʊt ɒn ðə ˈprɒpəti | bəʊθ bɪˈfɔː ðə ˈtrædʒədi | ən ˈɑːftə | ɪt ˈwɒzm̩ bikɒz ðə ˈneɪm əv ðə ˈhaʊs |*ˈfɔːweɪz | wɪtʃ wəz hər ˈʌŋklʃ ˈfeɪvrɪt ˈdʒæz sɒŋ | ˈstɜːd hə ˈmemri | ˈiːvn̩ ðəʊ hər ˈʌŋkl̩ ˈpleɪd ɪk̩ ˈkɒnstəntli | fə ˈsʌm[2] ˈriːzn̩ ʃid ˈɔːlweɪz ˈheɪtɪd ɪt wɪð ə ˈreə ˈvaələns | nɒt ət ˈɔːl ɪŋ ˈkærəktə wɪð hə ˈʌðəwaɪz ˈmaɪl[3] pɜːsəˈnæləti | ɪp ˈmaɪp bi ðə ˈtrelɪs wɪð ðə ˈpɔɪzn̩ ˈaɪvi twaɪnd əˈraʊnd ɪt | ðen əˈgen | ˈðæk[4] kʊb bi hər ˈɑːnts ˈɪnfluəns | ˈnəʊ | ɪn hə ˈhɑːt ʃi ˈnjuː əʒ ˈʃɔːli əʒ ʃi kəd ˈsiː ðə ˈblækt aʊp ˈpeɪnz ɪn ðə kənˈsɜːvətri ˈwɪndəʊz | ðət ˈðɪs wəz ðə ˈhaʊs ɪn ˈwɪtʃ ʃi əb biːm ˈbɔːn | ði ˈɑːskɪŋ ˈpraɪs wəz ˈmɔː ɒn ʃi əb ˈplæn tə ˈspend | ɪn ˈfækt ɪf ʃi ˈspent ˈðɪs mʌtʃ | ðə wʊb bi ˈnəʊ mʌni ˈlef fə ˈfɜːnɪtʃər ɔːr ˈeniθɪŋ wɪtʃ ˈniːdɪd ˈduːɪŋ | ˈʃig ˈgɒn ɪn wɪð ði ˈeɪdʒənt | ən wɪðɪn ˈsekŋz | hə ˈmaɪn wəz meɪd ˈʌp | ʃi ˈmʌst[5] ˈhæv[6] ɪt | ənd ɑːftər ˈɔːl sed ði ˈeɪdʒənt | ˈevriθɪŋ ɪz ɪm ˈprɪti gʊg kənˈdɪʃn̩ | ət ˈliːs ði ɪmˈpɔːtn̩t ˈθɪŋz | ən ɪt ɪz ˈfʊli ˈfɜːnɪʃt | ʃʊdʒu ˈteɪk ɪt | ˈɔːl jud ˈhæv[6] tə ˈspend | ɪz ˈtaɪm gɪvɪŋ ɪt ə ˈθʌrə ˈkliːnɪŋ | ən ði ˈəʊnə wɪl ˈletʃu ˈkiːp ɔːl ðə ˈkɒntənts | ən hi wəz ˈraɪt | ɪn ˈfækt | ˈwʌns ðə ˈlɪnəŋ ˈkʌvəz wə ˈteɪkŋ[7] ˈɒf | ɪk̩ kʊd ˈlʊk əz ɪf ɪt wəz ˈstɪl ˈlɪvd ɪn | ˈrʌgz əŋ[1] ˈkʊʃnz | ˈɔːnəmənts ɒn ðə ˈmæntl̩piːs ən ɒn ˈsaɪd teɪbl̩z | ðə ˈkɪtʃn̩ wəz rɪˈkwɪp tə ðə ˈlɑːs ˈsɔːspən əmb[8–9] ˈpleɪt | əʒ ʃi ˈstɒpt ət ðə ˈdɔːweɪ | ən ˈɪmɪdʒ tʊk ˈəʊvə hə ˈmaɪŋ[1] kəmˈpliːtli | ə ˈjʌn ˈwʊmən wəz ˈstændɪŋ wɪð hə ˈbæk tə ðə ˈdɔː | ˈbendɪŋ əʊvə ðə ˈstəʊv | əŋ[1] ˈgetɪŋ ˈsʌmθɪŋ ˈaʊt əv ði ˈʌvn̩ | *ˈdʒəʊn felt ˈdɪzi | ʃi ˈliːnd əgens ðə ˈdɔːfreɪm fə stəˈbɪlɪti | əz ˈsuːn əz ɪt əg̩ ˈkʌm | ðə ˈvɪʒn̩ wəz[10] dʒəs[3] ˈgɒn | ðə ˈkɪtʃn̩ wəz ʌnɪnˈhæbɪtɪd wʌns ˈmɔː | ɪp ˈmʌst[11] əv biːn ə ˈmɪkstʃər əv ˈlæk əv ˈfuːd | ən ˈəʊvər ˈæktɪv ɪmædʒɪˈneɪʃn̩ | ʃi went ˈaʊt tə ðə ˈhɔːlweɪ | ði ˈeɪdʒn̩t wəz ˈnəʊweər ɪn ˈsaɪt[12] | ˈkɔːʃəsli | *ˈdʒəʊm prəˈsiːdɪd wɪð hər ɪnˈspekʃn̩ | ʃi ˈwent təwɔːdz ðə ˈbæk əv ðə ˈhaʊs | ənd ɪntə ə ˈlɑːdʒ ˈruːm əʊvəˈlʊkɪŋ ðə ˈgɑːdn̩ | fə ˈsʌm[2] ˈriːzn̩ ʃi ˈnjuː ɪt əb biːŋ ˈkɔːl ðə ˈsʌnruːm[13] | ðə wə ˈsevrəl ˈwɪkər ˈɑːmtʃeəz wɪð ˈflaəri ˈkɒkŋ[8] ˈkʌvəz | ˈtuː ˈglɑːs tɒp ˈkɒfi teɪbl̩z | əm[1] ˈpɒtɪb ˈplɑːnts ˈevriweə | ðə wəz ən ˈæpməsfɪər əv ˈkʌmfətəbl̩ ˈlɪvd ɪn ˈtaɪdɪnəs | ət ðə ˈraɪt ˈemb[8–9] baɪ ðə ˈfrentʃ ˈwɪndəʊz | stud ə ˈgræm[1] piˈænəʊ | wɪð ˈsevrəl ˈfreɪmz ɒn ˈtɒp əv ɪt | *ˈdʒəʊn went ˈɪn tə ˈhæv[6] ə ˈkləʊsə ˈlʊk | ˈblæk ənd waɪt ˈfəʊtəgrɑːfs | ɪn ˈɔːl əv ðəm | ðə ˈseɪm piːpl̩ əˈpɪəd ɪn ˈdɪfrənt sɪˈnɑːriəʊz əm[1] ˈpɒstʃəz | ðə ˈwʊmən ʃid rɪˈmædʒɪnd ɪn ðə

'kɪtʃn̩ | ə 'mæn ɪn ɪz 'leɪt 'θɜːtiz | ən ə 'lɪtl̩ 'blɒŋg⁸⁻⁹ 'gɜːl | ðə 'ruːm 'riːld ə'raʊn
*'dʒəʊn | ən ʃi gɒt ðə 'seɪm 'nɔːzɪəs 'fiːlɪŋ ə'gen | wen ʃi wəz 'eɪbl̩ tu 'əʊpm̩ hər
'aɪʒ ʃi 'sɔːr¹⁴ ɪt 'ɔːl ɪn ə 'flæʃ | ðə 'mæn wəz ət ðə pi'ænəʊ wɪð ðə 'lɪtl̩ 'gɜːl sɪtɪŋ
'baɪ ɪm | hə 'fɪŋgəz¹⁵ 'smɔːl ən 'tʃʌbi bɪsaɪd 'hɪz¹⁶ ɒn ðə 'kiːz | ɪt wəz 'hɜː⁵ | ən ðə
'mæn wəz hə 'faːðə | ðə 'melədi wəz biːɪŋ 'pɔːli 'pleɪb bɪkɒz əv 'hɜː⁵
kɒntrɪ'bjuːʃn̩¹² | bət 'stɪl 'rekəgnaɪzəbl̩ | ɪt wəz *'fɔːweɪz | waɪl ʃi wəz 'steərɪŋ
ət ðəm | 'sʌm² 'ɪnstɪŋk 'təʊld ə tə 'lʊk aʊt əv ðə 'wɪndəʊ | ðə 'wʊmən |
*'dʒəʊnz 'mʌðə | həg kʌm 'aʊt ɪntə ðə 'gaːdn̩ | ʃi wəz¹⁰ 'dʒʌst¹¹ əbaʊt tə 'pɪk
səm 'hɜːbz | wen 'sʌdn̩li ʃi 'stʊd ʌp ən 'lʊkt ə'raʊnd | 'ɒbvɪəsli ə'lɜːtɪb baɪ
sʌm² 'saʊnd | frəm ðə 'bɒtəm əv ðə 'gaːdn̩ ə 'mæŋ keɪm | 'wɔːkɪŋ wɪð 'faːs
lɒŋ 'straɪdz | hi 'kærɪd ə 'hjuːdʒ 'ʃɒkgʌn | *'dʒəʊn traɪd tə 'skriːm | bək
'kʊbmp¹⁷⁻⁹ meɪk ə 'saʊnd | hə 'hed staːtɪd 'spɪnɪŋ ən ʃi 'feɪntɪd |

Comments to transcription

1. The alveolar plosive could have been assimilated instead of elided giving thus rise to a double assimilation.
2. *some* is used in the strong form when it modifies a countable noun in the singular (see Lesson 3).
3. The alveolar plosive could have been assimilated instead of elided.
4. Strong form because *that* is used as a demonstrative. ***
5. Strong form because the word is emphasised and therefore stressed.
6. Strong form because the verb is not an auxiliary here.
7. Progressive assimilation is not possible because the nasal is followed by a vowel.
8. Double assimilation.
9. The alveolar plosive could have been elided instead of assimilated.
10. In RP the alveolar fricatives do not assimilate to a following post-alveolar affricate.
11. The grammatical word is stressed (and therefore, used in strong form) for rhythmic reasons: to avoid a long sequence of unstressed syllables.
12. Assimilation is inhibited by the potential pause.
13. 'room' can also be pronounced /rʊm/ in compound words.
14. Notice the intrusive r (see Lesson 4).
15. Notice the pronunciation /fɪŋgə/ with a /g/. Another such word is /æŋgə/. On the other hand, words such as *sing* and *singer* do not have a /g/. This is because the velar nasal is at the end of a morpheme, even if another morpheme has been added as in *singer*.
16. Possessive pronouns are not weakened, therefore, /h/ may not be deleted either.
17. Triple assimilation.

Exercise 7.5

| 'wɒt dɪdʒu 'duː¹ wɪð ðə 'njuːʃpeɪpə² | ju 'hævn̩ 'θrəʊn ɪt ə'weɪ | 'hæv³ ju
|'njuːʃpeɪpə² | 'wɒt 'njuːʃpeɪpə² | ðə 'njuːʃpeɪpər² aɪ wəz 'riːdɪŋ | 'wɪtʃ wʌn
dʒu⁴ 'θɪŋk | 'əʊ | ɪts ɒn ðə 'teɪbl̩ ɪn ðə 'kɪtʃn̩ | 'ɪznt ɪt | 'ðætʃ⁵ 'jestədeɪz
'njuːʃpeɪpə² | aɪ 'daʊnt wɒnt tə 'riːd 'ðæt⁵| 'duː³ aɪ | əʊ 'dɪə | aɪv 'dʒʌʃ⁶⁻⁷
'juːzd ə 'njuːʃpeɪpə² tə 'ræp ʌp ði 'æʃɪz frəm ðə 'faə | həv ju 'θrəʊm̩ maɪ
'njuːʃpeɪpər² ə'weɪ ə'gen | jɔːr 'ɔːlweɪz 'duːɪŋ 'ðæt⁵ | 'lʊk | aɪm 'nɒt 'ɔːlweɪz
'duːɪŋ ɪt | aɪv 'dʌn ɪt 'wʌns ɔː 'twaɪs | 'ðæts⁵ 'ɔːl | 'wʌns ɔː 'twaɪs⁸ | ju 'dɪd ɪt
ɒn 'sʌndeɪ | 'dɪdn̩tʃu⁹ | ən 'wʌn deɪ laːs 'wiːk | 'dɪd aɪ | 'wel | 'ðæts⁵ 'əʊnli

'twaɪs[8] | 'jes | bət tə'deɪ 'meɪks ɪt 'θri: 'taɪmz | 'dʌznt ɪt[10] | 'jes | aɪ sə'pəʊz ɪt
'dʌz[1] | 'sɒri | bətʃu 'stɪl 'kɑːŋk[11-12] 'kleɪm ðət aɪm 'ɔːlweɪz 'duːɪŋ ɪt[8] | 'kænt[3] ju
| əʊ 'ɔːl raɪt[10] | ju 'ɔːlweɪz 'hæf[13-1] tə bi 'raɪt | 'dəʊntʃu[9] | aɪ 'miːn | ju 'θrəʊ
aʊp maɪ 'njuːʃpeɪpə[2] jet ə'gen | ənʤu[9] 'stɪl hæf[13-1] tə 'hæv[1] ðə 'lɑːs 'wɜːd |
ɪts 'rɪəli ə'nɔɪɪŋ | 'kʌm 'ɒn | aɪ 'dɪd seɪ aɪ wəz 'sɒri | wɒt 'els ʤu[4] 'wɒmp[12] mi
tə 'duː[1] | aɪl 'gəʊ aʊt əŋ[14] 'getʃu ə'nʌðə wʌn | 'ʃæl[3] aɪ |'nəʊ | 'dəʊmp[11-12]
'bɒðə | aɪl 'gəʊ maɪ'self | aɪ wəz 'æktʃuəli 'θɪŋkɪŋ əbaʊk 'gəʊɪŋ fər ə 'wɔːk
'eniweɪ | 'wel | 'ðeə ju 'ɑː[15] ðen | ju kʊg 'get səm 'bred əm[14] 'mɪlk 'tuː | 'naʊ |
aɪ 'dɪdn̩ seɪ aɪ wəz 'plænɪŋ tə 'duː[1] ðə 'wiːkli 'ʃɒpɪŋ | 'dɪd aɪ | fə 'gʊdnəs 'seɪk
| 'jɔːr ɪn ə 'faʊl 'muːd | 'wɒts ðə 'mætə wɪð ju | həv ju 'gɒt ə 'tuːθeɪk ɔː
'sʌmθɪŋ | 'meɪbi 'reɪbiz | 'veri 'fʌni | ʤəsp[11] bikɒz aɪ dɪs'laɪk hævɪŋ maɪ
'plænz əv 'spendɪŋ ə 'kwaət 'sʌndeɪ ɑːftə'nuːn dɪ'stɜːbd | ɪt 'tɜːnz aʊt aɪm
'bæd 'tempəd | əʊ aɪ 'beg jɔː 'pɑːdn̩ fər ɪntə'rʌptɪŋ jɔː 'rest | aɪ 'wʊbmp[11-16]
'maɪnd hævɪŋ səm 'taɪm tə ri'læks 'tuː | bət ɪt səʊ 'hæpm̩z aɪv biːn 'duːɪŋ
θɪŋz 'ɔːl ðə 'taɪm | laɪk 'kliːnɪŋ ðə 'faəpleɪs | maɪ 'feɪvrɪp 'pɑːs taɪm fər ə
wiːk'end | ɪp 'biːts 'duːɪŋ ðə 'bɑːθruːmz 'eniweɪ | wɪtʃ ɪz 'wɒt aɪ 'drɪb bifɔː
'lʌntʃ | jɔː 'nɒk gəʊɪŋ tə 'stɑːt ɒn 'ðæt[5] ə'gen | aɪv 'hɜːd ɪt 'sevrəl 'θaʊznd
'taɪmz bi'fɔː | ju 'hæv[15] | wel 'meɪbi aɪ ʃʊd 'stɑːp 'pʊtɪŋ ɪt ɪn 'raɪtɪŋ ðen | 'slɪp
ɪt ɪn'saɪʤɔː 'preʃəs 'peɪpə | 'ðæt[5] wʊd 'meɪk ju 'nəʊtɪs ɪt | əm[14] 'baɪ ðə 'weɪ
| 'neks taɪm 'juː[17] kŋ 'swiːp ðə 'faəpleɪs jɔː'self | 'ðæt[5] wɪl 'ʃɔːli 'stɒp mi frəm
'θrəʊɪŋ jɔː 'njuːʃpeɪpər[2] 'aʊt ə'gen |əʊ 'lɔːd | 'waɪ dɪd aɪ 'evə 'menʃn̩ ɪt |

Comments to transcription

1. Strong form because the verb is not used as an auxiliary here.
2. This is an exceptional case in which voice assimilation is possible within this compound word changing /z/ to /s/ because the following sound /p/ is voiceless.
3. Strong form because the grammatical word is stressed. This is the usual pattern in tag questions.
4. Colloquial pronunciation: *do* is weakened to /d/ and then coalesces with the following /j/ giving /ʤ/ as a result.
5. Strong form because *that* is used as a demonstrative here. ***
6. Fricative assimilation is possible because the plosive has been deleted, leaving the fricative and /j/ in contact.
7. When it means 'a short time ago', the word *just* can be weak if unstressed, but if it is stressed as in this case, it must be strong (see Lesson 3).
8. Assimilation is inhibited by the potential pause.
9. Instead of coalescing with /j/, the alveolar plosive could have been deleted.
10. Coalescence is inhibited by the potential pause.
11. The alveolar plosive could have been deleted instead of assimilated.
12. Double assimilation.
13. This is one of the few instances in which voicing assimilation is found in current RP English.
14. Assimilation could have been applied here instead of elision of the alveolar plosive, giving rise to a double assimilation.
15. Strong form because the grammatical word is stranded.
16. Triple assimilation.
17. Strong form because the grammatical word is emphasised and therefore stressed.

Exercise 7.6

| ðə wəz ˈwʌns ə ˈspaɪdə kɔːlg[1] *ˈkel | hu ˈlɪvb[1] baɪ ə ˈrɪvər ɪn ðə ˈwʊdz | hi əb
ˈbɪlk kwaɪt ə ˈkəʊzi lɪtl̩ ˈnest ət ðə ˈtɒp əv ə ˈtriː | ðə ˈspaɪdə wəz wel ˈnəʊm fər ɪz
ɪkˈstrɔːdɪnri ˈwiːvɪŋ | ðə wəz[2] dʒəs ˈnəʊbɒdi hu kʊb ˈmeɪk ˈbetər ɔː ˈstrɒŋgə[3]
ˈwebz ɪn ðə ˈhəʊl ˈfɒrɪst[4] | *ˈkel felp ˈpraʊd əv ɪz ˈkrɑːft | ən diˈvəʊtɪb ˈməʊst
əv ɪz ˈtaɪm tu ɪt | ˈɔːl deɪ ˈlɒŋ i ˈwɜːkt | ˈwiːvɪŋ ənd ˈwiːvɪŋ | ˈhɑːdli ˈstɒpɪŋ tu
ˈiːt ɔː ˈdrɪŋk | ət ˈnaɪt i ˈdremt əv ˈɔːl ðə ˈnjuː diˈzaɪnz i wʊg kriˈeɪt | əv ˈhaʊ tə
ˈmeɪk ðəm ˈhəʊld ən ˈʃaɪn ˈwʌndəfli[5] | ˈwʌn deɪ ɪz ˈfren ðə ˈrɒbɪŋ keɪm əˈraʊn
tə vɪzɪt[4] | bək *ˈkel wəz[2] ˈstrʌglɪŋ wɪð ə ˈspeʃli[5] ˈdɪfɪklt ˈnɒt | ˈsɒri ˈrɒbɪn | aɪm
ˈveri ˈbɪzi seg *ˈkel | əʊ ju kŋ ˈʃɔːli ˈteɪk ə ˈbreɪk | ən ˈtɔːk tə mi fər ə ˈwaɪl riˈplaɪd
ðə ˈrɒbɪn | wel ˈnɒt ˈnaʊ | ˈspaɪdə ˈwebz ə ˈmɔː ˈdɪfɪklt ðm ˈməʊsp[1] piːpl̩ ˈθɪŋk |
ðeɪ ʃʊb bi ˈstrɒŋ əz ˈwel əz ˈlaɪt | ən ˈðæp[6] miːnz ə ˈlɒt əv sɪərɪəs ˈθɪŋkɪŋ ənd
ˈhɑːd ˈwɜːk | ˈraɪt naʊ aɪm ˈtraɪɪŋ tə ˈwɜːk aʊt ðɪs ˈnɒt | səʊ aɪ ˈkɑːn stɒp tə
ˈtʃæt | ˈevri taɪm ˈsʌmbədi tɜːnz ˈʌp | ðə ˈrɒbɪn went əˈweɪ fiːlɪŋ ˈveri ʌpˈset[4] |
bikɒʒ ʃi əb pəˈtɪkjuləli ˈwɒntəd tə ˈspen səm ˈtaɪm wɪð hə ˈfrend | ˈneksp[1]
ˈmɔːnɪŋ ðə ˈspaɪdə ˈwəʊk ʌp ˈfiːlɪŋ ˈrestləs | ɪt wəz ə ˈsʌni ˈsprɪŋ ˈdeɪ | ənd i
ˈdɪgŋk[1-7] ˈkeə tə ˈduː[8] eni ˈwɜːk | hi wʊg ˈgəʊ tə ˈsiː wʌn əv ɪz ˈfrenz | ðen i
riˈmembəd ɪz ˈwɜːdz tə ðə ˈrɒbɪn | ən ˈrɪəlaɪzd haʊ ʌnˈfeər i əb ˈbiːn | ˈnaʊ ðət
i ˈθɔːt əbaʊt ɪt | hi əd ˈdʌn ðə ˈseɪm tə ˈsevrəl əv ɪz ˈfrenz | nəʊ ˈwʌndə ðəp
ˈməʊst əv ðəm əg ˈgɪvn̩ ɪm ˈʌp | wel ˈsʌmθɪŋ ˈhæd[8] tə bi ˈdʌn | ənd i ˈhæd[8]
ən aɪˈdɪə | hi wʊg ˈgɪv ə ˈpɑːti | ðə ˈspaɪdə ˈstɑːtəd ˈwɜːkɪŋ ɒn ɪt ˈstreɪt əˈweɪ
| hi ˈtʃəʊz ə ˈklɪərɪŋ ɪn ðə ˈfɒrɪst səˈraʊndəb baɪ ˈtɔːl ˈæʃ triːz | ən ˈstɑːtəd
ˈwiːvɪŋ frəm ˈwʌn tə ði ˈʌðə | ən əˈkrɒs ðəm | hi ˈwəʊv ən ˈwəʊv nɒn ˈstɒp |
ˈdeɪ ən ˈnaɪp puʃɪŋ ˈɔːl ɪz ˈskɪlz tə ðə ˈlɪmɪt | ɑːftə ˈsevn̩ ˈdeɪz ðə ˈkænəpi wəz
ˈfɪnɪʃt | ɪk ˈkʌvəd ðə ˈhəʊl ˈklɪərɪŋ laɪk ə ˈdəʊm | əŋg[1-9] ˈgləʊd ɪn ðə ˈsʌn wɪð
ˈmɪljənz əv ˈdjuː ˈdrɒps | ðək *ˈkel əg ˈkæptʃəd ɪn ɪz ˈnɒts | ʌndəˈniːθ ði ˈɔːnɪŋ
i əb meɪg ˈkɜːtn̩z əv ˈwebz | ˈhæŋɪŋ ɔːl əˈraʊnd | ðə wər ˈɔːlsəʊ ˈweb
ˈstriːməz | ənd ət ˈliːst ə ˈhʌndrəb bəˈluːnz | ɪŋ ˈkʌləz ˈteɪkŋ frəm ðə ˈreɪmbəʊ
| weŋ *ˈkel felt ˈsætɪsfaɪd wɪð ðə riˈzʌlt | hi ˈwent tə ðə ˈfɒrɪst ˈɔːtʃədz | əŋ[10]
ˈgæðəb ˈmæsəz əv ˈfruːts ən ˈsiːdz | wɪtʃ i ˈðeŋ ˈkærɪd tə ðə ˈtent | əmb[1-9]
pleɪsk[1] ˈkeəfli[5] ɒm ˈmeni lɪtl̩ ˈliːvz | fər ˈevribɒdi tu ˈiːt | ˈɑːftər ˈfɪnɪʃɪŋ ðiːz
əˈreɪndʒmənts | hi ˈwent tə ˈfaɪn ðə ˈrɒbɪn | ˈlʌkili ʃi wəz ət ˈhəʊm | əŋ[10] *ˈkel
| ˈɑːftər əˈpɒlədʒaɪzɪŋ fər ɪz biˈheɪvjə | ˈɑːskt ə tə ˈflaɪ ət ˈɔːl ˈspiːd | əŋg[1-9]
ˈkɔːl ɔːl ðeə ˈfrenz | ðə ˈrɒbɪn wəz diˈlaɪtɪd tə ˈsiː ðə ˈspaɪdə wəz ˈfiːlɪŋ mɔː
ˈsəʊʃəbl̩ | ən ˈrʌʃ tə ˈduː[8] əʒ ʃi wəz riˈkwestəd | wɪðɪn ə ˈʃɔːt ˈtaɪm | ˈevribɒdi
əg ˈgæðəd əraʊn ˈrɒbɪnz ˈhaʊs | ðen ðə ˈspaɪdə ˈsed | aɪm ˈveri ˈsɒri tu əv
ɪgˈnɔːdʒu ˈɔːl fə səʊ ˈlɒŋ | aɪ ˈsʌmtaɪmz ˈwʌri tuː ˈmʌtʃ əbaʊp maɪ ˈwiːvɪŋ |
əŋ[10] gek ˈkærɪd əˈweɪ wɪð ɪt[4] | bət ɪt ˈdʌzm[10] ˈmiːn aɪ fəˈgep maɪ ˈfrenz | səʊ
aɪ əv ˈdʌn sʌmθɪŋ ˈspeʃl fə ju | ˈfɒləʊ ˈmiː[11] ənd aɪl ˈʃəʊ ju | wen ði ˈænɪml̩z
əˈraɪvd ət ðə ˈklɪərɪŋ | ðeɪ wər ˈɔːl səʊ əˈmeɪz[12] baɪ ðə ˈdæzlɪŋ[5] ˈsaɪp bifɔː
ðeər ˈaɪz | ðət ðeɪ ˈkʊbm[9-12] ˈmuːv ɔː ˈspiːk | ˈɑːftər ə ˈwaɪl | ˈsʌm[13] əv ðəm
ˈstɑːtəg ˈgɑːspɪŋ | ˈsaɪɪŋ ən ˈtʃɪərɪŋ ət ðə ˈspaɪdəz ˈwɜːk əv ˈɑːt | ðen ˈevriwʌn
went ɪnˈsaɪd ðə ˈwʌndəfl̩ ˈtent | ənd ˈselɪbreɪtəg *ˈkelz riˈtɜːn tu ɪz ˈfrenz |
haʊˈevər ɪt wəz ðə ˈspaɪdər ɪmˈself hu wəz ˈhæpɪəst[4] | bikəz[14] ɪz ˈefəts əd fə
ˈwʌns gɪvm̩ ˈpleʒə tu ˈʌðəz | əmb[1] ˈmeɪd ðəm fəˈgɪv ɪm fər ɪz ˈlæk əv kənsɪ-
dəˈreɪʃn fə ðəm |

Comments to transcription

1. Instead of assimilating the alveolar plosive, we could have elided it.
2. In RP, the alveolar fricatives do not assimilate to a following post-alveolar affricate.
3. *strong* together with *young* and *long* are exceptional words in that they add the velar plosive /g/ when forming the comparative and superlative.
4. Assimilation may be inhibited by the potential pause.
5. Instead of /ə/ elision we could have applied syllabicity.
6. Strong form because *that* is a demonstrative here. ***
7. Triple assimilation.
8. Strong form because the verb is not being used as an auxiliary in this case.
9. Double assimilation.
10. Assimilation could have been applied instead of elision, giving rise to double assimilation.
11. Strong form because the grammatical word is emphasised, and therefore stressed.
12. Instead of deleting the alveolar plosive, we could have assimilated it.
13. Strong form because *some* is used as a pronoun here (see Lesson 3).
14. /bikɒz/ is an alternative pronunciation. The first syllable could also be pronounced /bə/.

Answers to Lesson 8: glottaling

Orthographic version for the sample transcription passage

For several years now, I have driven to the station most mornings of the week and parked my car in more or less the same place in the car park. I have then caught the train to London and done my day's work. In the evening I have returned, found my car and driven home. It probably doesn't sound like a very interesting routine, I admit that, but one can't have excitement every day. One evening last week I got back to the station at half past eight. It was a Monday evening and I had had quite a hard day. I walked wearily to the car park, looking forward to my evening at home. I'd get something to drink, eat dinner and maybe do some work on a bookcase I had bought secondhand. But to my utter amazement, there, where my car should have been was a strange car. I couldn't believe my eyes. I looked up and down the entire row of cars, but mine was not to be seen anywhere. It was several minutes before I could consider the possibility that the car had been stolen. For a while I thought that my mind was going. Had I parked in a different place that morning? I simply couldn't accept the fact that it was gone. Now it's clear that I'll never get my car back. My feelings of puzzlement and confusion have turned into anger. The insurance company took care of everything. I just hope that they let me have a new car soon and that my old one breaks down on whoever has got the use of it now. Call it silly, but I have a right to a little harmless revenge, I think. That was not the only misfortune I have recently experienced with cars. My wife's was broken into a few months ago. They smashed a window and tried to get the stereo, but with no luck. All of this went on while we sat having dinner in the house, not eight yards away from the back garden where my wife had parked. After all this, you can imagine what my attitude to car crime is. Once I've bought my new one, I'm going to put so many locks, alarm systems and security devices on it that the most determined and devoted of thieves will not succeed in taking it from me.

Exercise 8.1

(1) first class = a, b
/t/ cannot be glottaled because it is preceded by an obstruent.

(2) salt solution = c
/t/ in the word *salt* cannot be deleted because it is preceded by a consonant which does not agree in voicing with it. It cannot be assimilated because there is neither a velar nor a bilabial consonant following.

(3) hit parade = a, c
/t/ cannot be deleted because it is not preceded by a voiceless consonant.

(4) white shoes = c
/t/ cannot be deleted because it is not preceded by a voiceless consonant. It cannot be assimilated because there is neither a velar nor a bilabial consonant following.

(5.1) most = d
/t/ in the word *most* cannot be assimilated because there is neither a velar nor a bilabial consonant following. It cannot be deleted because it is followed by a vowel. It cannot be glottaled because it is not preceded by a sonorant and also because it is followed by a vowel.

(5.2) important = c
/t/ in the middle of the word *important* can be neither deleted, assimilated nor glottaled because it is followed by a vowel. However, if we apply syllabicity /ɪmpɔːtn̩t/, it could be glottaled, thought not deleted since it is preceded by a vowel.

(5.3) important = d
/t/ at the end of the word *important* can't be deleted because it is not preceded by a voiceless consonant and also because it is not followed by a consonant. Although it is preceded by a sonorant it cannot be glottaled because it is not followed by a consonant.

Exercise 8.2: Edited orthographic version (*Glottaling is marked in bold type.*)

I've had some terrible car journeys in my time, but I think the very worst one was in Athens. We'd booked a holiday on a small island not far away from Athens and had to catch a ferry to **get** there. Well, of course the plane was late and we landed at the airport about three-quarters of an hour before the ferry was due to leave. Fortunately we found a taxi driver who spoke a bit of English and managed to make him understand what our problem was. **It** was the middle of the day and all the roads in the city were jammed solid. The driver didn'**t let** this put him off. He drove most of the way to the port on the pavement. My wife and I sat in the back with our hands over our eyes, while he narrowly missed trees and pedestrians. Every time he came to a traffic light he simply drove onto the pavement and shot forward until he was level with the front of the queue. When the light changed to green, he cut in front of the first vehicle and drove on. We got to the ferry with about five minutes to spare and sat there shaking. Finally, the ship's hooter sounded to signal that we were about to sail. All the Greek passengers around us crossed themselves and muttered a prayer for a safe journey. I strongly advise you to do the same if ever you take a taxi from Athens airport.

Exercise 8.2

| aɪv ˈhæd[1] səm ˈterɪbl̩ ˈkɑː dʒɜːniz ɪm maɪ ˈtaɪm | bət[2] aɪ ˈθɪŋk ðə ˈveri ˈwɜːs[3] wʌn wəz ɪn *ˈæθənz | wɪb ˈbʊkt[4-2] ə ˈhɒlədeɪ ɒn ə ˈsmɔːl ˈaɪlən nɒʔ ˈfɑːr əweɪ frəm *ˈæθənz | ən ˈhæd[1] tə ˈkætʃ ə ˈferi tə ˈgeʔ ðeə | wel əf[5] ˈkɔːs ðə ˈpleɪn wəz ˈleɪt[6] | ən wi ˈlændəd əʔ ði ˈeəpɔːt[6] | əbauʔ ˈθriː kwɔːtəz[2] əv ən ˈɑə bifɔː ðə ˈferi wəz ˈdjuː tə ˈliːv | ˈfɔːtʃnətli[7] wi ˈfaʊnd ə ˈtæksi draɪvə hu ˈspəʊk ə bɪt[2] əv *ˈɪŋglɪʃ | əm ˈmænɪdʒ tə ˈmeɪk ɪm ʌndəˈstæn wɒt[2] ɑə ˈprɒbləm wɒz[8] | ɪʔ wəz ðə ˈmɪdl̩ əv ðə ˈdeɪ | ənd ˈɔːl ðə ˈrəʊdz ɪn ðə ˈsɪti[2] wə ˈdʒæm ˈsɒlɪd | ðə ˈdraɪvə ˈdɪdn̩ʔ[9] leʔ ˈðɪs pʊt[2] ɪm ˈɒf | hi drəʊv ˈməʊst[2-4] əv ðə ˈweɪ tə ðə ˈpɔːt[2] ɒn ðə ˈpeɪvmənt[6] | maɪ ˈwaɪf ənd ˈaɪ ˈsæt[2] ɪn ðə ˈbæk wɪð ɑə ˈhænz əʊvər ɑər ˈaɪz | waɪl hi ˈnɜːrəli mɪs[3] ˈtriːz əm pəˈdestriənz | ˈevri ˈtaɪm i ˈkeɪm tu ə ˈtræfɪk laɪt[6] | hi ˈsɪmpli ˈdrəʊv ɒntə[2] ðə ˈpeɪvmənt[6] | ən ˈʃɒʔ ˈfɔːwəd | ʌntɪl[2] i wəz ˈlevl̩ wɪð ðə ˈfrʌnt[2] əv ðə ˈkjuː | wen ðə ˈlaɪʔ tʃeɪndʒ tə ˈgriːn | hi ˈkʌt[2] ɪn ˈfrʌnt əv ðə ˈfɜːs[3] ˈvɪəkl̩ | ən ˈdrəʊv ˈɒn | wi ˈgɒʔ tə ðə ˈferi wɪð əbauʔ ˈfaɪv ˈmɪnɪʔs tə ˈspeə | ən ˈsæʔ ðeə ˈʃeɪkɪŋ | ˈfaɪnli[10] ðə ˈʃɪps ˈhuːtə[2] ˈsaʊndɪd | tə ˈsɪgnəl ðəʔ wi wər əˈbauʔ tə ˈseɪl | ˈɔːl ðə *ˈgriːk ˈpæsɪndʒəz əˈraʊnd əs ˈkrɒs[3] ðəmˈselvz | əm ˈmʌtəd[2] ə ˈpreə fər ə ˈseɪf ˈdʒɜːni | aɪ ˈstrɒŋli ədˈvaɪʒ ju tə ˈduː[1] ðə ˈseɪm | ɪf ˈevə ju ˈteɪk ə ˈtæksi frəm *ˈæθənz ˈeəpɔːt[6] |

Comments to transcription

1. Strong form because the verb is not an auxiliary here.
2. Glottaling is not possible because /t/ is followed by a vowel.
3. Glottaling is not possible because /t/ is not preceded by a sonorant, instead it has been deleted.
4. Glottaling is not possible because /t/ is preceded by an obstruent, not by a sonorant.
5. One of the few cases of voicing assimilation in current RP (see Lesson 7).
6. Glottaling is not possible because /t/ is followed by a potential pause.
7. Syllabicity could have been applied to the nasal instead of /ə/ elision.
8. Strong form because the grammatical word is stranded.
9. In negative contractions /t/ may be elided or, if it is followed by a consonant other than /h/, it may be glottaled instead.
10. /faɪnl̩i/ is an exception in that it cannot lose syllabicity even though it is followed by an unstressed vowel in the same word.

Exercise 8.3: Transcription

| fər əz ˈlɒŋ əʒ ʃi kʊd riˈmembə | ˈðɪs əd ˈɔːlweɪz biːn ˈwʌn əv hə ˈfeɪvrɪʔ[1] ˈpleɪsɪz | ʃi ˈsɔː *ˈdeɪzi kwaɪʔ[1] ˈklɪəli ˈkʌmɪŋ təˈwɔːdz ðə ˈfænlaɪʔ wɪð ə ˈlʊk əv ˈpɜːpəs | ˈmædəm sez ˈmɪʃ ʃʊq qeʔ[1] ˈbæk tə hə ˈniːdl̩ wɜːk | ən ˈstɒp ˈweɪstɪŋ[2-3] hə ˈtaɪm | ɪʔ wəz nəʊ ˈwʌndə ðət[4] hə ˈmʌðə ˈnjuː wɒt[4] *ˈhæɪə? wəz ˈæktʃuəli ˈduːɪŋ | ˈwɒʔ wʊd əv biːn səˈpraɪzɪŋ | wəz ˈfaɪndɪŋ ðəʔ ʃi wəz ˈduːɪŋ sʌmθɪŋ ˈʌðə ðn̩ ˈsteərɪŋ əʔ ðə ˈwɜːlb bɪjɒn ðəʊz ˈwɪndəʊz | ˈevrɪbɒdi ˈθɔːʔ ʃi wəz ən

ʌn'ɪntrəstɪŋ əŋ 'kwaəʔ 'tʃaɪld | ə 'lɪtl̩[5] 'leɪzi 'iːvn̩ | sɪns ɪʔ 'tʊk ə 'lɒʔ tə 'meɪk ə 'liːv ðə 'wɪndəʊ 'siːt[6] | weə ʃi 'siːm tə 'spen səʊ mʌtʃ 'taɪm ɪn ði 'iːvnɪŋz | 'lʊkɪŋ 'aʊʔ θruː ðə 'wɪndəʊ peɪnz əʔ ðə 'gɑːdn̩ | *'hærɪəʔ 'njuː wɒʔ ðeɪ 'θɔːt[6] | bəʔ ʃi 'dɪdn̩ʔ[7] leʔ ðəm 'bɒðər ə | ðeɪ 'rɪəli ʃʊd 'nɒʔ[1] bi 'bleɪmd | bɪkɒz ðeɪ 'kʊdn̩[7-1]'iːvn̩ 'ges | dʒəst[2-3] ə 'ʃɔːʔ lʊk ɪntə[3] hə 'wɜːl wʊd əv 'ʃəʊn ðəm | haʊ 'resləs[8] ən 'laɪvli hə 'maɪn wɒz[9] | bəʔ ðeɪ wʊd 'nevə 'traɪ tə 'siː | 'eniθɪŋ ðəʔ[1] 'kʊbm̩[10-11] bi 'tʌtʃt[2-3] ɔːr ɪk'spleɪn saən'tɪfɪkli[12] | 'dɪdn̩[7-3] ɪg'zɪs[8] fə ðəm | ən ðəʊ ðeɪ 'lʊk[8] θruː ðə 'seɪm 'wɪndəʊ | ən 'θɔːʔ ðeɪ 'sɔː ðə 'seɪm 'θɪŋz | 'nəʊbɒdi ɪn hə 'fæmli[12] əd 'evə kɔːʔ ðə 'slaɪtɪs[13-8-11] 'glɪmps | ən ðeɪ wʊd 'nevər əv 'ges[8] wɒʔ wəz 'hæpnɪŋ[12] evri 'naɪʔ[1] bɪhaɪn ðəʊz 'bʊʃɪz | ʃi 'hɜːd ðə 'meɪg kləʊz ðə 'geɪʔ[1] bɪ'haɪnd ər əʒ ʃi 'went[3] ə'weɪ | ɪʔ wəz 'kwaɪʔ 'seɪf 'naʊ | ðeɪ kʊd 'stɑːʔ[1] 'kʌmɪŋ | ʃi sæʔ 'stɪl ən 'redi tə 'weɪʔ fə ðə 'mɪrəkl̩ | haʊ 'kʊd ʃi let[4] hə 'fæmli[12] 'nəʊ əbaʊʔ ðə 'grɑːs 'kɪŋdəm | ən ðə 'kɔːt[4] hu 'meʔ daʊn əʔ ði 'əʊk 'kɑːsl̩ | ɔːr əbaʊʔ ðə 'treʒə 'hɪdn̩ ʌndə ðə 'ɜːd 'stəʊn | ɪʔ wəz 'prɒbli[14] 'betə[3] ðəʔ ðeɪ 'dɪdn̩[7] 'nəʊ | *'hærɪəʔ[1] 'kʊdn̩[7] fə'geʔ ðə 'siːgʌl 'prɪns ənd ɪz 'prɒmɪs | ðəʔ 'wʌn naɪʔ wʊg 'kʌm wen i wʊd 'teɪk ə tu ɪz 'kɪŋdəm | 'fɑːr ə'weɪ | bɪ'haɪn ðəʊz 'bʊʃɪz |

Comments to transcription

1. The alveolar plosive could have been assimilated instead of glottaled.
2. Glottaling is not possible because /t/ is not preceded by a sonorant.
3. Glottaling is not possible because the alveolar plosive is followed by a vowel.
4. Glottaling is not possible because the next sound is /h/.
5. In RP glottaling before a syllabic /l/ is not usual.
6. Glottaling is not possible because the alveolar plosive is followed by a potential pause.
7. In negative contractions /t/ may be elided or, if followed by a consonant other than /h/, it may be glottaled instead.
8. Glottaling cannot be applied because the sound preceding /t/ is not a sonorant. However, /t/ can be elided here.
9. The strong form is used because the grammatical word is stranded.
10. If glottaling had been applied instead of deletion, assimilation would still have been possible because glottal stop does not prevent assimilation.
11. /t/ could have been assimilated instead of deleted.
12. Syllabicity could have been applied instead of /ə/ elision.
13. The first /t/ in *slightest* cannot be glottaled because it is followed by a vowel.
14. This is a colloquial, quite rapid pronunciation for /prɒbəbli/ in which exceptionally /ə/ has been elided, even though it is not followed by a liquid or /n/, resulting in two adjacent /b/ sounds, and one of the /b/ sounds is elided as well.

Orthographic version

For as long as she could remember, this had always been one of her favourite places. She saw Daisy quite clearly coming towards the fanlight with a look of purpose. 'Madam says Miss should get back to her needlework and stop wasting her time.' It was no wonder that her mother knew what Harriet was actually doing. What would have been surprising was finding that she was doing something other than staring at the world beyond those windows. Everybody thought that she was an uninteresting and quiet child, a little lazy even, since it took a lot to make her leave the window seat where she seemed to spend so much time in the evenings looking out through the window panes at the garden. Harriet knew what they thought, but she didn't let them bother her. They really should not be blamed, because they couldn't even guess. Just a short look into her world would have shown them how restless and lively her mind was. But they would never try to see. Anything that couldn't be touched or explained scientifically didn't exist for them. And though they looked through the same window and thought they saw the same things, nobody in her family had ever caught the slightest glimpse and they would never have guessed what was happening every night behind those bushes. She heard the maid close the gate behind her as she went away. It was safe now. They could start coming. She sat still and ready to wait for the miracle. How could she let her family know about the grass kingdom and the court that met down at the oak castle or about the treasure hidden under the third stone? It was probably better that they didn't know. Harriet couldn't forget the seagull prince and his promise that one night would come when he would take her to his kingdom, far away, behind those bushes.

Exercise 8.4

| ɪʔ wəz ˈsætədi[1-2] ˈmɔːnɪŋ wen aɪ wəuk ˈʌp tə ðə ˈsaund əv ði əˈlaːm ˈrɪŋɪŋ ɪm maɪ ˈɪəz | aɪ ˈkwɪkli dʒʌmpt[3-2] ˈaut[2] əv ˈbed | riˈmembrɪŋ ðəʔ wi wə ˈɡəuɪŋ ɒf tə *ˈweɪlz ɪn ˈles ðn̩ ən ˈaəz ˈtaɪm | aɪ ˈræn ʌpˈsteəz tə ðə ˈspeə ˈbedrum[4] | tə ˈweɪk maɪ ˈsɪstər[3-2] ˈʌp | aɪ ˈʃuk ə ˈvɪɡrəsli | ən ˈʃautɪɡ[3] ˈkʌm ɒm *ˈmædlən | get[2] ˈʌp ɔː wɪl ˈmɪs ðə ˈtreɪn | əz aɪ ˈrʌʃt[3-2] ɪntə[3] ðə ˈbaːθrum[4] aɪ ˈhɜːd ə ˈmʌmblɪŋ ˈwɒʔ ˈtreɪn | ʃi əd ˈɒbvɪəsli fəˈɡɒʔn̩ ˈwɒʔ wi əb ˈplæn ðə ˈnaɪʔ[5] biˈfɔː | aɪ ˈʃautəd[3] əʔ ðə ˈtɒp əv maɪ ˈvɔɪs | ðə ˈtreɪn tə *ˈweɪlz | wi ə ˈspəuz[6] tə bi ˈkætʃɪŋ ə ˈtreɪn ət[2] ˈeɪʔ ˈθɜːti[3] | tə ˈɡəu ˈhəum tə ˈsiː ˈmʌm | riˈmembə | ɪt[2] ˈɔːl weŋk[7] ˈkwaəʔ fər ə ˈwaɪl | ʌntɪl[3] ʃi ˈrɪəlaɪz ʃi ˈwɒzn̩[8] ˈdriːmɪŋ | ʃi ˈɔːlməus[9] ˈfluː aut[2] əv ðə ˈbedrum[4] | ən ˈstaːtɪd[3] tə ˈpænɪk əʒ ˈjuːʒuəl | ˈwɒʔ ˈtaɪm ɪz ɪʔ nau | ˈwaɪ dɪdn̩tʃu[8-10] ˈweɪk mi ˈɜːlɪə | aɪ ˈmʌst[11-12] hæv[13] ə ˈkʌp əv ˈkɒfi ˈfɜːst[3-14] | ˈʌðəwaɪz aɪl ˈnevə ˈmeɪk ɪʔ θruː ðə ˈdeɪ ʃi sed ˈdesprəʔli | ˈðɪs wəz ə ˈtɪpɪkl̩ riˈækʃn̩ frəm maɪ ˈsɪstə[3-2] | hu ˈdʌzn̩[8-11] hæv[13] ə ˈkeər ɪn ðə ˈwɜːld | ˈnevə ˈmaɪn ðə ˈkɒfi aɪ ˈskriːmd | ˈfəun fər ə ˈtæksi | aɪ ˈleft[3-2] ə ˈtuː[15] ɪt[14] | ən ˈwenʔ daunˈsteəz tə ˈpuʔ ðə ˈketl̩[16] ɒn | baɪ ˈðɪs taɪm aɪ wəz ˈɔːlsəu fiːlɪŋ ˈæŋkʃəs | ən ˈwɪʃ[9] wi ˈhædn̩ʔ[8] diˈsaɪdɪd tə ˈɡəu ɒn ðɪs ˈtrɪp ət[2] ˈɔːl | ðə ˈtæksi wɪl bi ˈhɪər ɪn ˈfaɪv ˈmɪnɪʔs[5] | fəˈget[2] əbauʔ ðə ˈkɒfi | ˈweəz maɪ ˈhæmbæɡ ʃi ˈjeld | ðə ˈdɔːbel ˈræŋ | əu ˈnəu | ɪʔ[5] məs[9] bi ðə ˈtæksi ˈdraɪvə | ˈiːvn̩ aɪ wɒzn̩[8] ˈredi dʒəʔ[9-17] ˈjet[14] | aɪ ˈrʌʃ tu ˈaːnsə ðə ˈdɔː tə dɪˈskʌvər ɪʔ wəz ðə ˈpəusmən[9] | ˈaːskɪŋ mi tu əkˈsept[3-2] ə diˈlɪvri ɒm biˈhaːf əv maɪ ˈneɪbə | əʒ ʃi ˈwɒzn̩[8-2] ˈɪn | aɪ ˈtuk ðə ˈpaːsl̩ ən ˈsaɪn fər ɪt[14] | ðə ˈdɔːbel ˈræŋ əˈgen | ˈðɪs taɪm ɪʔ ˈwɒz[12] ðə ˈtæksi draɪvə | ə ju ˈredi aɪ ˈaːsk[9] maɪ ˈsɪstə[3-2] | ðə ˈtæksi ɪz ˈhɪə | ʃi wəz ˈrʌnɪŋ əˈraun laɪk ə ˈhedləs ˈtʃɪkɪn | bəʔ ʃi ˈgræbd hə ˈkəut[2] əz aɪ ˈklʌtʃ[9] maɪ ˈhæmbæg | ən wi ˈbəuθ hʌrid ˈauʔ tə ðə ˈkaː | əʔ ˈlaːs[9] wi wər ˈɒn aə ˈweɪ | ɔː ˈsəu aɪ ˈθɔːʔ[5] ðen | wi əd ˈəunli ˈgɒʔ tə ðə ˈbɒtəm[3] əv ðə ˈstriːʔ wen aɪ ˈhæd[13] ə ˈsɪŋkɪŋ ˈfiːlɪŋ | ˈtɜːm ˈbæk | aɪ ˈhævn̩ʔ[8] ˈlɒk[9] ðə ˈdɔː | ðə ˈdraɪvə ˈkwɪkli ˈmeɪd ə daɪˈvɜːʃn̩ | ən ˈhedɪb ˈbæk tu aə ˈhaus | ˈtaɪm wəz ˈtɪkɪŋ əˈweɪ | ən wi wə ˈbəuθ ˈwʌndrɪŋ ɪf ɪʔ wəz ə ˈsensɪbl̩ aɪˈdɪə tə kənˈtɪnju wɪð aə

ˈplæn ɔː nɒt¹⁴ | haʊˈevər aɪ ˈhel ðə ˈkiːz ɪm maɪ ˈhænd əz wi əˈprəʊtʃ⁹ ðə ˈhaʊs |
aɪ wəz ˈaʊt² əv ðə ˈkɑːr iːvm̩ biˈfɔːr ɪʔ⁵ ˈkeɪm tu ə ˈtəʊtl̩¹⁶ ˈstɒp | wɪðɪn ˈsekŋz wi
wə ˈbæk ɒn aə ˈdʒɜːni tə ðə ˈsteɪʃn̩ | bəʔ ˈðɪs taɪm ðə ˈtæksi draɪvə ˈpɪkt³⁻² ʌp ɪz
ˈspiːd | ðə wər ˈəʊnli ə fjuː ˈmɪnɪʔs ˈlef⁹ bifɔː ðə ˈtreɪn wəz ˈdjuː tə ˈliːv ðə
ˈplæʔfɔːm | aɪ ˈrɪəlaɪz wi məs⁹⁻¹⁸ bi ˈgetɪŋ² veri ˈnɪə ðə ˈsteɪʃn̩ | əz aɪ kʊd ˈhɪə
ðə ˈsteɪʃm̩ ˈmɑːstə³⁻² ˈmʌmblɪŋ ˈsʌmθɪŋ əʊvə ðə ˈtænɔɪ ˈsɪstəm³⁻² | wi ˈfaɪnli
əˈraɪvd | ˈpeɪd ðə ˈdraɪvə | kəˈlektəd³⁻² ðə ˈtɪkɪʔs frəm ði ˈɒfɪs | ən ˈdæʃ⁹ tə
ðə ˈplæʔfɔːm | tə ˈfaɪn ðəʔ ðə ˈwɒzn⁸⁻² ə ˈtreɪn ˈðeə | wi əb ˈmɪst³⁻² ɪʔ
dɪˈspaɪʔ duːɪŋ wɒʔ ˈfelʔ laɪk ə ˈmærəθn̩ | ˈsʌdn̩li ə ˈvɔɪs riˈpiːtəd² ði ˈɜːlɪə
ˈmesɪdʒ | ði ˈeɪʔ θɜːti² *ˈswɒnziː ˈtreɪn | dɪˈpɑːtɪŋ² frəm ˈplæʔfɔːm ˈtuː | əz
biːn dɪˈleɪd ʌntɪl² ˈeɪʔ fɪfti³⁻² ˈsevn̩ | wi əˈpɒlədʒaɪz fə ði ɪŋkənˈviːnɪəns | ˈwɒt²
ə riˈliːf wi bəʊθ ˈsaɪd | wi kʊd ˈnaʊ ənˈdʒɔɪ səm ˈkɒfi əʔ ˈlɑːst³⁻¹⁴ | ən ˈsʌmθɪŋ
mɔː səbˈstænʃl̩ ˈtuː | ˈaftər ɔːl ði ˈenədʒi wi əd ˈspenʔ tə ˈgeʔ ðeə |

Comments to transcription

1. As we have pointed out in previous annotations, the days of the week may be
   pronounced with an ending in /deɪ/ or /di/.
2. Glottaling is not possible because /t/ is followed by a vowel.
3. Glottaling is not possible because /t/ is preceded by an obstruent.
4. /rʊm/ and /ruːm/ are alternative pronunciations when the word is used in a
   compound.
5. Instead of glottaling /t/ we could have assimilated it.
6. Exceptional /ə/ elision because it happens in the syllable preceding the stress and
   without /ə/ being followed by a liquid.
7. Either /t/ assimilation or glottaling would have been possible here. Either way the
   sound preceding /t/ can be assimilated because a glottal stop does not prevent
   assimilation.
8. In negative contractions /t/ can be elided or, if it is followed by a consonant other
   than /h/, it may be glottaled.
9. Glottaling is not possible because /t/ is not preceded by a sonorant, but it may be
   deleted.
10. Instead of coalescing /t/ with /j/, we could have glottaled it.
11. /t/ cannot be glottaled because it is followed by /h/.
12. Strong form because the grammatical word is emphasised and therefore stressed.
13. The verb is used in the strong form because here it is not an auxiliary.
14. Glottaling is not possible because /t/ is followed by a potential pause.
15. Strong form because the grammatical item is stressed, as it usually is in this
    idiomatic usage.
16. Glottaling is not usual in RP before a syllabic /l/.
17. Fricative assimilation is possible because the alveolar plosive has been deleted
    leaving the fricative and the palatal in contact.
18. Either assimilation or deletion is possible here.

Exercise 8.5

| aɪ ˈrɪəli ˈheɪʔ ˈflaɪɪŋ | ɪʔs ˈnɒʔ ðət¹ aɪm əˈfreɪd ɔːr ˈeniθɪŋ | ðəʊ aɪ ˈduː² getˡ ə bɪʔ
ˈnɜːvəs ɪf ðə ˈflaɪʔs ˈbʌmpi | ðə ˈθɪŋ aɪ ˈrɪəli əbdˈʒekt³ tuː⁴ | ɪz ðəʔ ˈflaɪɪŋ ɪz ˈsəʊ
ˈbɔːrɪŋ | ən ˈsəʊ ʌŋˈkʌmfətəbl̩ˡ | ðə ˈlɑːs³ ˈlɒŋ ˈflaɪʔ ðəʔ wi ˈdɪd | wəz frəm

*lɒsˈændʒəliːz tə *njuːˈziːlənd | ɪʔ ˈtuk əˈbauʔ ˈtwelv ənd ə hɑːf ˈɑəz əuvəˈnaɪt⁵ | əf⁶ kɔːs ˈaɪ wəz ˈsiːtɪd ˈneks³ tə ˈsʌmwʌn hu ˈdrɒpt⁷⁻¹ ɒf tə ˈsliːp | ɪˈmiːdɪəʔli ˈɑːftə⁷⁻¹ wi əd ˈteɪkn ˈɒf | ən ˈspemʔ⁸ ˈməust⁷⁻¹ əv ðə ˈnaɪʔ ˈsnɔːrɪŋ | aɪ ˈfaɪnd ɪʔ ˈrɪəli ˈdɪfɪklʔ tə ˈsliːp ɒm ˈpleɪnz | ɪʔs dʒəs³ ˈtəutli⁹ ɪmˈpɒsɪbl̩ tə geʔ¹⁰ ˈkʌmfətəbl̩ iˈnʌf | wen aɪ ˈdɪb ˈmænɪdʒ tə ˈgeʔ tə ˈsliːp | ðə ˈpɜːsn̩ siːtɪŋ¹ ˈneks³ tə mi wəuk ˈʌp | ən ˈwɒntɪd¹ tə getˈ ˈauʔ tə ˈgəu tə ðə ˈtɔɪlət⁵ | ðen ðə ˈstjuːədz kep¹¹ ˈkʌmɪŋ raund ˈevri hɑːf ˈɑə | ənd ˈɒfrɪŋ əs ˈtiː ɔː ˈwɔːtər¹ ɔːr ˈɒrɪndʒ dʒuːs | ðeɪ wə ˈmeɪkɪŋ ˈʃɔː ˈnəubədi əˈraɪv dihaɪˈdreɪtɪd¹ | bəʔ ðeɪ ˈɔːlsəu priˈventɪb¹ mi frəm ˈgetɪŋ¹ eni ˈrest⁷⁻⁵ | ɒn əˈnʌðər əˈkeɪʒn̩ | aɪ wəz ɒn ən ˈeɪt¹ ɑə ˈflaɪʔ tə *ˈnɔːθ əˈmerɪkə | ðɪs wəz biˈfɔːr aɪ əg ˈgɪvn̩ ʌp ˈsməukɪŋ | əz ˈlʌk wud ˈhæv¹² ɪt⁵ | maɪ ˈtrævl̩ eɪdʒm̩ʔ⁸ ˈbuk¹¹ mi wɪð ˈwʌn əv ðə ˈfjuː ˈkʌmpniz | hu hæd¹² ə ˈnɒn ˈsməukɪŋ ˈpɒləsi ɒn ˈɔːl ðeə ˈflaɪʔs | aɪ ˈdɪdnʔ¹³ faɪnd ˈaut¹ əbauʔ ˈðɪs | ʌntɪl¹ aɪ ˈtʃekt⁷⁻¹ ˈɪn | ˈðeəfɔːr aɪ wəz kəmˈpliːʔli ʌmpriˈpeəd fə ði ɪkˈspɪərɪəns | ðə ˈfɜːs³ fjuː ˈɑəz wə nɒʔ ˈtuː ˈbæd | aɪ ˈetˈ ən ˈdræŋk ˈevriθɪŋ aɪ wəz ˈɒfəd | ˈiːvn̩ ðəu aɪ ˈwɒzn̩¹³⁻¹⁴ ˈhʌŋgri ɪn ðə ˈslaɪtɪst⁷⁻⁵ | ɑːftə⁷⁻¹ ðə ˈsekm̩ meɪm ˈmiːl ən ˈkɒfi | aɪ ˈstaːtɪd¹ fiːlɪŋ ˈedʒi | səu aɪ ˈwenʔ fə ðə ˈswiːʔs | aɪ ˈeʔ səu ˈmeni | ðətˈ ɪʔs ə ˈwʌndə maɪ ˈtiːθ dɪdnʔ¹³ fɔːl ˈauʔ ðeər ən ˈðen | wɪð əunli ˈwʌn ɑə tə ˈgəu əˈkɔːdɪŋ tə ˈʃedjul | wi wər ɪnˈfɔːm baɪ ðə ˈpaɪləʔ ðəʔ wib bi ˈrʌnɪŋ əbautˈ ən ˈɑə ˈleɪt⁵ | ˈðæʔ ˈdɪd ɪʔ fə mi | aɪ gɒʔ ˈrɪəli ˈæŋgri | ən wəz ˈsɪərɪəsli ˈtemptɪd⁷⁻¹ tə ˈhaɪd sʌmweər ən ˈlaɪtˈ ʌp ə sɪgəˈret⁵ | ə ˈstjuədes | ˈnəutɪsɪŋ¹ maɪ ædʒɪˈteɪʃn̩ | ˈɒfəb mi səm ˈnɪkətiːn¹ ˈtʃuːɪŋ gʌm | ʃi wəz ə ˈsməukə həˈself | ənd ˈɔːlweɪz¹⁵ hæd¹² ə ˈterɪbl̩ ˈtaɪm | wen ʃi wəz ˈwɜːkɪŋ ɒn ˈwʌn əv ðə trænzəʔˈlæntɪk¹ ˈflaɪʔs | wi ˈfaɪnli¹⁶ ˈlændɪd | ənd aɪ ˈrʌʃ³ tə ði ˈeəpɔːʔs ˈsməukɪŋ ˈeərɪə | fə maɪ riˈtɜːn ˈdʒɜːni aɪ meɪd ˈʃɔːr aɪ wəz ˈveri veri ˈtaəd | səu ðətˈ aɪ spemʔ⁸ ˈməust⁷⁻¹ əv ðə ˈtaɪm əˈsliːp |

Comments to transcription

1. Glottaling is not possible because /t/ is followed by a vowel.
2. Strong form because the grammatical word is emphasised and therefore stressed.
3. Glottaling is not possible because /t/ is not preceded by a sonorant, but it may be deleted.
4. Strong form because the grammatical word is stranded.
5. Glottaling is not possible because /t/ is followed by a potential pause.
6. This is one of the few cases in which voicing assimilation is possible in current RP English.
7. Glottaling is not possible because /t/ is not preceded by a sonorant.
8. Either /t/ assimilation or glottaling would have been possible here. Either way the sound preceding /t/ can be assimilated because a glottal stop does not prevent assimilation.
9. In RP glottaling is not usual before a syllabic /l/.
10. Instead of glottaling /t/ we could have assimilated it.
11. /t/ cannot be glottaled because it is preceded by an obstruent, but it may be assimilated or deleted.
12. Strong form because the verb is not used as an auxiliary here.
13. In negative contractions /t/ can be elided or, if it is followed by a consonant other than /h/, it may be glottaled.

14. /t/ cannot be glottaled because it is followed by /h/.

15. /ɔːlwɪz/ and /ɔːlwəz/ are alternative pronunciations. The sound /l/ may be dropped too.

16. /faɪnl̩i/ is an exception in that /l/ cannot lose syllabicity even though it is followed by an unstressed vowel in the same word.

Exercise 8.6

| ˈwen aɪ wəʊk ˈʌp | aɪ ˈnjuː ðæʔ[1] ˈdeɪ wʊb bi ˈwʌn əv ðə ˈməʊst[1-2] ɪmˈpɔːʔn̩ʔ ˈdeɪz ɪm maɪ ˈlaɪf | ənd ɪʔ ˈwɒz[3] | bəʔ fə ˈveri ˈdɪfrənʔ ˈriːznz tə ˈwɒʔ wəz ˈplænd | ɪʔ ˈsiːm laɪk aɪ əb ˈmeɪd ɪt[1] əʔ ˈlɑːst[2-4] | aɪ əb biːn ˈɒfəd ə ˈpɑːt[1] ɪn ə ˈfɪlm | ˈðæʔ ˈnaɪʔ ðə prəˈdjuːsəz | ˈdaɪrektər[5] ənd ˈaɪ | wə tə ˈmiːʔ tə ˈsaɪn ðə ˈkɒntrækt[2-4] | ˈiːvn̩ ðə ˈweðə wəz ɒm maɪ ˈsaɪd | ɪʔ ˈstɑːtɪd[1] əz ə ˈgreɪʔ ˈdeɪ | ˈmʌtʃ ˈbetə[1] ðn̩ wʌn wʊd ɪkˈspekt[1-2] əʔ ˈðæʔ taɪm əv ðə ˈjɪə | bəʔ təˈwɔːdz ði ˈiːvnɪŋ ði ˈæʔməsfɪə[6] bigæn ˈʃəʊɪŋ saɪnz əv ˈtʃeɪndʒ | ɪʔ[6] bikeɪm ˈhevi ənd iˈlektrɪk | aɪ ˈdɪdn̩[7-8] ˈhæv[9] eni preməˈnɪʃn̩ əz ˈsʌtʃ | bət[1] aɪ ˈduː[10] riˈmembər ə ˈkaɪnd əv ˈtɪklɪŋ ɒm maɪ ˈskɪn | ə ˈfiːlɪŋ ðəʔ[6] ˈpʊp[11] mi ɒn ˈedʒ | əz ɪf maɪ ˈbɒdi wəz ˈtraɪɪŋ tə ˈwɔːm mi | aɪ ˈstɑːtɪd[1] getɪŋ[1] ˈredi veri ˈɜːli | aɪ ˈwɒntɪd[1] tə bi ɒn ˈtaɪm | ənd aɪ ˈwɒzn̩[7] ðə məʊs[12] ˈkɒnfɪdn̩t[1] əv ˈdraɪvəz əʔ ˈnaɪt[4] | ət[1] ə ˈkwɔːtə[1] tə ˈsevn̩ aɪ wəz ɔːlˈredi ɒn ðə ˈrəʊd | ðə ˈrestrɒnʔ[13] wɒzn̩[7-1] ɔːl ˈðæʔ fɑː frəm maɪ ˈhaʊs | bəʔ ðə ˈrəʊd aɪ hæd[9] tə ˈteɪk wəz ˈəʊnli ə ˈkʌntri ˈleɪn | ənd ɪʔ wʊd ˈteɪk mi əʔ ˈliːst[2-8] hɑːf ən ˈɑːə tə ˈgeʔ ðeə | ˈnaɪʔ ˈfel | ənd aɪ ˈtɜːnd ɒn ðə ˈhed laɪʔs | ˈsʌdn̩li ðə ˈkɑː ˈstɒpt[2-4] | aɪ gɒt[1] ˈaʊʔ tə ˈsiː wɒʔ wəz ˈrɒŋ wɪð ɪt[4] | ˈkɜːsɪŋ ɪʔ[6] ˈmaɪldli ʌndə maɪ ˈbreθ | aɪ wʊd ˈheɪʔ tə bi ˈleɪʔ fə ˈðɪs əˈpɔɪmʔ[14]mənt[4] | ju km̩[15] ˈbreɪk ˈdaʊn ˈeni ʌðə ˈtaɪm | bəʔ ˈnɒʔ təˈdeɪ pliːz aɪ ˈpliːdɪd | ðen aɪ ˈfaʊnd aɪ wəz ʌnˈeɪbl̩ tə ˈwɔːk | ðəʔ[6] maɪ ˈlegz wʊbm̩ʔ[7-14] ˈmuːv | ə ˈterɪbl̩ ˈlaɪʔ[6] ˈblaɪndɪb mi fər ə fjuː ˈseknz | ðen ɪʔ ˈlesnd | ənd ə ˈhjuːdʒ metl̩[16] ˈgləʊb əˈpɪəd ɪn ˈfrʌnt[1] əv mi | ɪʔ wəz ˈkʌmɪŋ ˈdaʊn | ənd əz ɪʔ ˈdɪd səʊ | ə ˈbɪg klaʊd əv ˈdʌst[2-1] ən ˈstiːm ˈrəʊz ɒf ðə ˈgraʊnd | aɪ ˈhɜːd sʌm[17] ˈwɪslɪŋ kaɪnd əv ˈsaʊnd | ɪʔ wəz ˈbjuːtɪfl̩[1] | ən ɪp[11] ˈmeɪd mi stɑːʔ ˈwɔːkɪŋ təwɔːdz ðə ˈgləʊb | pəˈhæps aɪ gɒʔ[6] ˈkləʊs | meɪbi ˈiːvn̩ went[1] ɪnˈsaɪd | bəʔ ˈnʌθɪŋ els wəz ˈredʒɪstəd[2-1] ɪm maɪ ˈmaɪnd | ɑːftə[2-1] ˈwɒʔ siːm ˈseknz aɪ wəz ˈbæk ɪn ðə ˈkɑː | ðə ˈlaɪʔ[6] gləʊb əd dɪsəˈpɪəd | aɪ ˈsæʔ ðeə waɪl ə ˈdriːmlaɪk ˈfiːlɪŋ əʊvəˈwelm mi | ɪʔ ˈwʊdn̩[7] leʔ[6] mi ˈθɪŋk | əʔ ˈlɑːst[2-1] aɪ ˈmeɪb maɪ ˈbɒdi stɑːʔ ðə ˈkɑː | maɪ ˈwɒtʃ wɒzn̩ʔ[7] ˈwɜːkɪŋ | səʊ aɪ hæd[9] ˈnəʊ weɪ əv ˈtelɪŋ wɒʔ ðə ˈtaɪm wɒz[18] | wen aɪ ˈgɒʔ tə ðə ˈrestrɒnt[13-4] | ɪʔ wəz ˈempti[2-1] | aɪ ˈθɔːʔ ðət[1] ɪʔ[6] məs[12] bi ˈkwaɪʔ ˈleɪʔ fə ðəm tə bi ˈkləʊzɪŋ | aɪ ɑːskt[2-1] ə ˈmæn hu wəz ˈpʊtɪŋ[1] aʊʔ ðə ˈbɪnz | ɪʔs ˈpɑːs[12] ˈmɪdnaɪʔ[6] ˈmædəm i ˈsed | ˈrɪəli ˈleɪʔ ðen | ðə wəz ˈnəʊ pɔɪnt[8] ˈhæŋɪŋ əˈraʊnd | səʊ aɪ ˈwemʔ[14] bæk ˈhəʊm | wen aɪ ˈwɔːkt[2-1] ɪn aɪ ˈrɪəlaɪz ðə wəz ˈdʌst[2-1] ˈevriweə | əz ɪf ðə ˈpleɪs hæbm̩ʔ[7-14] biːŋ ˈkliːn fər ˈeɪdʒɪz | ˈðæʔ wəz nɒʔ[6] ˈpɒsɪbl̩ | aɪ əg ˈgɪvn̩ ðə ˈhaʊs ə ˈθʌrə ˈkliːnɪŋ ðə ˈdeɪ biˈfɔː | aɪ ˈwenʔ tə maɪ ˈɑːnsrɪŋ məˈʃiːn | ˈmeɪbi ðeɪ əd ˈtraɪd tə leʔ[6] mi ˈnəʊ weə ðeɪ wʊd ˈbiː[3] | ðə kəmˈpjuːtəlaɪk[1] ˈvɔɪs sed | ˈwenzdeɪ sepˈtembə[19] ði ˈeɪʔθ | ju hæv[9] ˈtwenti[1] ˈmesɪdʒɪz | nəʊ ˈðæʔ[6] kʊd ˈnɒʔ[6] bi raɪʔ ˈʃɔːli | ɪʔ wəz ˈmɑːtʃ | aɪ ˈtɜːnd ɒn ðə ˈtelivɪʒn̩ tə ˈtʃek ðə ˈsiːfæks ˈpeɪdʒɪz | ðə ˈseɪm ˈdeɪʔ[6] keɪm ˈʌp ɒn ðə ˈskriːn | aɪ əb biːn əˈweɪ fə ˈsɪks ˈmʌnθs | aɪ ˈfelʔ veri ˈdɪzi | səʊ aɪ ˈsæʔ ˈdaʊn | əm pʊʔ[6] maɪ ˈhed ɪm maɪ ˈhænz | ˈwɒʔ wəz aɪ ˈgəʊɪŋ tə ˈduː[9] | ˈweər əd aɪ ˈbiːn |

Comments to transcription

1. Glottaling is not possible because /t/ is followed by a vowel.
2. Glottaling is not possible because /t/ is preceded by an obstruent.
3. Strong form because the grammatical word is stranded and also because it is stressed for rhythmical reasons.
4. Glottaling is not possible because /t/ is followed by a potential pause.
5. /dɪrektə/ and /daɪrektə/ are alternative pronunciations.
6. /t/ could have been assimilated instead of glottaled.
7. In negative contractions /t/ can be elided or, if it is followed by a consonant other than /h/, it may be glottaled.
8. Glottaling is not possible when /t/ is followed by /h/.
9. Strong form because the verb is not used as an auxiliary here.
10. Strong form because the grammatical word is emphasised and therefore stressed.
11. Instead of assimilating /t/, we could have glottaled it.
12. Glottaling is not possible because /t/ is preceded by an obstruent, but it may be deleted or assimilated here.
13. /ˈrestərɒnt/ without schwa deletion is an alternative pronunciation. In either case the /t/ in 'rest' cannot be glottaled because (i) it is preceded by an obstruent, (ii) it is followed by a vowel or (iii) by /r/ in the same word (see glottaling conditions in the lesson).
14. Either /t/ assimilation or glottaling would have been possible here. Either way the sound preceding /t/ can be assimilated because a glottal stop does not prevent assimilation.
15. In this case either progressive or regressive assimilation would have been possible.
16. In RP glottaling before a syllabic /l/ is not usual.
17. *some* is used in the strong form when it modifies a countable noun in the singular (see Lesson 3).
18. Strong form because the grammatical word is stranded.
19. /səpˈtembə/ is an alternative pronunciation.

Answers to Lesson 9: further practice

Exercise 9.1

| aɪ ˈjuːs tə ˈvɪzɪʔ ðɪs ˈeldl̩i[1] ˈneɪbər əv ˈmaɪn | tə ˈwɒʃ n̩[2] ˈset hə ˈheə | ˈwʌm pəˈtɪkjulər ˈiːvnɪŋ | aɪ wəz ˈðeə wen hə ˈdɔːtər *əˈniːtər əˈraɪvd | ʃid ˈdʒʌs riˈtɜːn frəm ðə ˈtaunz ˈtɒp klɑːs ˈheədresə | ən ʃi əˈprəutʃ[3] mi wɪð ˈwɒt aɪ ˈθɔːʔ wəz ən ɪŋˈkredɪbl̩ ɒpəˈtjuːnɪti | ʃi ˈɑːskt mi ɪf aɪ wəd[4] kənˈsɪdə biːɪŋ ˈwʌn əv hə ˈheədresəz əˈprentɪsəz | hi əb biːŋ kəmˈpleɪnɪŋ əbaut hau ˈʃɔːʔ ˈstɑːft i wɒz | sɪns ˈtuː əv ɪz əˈsɪstən?s əd ˈleft | *əˈniːtər[5] əd riˈmembəb ˈmiː | ən[2] ˈθɔːʔ ðət aɪ ˈmaɪʔ[6] bi ˈɪntrəstəd| səu ʃi ˈmenʃəm[3] maɪ ˈneɪm tu ɪm | ˈnætʃrəli aɪ wəz diˈlaɪtəd wɪð ðɪs aɪˈdɪə | səu ʃi ˈkɔːld ɪm əʔ ðə ˈsælɒn | ən wɪðɪn ˈfɪftiːm ˈmɪnɪʔs | ðeɪ əd əˈreɪndʒ fə mi tə ˈstɑːʔ ˈwɜːk ðə ˈfɒləuɪŋ wiːkˈend | aɪ wəz ˈəunli fɔːˈtiːn əʔ ðə ˈtaɪm | əm[2−3] ˈbiːɪŋ ˈɒfəd ə ˈsætədeɪ[7] ˈdʒɒb ɪn ˈwʌn əv ðə ˈtɒp əˈstæblɪʃmənʔs ɪn ˈtaun | siːm laɪk ðə ˈtʃɑːns əv ə ˈlaɪftaɪm | ɪʔ[6]

'men? ðət aɪ wʊd⁴ hæv ði ɒpə'tjuːnɪti tə 'wɜːk wɪð prə'feʃnl̩ 'staɪlɪsts | ən² 'ɜːn
səm 'pɒkɪ?⁶ mʌni | wɪtʃ wəz 'desprə?li 'niːdəd ə? ðə 'taɪm | aɪ hæv 'fɒm³
'memrɪz əv maɪ 'fɜːs 'deɪ ðeə | di'spaɪ? ðə 'fæk ðət ɪ? 'dɪbm̩⁸ bi'gɪn veri
'prɒmɪsɪŋli | aɪ wəz sə'pəʊz tə staː?⁶ 'prɒmptli ət 'haːf paːst 'eɪt | aɪ əd 'nevə
'me? ði 'əʊnər əv ðə 'sæləm bi'fɔː | ən² aɪ wəz 'veri 'nɜːvəs | aɪ 'njuː i wəz
kɔːld *'ældəʊ | əv ɪ'tæljən næʃ'nælɪti⁹ | əbaʊ? 'fɔːti jɪəz 'əʊld | ən² 'veri wel
'ɒf | bət aɪ 'dɪdn̩¹⁰ nəʊ 'mʌtʃ əbaʊ? 'wɒt i wəz 'laɪk əz ən ɪm'plɔə¹¹ | aɪ 'faʊm³
maɪ 'weɪ tə ðə 'pleɪs | ən² ə'raɪv 'raɪt ɒn 'taɪm | bə? ðə 'frʌn? 'dɔː wəz 'lɒkt |
aɪ 'weɪtəd 'nɜːvəsli fər ə 'waɪl | ənd² əz ðə 'mɪnɪ?s tɪk³ 'baɪ aɪ 'staːtəd 'wʌndrɪŋ
ɪf aɪ wəz ɪn ðə 'raɪ?⁶ 'pleɪs | waɪlst aɪ 'peɪst ʌp n̩² 'daʊn ðə 'peɪvmən? 'weɪtɪŋ fə
'sʌmwʌn tu ə'raɪv | 'kɒnstən?li 'tʃekɪŋ maɪ 'wɒtʃ | aɪ wəz 'fiːlɪŋ məʊst 'æŋkʃəs
| əz ɪ? wəz 'naʊ ə 'kwɔːtə tə 'naɪn | ən² 'stɪl 'nəʊwʌn ɪn 'saɪt | 'ðen frəm ðə
'bɒtəm əv ðə 'striːt | ə 'kaː keɪm 'spiːdɪŋ tə'wɔːdz mi | wɪð ə 'skriːtʃ əv
'breɪks ðə 'kaː 'hɔːltəd | ənd² 'aʊ? dʒʌmp ðɪs 'tɔːl 'daːk heəb 'mæn wɪð ə
'bɪəd | ðɪs 'mʌs³⁻¹³ bi 'hɪm aɪ 'θɔː? tə maɪ'self | gʊb 'mɔːnɪŋ i 'sed | 'fʌmblɪŋ
wɪð ðə 'kiːz əz i 'traɪd tu 'əʊpm̩ ðə 'dɔː | 'sɒri aɪm 'leɪt | 'kʌm ɒn 'ɪn | aɪ
'fɒləʊd ɪm ʌp'steəz | hi 'aːsk³ mi tə 'teɪk ɒf maɪ 'kəʊt | 'tʊk ɪ? 'frɒm¹⁴ mi | ən²
aːftə 'pʊtɪŋ ɪt ɒn ə 'hæŋə | hi 'kærid ɪ? tə ðə 'kləʊkrʊm ʌp'steəz | aɪ wəz
'rɪəli¹⁵ ɪm'pres³ baɪ ɪz 'gʊb 'mænəz | hi ə'skɔːtəb mi 'ɪntə ðə 'sæləɒn | ənd²
'aːsk³ mi tə 'teɪk ə 'siː? waɪlst i 'swɪtʃt ɒn ðə 'laɪ?s | ðə 'rest əv ðə 'staːf | ən²
'sevrəl 'klaːn?s 'staːtəd tu ə'raɪv | aɪ 'kʊdn̩ help 'nəʊtɪsɪŋ haʊ 'pɒʃ 'evrɪwʌn
'lʊkt | ən¹ haʊ 'bɪg ŋ²⁻³ 'kliːn ðə 'ruːm wɒz | ɪ? wəz 'ɔːlsəʊ veri 'smaː?li
'dekəreɪtəd | wɪð 'lɒ?s əv 'fænsi 'mɪrəz | əm²⁻³ 'plʌʃ 'pædəd 'tʃeəz | əz aɪ
'sæ? daʊm baɪ ðə 'bækwɒʃ | hi 'ɒfəb mi ə 'gaʊn tə pʊt 'ɒn waɪlst i 'dʒentli
'ləʊəb maɪ 'hed | maɪ 'lɒŋ 'heə 'dæŋgl̩d ɪntə ðə 'bæk əv ðə 'beɪsɪn | aɪ kəd⁴
'hɪə ðə 'wɔːtə 'rʌnɪŋ frəm ðə 'tæp bi'haɪm³ mi | ən²⁻³ 'gɒ? veri 'wʌrid | ə'speʃli¹
wen i 'sed tə mi | 'wɒ? taɪm ɪz ðə 'wedɪŋ | aɪ 'mʌmbl̩ 'nɜːvəsli 'wɒ? 'wedɪŋ | 'jɔː
wedɪŋ i ri'plaɪd | 'aːntʃu¹⁶ getɪŋ 'mærid tə'deɪ | ju kn̩ ɪ'mædʒɪn haʊ ɪm'bærəst aɪ
'wɒz wen aɪ 'aːnsəd 'nəʊ | aɪv 'kʌm tə 'wɜːk hɪə | baɪ 'ðɪs taɪm ðə 'sæləɒn wəz
'kwaɪk⁶'kraʊdəd | aɪ 'kʊdn̩¹⁰ stɒp 'blʌʃɪŋ əz aɪ wəz 'teɪkn̩ tə ðə 'bæk 'ruːm | weər
aɪ wəz 'ɪntrədjuːs tə *'helən | ðə 'suːpəvaɪzə | ʃi 'geɪv mi ə 'taəl tə 'rʌb əʊvə ðə
'wet 'endz əv maɪ 'heə | ən² 'traɪd tə 'kʌmfə?⁶ mi ə 'lɪtl̩ | ʌntɪl aɪ 'fel?⁶ mɔː
ri'lækst | ʃi 'tʊk mi ə'raʊnd | 'ʃəʊɪŋ mi ðə 'θɪŋz aɪ wəz ɪk'spektəd tə 'duː | aɪ
wəz 'gɪvn̩ ə 'juːnɪfɔːm tə 'weə | ən² 'wen? tə 'wɜːk ɪn ðə ri'sepʃn̩⁹ 'eərjə¹² | ə?
ði 'end əv ðə 'deɪ aɪ gɒp 'peɪd | əm²⁻³ 'mɔː ðŋ̩ aɪ əd 'driːmd ɒv | sɪns 'meni
əv ðə 'klaːn?s wə 'veri 'dʒenrəs | ənd² aɪ 'endəd 'ʌp wɪð ə 'lɒt əv 'ekstrə
'mʌni frəm 'tɪps | dɪs'paɪ? ðə 'lɒŋ 'aəz ðət aɪ 'wɜːkt | ən² ðə di'zaːstrəs 'staː?
tə ðə 'deɪ | ɪt 'ɔːl 'pruːv tə bi 'rɪəli 'tʃæləndʒɪŋ ənd² ɪn'dʒɔəbl̩¹¹ | aɪ kən'tiːnjuːd
tə 'wɜːk ðeər 'evri wiːk'end | ən² 'leɪtər 'ɒn | 'fʊl 'taɪm | ʌntɪl aɪ kəm'pliːtəd ðə
'θriː jɪər ə'prentɪʃʃɪp | əm²⁻³ bi'keɪm ə 'kwɒlɪfaɪd 'staəlɪst |

Comments to transcription

1. Either /ə/ elision or syllabicity is possible here.
2. Remember that /ənd/, /ən/, /n̩d/ and /n̩/ are alternative weak forms independently
   of whether the sequence meets the general conditions for alveolar plosive elision
   outlined in Lesson 6.
3. The alveolar plosive could have been assimilated instead of elided.

4. Remember that grammatical words which have /ʊ/ in their citation form, such as *would*, *should* and *could*, can remain unchanged even if they are unstressed because /ʊ/ is already a weak vowel, but they may also be further weakened to /ə/ in quicker pronunciations.
5. Sandhi r would not have been possible if the following /h/ had not been elided.
6. The alveolar plosive could have been either assimilated or glottaled.
7. The ending '-day' used in the days of the week may be pronounced /di/ or /deɪ/.
8. The alveolar plosive could have been elided, glottaled or assimilated here.
9. /ə/ elision or syllabicity frequently take place in the suffix *-tion*, even if there are two consonants before schwa or if /ən/ precedes the stressed syllable.
10. The alveolar plosive could have been either glottaled or elided.
11. The sequence /ɔɪə/ can be pronounced /ɔə/. This is the same type of smoothing process we have been using for /aɪə/ and /aʊə/ but since /ɔɪə/ appears less frequently than these other triphthongs we have not used it through the book to simplify things.
12. This is a common process for the diphthong /ɪə/ which has already been mentioned in some previous transcriptions. In unstressed positions, the first element of the diphthong may lose its prominence and become /jə/.
13. *must* is pronounced in strong form when it is stressed, like any other grammatical word. However, *must* tends to be stressed when it means 'deduction' as in *she must be tired* or *he must have left early*. In some of these cases, *must* may also be stressed because of rhythmical reasons (to avoid a very long sequence of unstressed syllables).
14. The preposition could have been unstressed and in the weak form.
15. The word *really* can also be pronounced /riːli/.
16. Instead of coalescing /t/, we could have glottaled or elided it.

Exercise 9.2

| ɪʔ wəz ə ˈθɜːzdeɪ ɑːftəˈnuːn | aɪ wəz ˈɒm maɪ weɪ ˈhəum frəm ˈwɜːk ɒn ði ˈʌndəgraʊnd | ðe ˈtreɪn kærɪdʒ wəz ˈempti[1] | bikɒz[2] aɪ wəz ˈgəʊɪŋ həʊm ˈɜːli | aɪ ˈhægn̩[3] gɒp[4] mʌtʃ ˈsliːp ðə ˈnaɪp[4] biˈfɔː | bikɒz[2] ə ˈterɪbl̩ ˈkəʊlg[5] kep[5] ˈmeɪkɪŋ mi ˈkɒf | ən ðə ˈkɒf kep ˈweɪkɪŋ mi ˈʌp | ðə ˈhəʊl ˈmɔːnɪŋ ɪn ði ˈɒfɪs əg ˈgɒn ɪn ə ˈdeɪz | aɪ felʔ ˈtæəd n̩ ˈdɪzi | ɪʔ ˈsiːmd aɪ wəz gəʊɪŋ ˈdaʊn wɪð ˈfluː | səʊ aɪ ˈpækt ˈʌp əraʊn ˈθriː əˈklɒk | ən ˈtəʊl[5] maɪ ˈsekrətri ðət aɪ ˈmaɪʔ nɒp[4] bi ˈɪn ðə ˈfɒləʊɪŋ ˈdeɪ ət ˈɔːl | ɪf aɪ ˈwɒzn̩[6] ˈfiːlɪŋ eni ˈbetə | səʊ aɪ ˈsæt ɪn ðə ˈtreɪn | ˈθɪŋkɪŋ əv ə ˈhɒk[4] kʌp əv ˈtiː | ən ðə ˈlʌvli ˈfaər aɪ wʊg gek[4] ˈgəʊɪŋ | əz ˈsuːn əz aɪ əˈraɪvd ˈhəʊm | aɪ əˈvɔɪdɪd ɔːl ˈθɔːʔs əv ðə ˈtwenti mɪnɪ ˈwɔːk frəm ðə ˈsteɪʃn̩ | aɪ wʊd ˈteɪk ə ˈtæksi | ɪf ðə ˈwɒz wʌn | bə? ˈðæʔ wəz ʌnˈlaɪkli ɪm ˈmaɪ ˈvɪlɪdʒ | səʊ ɪʔ wʊd ˈhæf[7] tə bi ði ˈəʊl trek ˈhəʊm | aɪ ˈdɪdn̩[6] juːʒuəli ˈmaɪnd ɪʔ[4] ˈmʌtʃ | bə? ðə ˈpɑːθs wʊb bi ˈmʌdi frəm ˈjestədeɪz ˈreɪn | ənd aɪ ˈwɒntɪd tə bi ˈhəʊm əz ˈsuːn əz ˈpɒsɪbl̩ | ˈɔːl ðɪs wəz ˈgəʊɪŋ θruː maɪ ˈmaɪnd | wen aɪ ˈrɪəlaɪzd aɪ ˈwɒzn̩ əˈləʊn ɪn ðə ˈkærɪdʒ eni ˈmɔː | ˈsʌmwʌn wəz ˈsɪtɪŋ ˈɒpəzɪp[4] mi | ɪʔ wəz ə ˈblɒn ˈtʃæp ɪn ɪz ˈɜːli ˈθɜːtiz | hi məst əv ˈgɒt ɒn ˈwaɪl aɪ wəz ˈmjuːzɪŋ əbaʊp[4] maɪ ˈfaə | bikɒz[2] aɪ ˈhædn̩[6] ˈnəʊtɪst ɪm biˈfɔː | aɪ ˈlʊkt ət ɪm ˈbriːfli əz wʌn ˈdʌz | bəʔ ðem maɪ ˈaɪz ˈlɪŋgəd[8] ɒn ɪz ˈfeɪs | aɪ ˈnəʊ ðɪs ˈmæn aɪ ˈθɔːt | biˈfɔː meɪkɪŋ ə ˈfuːl əv maɪˈself baɪ ˈgriːtɪŋ ə ˈtəʊtl̩ ˈstreɪndʒə | aɪ ˈtraɪd tə ˈθɪŋk weər aɪ ˈnjuː ɪm frɒm | ˈnɒʔ ðə ˈvɪlɪdʒ | bikɒz[2] ɪʔ wəz ˈsəʊ

'smɔːl | wi 'ɔːl njuː iːtʃ 'ʌðə veri 'wel | iːvn̩ 'tuː 'wel fə 'maɪ 'laɪkɪŋ | ɪʔ⁴ 'mʌs⁵ bi frəm 'wɜːk ðen | aɪ 'spent ə 'fjuː 'mɪnɪʔs 'mentl̩i⁹ ri'vjuːɪŋ 'ɔːl ðə di'pɑːp⁴mənʔs | bət i 'dɪdn̩⁶ fɪt ɪn 'eni əv ðəm | aɪ 'glɑːnst ɪn ɪz daɪ'rekʃn̩¹⁰ ə'gen | 'traɪɪŋ tə bi 'sʌtl̩ | hɪz 'kləʊðz ʃʊd əv 'təʊl⁵ mi ðət i 'wɒzn̩⁶ frəm 'maɪ 'fɜːm | wi hæv 'kwaɪt ə 'strɪk 'dres kəʊd | ən 'hiː wəz 'weərɪŋ 'əʊl feɪdɪd 'sweʔ⁴ pænʔs | 'treɪnəz | ən ə 'dʒækɪt əv ɪn'defənɪk⁴ 'kʌlə | 'wɒz ɪt ə 'frend əv ə 'frend | nəʊ aɪ 'dɪdn̩⁶ 'θɪŋk səʊ | 'sʌdn̩li ɪʔ 'dɔːnd ɒm mi | aɪ 'njuː weər aɪ əd 'siːn ɪz 'feɪs bi'fɔː | ɪʔ wəz ɒn 'telivɪʒn̩ | ɪn ə 'pliːs¹¹ 'prəʊgræm | hɪz 'fəʊtəʊgrɑːf əb biːn 'ʃəʊn əz 'ðæt əv ə 'wɒntɪg 'krɪmɪnl̩ | əz aɪ 'lʊkt ət ɪm ə'gen frəm bi'niːθ maɪ 'aɪbrauz | 'ɔːl ðə 'diːteɪlz əv ðə 'prəʊgræm keɪm 'bæk tə mi | hi wəz 'wɒntɪd fə 'kwestʃənɪŋ | wɪtʃ ɪn 'ʌðə wɜːdz 'ment ə'rest | əʊvər ə 'bruːtl̩ 'mɜːdə | hi əd 'priːvjəsli¹² dʌn 'taɪm ɪn 'prɪzn̩ fə 'mænslɔːtə | ðə 'pliːs¹¹ wɔːnd 'enibɒdi hu 'maɪʔ⁴ kʌm ə'krɒs ɪm | tə bi ɪk'striːmli 'keəfl̩ | bikɒz² i wəz 'nəʊn fər¹³ ɪz 'vaələnt ʌn'steɪbl̩ 'tempə | ðen aɪ 'rɪəlaɪzd aɪb biːn 'steərɪŋ ət ɪm | ən i wəz 'lʊkɪŋ 'bæk | aɪ felʔ 'səʊ 'fraɪʔn̩ ðət aɪ 'stɑːtɪd 'ʃeɪkɪŋ | bət ə' ðə 'seɪm 'taɪm | wəz ʌn'eɪbl̩ tə get 'ʌp ən 'duː sʌmθɪŋ | laɪk 'pʊl ði ə'lɑːm | ɪz ðeə 'sʌmθɪŋ ðə 'mætər¹³ i sed 'sʌdn̩li | 'skeərɪŋ ðə 'laɪf aʊt əv mi | 'wɒʔs ðə 'mætə wɪð ju i ri'piːtɪd | aɪ 'traɪd tə 'seɪ sʌmθɪŋ | bəʔ 'faʊn ðəp⁴ maɪ 'lɪp muːvmənʔs wə 'nɒt ə'kʌmpənɪb baɪ eni 'saʊnd | aɪ felʔ⁴ 'kəʊld ən 'hɒt | ən wəz 'traɪŋ 'hɑːd fər ə 'skriːm | 'lʊk i 'sed | ə ju ɔːl'raɪt | ju lʊk əz 'peɪl əz ə 'gəʊst | kn̩ aɪ 'help ju ət 'ɔːl | 'wel | ju kn̩ ɪ'mædʒɪn ðə 'ʃɒk aɪ 'gɒt əʔ 'ðæt | ə 'hɑːgn̩⁵ 'krɪmɪnl̩ 'ɒfrɪŋ mi ə'sɪstəns | aɪ 'kʊdn̩⁶ 'teɪk eni 'mɔː | maɪ 'hed stɑːtɪd 'fiːlɪŋ 'laɪt | ənd aɪ 'njuː aɪ wəz 'gəʊɪŋ tə 'feɪnt | aɪ 'mænɪdʒ tə 'seɪ 'təʊtl̩i ðə 'rɒŋ 'θɪŋ | bifɔː 'pɑːsɪŋ 'aʊt | aɪ 'nəʊ 'juː | 'sʌmtaɪm 'leɪtər aɪ wəʊk 'ʌp tə 'sʌmbədi¹⁴ 'slæpɪŋ mi | aɪ ri'membəb maɪ 'lɑːs 'wɜːdz | ən 'rɪəlaɪzd aɪ wəz 'ʃɔːli 'dʌn fɔː | wen aɪ 'sɔːr¹³ ɪm 'liːnɪŋ 'əʊvə mi | du¹⁵ ju 'fiːl 'betər¹³ i 'ɑːsk⁵ mi | aɪ 'nɒdɪd | 'gɒd nəʊz 'waɪ | aɪ 'wɒzn̩⁶ 'ʃɔː jud ri'membə mi i 'sed | maɪ 'feɪs məst əv 'ʃəʊb maɪ 'təʊtl̩ bi'wɪldəmənt | bikəz² i ɪn'laɪpm⁵ mi | ðə 'dʒɪm ju 'nəʊ | ðə 'dʒɪm aɪ 'krəʊkt | 'jes i ri'plaɪd 'tʃɪəfli⁹ | wi 'gəʊ tə ðə 'seɪm 'dʒɪm ɪn 'taʊn | ə ju 'ɒn jɔː weɪ 'həʊm tə *'tʃelnəm | ɪʔs 'fʌni ju ʃʊd 'lɪv aʊt 'hɪə | aɪv dʒəs⁵ 'muːvdʒu¹⁶ 'nəʊ | aɪ kəg 'gɪv ju ə 'lɪft 'həʊm wen wi 'geʔ ðeə | ju 'dəʊn⁶ lʊk əz 'ɪf ju ʃʊd 'traɪ tə 'meɪk ɪt ɒn jɔːr 'əʊn | əz i 'tɔːkt | 'evrɪθɪŋ 'fel ɪntə 'pleɪs | əf⁷ 'kɔːs aɪ 'njuː ɪm frəm ðə 'dʒɪm | wi 'ɒfn̩ wɜːkt 'aʊt əʔ ðə 'seɪm 'taɪm | aɪ felʔ 'terɪbli 'fuːlɪʃ | aɪ 'θɪŋk aɪv gɒʔ ðə 'fluː aɪ 'təʊld ɪm | jes 'ðæʔs wɒt aɪ 'θɔːp⁴ maɪ'self | 'dəʊn⁶ 'wʌri | 'aɪl getʃu¹⁷ həʊm 'suːn i'nʌf |

Comments to transcription

1. /emti/ is also a possible pronunciation.

2. /bikɒz/ and /bikəz/ are alternative pronunciations.

3. /t/ could have been elided, glottaled or assimilated here.

4. /t/ could have been either assimilated or glottaled.

5. The alveolar plosive could have been assimilated or elided.

6. The alveolar plosive could have been either glottaled or elided.

7. Voice assimilation in current RP English is only possible in a few cases, like this one.

8. Notice the pronunciation /lɪŋgə/ with a /g/ which is pronounced because the velar nasal /ŋ/ is **not** morpheme-final. On the other hand, words such as *sing* and *singer* do not have a /g/ because the velar nasal is at the end of a morpheme, even if

another morpheme has been added as in *singer* /sɪŋə/. The only exceptions to this rule are the adjectives *long*, *strong* and *young* since although /ŋ/ is morpheme-final, /g/ is added after /ŋ/ in the comparative and superlative forms, so that we say /lɒŋ/and /lɒŋgə/.

9. Either /ə/ elision or syllabicity is possible here.
10. /dɪˈrekʃn̩/ and /dəˈrekʃn̩/ are alternative pronunciations.
11. Special case of /ə/ elision because it precedes the stressed syllable (see Lesson 6).
12. In unstressed positions, the first element of the diphthong /ɪə/ may lose its prominence and become /jə/.
13. Sandhi r would not have been possible if the following /h/ had not been elided.
14. /sʌmbɒdi/ is an alternative pronunciation.
15. *do* could be weakened further to /də/ or even, in fast speech, to /d/ in which case it could coalesce with the following /j/ giving the sequence /dʒu/.
16. /d/ elision is an alternative to coalescence here.
17. /t/ glottaling or coalescence with /j/ are two possible alternatives here.

Exercise 9.3

| ˈsʌm[1] piːpl̩ hæv ə ˈspeʃl̩ ˈnætʃrəl ˈtælən? ðəp[2] ˈmeɪks ɔːl ðə ˈdɪfrəns | ðeɪ meɪ ˈlʊk laɪk ˈnɔːml̩ ˈhjuːmənz | hu ˈgəʊ tə ˈwɜːk | ˈiːt | ˈsliːp | ˈnʌθɪŋ ˈaʊt əv ði ˈɔːdn̩ri | ʌnˈtɪl ju faɪnd ˈaʊt əbaʊ? ðeər əˈbɪləti | ˈðen ðeɪ ˈʃaɪn ɪn ðeər ˈəʊn dəˈmeɪn[3] | wɪð ə ˈkaɪnd əv ˈluːmɪnəs[4] ˈreɪdjəns[5] ðəp[2] ˈmeɪks ðəm juˈniːk | ɪn ˈaə ˈhaʊs | ˈevribədi ˈsiːm tə hæv ə dɪˈstɪŋk ˈfleə | maɪ ˈfɑːðə wəz ə ˈgɪftɪd ˈstɔːri telə | hi kʊb meɪk ˈeni ˈænɪkdəʊk[2] ˈkʌm tə ˈlaɪf | wi wʊd ˈsɪ? fər aəz ˈlɪsnɪŋ[6] tu ɪm ˈtelɪŋ əs əbaʊ? ðə ˈpɑːst | əbaʊ? ðə ˈhɪstri əv aə ˈkʌntri | ˈwɒ? wʊd əv biːn ˈdraɪ ˈkrɒnɪkl̩z | ˈkʌmɪŋ frəm ˈenibədi ˈels | wə trænsˈfɔːm[7] baɪ ɪz ˈtelɪŋ | ɪntə rəˈmæntɪk[3] ˈteɪlz əv ˈkɪŋz əŋ[7] ˈkwiːnz | ˈlɔːdz əmb[7] ˈpezn̩?s | ˈblʌd ˈenəmiz əm[7] ˈbrəʊkn̩ ˈvaʊz | maɪ ˈsɪstər ɪnˈherɪtɪd ɪz ˈskɪlz | bɪkɒʒ ʃi ˈəʊnd ə ˈpaəfl̩ ɪmædʒɪˈneɪʃn̩ | wɪtʃ ʃi ˈjuːzd ɪn ˈveərjəs[5] ˈweɪz | ə? ˈskuːl ɪt ˈsɜːvd ə ˈwel | bɪkɒʒ ʃi ɪkˈseld ɪn ˈfɪkʃn̩ ˈraɪtɪŋ | ˈwen aɪ wəz ˈlɪtl̩ | ə? ˈtaɪmz ʃi wʊg ˈgep[2] mi ˈmezmeraɪzd[8] | ɔ: ˈskeəd aʊt əv maɪ ˈwɪ?s | dɪˈpendɪŋ ɒn ðə ˈstɔːri ʃi wəz riˈkaʊntɪŋ | ən ʃi ˈɔːlweɪz ˈdɪd səʊ | əz ˈɪf ʃi wəz ˈspiːkɪŋ əv ˈpjʊə ˈfæks | ˈʌðə ˈtaɪmz | ʃi wʊg kənˈkɒk ðə məʊst ɪnˈtrɑːnsɪŋ ˈgeɪmz fər əs tə ˈpleɪ | aə ˈdɒlz wʊd əˈkwɛər ə ˈlaɪf əv ðeər ˈəʊn | ˈfʊl əv ədˈventʃəz | ɪn wɪtʃ ˈwiː ˈɔːlsəʊ | wʊb bɪˈkʌm ˈkærəktəz | ði ˈəʊnli ˈtaɪmz aɪ kn̩ riˈmembər evə biːɪŋ ˈbɔːd | wə ˈðəʊz wen ʃi ˈwɒzn̩ ət ˈhænd | aə ˈmʌðə hæd ə ˈfleə fə ˈmeɪkɪŋ ˈevriwʌn ˈkʌmftəbl̩[9] | ɪn ən ˈʌnəbtruːsɪv ˈweɪ | ʃi wʊg ˈgetʃu[10] ˈfiːlɪŋ ət ˈhəʊm | wɪðɪn ˈmɪnɪ?s əv əˈraɪvɪŋ ə? ðə ˈhaʊs | ɪ? wəz ˈpɑː?li ðə ˈfæk ðə? ʃi wəz ˈɔːlwɪz ˈdʒenjuɪnli ˈɪntrəstɪd ɪm ˈpiːpl̩ | wɪtʃ ˈmeɪd ər ə sɪmpəˈθetɪk n̩ əˈpriːʃətɪv ˈlɪsnə[6] | bə? ðə wəz ˈsʌmθɪŋ ˈels mɔ: ˈdɪfɪkl̩ tə pɪn ˈdaʊn | ˈmeɪbi ə ˈhɑː?felk[2] ˈglædnəs əbaut ˈhævɪŋ ðəp[2] ˈpɜːsn̩ əˈraʊnd | wɒtˈevər ɪ? ˈwɒz | ɪt ɪnˈveərjəbli[5] ˈwɜːkt | səʊ ðət ˈɔːl aə ˈfrenz felt ɪˈmiːdjətli[5] ˈwelkəm | ən ˈnevə ˈfeɪl tə riˈtɜːn | aə ˈgræmmʌðə[7] hæd ə ˈgɪf fər ˈænɪml̩z | ɪ? wəz ˈkwaɪt əˈmeɪzɪŋ haʊ ðeɪ wʊd ˈteɪk tu ər ˈɪnstən?li | ˈðɪs wəz ɪˈspeʃli[6] ˈtruː əv ðə ˈsɪk wʌnz | ðə wəz ˈwʌn əˈkeɪʒn̩ ðə?[2] pəˈtɪkjələli ɪmˈprest evriwʌn | aər ˈʌŋkl̩z ælˈseɪʃn̩ əd ˈiː?n̩ səm ˈræp[2] ˈpɔɪzn̩ | lef ˈlaɪɪŋ ɪn ðə ˈstriː?s | ðə ˈve?[2] priˈskraɪb ˈsɜː?n̩ ˈtæbləʔs | ðəp[2] ˈmaɪ? dʒəs ˈwɜːk | əŋ[7] ˈgɪv ɪm ə ˈtʃɑːns tə pʊl ˈθruː | ðə ˈprɒbləm ˈwɒz | ðət i ˈwʊdn̩ ˈiːt ət ˈɔːl | səʊ ðə wəz ˈnəʊ pɔɪm?[2] ˈmɪksɪŋ ðə ˈmedsn̩[11] wɪð ɪz ˈfuːd | maɪ ˈʌŋkl̩ traɪd ˈfiːdɪŋ ɪm

ðə ˈtæblə?s | bə? ðə ˈpɔː ˈdɒg ˈwʊdn̩[12] let ˈeniwʌn ˈnɪər[13] ɪm | ˈaɪðə | ɪk[2] ˈgɒ? tu ə
ˈsteɪdʒ weər[13] i wəz ˈsəʊ ˈsɪk n̩ iˈmeɪʃieɪtɪd | ðə? wi wə ˈʃɔːr[13] ɪd ˈdaɪ wɪðɪn ə ˈfjuː
ˈdeɪz | ˈðæ? wəz wem maɪ ˈgræmmʌðər[7] əˈraɪvd | ˈveri ˈfreɪl ənd ʌnˈsteɪbl̩ ɒn hə
ˈfiːt | ʃi went ˈʌp tə ðə ˈdɒg | ˈəʊpn̩d ɪz ˈmaʊθ wɪð ˈwʌn ˈhænd | əm[7] ˈpɒpt ɪn ə
ˈtæblə? wɪð ðɪ ˈʌðə wʌn | ˈpʊʃɪŋ ɪ? ˈraɪ? daʊn ɪz ˈθrəʊt | səʊ ðət i ˈwʊdn̩[12] spɪt ɪt
ˈaʊt | ɑːftə ˈðæ? ʃi ˈfed ɪm | ˈstɪl baɪ ˈhænd | səm ˈmɪlksɒps | ˈðɪs went ˈɒn fə
ˈsevrəl ˈdeɪz | ʌntɪl ðə ˈdɒg wəz ˈfʊli riˈkʌvəd | ən i wəz ət hə ˈbek ən[7] ˈkɔːl
evər ˈɑːftə | əf ˈkɔːs ðər ə ˈpiːpl̩ hu pəˈzes ˈtruːli ɪkˈstrɔːdɪnri əˈbɪlətiz | laɪk ə
ˈpɜːfəkt ˈɪə fə ˈmjuːzɪk | səʊ ðə? ðeɪ kn̩ ˈtel wɒt ə ˈnəʊt ɪz ɪgˈzækli[14] | ˈiːvn̩
wen ðeɪ ˈhɪər ɪt ɪn aɪsəˈleɪʃn̩ | ˈʌðəz hæv fəʊtəˈgræfɪk ˈmemriz | aɪ ˈjuːs tə
ˈenvi ðəm | ˈspeʃli[6] wen ˈstʌdiŋ fər ən ɪgˈzæm[14] | həv ju ˈevə ˈθɔː? wɒt ən
ədˈvɑːntɪdʒ ɪp[2] məs[7] ˈbiː | tə bi ˈkeɪpəbl̩ əv riˈmembrɪŋ sʌmθɪŋ | ˈdʒʌs[7–15] baɪ
ˈlʊkɪŋ· ət ɪt ə ˈkʌpl̩ əv ˈtaɪmz | bət ɪf ˈaɪ wəz ˈgɪvn̩ ði ɒpəˈtjuːnɪti tə ˈtʃuːz | ˈaɪ
wʊd ˈsetl̩ fə ˈmjuːzɪkl̩ ˈtælənt | laɪk ˈhævɪŋ ə ˈgʊd ˈsɪŋɪŋ[16] ˈvɔɪs | ɔː ˈpleɪɪŋ ən
ˈɪnstrəmən? ˈrɪəli ˈwel | əf ˈkɔːs ðəʊz ˈskɪlz kʌm wɪð ˈpræktɪs |ˈtuː | bə? ˈnəʊ
daʊt ə ˈnætʃrəl ˈgɪf fər ɪt | ˈgɪvz ju ə ˈhed ˈstɑːt |

Comments to transcription

1. *some* is used in the strong form because it means 'some, but not all' (see Lesson 3).
2. The alveolar plosive could have been either assimilated or glottaled.
3. When the diphthong /əʊ/ appears in an unstressed position preceding the stressed syllable, it is often simplified to /ə/ as in this case.
4. /ljuːmɪnəs/ is an alternative pronunciation.
5. In unstressed positions, the first element of the diphthong /ɪə/ may lose its prominence and become /jə/.
6. Either syllabicity or /ə/ elision is possible here.
7. The alveolar plosive could have been assimilated or elided.
8. /ə/ elision is not likely here because the resulting sequence of consonants /zmr/ does not occur within words in RP English
9. /ə/ elision in the syllable /fət/ is frequent although exceptional since /ə/ is not followed by a liquid.
10. /t/ glottaling or coalescence with /j/ are alternative processes here.
11. There is an alternative pronunciation /medɪsən/. The final syllable may also be pronounced /sɪn/ in which case syllabicity would not be possible.
12. The alveolar plosive could have been either glottaled or elided.
13. Sandhi r would not have been possible if the following /h/ had not been elided.
14. The first syllable in this word may also be pronounced /eg/ /əg/ /ek/ /ək/ or /ɪk/.
15. The strong form is used because the word is emphasised.
16. Remember that words such as *sing* do not have a /g/ because the velar nasal is at the end of a morpheme, even if another morpheme has been added as in *singing* /sɪŋɪŋ/. The adjectives *long*, *strong* and *young* are exceptions since although /ŋ/ is morpheme-final, /g/ is added after /ŋ/ in the comparative and superlative forms.

Exercise 9.4

| *ˈmɑːgrə? stʊd ˈhəʊldɪŋ ðə ˈniː?li ræp[1] ˈprezn̩? ˈtaɪt | ðə ˈsmɔːl ˈbɒks fɪtɪd
ˈnaɪsli ɪntə ðə ˈpɑːmz əv hə ˈhænz | ən ʃi ˈfel?[2] kwaɪk[2] kənˈten? ˈstændɪŋ ðeər
ɒn ðə ˈplæ?fɔːm əv ðə ˈtjuːb steɪʃn̩ | ðə ˈbəʊ ɒn ðə ˈbɒks | ˈrɪpl̩ ˈdʒen?li ɪn ðə

ˈwɔːm ˈeə | ðəʔ² ˈkeɪm frəm ɪnˈsaɪd ðə ˈtʌnl̩ | ˈweɪtɪŋ fə ðə ˈnɔːθbaʊn ˈtreɪn tə
ˈteɪk ər əˈweɪ | ən wɪð ˈnʌθɪŋ tə dɪˈstrækt hər əˈtenʃn̩ | ˈɔːl ðə ˈpəʊstəz wər
ˈəʊld | ənd ˈædvətaɪzd ˈhɒlɪdeɪz ɔːr ɪgˈzɒtɪk³ ˈdrɪŋks | ˈθɪŋz ʃi kəd ˈnɒʔ² get
ˈɪntrəstɪd ˈɪn | *ˈmɑːgrəʔs ˈmaɪn ˈwɒndəd | ʃi ˈnjuː ʃi dɪd ˈnɒt hæv ˈlɒŋ tə
ˈweɪʔ ˈnaʊ | ðə ˈstreŋθ əv ðə ˈwɪn ˈtəʊld əv ði ˈɪmɪnənt əˈraɪvl̩ əv ðə ˈtreɪn | ʃi
ˈhəʊp fər ə ˈsiːʔ tə bi ˈfriː | səʊ ðəʔ ðə ˈtwenti ˈmɪnɪʔ ˈdʒɜːni | wʊd əʔ ˈliːs⁴
pɑːs ɪŋ ˈkʌmfəʔ fə ˈwʌns | ˈdeɪdriːmɪŋ wəz ˈdɪfɪkl̩ʔ wen wʌn wəz ʌŋˈkʌmftəbl̩⁵
| ʃi ˈpɒndəd ɒn ðə ˈneɪtʃər əv hə ˈfeɪvrɪʔ² ˈpɑːstaɪm | ˈdeɪdriːmɪŋ ˈsɜːʔnli
wɒzn̩⁶ ˈsʌmθɪŋ ðək² kʊb bi ˈdʌn dʒəst ˈeniweə | ɔː ˈkʊd ɪt | ðə səˈraʊndɪŋz
hæd tə bi sɪmpəˈθetɪk | aɪ ˈwʌndə wɒʔ wʊd bi ðə ˈbes⁴ kaɪnz əv ˈpleɪsɪz fə
ˈdeɪdriːmɪŋ | ðə ˈwʌnz ðəʔ wʊd ˈlet ə ˈsmɔːl ˈlɪŋgrɪŋ⁷ ˈθɔːʔ dɪˈveləp | ɪntu ə
ˈfʊlskeɪl ˈdrɑːmər ɪnˈvɒlvɪŋ ˈlʌv ən ˈɪntriːg | ˈwɒt ɪf ðə səˈraʊndɪŋz hæd ən
ˈɪnflwəns⁸ ɒn ðə ˈtaɪp əv ˈdriːm | meɪbi ˈdɪfrəŋk² ˈkaɪnz əv ˈpleɪsɪz | prədjuːs
ˈdɪfrəŋʔ² ˈkaɪnz əv ˈdeɪdriːmz | hə ˈmaɪn wəz ˈwɜːkɪŋ ˈhɑːd | ˈðɪs wəz ən
ˈævənjuː əv ekspləˈreɪʃn ðəʔ ˈsiːm səʊ ˈɒbvjəs⁹ | jet ɪn ˈɔːl hə ˈjɪəz əv ˈdeɪdriːmɪŋ
| ˈnevər¹⁰ əd ɪʔ əˈkɜːd tu ə | wen ˈpiːpl̩ ər əˈsliːp | ən ðeɪ ˈsmel ˈsməʊk | ðeɪ ˈdriːm
əv ˈfaə | ʃi rɪˈmembəd ˈsʌmwʌn ˈtelɪŋ ə | ˈsʌmtaɪmz ˈdeɪdriːmz kʊb bi ˈrɪəli¹¹
ʌmˈpleznt | wəz ðeə ˈsʌtʃ ə ˈθɪŋ əz ə ˈdeɪ ˈnaɪʔmeə² | ʃi ˈkləʊzd hər ˈaɪz | ən
tʊk ə ˈdiːp ˈbreθ | ˈɑːftər ə ˈsekn̩d ɔː ˈtuː | hə ˈmaɪn felʔ² ˈklɪər əŋ⁴ ˈkɑːm | ʃi
ˈəʊpm̩d hər ˈaɪz əˈgen | ənd wəz ˈgriːtɪb baɪ ðə ˈsaɪt əv ðə ˈtjuːb treɪn ˈsləʊɪŋ
ˈdaʊn | əz ɪʔ² ˈpɑːst əlɒŋ ðə ˈplæʔfɔːm | ˈgrædʒwəli⁸⁻¹² ɪʔ² ˈkeɪm tu ə ˈstɒp |
ən ˈlʌkili iˈnʌf | ðə ˈdɔːz əʊpm̩ ˈdaərəkli¹³ ˈɒpəzɪt¹⁴ ə | ə ˈsmaɪl gruː ɒn hə ˈlɪps |

Comments to transcription

1. The alveolar plosive could be assimilated or elided but in this case assimilation would result in a /ppp/ sequence which is indistinguishable from the sequence /pp/ we would get if the alveolar was deleted.
2. The alveolar plosive could have been either assimilated or glottaled.
3. The first syllable in this word may be pronounced as in the transcription or /eg/ /əg/ /ek/ /ək/ /ɪk/.
4. The alveolar plosive could have been assimilated or elided.
5. Frequent though exceptional case of /ə/ elision in the syllable /fət/ because it is not followed by a liquid.
6. The alveolar plosive could have been either glottaled or elided.
7. Notice the pronunciation /lɪŋgrɪŋ/ with a /g/ which is pronounced because the first velar nasal /ŋ/ is **not** morpheme-final. On the other hand, words such as *sing* and *singer* do not have a /g/ because the velar nasal is at the end of a morpheme, even if another morpheme has been added as in *singer* /sɪŋə/. The only exceptions to this rule are the adjectives *long*, *strong* and *young* since although /ŋ/ is morpheme-final, /g/ is added after /ŋ/ in the comparative and superlative forms.
8. In the same way we have seen for /ɪə/, the first element in the diphthong /ʊə/ may in unstressed positions lose its prominence and become /wə/.
9. This is a common process for the diphthong /ɪə/ which has already been mentioned in some previous transcriptions. In unstressed positions, the first element of the diphthong may lose its prominence and become /jə/.
10. Sandhi r would not have been possible if the following /h/ had not been elided.
11. This word could also be pronounced /riːli/.

12. Notice the word internal coalescence of /d/ and /j/ giving /dʒ/.
13. Notice that /t/ has been deleted word internally.
14. /ɒpəsɪt/ is an alternative pronunciation.

Exercise 9.5

| ɪʔ wəz ˈəʊvər ə ˈjɪər əgəʊ ðə? *ˈmeəri lɑːs ˈwenʔ tə ˈtʃɜːtʃ | haʊevə ˈnəʊbədi[1]
deəg ˈkrɪtɪsaɪz ə fɔːr[2] ɪt | nɒt ˈiːvn̩ ðə məʊst ɪnˈvetrək[3] ˈgɒsɪps ˈtɔːkt əbaʊt ɪt |
*ˈmeəri dɪdn̩[4] gəʊ tə ˈtʃɜːtʃ eni ˈmɔː | ən ðə həʊl ˈvɪlɪdʒ riˈspektɪd[5] hə diˈsɪʒn̩ |
ðæt ˈɪz | ˈevriwʌn ɪkˈsep fə ðə ˈvɪkə | ˈhiː kʊdn̩ əˈpruːv əv hə riˈzɒlv | wɪtʃ
ˈwent əgenst ˈɔːl rɪˈstæblɪʃ[6] ˈkʌstəmz | ən ˈʃiː dɪd nɒʔ rɪˈspek ðə ˈvɪkəz
ˈætɪtjuːd | ðeə ˈlɑːs səʊ kɔːld ˈɑːgjʊmən? tʊk pleɪs ˈmʌnθs əgəʊ | ɒn
*ˈɔːlˈsəʊlz deɪ | *ˈmeəri əg ˈgɒn tə ðə ˈsɜːvɪs | əz ʃi ˈɔːlwɪz ˈdɪd | tə ˈpreɪ fə ðə
ˈsəʊlz əv ðəʊz diˈpɑːtɪd[5] | hə ˈfɑːðə | ðen hə ˈbrʌðər ən ðen hə ˈmʌðə | aɪðə[7]
ðə ˈsiː ɔː ˈsɒrəu | wɪtʃ ˈsʌmtaɪmz wə ˈwʌn ən ðə ˈseɪm θɪŋ | həd ˈteɪkŋ ðəm
ˈwʌn baɪ ˈwʌn | ðə ˈsiː ˈgɪvz | bət ɪʔ ˈteɪks əweɪ ˈmɔː | ˈmʌtʃ mɔː hə ˈmʌðə
juːs tə ˈseɪ | ən ʃi wʊd[8] ˈsteər ˈaʊt | hər ˈaɪz ˈlɒst ɪn ðə ˈvɑːsnəs[5] əv ðə ˈsiː |
frəm weər ˈɔːl hə ˈdʒɔɪz ən ˈsɒrəʊz əd ˈɔːwɪz ˈsprʌŋ | hər ˈaɪz ˈmɜːki ˈnaʊ |
həd ˈɒfn̩ ˈhel ðeər ˈəʊn | ˈtʃæləndʒɪŋ ðə ˈsiː | ə ˈsaɪ brəʊk aʊt əv *ˈmeəri |
wen ʃi keɪm ˈbæk tə ðə ˈrɪəl ˈwɜːld | əʔ ði ˈend əv ðə ˈmæs ðæt *ˈɔːl ˈsəʊlz
deɪ | ə ˈsaɪ ðəp[3] brɔːʔ tə ði ˈɔːltər əz ən ˈɒfrɪŋ | ɔːl hə ˈmemriz | ˈfɑːðə |
ˈmʌðə | ˈbrʌðə | *ˈtəʊni | ˈnəʊ | ˈnɒʔ *ˈtəʊni | ʃi ˈhɜːd əself ˈʃaʊt əz ðə ˈvɪkə
sed ə ˈpreə fə ðə ˈseɪləz | ˈlɒs wɪð ðə ˈfɪʃɪŋ bəʊp[3] *ˈmaʊnti | ˈneɪmɪŋ iːtʃ ˈwʌn
əv ðəm | ən ˈlɑːst əv ɔːl *ˈtəʊni | ˈnɒ? *ˈtəʊni | ˈnɒt ˈhɪm ʃi kept ɒn ˈʃaʊtɪŋ |
waɪlʃ[9] ʃi ˈstrəʊd aʊt əv ðə ˈtʃɜːtʃ | *ˈtəʊni ɪz əˈlaɪv | ənd[10] ˈjuː ˈwəʊmp[4] bi ðə
ˈwʌnz tə ˈkɪl ɪm | *ˈtəʊni wɪl kʌm ˈbæk tə mi ˈsuːn | əndʒu[11] ˈwəʊm[4] bi ˈeɪbl̩
tə ˈteɪk ɪm əˈweɪ frɒm[2] mi | ən ˈðæʔ ˈdeɪ | ʃi ˈlef ðə ˈtʃɜːtʃ | ˈnevə tə rɪˈtɜːn | əz
ʃi ˈwɔːk[6] pɑːs ðə ˈsemətri ˈgeɪʔs | ʃi ˈtɜːnd hə ˈhed ði ˈʌðə ˈweɪ | səʊ ðə? ʃi
ˈwʊdn̩ hæf[12] tə ˈhiːd ðə ˈkɔːl frəm biˈhaɪn ðə ˈgeɪʔs | ðə ˈkɔːl wɪtʃ ˈbekŋd ə tə
ˈstɒp | ən[6] gɪv ʌp hə ˈfɜːm biˈliːf | *ˈmeəri ˈsæt ɒn ə ˈstəʊm ˈbentʃ | ˈfeɪsɪŋ ðə
ˈmɪsti ˈsiː | ʃi riˈfjuːz tə gəʊ ˈbæk | nɒt ˈiːvn̩ fə hə ˈfæmli wʊd[8] ʃi ˈduː ɪt | ðə
ˈflɑːʒ ʃi əb priˈpeəd tə ˈpʊp[3] baɪ ðeə ˈgreɪvz | wə ˈlef[6] biˈhaɪnd ɒn ðə ˈtʃɜːtʃ
ˈpjuː | ðeɪ əb biːm ˈmærid fər ə ˈfjuː ˈmʌnθs | ðæ? ˈdeɪ wen *ˈtəʊni keɪm
ˈbæk ɪn ði ˈiːvnɪŋ | ˈbɜːstɪŋ tə ˈʃeər[13] ɪz ˈnjuːz | hi əb biːŋ ˈgɪvn̩ ə ˈdʒɒb ɒn ðə
*ˈmaʊnti | ðə ˈbest əmb[6] məʊsp[6] ˈmɒbm̩ ˈbəʊt ɪn ðə ˈhəʊl ˈeəriə[14] | ɪʔ wəz
ˈeni ˈfɪʃəmənz ˈdriːm ˈʃɪp i ˈbiːmd | ən ɪmpəˈseptɪbl̩ ˈʃædəʊ krɒs[6] *ˈmeəriz
ˈbraʊ əz i ˈspəʊk | ʃi diˈsaɪdɪd[5] tu ɪgˈnɔːr ɪt | əm[6] ˈbrɪŋ hə ˈsmaɪl ˈbæk tə ðə
ˈsɜːfɪs | ʃi ˈwʊdn̩[15] dwel ɒn ˈfæntəmz | ˈnɒ? wen *ˈtəʊni wəz səʊ ˈhæpi |
haʊˈevə | ˈmeɪbi ˈsensɪŋ hə ˈmuːd | hi rɪəˈʃɔːd ə | ɪʔ wəz ðə ˈseɪfəs[5-6] ˈbəʊt ɪn
ðə ˈhəʊl ˈfliːt | hib bi əˈweɪ fər ə ˈfjuː wiːks ˈəʊnli | ˈθriː ˈmʌnθs əʔ ðə ˈməʊst |
ðə ˈpeɪ wəb bi ˈveri ˈgʊd | ən wen i rɪˈtɜːnd | ðeɪ kəd[8] ˈθɪŋk əv ˈstɑːtɪŋ ʌp ə
ˈfæmli | *ˈmeəri gɒt ˈʌp frəm ðə ˈbentʃ | ən ˈstɑːtɪd[5] ˈwɔːkɪŋ ˈhəʊm | hə
ˈdʒɔːz ˈklentʃ wɪð dɪtɜːmɪˈneɪʃn̩ | ˈðæʔ wəz ə ˈde? ˈdestəni ˈəʊd ə | ən ʃi hæd
ˈnəʊ ɪnˈtenʃn̩ əv gɪvɪŋ ˈʌp ɒn ɪt | ə ˈjɪə wemp[3] ˈbaɪ | ə ˈjɪə sɪns ðə *ˈmaʊnti
dɪsəˈpɪəd | *ˈmeəri kept ɒn ˈweɪtɪŋ | ˈevri ˈdeɪ wɪðaʊʔ ˈfeɪl | ʃi wəg[8] gəʊ
ˈdaʊn tə ðə ˈhɑːbə | wɪð ˈhʌrid ˈsteps ʃi wəd[8] ˈskɪp ðə ˈneʔs | wɪtʃ ðə ˈwɪmɪn
wə ˈmendɪŋ | ðeɪ wʊd[8] lʊk ʌp m̩[16] ˈʃeɪk ðeə ˈhedz ˈsædli | ˈwʌn ɔː ˈtuː wʊg[8]
ˈgriːt ə | ˈgetɪŋ ɪn rɪˈtɜːn ðə ˈflɪkər əv ə ˈsmaɪl | ɔːr ə ˈmɜːmə frəm *ˈmeəri | ʃi

kənˈtɪnjuːd ɒn hə ˈweɪ | ðə ˈseɪm ˈevri ˈsɪŋ!̩ ˈdeɪ | tə ðə ˈveri ˈend əv ðə ˈpɪə | ˈðeə | baɪ ðə ˈlaɪthaʊs | ʃid ˈstæn fər ə ˈlɒŋ ˈtaɪm | ˈsteərɪŋ ˈhɑːd aʊʔ təˈwɔːdz[17] ðə həˈraɪzn̩ | ˈskriːnɪŋ ðə ˈsiːz | ðen ʃi wʊd[8] ˈtɜːm ˈbæk | ən riˈtreɪs hə ˈsteps | ˈsləʊli ˈnaʊ | əz ɪf ʃi əd ˈdʌn ə ˈrɪtʃʊəl[18] ˈdjuːti | ʃiɡ ɡəʊ ˈʌp ðə ˈhɪl ˈlɪt!̩ baɪ ˈlɪt!̩ | diˈleɪɪŋ hə riˈtɜːn tə ðə ˈkɒtɪdʒ | ˈnəʊbədi[1] wʊd[8] ˈsiː ər ʌntɪl ðə ˈfɒləʊɪŋ ˈmɔːnɪŋ ˈbæk ət ðə ˈpɪə | ˈwʌn ˈdɑːk ˈreɪni ˈdeɪ ɪn nəˈvembə[19] | ɒn wɪtʃ ðə ˈwɪm[6] bluː | laɪk ən ˈəʊmən | *ˈmeəri ˈlef ðə ˈhaʊs | hə ˈfeɪs ˈflʌʃt[20] ŋ̍[6] ˈɡləʊɪŋ wɪð ɪkˈsaɪpmənt[3] | ʃi ˈwɔː ðə ˈɡəʊl[6] ˈbrəʊtʃ hə ˈmʌðər[13] əɡ ˈɡɪvn̩ ər ɒn hə ˈbesk[6] ˈkaʊt | ənd ə ˈfjuː ˈdrɒps əv ðæʔ ˈrɪəli ɡʊb ˈpɜːfjʊm *ˈtəʊni əb ˈbrɔːt ə frəm ˈwʌn əv ɪz ˈtrɪps | ʃi ˈəʊpm̩d ən ʌmˈbrələr əɡens ðə ˈreɪn | ən ˈstɑːtəd[5] ˈwɔːkɪŋ | ˈlaɪʔ[3-21] ŋ̍[6] ˈkwɪk | təwɔːdz[17] ðə ˈpɪə | ˈəʊnli əʊl *ˈtɒm sɔːr[13] ə ɡəʊ ˈbaɪ | *ˈmeəri ˈsmaɪld ən ˈweɪvd æt[2] ɪm ˈtʃɪəfli[22] | wɪðaʊʔ ˈstɒpɪŋ | wen ʃi ˈriːtʃ ðə ˈlaɪthaʊs | ʃi ˈkləʊz ði ʌmˈbrələr əm pleɪst ɪk[3] ˈkeəfli[22] əɡens ˈwʌn əv ðə ˈstəʊn ˈwɔːlz | ʃi tʊk ə ˈmɪrər aʊt əv hə ˈhæmbæɡ[6] | ən ˈtʌtʃt ʌp hə ˈheə | ˈveri ˈsləʊli | əz ˈsləʊli əz ˈwʌn hu biˈliːvʒ ʃiz ˈwɔːkɪŋ ɒn ˈwɔːtə | *ˈmeəri went ˈɪntə ðə ˈfəʊm | ˈsmaɪlɪŋ laɪk ə ˈtʃerəb | lʊkɪŋ ˈfɪələsli ə? ðə ˈdɑːk ˈtɜːbjʊlən? ˈsiː | ðen ə ˈbɪɡ ˈweɪv | ˈsʌdn̩ ən ˈrʌf | ˈlæʃt ət hə ˈweɪst | ˈtʊk ər ɪn ɪ?s ɪmˈbreɪs | əŋ[6] ˈkærid ər əˈweɪ |

Comments to transcription

1. /nəʊbɒdi/ is an alternative pronunciation.
2. A preposition may be in the strong or weak form before an unstressed pronoun.
3. The alveolar plosive could have been either assimilated or glottaled.
4. The alveolar plosive could have been elided, glottaled or assimilated here.
5. Remember that /ɪ/ and /ə/ are alternative pronunciations in the plural, third person and past tense morphemes and in others like '-less' and '-ness'.
6. The alveolar plosive could have been assimilated or elided.
7. /iːðə/ is an alternative pronunciation.
8. Remember that grammatical words which have /ʊ/ in their citation form, such as *would*, *should* and *could*, can remain unchanged even if they are unstressed because /ʊ/ is already a weak vowel, but they may also be further weakened to /ə/ in quicker pronunciations.
9. In this case, fricative assimilation is possible because the alveolar plosive has been deleted.
10. Coalescence is less likely because /j/ is in a stressed word.
11. /d/ elision or coalescence with /j/ are alternative processes here.
12. Notice this is one of the few cases of voice assimilation in connected speech.
13. Sandhi r would not have been possible if the following /h/ had not been elided.
14. In unstressed positions, the first element of the diphthong /ɪə/ may lose its prominence and become /jə/.
15. The alveolar plosive could have been glottaled or deleted.
16. Notice the progressive assimilation which occurs across words.
17. /tuˈwɔːdz/ and /ˈtɔːdz/ are other possible pronunciations for this word.
18. This word could also be pronounced without coalescence /ˈrɪtjʊəl/. Additionally, the first element of the diphthong /ʊə/ may lose its prominence and become /wə/.
19. When the diphthong /əʊ/ is preceding the stressed syllable, the second element of the diphthong (/ʊ/) often disappears.

20. Theoretically, /t/ could be assimilated. However, the resulting sequence of /ʃk ŋ gl/ is unlikely. It may not be deleted because the consonant following it is a syllabic one.
21. Glottaling is possible because the following word does not begin with vowel since we have applied syllabicity to *and*.
22. Either /ə/ elision or syllabicity is possible here.

Exercise 9.6

| ˈtrævlɪŋ[1] ɪz ˈwɒt aɪ ˈlaɪk duːɪŋ ˈbest | ɪt ɪz ˈwʌndəfl̩ tə ˈfaɪn[2] jəself[3] ˈsʌdn̩li | aːftər ə ˈfjuː aəz ˈpleɪn dʒɜːni | ɪn ə ˈtəʊtli[1] ˈdɪfrən?[4] ˈkʌltʃə | ən ˈæpməsfɪər[4] ʌnˈlaɪk ˈjɔːz | weər ˈevriθɪŋ səˈpraɪzɪz ju | ˈevriθɪŋ ɪz ˈnjuː | əndʒu kŋ diˈtætʃ jɔːˈself[3] frəm jɔːr ˈevrideɪ ˈlaɪf | wen wi ˈɡəʊ əˈbrɔːd | wi ˈlaɪk tə ˈmeɪk ɑər ˈəʊn əˈreɪndʒmənʔs | wɪtʃ ɪz ˈsɜːʔn̩li ˈhɑːdə | bɪkɒz ju ˈfeɪs meni mɔː ˈprɒbləmz ən ˈdɪfɪkl̩tiz | əndʒu[2] ˈhæv mɔː ˈkɒntæk wɪð ði ɒfn̩ ˈkruəl riˈælɪti əv ðə ˈpleɪsɪz ju ˈvɪzɪt | bəʔ ˈðæt ɪz dʒəs ˈwaɪ aɪ ˈlaɪk ˈtrævlɪŋ[1] laɪk ˈðæt | ju ˈɡeʔ tə nəʊ ˈʌðə weɪz əv ˈlaɪf | wen trævlɪŋ[1] | ju ˈhæf[5] tə hæv ən ˈəʊpm̩ ˈmaɪnd | əm[6] bi ˈeɪbl̩ tu əˈdʒʌs tu ˈɔːl sɔːʔs əv sɪtʃuˈeɪʃnz[7] | ənd ˈiːvn̩ wen ju ə ˈhævɪŋ ə ˈbæd ˈtaɪm | ɪnˈdʒɔɪ ɪt əz pɑːt əv ði ɪkˈspɪərjəns[8] | ə ˈlɒt əv ˈpiːpl̩ ˈfaɪn ˈstreɪndʒ ˈfuːdz n̩ ˈsmelz ʌmˈplezn̩t | ɔː ðeɪ ˈkɑːm[9] beə ˈsiːɪŋ ˈpɒvəti | ən ˈsʌm[10] piːpl̩ ə ˈnɒp[4] priˈpeəd tə bi ʌŋˈkʌmftəbl̩[11] | ˈsliːp ˈeniweə | ˈpʊt ʌp wɪð ˈɪnseks | ɔː ˈfeɪs ˈdeɪndʒə | aɪ ˈdəʊn[9] ɡeʔ ˈskeəd ˈiːzili | ən ˈdəʊm[9] maɪŋ[6] ˈɡəʊɪŋ ˈɒf ðə ˈbiːʔn̩ ˈtræk | ˈiːvn̩ ɪf ɪʔs ˈspəʊz[11] tə bi ˈdeɪndʒrəs | ˈwʌns wi wenʔ tə ˈvɪzɪt ə *mɑːˈsaɪ ˈvɪlɪdʒ | əˈweɪ frəm ðə səˈfɑːri ˈsɜːkɪʔs | wi wə ˈteɪkŋ ðeə baɪ ə ˈmæn frəm ðə ˈvɪlɪdʒ | hu ˈwɜːk fər ə ˈfrend əv ˈaəz | ən hu wəz ˈbrɪŋɪŋ ˈprezn̩ʔs fə ðə ˈɡɜːl i wəz ɪnˈɡeɪdʒ tuː | hi ɪntrəˈdjuːst əs tu ˈɔːl ɪz ˈfæmli | ən wi wə ˈwelkəmd əz ˈfrenz | wi ˈvɪzɪtɪd sʌm[10] əv ðə ˈhʌʔs biˈlɒŋɪŋ tu ɪz ˈfɑːðəz ˈwaɪvz | | ðə ˈhʌʔs wə meɪd əv ˈpres[6] ˈkaʊ dʌŋ | ɔːlˈðəʊ ə ˈmæn kŋ hæv ˈsevrəl ˈwaɪvz | ˈiːtʃ ˈwʊmən məst hæv hər ˈəʊn ˈdwelɪŋ | ˈevriweə wi ˈwenʔ wi wər ˈɒfəd ˈtiː | ən ðeɪ ˈkɪld ə ˈɡəʊt ɪn ɑər ˈɒnə | ðeɪ ˈduː səʊ baɪ ˈslɪtɪŋ ɪʔs ˈθrəʊt | səʊ ðət ɪʔ[4] ˈbliːdz tə ˈdeθ | ðeɪ ˈdrɪŋk ðə ˈblʌd | bɪkəz ðə *mɑˈsaɪ biˈliːv ðət ˈænɪml̩ ˈblʌɡ ɡɪvz ðəm ðə ˈstreŋθ | tə ˈmeɪk ðəm ðə ˈɡʊd ˈwɔːrjəz[8] ðeɪ ˈɑː | ˈwaɪl ðeɪ wə ˈfɪlɪŋ ˈdʒɑːz wɪð ðə ˈblʌd | wi ˈθɔːʔ wi wə ˈɡəʊɪŋ tə bi ˈɒfəd sʌm[10] | ˈfɔːtʃnəʔli[1] | ðeɪ ˈkʊk ði ˈænɪml̩z ˈmiːt ɒn ən ˈəʊpm̩ ˈfaə fər ˈʌs | ˈðər ɪz ˈnəʊ sɪŋl̩ ˈpleɪs aɪ ˈwʊdn̩[12] wɒnʔ tə ˈɡəʊ tuː | ˈhæm[6] mi ə ˈpleɪn tɪkɪt | ən aɪm ˈɒm maɪ ˈweɪ | ˈaɪ dəʊn[9] ˈkeə | ðə ˈsɪmpl̩ ˈfækt əv ˈkrɒsɪŋ ðə ˈbɔːdə | ənd ˈlɪsnɪŋ[1] tə ðə ˈreɪdjəʊ[8] | ɔː ˈlʊkɪŋ əp[4] ˈpetrəl steɪʃn̩ ˈsaɪnz ɪn ə ˈfɒrɪn ˈlæŋɡwɪdʒ | ɪz ˈsʌmθɪŋ aɪ əˈdɔː | aɪ ˈlʌv ˈeəpɔːʔs | ˈwɔːkɪŋ daʊn ðə ˈstriːʔs əv ˈfɒrɪn ˈtaʊnz | ˈwɒtʃɪŋ piːpl̩ | ən ˈðæʔs sʌmθɪŋ ju kŋ ˈduː ɪn ˈθɜːd wɜːl[6] ˈkʌntriz ɔːr ɪn diˈveləp wʌnz | ɪn diˈveləp[6] ˈkʌntriz ju hæv ə ˈbetə ˈtʃɑːns əv ənˈdʒɔɪɪŋ ˈmæmmeɪd ˈwɜːks | ˈɑːkɪtektʃə | ˈpeɪntɪŋz | ðə ˈhɪstri əv ˈsɪtiz ən sɪvɪlaɪˈzeɪʃnz | pəhæps[13] ɪn ˈʌðə pɑːʔs əv ðə ˈwɜːl laɪk ˈsentrəl *ˈæfrɪkə | wɪtʃ ɪz maɪ ˈfeɪvrɪt | wɒtʃu[14] kŋ ənˈdʒɔɪ ɪz ˈneɪtʃə | wɪtʃ ɪz suːˈpɜːb | ən ðə ˈpiːpl̩ ən ðeə ˈweɪ əv ˈlaɪf | bəʔ ðər ˈɑːŋ[9] ɡreɪp[4] mjuːˈzɪəmz tə ˈɡəʊ tuː | ˈðəʊz ə ˈtuː ˈdɪfrən?[4] kaɪnz əv ˈtrɪp | aɪ ˈlaɪk ðəm ˈbəʊθ | bəʔ[4] pəhæps[13] əz ə ˈbetə weɪ əv ˈbreɪkɪŋ əweɪ frəm ˈevriθɪŋ | aɪ prɪˈfɜː ðə mɔːr ədˈventʃrəs ˈtaɪp | maɪ ˈleɪtəs ˈtrɪp | lɑːs ˈwɪntə | wəz tə *zɪmˈbɑːbwi | ˈwʌn əv ðə ˈθɪŋz ðət ɪmˈpres[6] mi ˈməʊst | wəz ˈflaɪɪŋ ˈəʊvə ðə *vɪkˈtɔːrjə[8] ˈfɔːlz | ɪʔ wəz ən ɪndɪˈskraɪbəbli mæɡˈnɪfɪsn̩ʔ[15] ˈsiːn | wi wə ˈstɪl meni ˈmaɪlz əweɪ frəm

ðə 'fɔːlz | wen wi 'sɔː wɒʔ 'siːm tə bi ðə 'sməuk frəm ə 'hjuːdʒ 'fɒrɪs 'faə | 'raɪzɪŋ ɪŋ'kredɪbli 'haɪ | əz wi gɒʔ[4] 'kləusə | wi 'rɪəlaɪzd ɪʔ wəz ðə 'stiːm kʌmɪŋ 'ʌp frəm ðə 'fɔːlz | wi wə 'lʌkili gɪvm̩ pə'mɪʃn̩ tə 'flaɪ əuvə ðə 'fɔːlz | wɪtʃ ɪʒ 'juːʒuəli[16–17] fə'bɪdn̩ | tə 'kraun ɪt 'ɔːl | wi sɔː 'tuː 'təutli[1] 'sɜːkjulə 'reɪmbəuz əuvə ðə 'wɔːtə | 'ðæʔ wəz ə 'rɪəli 'muːvɪŋ ɪk'spɪərjəns[8] | 'feɪsɪŋ sʌtʃ 'splendɪd 'nætʃrəl fə'nɒmənə | 'puʔʃ ju ɪn ə ri'flektɪv 'muːd | ɪp[4] 'meɪkʃ ju 'stɒp m̩[18] 'θɪŋk əbauʔ jə'self[3] | ɪʔs əz 'ɪf ju wə 'sent ɪntu ə 'traːns | 'trævlɪŋ[1] fə 'miː | ɪz ə 'tʃaːns tə nəu 'mɔː | aər ɪ'miːdjət[8] ən'vaərəmmənt[19] ɪz səu ri'strɪktɪd | laɪk ə 'greɪn əv 'sænd | 'nəuɪŋ ʌðə sɪtju'eɪʃn̩z meɪkʃ ju ə mʌtʃ 'rɪtʃə 'pɜːsn̩ | ju 'rɪəlaɪz ðə?[4] 'piːplz 'vjuːz ən 'hæbɪʔs | 'veəri ə 'lɒʔ frəm 'wʌn pleɪs tu ə'nʌðə | ən ðəʔ ðər ɪz 'nəu 'æbsəljuːʔ 'truːθ | ðət 'eniθɪŋ meɪbi 'vælɪd | 'eni taɪp əv bi'heɪvjə[8] | 'eni rɪ'lɪdʒn̩ | 'ðæt ɪz waɪ wi kaːn[12] 'dʒʌdʒ frəm 'weə wi 'aː | 'njuːz wi 'get əbauʔ θɪŋz 'hæpnɪŋ[1] ɪn ə'nʌðə paːt əv ðə 'wɜːld | ɪf wi 'hævm̩[9] 'biːn | ən hævn̩[12] 'siːn wɒʔ 'θɪŋz ə 'laɪk ðeə | 'trævlɪŋ[1] ɪz maɪ 'pæʃn̩ | ɪʔs əz ɪf 'wʌŋ kud lɪv 'sevrəl dɪfrənʔ 'laɪvz | aɪ 'laɪk hævɪŋ ðæʔ 'stɔːr əv 'memrɪz tə delv 'ɪntu evri 'nau ən 'ðen | aɪ 'həup maɪ 'tʃɪldrən fiːl ðɪs weɪ 'tuː | ɪʔ wɪl 'tiːtʃ ðəm tu ə'priːʃɪeɪt ən 'vælju ʌðə 'kʌltʃəz | ən 'nɒʔ tə dɪ'spaɪz 'eniθɪŋ | 'dʒʌs[6] bikɒz ɪt ɪz 'nɒʔ wɒʔ 'ðeɪ ə 'juːs tuː |

Comments to transcription

1. Either syllabicity or /ə/ elision is possible here.
2. /d/ deletion or coalescence with /j/ are alternative processes here.
3. /jə'self/ and /jɔː'self/ are alternative pronunciations, the one with schwa being more colloquial.
4. The alveolar plosive could have been either assimilated or glottaled.
5. Notice this is one of the few cases of voice assimilation in RP connected speech.
6. The alveolar plosive could have been assimilated or elided.
7. /sɪtjueɪʃn̩z/ is an alternative pronunciation without word internal coalescence.
8. In unstressed positions, the first element of the diphthong /ɪə/ may lose its prominence and become /jə/.
9. The alveolar plosive could have been elided, glottaled or assimilated here.
10. *some* is used in the strong form when it means 'a group within the whole' or when it modifies a countable noun in the singular, when it is used as a pronoun etc. (see Lesson 3).
11. Exceptional case of /ə/ elision because it is not followed by a liquid.
12. The alveolar plosive could have been either glottaled or elided.
13. /pə'ræps/ and /'præps/ are other possible pronunciations.
14. The alveolar plosive could have been glottaled or coalesced with /j/.
15. /məg/ is an alternative pronunciation of the first syllable of this word.
16. In unstressed positions, the first element of the diphthong /uə/ may lose its prominence and become /wə/.
17. Instead of /'juːʒuəli/ we could have chosen /'juːʒəli/ as an alternative pronunciation which could then have been subject to syllabicity or /ə/ elision giving /'juːʒli/.
18. Notice the progressive assimilation which occurs across words.
19. Notice the word-internal regressive assimilation of the alveolar nasal to bilabial.

Glossary

accent: a variety of pronunciation of a language. Received Pronunciation (RP) is only one of the many accents with which Modern English is spoken. Others include: General American, Australian, Scottish, Irish, Welsh, Northern English, South Western English. There are many more.

affricate: an oral stop with a slow release during which there is audible friction. RP English has two affricate sounds /tʃ/ (example: the two consonants in *church*) and /dʒ/ (example: the two consonants in *judge*).

alveolar plosive elision: a connected speech process where /t/ or /d/ is deleted.

alveolar: a place of articulation. The passive articulator is the alveolar ridge and the active articulator the tip or the blade of the tongue. The alveolar consonants of RP English are: /t d n s z l/.

alveolar ridge: the bony ridge behind the upper front teeth. It is the passive articulator for alveolar sounds such as /s t n/.

anticipatory assimilation: a form of assimilation where the first sound in a sequence takes on one of the features of the next sound. Example: *bad boy* /bæd bɔɪ/ → /bæb bɔɪ/. Here the /d/ at the end of the word *bad* turns into a /b/ in anticipation of the bilabial place of articulation of the /b/ at the beginning of the following word.

APE: alveolar plosive elision.

approximant: a speech sound produced by leaving a wide opening between the active and passive articulators so that no friction noise is caused when air passes between the articulators. RP English has four approximants: /w r l j/.

assimilation: a feature of connected speech where one sound becomes more similar to an adjacent sound. An example from RP English is *one book* /wʌn bʊk/ → /wʌm bʊk/.

back vowel: a vowel produced by raising the back of the tongue towards the soft palate. /uː ʊ ɔː/ are examples of RP English back vowels.

bilabial: a place of articulation. The articulators concerned are the lips. The bilabial sounds of RP English are: /p b m/.

central vowel: a vowel produced with the centre of the tongue (the junction of the front and back parts of the tongue) raised highest. Examples of RP central vowels are /ɜː/ in *bird* and /ə/ in *bigger*.

citation form: the pronunciation of a word when it is unaffected by any connected speech processes such as weakening, assimilation, sandhi r, elision. The citation form is the form normally used when the word is pronounced in isolation. Example: *bad*: citation form /bæd/ non-citation forms: /bæb, bæg/.

close vowel: a vowel produced with the highest point of the tongue close to the roof of the mouth. /iː uː/ are examples of close vowels in RP English.

close–mid vowel: a vowel produced with the highest point of the tongue fairly close to the roof of the mouth. RP English /ɪ ʊ/ are approximately close–mid.

coalescence: a form of assimilation where two adjacent sounds merge to form a single sound. In RP English this may occur with the sequences /t/ + /j/ and /d/ + /j/, resulting in /tʃ/ and /dʒ/ respectively. Examples: *but you* /bətʃu/ and *did you* /dɪdʒu/.

coda: the part of the syllable after the vowel. RP English codas may contain no consonants, one, two, three or four consonants. Examples: *sea, set, sent, belts, texts*.

connected speech process: any one of a number of phenomena, such as assimilation and elision, which account for the influence that sounds may have on their neighbours when words are used in phrases or sentences.

connected speech: any stretch of speech consisting of more than one word.

dental: a place of articulation. For dental sounds the active articulator is the tip or blade of the tongue and the passive articulator is the upper front teeth. /θ ð/ are the dental consonants of RP English.

deletion: the same as elision.

de-syllabicity: a process where the syllabic nature of a consonant (see **syllabic** below) is removed and there is a reduction in the number of syllables. For example: *gardening* /ɡɑːdn̩ɪŋ/ → /ɡɑːdnɪŋ/.

diphthong: a vowel sound where there is a change in quality within a syllable. The diphthongs of RP English are /eɪ aɪ ɔɪ aʊ əʊ ɪə eə ʊə/.

elision: a connected speech process where a sound is deleted.

fricative: a manner of articulation. The active and passive articulators are very close together forming a narrow channel. When air passes through this it becomes turbulent and produces friction noise. The RP English fricative sounds are: /f v θ ð s z ʃ ʒ h/.

front vowel: a vowel produced by raising the front of the tongue towards the hard palate. /iː ɪ e/ are examples of RP English front vowels.

glottal: a place of articulation. The articulators concerned are the two vocal folds.

glottaling: the replacement of /t/ by /ʔ/ as in *not now* /nɒʔ naʊ/.

grammatical word: a word such as an auxiliary verb, pronoun, preposition or conjunction. Grammatical words very often have weak forms and are frequently unstressed.

height: a feature of vowel production. The height of a vowel is specified in terms of the distance between the highest point of the tongue and the roof of the oral cavity.

intrusive /r/: a form of sandhi r. When a word ending in a vowel in the set /ɑː ɔː ɪə eə ʊə ə/ is immediately followed by a word beginning with a vowel, an /r/ may be inserted to break up the vowel sequence, even though there is no letter *r* in the spelling of the word. Example: *I saw it* /aɪ sɔːr ɪt/. Intrusive /r/ may also occur word-internally as in *drawing* /drɔːrɪŋ/, although some speakers attempt to avoid it in this position.

labial–velar: a place of articulation where there are two simultaneous constrictions in the vocal tract, one at the lips and the other between the back of the tongue and the soft palate. The only labial–velar sound in RP English is /w/.

labiodental: a place of articulation. The passive articulator is the upper front teeth and the active articulator is the lower lip. /f v/ are the labiodental consonants of RP English.

larynx: a cartilaginous structure at the lower end of the vocal tract. The larynx contains the vocal folds.

lateral approximant: a manner of articulation. A lateral approximant has a closure on the midline of the vocal tract, but one or both sides of the tongue are lowered so that air can escape laterally without causing any friction noise. /l/ is the only RP English lateral approximant.

lexical stress: refers to the relative prominence of syllables within words when they are spoken in isolation.

lexical word: a word such as a noun, adjective or main verb. Lexical words do not have weak forms and are usually stressed. See also **grammatical word**.

linking /r/: a form of sandhi r in which r or re in the spelling of a word is pronounced as /r/, rather than being silent, because the next sound is a vowel.

lip posture: a feature of vowel production. Lip posture has two values: rounded and unrounded.

location: a feature of vowel production. The location of a vowel is specified in terms of where in the oral cavity, at the front or at the back, the highest point of the tongue is during the production of a vowel.

manner of articulation: a feature of the production of consonant sounds. The manner of articulation for a consonant is specified principally in terms of the narrowness of the constriction for the production of the consonant. RP English consonants are produced using the following manners of articulation: plosive, fricative, affricate, nasal, median approximant, lateral approximant.

median approximant: a manner of articulation. A median approximant consonant is produced with a fairly wide constriction between the passive and active articulators and there is no air turbulence causing friction noise. The air escapes down the midline of the vocal tract. /w r j/ are the median approximants of RP English.

mid vowel: a vowel produced with the highest point of the tongue approximately midway between the position for close vowels and that for open vowels. The RP English vowels /ə ɜː e ɔː/ are all approximately mid.

moa: manner of articulation.

monophthong: a vowel sound where there is no change of quality within a syllable. The monophthongs of RP English are /iː ɪ e æ ʌ ɑː ɒ ɔː ʊ uː ɜː ə/.

monophthonging: the replacement of a diphthong with a monophthong. An example is *tour* /tʊə/ → tɔː/.

nasal: a manner of articulation. There is a complete closure in the oral cavity, but the soft palate is lowered and air exits via the nasal cavity. The RP English nasals are /m n ŋ/.

neutralisation: the reduction or suspension in certain environments of the distinction which two sounds can normally make in a language.

obstruent: a consonant sound which is produced with a constriction between the articulators which causes a rise in air pressure in the vocal tract. Plosives, fricatives and affricates are all obstruents. The opposite of obstruent is **sonorant**.

onset: the part of the syllable before the vowel. Onsets in RP English may contain no consonants, one, two or three consonants. Examples: *egg, leg, stop, strange*.

open vowel: a vowel produced with a considerable distance between the highest point of the tongue and the roof of the oral cavity. /ɑː/ is an example of an RP English open vowel.

open–mid vowel: a vowel produced with a fairly large distance between the highest point of the tongue and the roof of the mouth. The RP English vowels /æ ʌ/ are both slightly below open mid.

orthography: the spelling of a word or words in written language.

palatal: a place of articulation. The active articulator is the front of the tongue and the passive articulator is the hard palate. /j/ is the only palatal consonant in RP English.

past tense morpheme: the suffix (usually spelled *-ed*) attached to regular verbs to signal past tense. In RP English the morpheme has three different pronunciations (1) /t/ which is attached to verbs which end in a voiceless sound except /t/, (2) /d/ which is attached to verbs which end in a voiced sound except /d/, (3) /ɪd/ or /əd/ (some speakers use the first and others use the second) which is attached to verbs which end in /t/ or /d/.

perseverative assimilation: a type of assimilation when the second of a sequence of consonants takes on a feature of the production of the previous consonant. For example *back and forth* can be pronounced /bæk ŋ fɔːθ/. The reason why the word *and* in this pronunciation is represented by a velar nasal is the influence of the preceding velar consonant. Perseverative assimilation is rarer than anticipatory assimilation in RP English.

phonological process: a phenomenon where a sound or morpheme is affected by the context in which it appears.

place of articulation: a feature of the production of consonants sounds. The place of articulation refers to the location of the narrowest constriction in the vocal tract during the production of a consonant. RP English uses the following places of articulation for consonants: bilabial, labiodental, dental, alveolar, post-alveolar, palatal, velar, glottal and labial–velar.

plosive: an oral stop consonant with a rapid release. The plosives of RP English are /p b t d k g/.

plural morpheme: the suffix (usually spelled *s* or *es*) added to the end of a noun to indicate plural number. The plural morpheme in RP English has three different pronunciations: (1) /s/ which is used when the noun ends in a voiceless non-sibilant sound, (2) /z/ which is used when the noun ends in a voiced non-sibilant sound, (3) /əz/ or /ɪz/ (some speakers use the first and others the second) which is used when the noun ends with a sibilant sound.

poa: place of articulation.

post-alveolar: a place or articulation. The active articulator is the tip or blade of the tongue and the passive articulator is the rear part of the alveolar ridge. /ʃ ʒ tʃ dʒ r/ are the post-alveolar consonants of RP English.

progressive assimilation: the same as perseverative assimilation.

Received Pronunciation: an accent of English used in England. Received Pronunciation (RP) is the accent most widely used for the purposes of teaching English as a foreign or second language and is the accent represented in nearly all pronouncing dictionaries produced in England.

regressive assimilation: the same as anticipatory assimilation.

rhythmic stress: the same as sentence stress.

rounded vowel: a vowel produced with rounded lips. /uː ɔː/ are examples of RP English rounded vowels.

RP: Received Pronunciation.

sandhi r: a term used to cover both intrusive /r/ and linking /r/.

SBS: Southern British Standard.

SCF: syllabic consonant formation.

schwa elision: a process whereby /ə/ is deleted. Example: *history* /hɪstəri/→/hɪstri/.

schwa: the name given to the mid central unrounded vowel symbolised /ə/. Examples are the first vowel in the word *perhaps* and the final vowel in the word *brother*.

sentence stress: the relative prominence of syllables found in the pronunciation of phrases or sentences. Sentence stress does not necessarily coincide with lexical stress.

sibilant: an alveolar or postalveolar consonant with an intense friction component. The sibilant sounds of RP English are /s z ʃ ʒ tʃ dʒ/.

smoothing: the deletion of the second in a sequence of three vowel qualities. In RP English this occurs most frequently when a diphthong is followed by /ə/. The second part of the diphthong is deleted. Example: *fire* /faɪə/→/faə/.

soft palate: the moveable back part of the roof of the oral cavity. Another name for this is the velum.

sonorant: a class of sounds comprising vowels, nasals, lateral approximants and median approximants. During the production of sonorant sounds there is no appreciable rise of air pressure within the vocal tract.

Southern British Standard: another term for Received Pronunciation.

stop: a consonant sound produced with a complete closure in the oral vocal tract. Nasals, plosives and affricates are all stops.

stranding: this is the situation where a preposition is not immediately followed by the noun to which it refers or an auxiliary or modal verb is not immediately followed by a main verb. This occurs because of a movement or a deletion process. Stranded prepositions and auxiliaries must have a strong form pronunciation even when they are not stressed. Examples: *What are you looking at?* /æt/. *I'll do it as soon as I can.* /kæn/.

stressed: a syllable is stressed if it is more prominent than the syllables around it. This prominence is caused by a combination of extra length and loudness.

strong form: the pronunciation which certain function words have when they bear sentence stress, when they are stranded or in citations. For example the strong form of the word *and* is /ænd/.

style: the variety of pronunciation suited to a particular occasion or situation. In a lecture or other formal situation the type of pronunciation used would probably be different form that used in an informal situation such as a relaxed conversation among friends.

syllabic: a term describing a consonant which forms a syllable without the help of an accompanying vowel. The two most common syllabic consonants in RP English are /n̩/ (as in the word *button*) and /l̩/ (as in the word *bottle*).

syllabic consonant formation: the coalescence of a sonorant consonant with a preceding /ə/ to form a syllabic consonant.

unrounded vowel: a vowel produced without rounding of the lips. Examples of RP English unrounded vowels are /iː e æ ɑː/.

unstressed: a syllable is unstressed if it does not bear prominence due to lexical or sentence stress.

velar: a place of articulation. The active articulator is the back of the tongue and the passive articulator is the soft palate. /k g ŋ/ are the velar consonants of RP English.

velum: the soft palate.

voiced: accompanied by vocal fold vibration. All RP English vowels are voiced and so are the following consonants: /b d g v ð z ʒ dʒ m n ŋ w r l j/.

voiceless: produced without accompanying vocal fold vibration. The following RP English consonants are voiceless: /p t k f θ s ʃ tʃ h/.

weak form: the pronunciation used for certaing function words when they are not stranded and do not bear sentence stress. For example the weak form of the word *for* is /fə/.

word group boundary: the beginning or end of a group of words which bear a complete intonation pattern. For the purposes of this course a word group boundary can be thought of as marking a brief pause. The symbol used is |.

Bibliography

Ashby, P. 1995: *Speech Sounds*. London: Routledge.

Bogle, D. 1996: *Practical Phonology*. Edinburgh: Moray House.

Bowler, B. And Cunningham, S. 1990: *Headway, Advanced Pronunciation*. Oxford: Oxford University Press.

Brazil, D. 1994: *Pronunciation for Advanced Learners of English*. Cambridge: Cambridge University Press.

Carney, E. 1997: *English Spelling*. London: Routledge.

Cruttenden, A. (Ed.) 1994: *Gimson's Introduction to the Pronunciation of English*. London: Edward Arnold.

Davenport, M. and Hannahs, S. J. 1998: *Introducing Phonetics and Phonology*. London: Edward Arnold.

Digby, C. and Myers, J. 1993: *Making Sense of Spelling and Pronunciation*. Hemel Hempsted: Prentice Hall International.

Edwards, H. T. 1992: *Applied Phonetics: The sounds of American English*. San Diego, CA: Singular Publishing Group.

Edwards, H. T. and Gregg, A. L. 1997: *Applied Phonetics Workbook: A Systematic Approach to Phonetic Transcription*. San Diego, CA: Singular Publishing Group.

Fletcher, C. 1990: *Longman Pronouncing Dictionary. Study Guide*. London: Longman.

Fudge, E. 1984: *English Word Stress*. London: George Allen & Unwin.

Hewings, M. 1993: *Pronunciation Tasks*. Cambridge: Cambridge University Press.

Jones, D. 1997: *English Pronouncing Dictionary*, edited by P. Roach & J. Hartman. Cambridge: Cambridge University Press.

Knowles, G. 1987: *Patterns of Spoken English*. London: Longman.

Ladefoged, P. 1993 [1975]: *A Course in Phonetics*. New York: Harcourt.

Morris-Wilson, I. 1984: *English Phonemic Transcription*. Oxford: Blackwell.

O'Connor, J. D. 1980 [1967]: *Better English Pronunciation*. Cambridge: Cambridge University Press.

O'Connor, J. D. and Fletcher, C. 1989: *Sounds English*. London: Longman.

Roach, P. 1991: *English Phonetics and Phonology*. Cambridge: Cambridge University Press.

Roach, P. 1992: *Introducing Phonetics*, London: Penguin.
Trask, L. 1996: *A Dictionary of Phonetics and Phonology*. London: Routledge.
Wells, J. C. and Colson, G. 1971: *Practical Phonetics*. London: Pitman.
Wells, J. C. 1990: *Longman Pronunciation Dictionary*. London: Longman.